DISQUIET, PLEASE!

DISQUIET, PLEASE!

MORE HUMOR WRITING FROM
THE NEW YORKER

EDITED BY

DAVID REMNICK AND HENRY FINDER

RANDOM HOUSE / NEW YORK

All of the pieces in this collection were originally published in *The New Yorker.*
The publication date of each piece is given at the end of the piece.

ISBN 978-1-4000-6801-2

www.atrandom.com

Printed in the United States of America on acid-free paper

2 4 6 8 9 7 5 3 1

FIRST EDITION

Book design by Casey Hampton

CONTENTS

TESTAMENTS AND DECLARATIONS

THE GREAT AND THE GOOD

EXPLANATIONS AND ADVISORIES

PAST IMPERFECT

FIELD NOTES FROM ALL OVER

PERSONAL HISTORY

INTRODUCTION

BEFORE the folks at *The New Yorker* could reliably make anybody else laugh, they specialized in entertaining themselves. The magazine was launched in February of 1925, and its early issues were, to be charitable, hit or miss. Harold Ross, the founding editor, figured that the only thing in the debut issue that really worked was Rea Irvin's cover portrait of Eustace Tilly, peering through his monocle at a butterfly.

But the workplace, by all accounts, was a riot. The irascible James Thurber caused a copy editor to faint when he burst in on him with a pistol in hand, yelling, "Are you the son of a bitch that keeps putting notes in red ink on the proofs of my Talk stories?" When Ross found Dorothy Parker at a speakeasy instead of at her desk, she had a ready—and, yes, often quoted—excuse: "Someone was using the pencil." Then there was the drunk-dialing incident, when Ross had had too much Scotch and telephoned the great cartoonist Peter Arno in the middle of the night to tell him he was fired. (*So* much funnier the next day.) Rea Irvin, the magazine's art editor, drew a not-for-public-consumption takeoff of the Eustace Tilly cover for the boss's birthday: It featured a silhouette of Ross—an upward shock of hair, a limp cigarette dangling from his mouth—peering at a globular insect with a distinct resemblance to the drama critic Alexander Woollcott. A mannequin from Wanamaker's (E. B. White had used pictures of it in a series of ads he composed for a 1927 circulation campaign) stood in Ross's office, complete with a filthy hairpiece, for years after the joke was forgotten, which, for Ross, was exactly what made it funny.

The freshest stuff that appeared in the magazine back then was often self-parody, possibly more amusing to the staff than to anyone else. Much was made of the "vast organization" of *The New Yorker;* a picture of Grand Central Station was described in a caption as the magazine's "sumptuous waiting room." The truth is, the staff's most inspired work in those days never made it beyond the vast organization; the in-house editorial memos (we reprint one of them, by the editor and writer Wolcott Gibbs) regularly outstripped anything that actually appeared in print. And then—the magazine found its voice, or voices.

A handful of people competing to make one another laugh: It's not the worst way for an original comic enterprise to begin. Maybe it's the only way. If something you did got a laugh from your friends, you wouldn't be discouraged by the fact that most people didn't get it; if you were on to something, plenty of those people would come around. More than anything, Ross wanted his magazine to be funny, but he didn't want it to be funny the way other magazines were funny. The debut issue of *The New Yorker* printed a lame Q&A-style joke, which ended with the Q. Many assumed it was a typographical error; more likely, it was an absurdist, defiant assertion that the magazine wasn't in the business of serving up conventional humor. In the magazine Ross wanted to create, there would be no setup/punch-line jokes—no knock-knocks, no "kids say the darnedest things" squibs, no after-dinner anecdotes, nothing about a priest and a rabbi walking into a bar.

It was one thing to avow what *New Yorker* humor wasn't; it took a little longer to establish what it *was.* That's where Thurber and White came in. In the Thumbelina realm of *New Yorker* history, Thurber and White were the framers of a comic constitution, our Adams and Jefferson, albeit without the cupping scars and slave children. They ranged widely in the forms they explored, and encouraged others to do so. Some of what the magazine published, as it hit its stride, was parody—of radio monologues, of what Ross called "journalese," of advertising copy, of etiquette manuals, of the mannerisms of the great novelists. There were depictions of the sad-sack sufferer, an updated version of the silent-movie schlemiel. There were stories of comic happenings, real or imagined. There were waggish commentaries that did figure eights on the line of irony. There were the rants, presented straight, of the wildly unhinged or the obliviously self-satisfied.

Needless to say, every good writer at the magazine had his or her own voice, and his or her own devils. Dorothy Parker's depictions of drunken or hungover heroines were no doubt influenced by her own boozy ways; and you can glimpse Thurber's blighted first marriage—it's like opening a freezer—in tales of connubial misery like "Quiet, Please," "Not Together," and (included in this anthology) "The Breaking Up of the Winships." Yet something distinctive arose from the juxtaposition of all these voices. The marriage, like the hangovers, came to an end; the work has pretty much survived. Within a few years of the magazine's launch, a contributor complained to a rejecting editor that a humor piece written for *The New Yorker* couldn't be placed elsewhere: The magazine's preferences were too idiosyncratic, too distant from what everyone else was up to. "We have evolved a system for the smooth operation of a literary bordello," White later wrote. "The system is this: We write as we please, and the magazine publishes as *it* pleases. When the two pleasures coincide, something gets into print."

There are no guns, toy or otherwise, at the magazine's offices these days. The whole firing-while-drunk thing happens only rarely. That mannequin has long since disappeared (though we have our suspicions). Staff members have learned the hard way not to make fun of the boss's coiffure, ever. But the bordello system that White described remains intact. It has functioned so well, in fact, that the magazine's archives are full to bursting with humor, a goodly amount of it still humorous. Putting together an anthology of *New Yorker* humor writing is so much fun we've done it twice.

THE publication of our previous sampler, *Fierce Pajamas*, gave us pleasure; but also pain. For every piece we included, we left out two that we liked just as much. Between the anthology's editors, second-guessing soon began in earnest. What could explain a blunder like (to name one of many) leaving out "Kimberley Solzhenitsyn's Calendar"? Exactly which one of us was asleep at the wheel? Years of recrimination ensued. Styptic glances gave way to glowering stares and then long, wintry silences. If *Disquiet, Please!* is a follow-up, every follow-up is also, in certain respects, a do-over. In making our selections, we have therefore adhered to an especially rigorous methodology. First, we gathered pieces, not found in the previous anthology, that made us laugh, or beam, or both. Then, when those proved too numerous to fit into a book, we arranged the pieces in a circle and spun a bottle. Afterward, we recycled the bottle.

For all that, we could not escape the guilty knowledge that many of the funniest pieces that *The New Yorker* publishes aren't exactly humor pieces. They are, rather, works of reporting, opinion, or criticism in which the comic eye and sensibility are fully engaged, and, as before, we couldn't do them justice. Humor has never been segregated in the magazine that Ross founded. And yet the anthologist looks for density, for concentration—for an array of comic effects on display in a relatively small space. The difference between a humor piece and a humorous piece is the difference between attar of rose and actual roses. This is not to the discredit of roses, whose breeding and cultivation we hold in high esteem. It's just that humorists are generally less encumbered than reporters or reviewers by the task of explaining how a bill was passed or a bridge was built, or what an actual person or movie is actually like. The journalist's challenge is to paint an urn that must hold water. The humorist can turn a lump of clay into an urn that pointedly fails to.

In compiling this book, we also took full advantage of the fact that, since the last time around, we had almost a decade's worth of new pieces to choose from, and we helped ourselves to those recent harvests with two hands, or maybe four. It's what the founders would have done. Whether it was genius or dumb luck, Ross, White, Thurber, Gibbs, and the rest managed to do something that eluded even the incomparably gifted H. L. Mencken and George S. Nathan, who jointly piloted the long-defunct (and slightly *New Yorker*-ish) magazine *Smart Set*. They managed to create a magazine with an identity potent enough, yet capacious enough, to outlast them—a magazine that could be renewed and remade and remain recognizably itself. We thereby honor the Founders, in this collection, by giving them short shrift. (You'll find them more decently represented in *Fierce Pajamas*, which also boasts a section of comic verse sufficient to forgo supplementation here.) We've instead devoted the balance of our space to their successors, their legatees. Most of the more recent comic talents we've included are still living, or very nearly; some are even young. In *Disquiet, Please!* we've taken the opportunity to present late-vintage wine from old vines (not *old;* established, really, or, let's say, *distinguished*). But we've also had the particular pleasure of introducing previously unpublished contributors, such as Yoni Brenner or Simon Rich, who, we understand, was not yet born when *Fierce Pajamas* came out, and is not old enough to drink that wine. We have erred on the side of newness.

AND yet the new is never so new as all that. Men and women still drive each other nuts, just as in olden days. Self-delusion still generates insight. The entertainment industry is still seductive and silly. Our children still bring out the best in us, and the worst. Puffed-up literary piety still invites piercing. In convention-bound prose—ad copy, class notes, Zagat reviews, drug disclaimers, popularizations of impenetrable science, tonight's specials, the gossip column—cliché is always just a few clicks away from preposterousness. Furry animals: You can never go wrong with them. And it's still the case that (as White learned long ago) you should never get into an argument with a libertarian. At the cutting edge of comedy, you'll find few moves that Thurber and White wouldn't have recognized, and few they didn't attempt.

Surveying the contributors to this anthology, across four generations, we've noticed other continuities, other patterns. We can now start to puzzle through a question we're often asked: What makes a *New Yorker* humor writer? Is there a particular course of study, some people have even wondered, that can actually produce a *New Yorker* humorist? (The answer is yes, but Hunter College no longer offers it.) What sort of career experiences are helpful? Having researched this matter, we can offer a few pointers. Peter De Vries, as a young man, once played a wounded gorilla on a radio drama, and we can think of no better preparation for *The New Yorker*'s editorial process. Granted, there are other contenders. The world of advertising seems to be a pretty good incubator for wisenheimers. White himself served time writing ad copy (one of his first *New Yorker* pieces imagined what would happen if spring, the season, were an advertising account), and it's a résumé he shares with such current contributors as Bruce McCall and John Kenney, who likewise know from the inside the codes and cadences they send up. Other humor writers have emerged from the world of newspapers (as Thurber did); a few from the underbelly of *The New Yorker* itself. So if you are unable to land a wounded-gorilla role, you might seek employment as a writer. And you needn't restrict yourself to print. A number of classic *New Yorker* humorists—such as Benchley, Parker, Perelman, and later, in an unexampled way, Woody Allen—spent time writing for movies or television. That's true, as well, about many more recent contributors, such as Paul Rudnick, Patricia Marx, Andy Borowitz, Larry Doyle, Paul Simms, and Yoni Brenner. For them, having suckled at the golden teat and grown rich off *The New Yorker*, working in Hollywood is a way of giving back to the community. It's a heartening tradition, and we salute their generosity.

We salute, as well, the generosity of all those who helped us assemble this collection with their unstinting, if at times heated, advice (in a few instances, to be honest, "advice" is the word only if you stipulate that General MacArthur advised Tojo to surrender). We cannot list every counselor, but we're particularly grateful to Leo Carey, whose comic sensibility is as finely tuned as a cello (a finely tuned cello, that is to say), and who has, rather precociously, become a redoubt of institutional memory; Susan Morrison, who has culled and edited the magazine's Shouts and Murmurs—and nurtured its writers—for more than a decade; and Adam Gopnik, who conveyed the dire threats of an Old Testament prophet should a certain Thurber piece be left out (we chose not to discover whether his omniscience is matched by omnipotence). Andrea Walker gamely foraged through *The New Yorker*'s half-a-billion-word archives, searching, sorting, reading, organizing, and juggling logistical challenges with an agility that would do NASA proud. We're grateful, as well, to the magazine's deputy editor, Pamela Maffei McCarthy, not least for arranging this book's publication, cunningly persuading Random House that, in return, it should pay *The New Yorker* a little something, rather than the other way around. Lynn Oberlander and Andrew Avery sorted through rights and permissions; Jon Michaud and Erin Overbey helped keep everything on track; Greg Captain lent a hand with the cover image. At Random House, Jennifer Hershey, Julia Cheiffetz, Millicent Bennett, and Evan Camfield helped turn a big messy stack of wrinkled, coffee-ringed photocopies into a tidily bound volume with a cover and everything, shipped to bookstores across the land. All these men and women did their part. Now it's your turn.

There's a story, possibly true, about the producer of a sitcom who once summoned a pair of staff writers to berate them about a script they'd just handed in. "The show's supposed to be funny, and this just isn't funny," the producer said. "There's not a laugh in it." The writers, taken aback, protested that the script had some of the funniest writing they'd done. With the producer's sufferance, they started to read it out loud. A page into it, the producer was convulsed with laughter. By the end of the first scene, he had fallen out of his chair and onto the floor, in helpless paroxysms, wildly signaling the writers to stop. At last, the producer recovered his breath, heaved himself back onto his chair, and grumbled, "Well, sure, if you're going to read it like *that*." Aside from begging your indulgence for this volume's inexplicable omissions, casualties of the spinning bottle, we have very few requests to make of you, the reader. You should feel free to dip into this anthology randomly, to read it backward, to give it a home next to a porcelain commode. (Better there than on a high shelf.) All we ask is that you read it like *that*.

COUPLES

JAMES THURBER

THE BREAKING UP OF THE WINSHIPS

THE trouble that broke up the Gordon Winships seemed to me, at first, as minor a problem as frost on a windowpane. Another day, a touch of sun, and it would be gone. I was inclined to laugh it off, and, indeed, as a friend of both Gordon and Marcia, I spent a great deal of time with each of them, separately, trying to get them to laugh it off, too—with him at his club, where he sat drinking Scotch and smoking too much, and with her in their apartment, that seemed so large and lonely without Gordon and his restless moving around and his quick laughter. But it was no good; they were both adamant. Their separation has lasted now more than two months. I doubt very much that they will ever go back together again.

It all started one night at Leonardo's, after dinner, over their Bénédictine. It started innocently enough, amiably even, with laughter from both of them, laughter that froze finally as the clock ran on and their words came out sharp and flat and stinging. They had been to see *Anna Karenina*. Gordon hadn't liked it very much: He said that Fredric March's haircut made the whole thing seem silly. Marcia had been crazy about it because she is crazy about Greta Garbo. She belongs to that considerable army of Garbo admirers whose enchantment borders almost on fanaticism and sometimes even touches the edges of frenzy. I think that, before everything happened, Gordon admired Garbo, too, but the depth of his wife's conviction that here was the greatest figure ever seen in our generation on sea or land, on screen or stage, exasperated him that night. Gordon hates (or used to) exaggeration, and he respects (or once did) detachment. It was his feeling that detachment is a necessary thread in the fabric of a woman's charm. He didn't like to see his wife get herself "into a sweat" over anything and, that night at Leonardo's, he unfortunately used that expression and made that accusation.

Marcia responded, as I get it, by saying, a little loudly (they had gone on to Scotch and soda), that a man who had no abandon of feeling and no passion for anything was not altogether a man, and that his so-called love of detachment simply covered up a lack of critical appreciation and understanding of the arts in general. Her sentences were becoming long and wavy, and her words formal. Gordon suddenly began to pooh-pooh her; he kept saying "Pooh!" (an annoying mannerism of his, I have always thought). He wouldn't answer her arguments or even listen to them. That, of course, infuriated her. "Oh, pooh to you, too!" she finally more or less shouted. He snapped at her, "Quiet, for God's sake! You're yelling like a losing prizefight manager!" Enraged at that, she had recourse to her eyes as weapons and looked steadily at him for a while with the expression of one who is viewing a small and horrible animal, such as a horned toad. They then sat in moody and brooding silence for a long time, without moving a muscle, at the end of which, getting a hold on herself, Marcia asked him, quietly enough, just exactly what actor on the screen or on the stage, living or dead, he considered greater than Garbo. Gordon thought a moment and then said, as quietly as she had put the question, "Donald Duck." I don't believe that he meant it at the time, or even thought that he meant it. However that may have been, she looked at him scornfully and said that that speech just about perfectly represented the shallowness of his intellect and the small range of his imagination. Gordon asked her not to make a spectacle of herself—she had raised her voice slightly—and went on to say that her failure to see the genius of Donald Duck proved conclusively to him that she was a woman without humor. That, he said, he had always suspected; now, he said, he knew it. She had a great desire to hit him, but instead she sat back and looked at him with her special Mona Lisa smile, a smile rather more of contempt than, as in the original, of mystery. Gordon hated that smile, so he said that Donald Duck happened to be exactly ten times as great as Garbo would ever be and that anybody with a brain in his head would admit it instantly. Thus the Winships went on and on, their resentment swelling, their sense of values blurring, until it ended up with her taking a taxi home alone (leaving her vanity bag and one glove behind her in the restaurant) and with him making the rounds of the late places and rolling up to his club around dawn. There, as he got out, he asked his taxi-driver which he liked better, Greta Garbo or Donald Duck, and the driver said he liked Greta Garbo best. Gordon said to him, bitterly, "Pooh to you, too, my good friend!" and went to bed.

The next day, as is usual with married couples, they were both contrite, but behind their contrition lay sleeping the ugly words each had used and the cold glances and the bitter gestures. She phoned him, because she was worried. She didn't want to be, but she was. When he hadn't come home, she was convinced he had gone to his club, but visions of him lying in a gutter or under a table, somehow horribly mangled, haunted her, and so at eight o'clock she called him up. Her heart lightened when he said, "Hullo," gruffly: He was alive, thank God! His heart may have lightened a little, too, but not very much, because he felt terrible. He felt terrible and he felt that it was her fault that he felt terrible. She said that she was sorry and that they had both been very silly, and he growled something about he was glad she realized *she'd* been silly, anyway. That attitude put a slight edge on the rest of her words. She asked him shortly if he was coming home. He said sure he was coming home; it was his home, wasn't it? She told him to go back to bed and not be such an old bear, and hung up.

THE next incident occurred at the Clarkes' party a few days later. The Winships had arrived in fairly good spirits to find themselves in a buzzing group of cocktail-drinkers that more or less revolved around the tall and languid figure of the guest of honor, an eminent lady novelist. Gordon late in the evening won her attention and drew her apart for one drink together and, feeling a little high and happy at that time, as is the way with husbands, mentioned, lightly enough (he wanted to get it out of his subconscious), the argument that he and his wife had had about the relative merits of Garbo and Duck. The tall lady, lowering her cigarette-holder, said, in the spirit of his own gaiety, that she could count her in on his side. Unfortunately, Marcia Winship, standing some ten feet away, talking to a man with a beard, caught not the spirit but only a few of the words of the conversation, and jumped to the conclusion that her husband was deliberately reopening the old wound, for the purpose of humiliating her in public. I think that in another moment Gordon might have brought her over, and put his arm around her, and admitted his "defeat"—he was feeling pretty fine. But when he caught her eye, she gazed through him, freezingly, and his heart went down. And then his anger rose.

Their fight, naturally enough, blazed out again in the taxi they took to go home from the party. Marcia wildly attacked the woman novelist (Marcia had had quite a few cocktails), defended Garbo, excoriated Gordon, and laid into Donald Duck. Gordon tried for a while to explain exactly what had happened, and then he met her resentment with a resentment that mounted even higher, the resentment of the misunderstood husband. In the midst of it all she slapped him. He looked at her for a second under lowered eyelids and then said, coldly, if a bit fuzzily, "This is the end, but I want you to go to your grave knowing that Donald Duck is *twenty times* the artist Garbo will ever be, the longest day you, or she, ever live, if you *do*—and I can't understand, with so little to live for, why you should!" Then he asked the driver to stop the car, and he got out, in wavering dignity. "Caricature! Cartoon!" she screamed after him. "You and Donald Duck both, you ——" The driver drove on.

The last time I saw Gordon—he moved his things to the club the next day, forgetting the trousers to his evening clothes and his razor— he had convinced himself that the point at issue between him and Marcia was one of extreme importance involving both his honor and his integrity. He said that now it could never be wiped out and forgotten. He said that he sincerely believed Donald Duck was as great a creation as any animal in all the works of Lewis Carroll, probably even greater, perhaps much greater. He was drinking and there was a wild light in his eye. I reminded him of his old love of detachment, and he said to the hell with detachment. I laughed at him, but he wouldn't laugh. "If," he said, grimly, "Marcia persists in her silly belief that that Swede is great and that Donald Duck is merely a caricature, I cannot conscientiously live with her again. I believe that he is great, that the man who created him is a genius, probably our only genius. I believe, further, that Greta Garbo is just another actress. As God is my judge, I believe that! What does she expect me to do, go whining back to her and pretend that I think Garbo is wonderful and that Donald Duck is simply a cartoon? Never!" He gulped down some Scotch straight. "Never!" I could not ridicule him out of his obsession. I left him and went over to see Marcia.

I found Marcia pale, but calm, and as firm in her stand as Gordon was in his. She insisted that he had deliberately tried to humiliate her before that gawky so-called novelist, whose clothes were the dowdiest she had ever seen and whose affectations obviously covered up a complete lack of individuality and intelligence. I tried to convince her that she was wrong about Gordon's attitude at the Clarkes' party, but she said she knew him like a book. Let him get a divorce and marry that creature if he wanted to. They can sit around all day, she said, and all night, too, for all I care, and talk about their precious Donald Duck, the damn comic strip! I told Marcia that she shouldn't allow herself to get so worked up about a trivial and nonsensical matter. She said it was not silly and nonsensical to her. It might have been once, yes, but it wasn't now. It had made her see Gordon clearly for what he was, a cheap, egotistical, resentful cad who would descend to ridiculing his wife in front of a scrawny, horrible stranger who could not write and never would be able to write. Furthermore, her belief in Garbo's greatness was a thing she could not deny and would not deny, simply for the sake of living under the same roof with Gordon Winship. The whole thing was part and parcel of her integrity as a woman and as an—as an, well, as a woman. She could go to work again; he would find out.

There was nothing more that I could say or do. I went home. That night, however, I found that I had not really dismissed the whole ridiculous affair, as I hoped I had, for I dreamed about it. I had tried to ignore the thing, but it had tunnelled deeply into my subconscious. I dreamed that I was out hunting with the Winships and that, as we crossed a snowy field, Marcia spotted a rabbit and, taking quick aim, fired and brought it down. We all ran across the snow toward the rabbit, but I reached it first. It was quite dead, but that was not what struck horror into me as I picked it up. What struck horror into me was that it was a white rabbit and was wearing a vest and carrying a watch. I woke up with a start. I don't know whether that dream means that I am on Gordon's side or on Marcia's. I don't want to analyze it. I am trying to forget the whole miserable business.

1936

PETER DE VRIES

THE HOUSE OF MIRTH

THE collaboration known as marriage could, I think, be profitably extended from the domestic to the social sphere, where a man and wife might brighten their contribution to, say, the give-and-take of dinner-table conversation by preparing a few exchanges in advance. "It's simply the principle of teamwork," I told my wife in partially describing the idea to her one evening as we were dressing to go to dinner at the home of some friends named Anthem. "For instance, tonight, Sue Anthem being as hipped as she is on family trees, we're bound to talk relatives at some point. Well, I'm going to tell about my seagoing grandfather who's so wonderful. In the middle of it, I'll pause and take up my napkin, and then I'd appreciate it if you'd ask me, 'Was he on your mother's side?' " (I planned to answer, "Yes, except in money matters, when he usually stuck up for my father." This wasn't much, but I was feeling my way around in the form, trying to get the hang of it before going on to something more nearly certifiable as wit.)

Dinner ran along the lines I had foreseen. Sue Anthem got off on kinship, and I launched my little account of this wonderful grandfather. I paused at the appointed moment and, glancing at my wife, reached for my napkin.

"I keep forgetting," she came in brightly. "Was he your maternal grandfather?"

"Yes, except in money matters, when he usually stuck up for my father," I replied.

A circle of blank looks met my gaze. I coughed into my napkin, and Sue picked up the thread of the discussion while I reviewed in my mind a couple of other gambits I had worked out with my wife, on the way over. One of these concerned a female friend, not present that evening, whom I will cut corners by calling a gay divorcée. She had just announced her engagement to a man so staid that news of the match took everyone who knew her by surprise. "Now, if the thing comes up, as it probably will," I had coached my wife, "say something about how you've only met him a few times but he seems a man of considerable reserve." I intended then to adroitly add, "Which Monica will get her hands on in short order." I expected that to go over big, the divorcée being a notorious gold-digger.

The gossip did get around to her soon after it left the subject of relatives, and my wife came in on cue punctually enough, but her exact words were "He's such a quiet, unassuming chap."

This time, I had the presence of mind to realize the quip was useless, and check myself. Another misfire followed almost immediately. In preparation for possible discussion of Italy, where Monica and her fiancé planned to honeymoon, I had primed my wife to tell about her own visit to the Gulf of Spezia, where the drowned Shelley had been washed up. "In a way, you know, he was lucky," I had planned to comment. "Most poets are washed up *before* they're dead." She told her story, but used the words "where Shelley was found," thus washing up *that* mot.

It was clear that I would have to explain the system to my wife in detail if I was ever to get the bugs out of it. I decided, in fact, that I had better reveal in each case what the capper was to be, so that she would realize the importance of delivering her line exactly as prearranged. I did this while we were driving to our next party, several evenings later. I had ducked her questions about the failures at the Anthems', preferring to wait till I had some new material worked up to hammer my point home with before I laid the whole thing on the line.

"At the Spiggetts' tonight," I said, "there's certain to be the usual talk about art. Here's a chance for you to get in those licks of yours about abstract painting—isn't it high time painters got back to nature, and so on. The sort of thing you said at the Fentons'. You might cite a few of the more traditional paintings, like the portraits of Mrs. Jack Gardner and Henry Marquand. Then turn to me and ask—now, get this, it's important—ask, 'Why can't we have portraits like that any more?' "

"Then what will you say?" she asked.

I slowed to make a left turn, after glancing in the rear-view mirror to make sure nobody was behind me. " 'It's no time for Sargents, my dear.' "

My wife reached over and pushed in the dash lighter, then sat waiting for it to pop, a cigarette in her hand.

"Of course I'll throw it away," I said. "Just sort of murmur it."

She lit the cigarette and put the lighter back in its socket. "Isn't this a little shabby?" she asked.

"Why? What's shabby about it? Isn't it better than the conversation you have to put up with normally—doesn't it make for something at least a cut above that?" I said. "What's wrong with trying to brighten life up? We can turn it around if you like. You can take the cappers while I feed you the straight lines—"

"Lord, no, leave it as it is."

"Can I count on you, then?"

"I suppose," she said, heaving a sigh. "But step on it. We're supposed to eat early and then go to that Shakespearean little theatre in Norwalk."

MY wife and I parted on entering the Spiggetts' house. I made off to where a new television comedienne, named Mary Cobble, was holding court with a dozen or so males. She was a small blonde, cute as a chipmunk and bright as a dollar. The men around her laughed heartily at everything she said. It was well known in Westport that her writers, of whom she kept a sizable stable, formed a loyal claque who followed her to every party, but it didn't seem to me that *all* the men around her could be writers. I knocked back a few quick Martinis and soon felt myself a gay part of the group. Once, I glanced around and saw my wife looking stonily my way over the shoulder of a man whose fame as a bore was so great that he was known around town as the Sandman. Matters weren't helped, I suppose, when, presently returning from the buffet with two plates of food, I carried one to Mary Cobble and sat down on the floor in front of her to eat the other. At the same time, I saw the Sandman fetching my wife a bite.

Midway through this lap dinner, there was one of those moments when all conversation suddenly stops at once. Lester Spiggett threw in a comment about a current show at a local art gallery. I saw my wife put down her fork and clear her throat. "Well, if there are any portraits in it, I hope the things on the canvases are faces," she said. She looked squarely at me. "Why is it we no longer have portraits that *portray*— that give you pictures of *people*? Like, oh, the *Mona Lisa,* or *The Man with the Hoe,* or even that *American Gothic* thing? Why is that?"

Everybody turned to regard me, as the one to whom the query had obviously been put. "That's a hard question for me to answer," I said, frowning into my plate. I nibbled thoughtfully on a fragment of cold salmon. "Your basic point is, of course, well taken—that the portraits we get are not deserving of the name. Look like somebody threw an egg at the canvas."

Fuming, I became lost in the ensuing free-for-all. Not so my wife, whom annoyance renders articulate. She more than held her own in the argument, which was cut short when Mary Cobble upset a glass of iced tea. She made some cheery remark to smooth over the incident. The remark wasn't funny, nor was it intended to be funny, but to a man her retinue threw back their heads and laughed.

Meaning to be nice, I laughed, too, and said, "Well, it goes to show you. A good comedienne has her wits about her."

"And pays them well," my wife remarked, in her corner. (Luckily, Mary Cobble didn't hear it, but two or three others did, and they repeated it until it achieved wide circulation, with a resulting increase in our dinner invitations. That, however, was later. The present problem was to get through the rest of the evening.)

We had to bolt our dessert and rush to the theatre, where they were doing *King Lear* in Bermuda shorts, or something, and my wife and I took another couple in our car, so I didn't get a chance to speak to her alone until after the show. Then I let her have it.

"That was a waspish remark," I said. "And do you know why you made it? Resentment. A feeling of being out of the swim. It's because you're not good at repartee that you say things like that, and are bitter."

"Things like what?" my wife asked.

I explained what, and repeated my charge.

In the wrangle, quite heated, that followed her denial of it, she gave me nothing but proof of its truth. I submitted that the idea of mine that had given rise to this hassle, and of which the hassle could safely be taken to be the corpse, had been a cozy and even a tender one: the idea that a man and wife could operate as a team in public. "What could be more domestic?" I said.

"Domesticity begins at home," she rather dryly returned.

I met this with a withering silence.

1956

NOAH BAUMBACH

THE ZAGAT HISTORY OF MY
LAST RELATIONSHIP

AASE'S

Bring a "first date" to this "postage stamp"–size bistro. Tables are so close you're practically "sitting in the laps" of the couple next to you, but the lush décor is "the color of love." Discuss your respective "dysfunctional families" and tell her one of your "fail-safe" stories about your father's "cheapness" and you're certain to "get a laugh." After the "to die for" soufflés, expect a good-night kiss, but don't push for more, because if you play your cards right there's a second date "right around the corner."

BRASSERIE PENELOPE

"Ambience and then some" at this Jamaican-Norwegian hybrid. Service might be a "tad cool," but the warmth you feel when you gaze into her baby blues will more than compensate for it. Conversation is "spicier than the jerk chicken," and before you know it you'll be back at her one-bedroom in the East Village, quite possibly "getting lucky."

THE CHICK & HEN

Perfect for breakfast "after sleeping together," with "killer coffee" that will "help cure your seven-beer/three-aquavit hangover." Not that you need it—your "amplified high spirits" after having had sex for the first time in "eight months" should do the trick.

DESARCINA'S

So what if she thought the movie was "pretentious and contrived" and you felt it was a "masterpiece" and are dying to inform her that "she doesn't know what she's talking about"? Remember, you were looking for a woman who wouldn't "yes" you all the time. And after one bite of chef Leonard Desarcina's "duck manqué" and a sip of the "generous" gin Margaritas you'll start to see that she might have a point.

GORDY'S

Don't be ashamed if you don't know what wine to order with your seared minnow; the "incredibly knowledgeable" waiters will be more than pleased to assist. But if she makes fun of "the way you never make eye contact with people," you might turn "snappish" and end up having your first "serious fight," one where feelings are "hurt."

PANCHO MAO

"Bring your wallet," say admirers of Louis Grenouille's pan-Asian-Mexican-style fare, because it's "so expensive you'll start to wonder why she hasn't yet picked up a tab." The "celeb meter is high," and "Peter Jennings" at the table next to yours might spark an "inane political argument" where you find yourself "irrationally defending Enron" and finally saying aloud, "You don't know what you're talking about!" Don't let her "stuff herself," as she might use that as an excuse to go to sleep "without doing it."

RIGMAROLE

At this Wall Street old boys' club, don't be surprised if you run into one of her "ex-boyfriends" who works in "finance." Be prepared for his "power play," when he sends over a pitcher of "the freshest-tasting sangria this side of Barcelona," prompting her to visit his table for "ten minutes" and to come back "laughing" and suddenly critical of your "cravat." The room is "snug," to say the least, and it's not the best place to say, full voice, "What the fuck were you thinking dating him?" But don't overlook the "best paella in town" and a din "so loud" you won't notice that neither of you is saying anything.

TATI

Prices so "steep" you might feel you made a serious "career gaffe" by taking the "high road" and being an academic rather than "selling out" like "every other asshole she's gone out with." The "plush seats" come in handy if she's forty-five minutes late and arrives looking a little "preoccupied" and wearing "a sly smile."

VANDERWEI'S

Be careful not to combine "four dry sakes" with your "creeping feeling of insecurity and dread," or you might find yourself saying, "Wipe that damn grin off your face!" The bathrooms are "big and glamorous," so you won't mind spending an hour with your cheek pressed against the "cool tiled floor" after she "walks out." And the hip East Village location can't be beat, since her apartment is "within walking distance," which makes it very convenient if you should choose to "lean on her buzzer for an hour" until she calls "the cops."

ZACHARIA AND SONS & CO.

This "out of the way," "dirt cheap," "near impossible to find," "innocuous" diner is ideal for "eating solo" and insuring that you "won't run into your ex, who has gone back to the bond trader." The "mediocre at best" burgers and "soggy fries" will make you wish you "never existed" and wonder why you're so "frustrated with your life" and unable to sustain a "normal," "healthy" "relationship."

2002

DAVID OWEN

8 SIMPLE RULES FOR DATING
MY EX-WIFE

I SHARE the blame for my divorce. I did a lot of things wrong in my marriage: worked too hard, cared too much, made too many sacrifices for my family. Tore my heart out and left it lying on the kitchen floor so that anybody who wasn't too busy stabbing me in the back could stomp it into the no-wax vinyl tiles that I myself laid down at a savings of more than two thousand dollars. I am guilty of that and more.

But forget it. Past is past. Let's move on. You are now dating my ex-wife, and her lawyer, my lawyer, and a state judge have all informed me in writing that you have a legal right to do so. So be it. I'm not a black-mailing pickpocket doubletalking divorce attorney, so I don't know the technicalities. But the two of us still need to have some kind of ground rules here:

1. Twenty-two years, pal. That's how long we were married. You've been dating her for a month. Tell you what. In twenty-one years and eleven months, let's you and me talk again.

2. Despite what you may have been told, I've got some self-respect left, and I don't need to have your face shoved into my face every time I turn around. From five o'clock on Friday afternoon until two o'clock on Sunday morning, the bar at the Ramada Inn belongs to me.

3. The oil in the Saturn wagon gets changed every three thousand miles—not five thousand miles, not seven thousand miles, not ten thousand miles—and I don't care what she or the owner's manual

or the guy in the service department or the Internet says. Three. Thousand. God. Damned. Miles.

4. The Wiffle ball hanging from the string in the right-hand bay of the garage is where the middle of the front of the hood of the Saturn wagon should be pointed when it's parked correctly. The Wiffle ball is not supposed to rest on the hood of the car. You aim at the ball. It makes parking easier.

5. The two of you don't walk together within a thousand feet of the golf course or the driving range. Not ever.

6. Before you even ask, allow me to explain why there's no cable TV. To install cable TV, they have to drill a hole through the house. Hey, fine, so let's get satellite TV instead. Well, guess what? To install satellite TV, they have to drill about twenty holes through the roof. Somebody ought to get the Nobel Prize for that idea—drilling holes through the roof.

7. The band saw in the basement belongs to me. You are not to use it, you are not to move it, you are not to put anything on it or let anyone else put anything on it, including even just one corner of a laundry basket while the person carrying the laundry basket scratches their nose. I can't remove the band saw from the basement just yet. For one thing, I don't have a workshop to put it in anymore, and if you're interested in knowing why I suggest you study the terms of my divorce. For another thing, I assembled that band saw myself. When I got the box home from Sears, I thought, Hey, great, I'll just lift out my brand-new band saw and start ripping pressure-treated railroad ties, but guess what? The box didn't contain a band saw. The box contained a large plastic bag filled with medium-sized plastic bags filled with small plastic bags filled with parts the size of bird shot. Putting that thing together took three solid months of the best years of my life, and to make the blade cut plumb I had to level the legs with a laser transit that I borrowed from a friend of mine who's a contractor. So hands the hell off.

8. This should go without saying, but—no funny business. Understood? She's fifty years old, for crying out loud.

2004

PATRICIA MARX

AUDIO TOUR

HELLO, and welcome to the rent-stabilized apartment of Todd Niesle. I'm Debby, a specialist in Todd Niesle, and I'm going to be your guide. Before you begin your journey through the World of Todd Niesle and His Stuff, may I ask you to reduce the volume on your Acoustiguide player to a polite level? Todd Niesle does not know that you are here. Moreover, the woman in 12-A has had a bee in her bonnet about me ever since I, Debby, while, okay, yes, a tiny bit drunk, mistook her door for Todd Niesle's late one night and jimmied it open. But that's another Acousti-story.

You are standing in Todd Niesle's foyer. The faux faux-marble table on your right is attributed to Todd Niesle's mother, circa last Christmas. It's a fine example of a piece that I, Debby, do not like. Take a moment to look through the mail on the faux faux-marble table. There should be a lot of it, because Todd Niesle is away, skiing in Vermont with his brother. Is there a letter postmarked Milwaukee? Just curious.

Proceed through the foyer and into the living room. In this room, we can see the influence of early Michelle. Notice how Michelle seems to like making bold statements with splashes of color, especially in upholstery. You can tell by the excess of passementerie on the throw pillows what an incorrigible bitch Michelle is. If you care to pause to look at some of the art and other knickknacks, simply press the red button on your Acoustiguide. We will continue at the medicine cabinet in the bathroom off the master bedroom.

To reach the master bedroom, you must traverse the cavernous room on your left. The sole function of that room is to provide a way to the next room. It doesn't seem fair that Todd Niesle pays only eleven hundred dollars a month for this spacious two-bedroom with a dining room, when I, Debby, happen to know that his income far exceeds the maximum allowed for a tenant in a rent-stabilized apartment. Furthermore, I, Debby, have heard Todd Niesle say on more than one occasion, "There's tons more closet space here than I know what to do with." And yet I, Debby, was never offered more than half a drawer, and even that humiliating amount I had to demand. The phone number for the Rent Info Hotline is 718-739-6400 (ask for Eligibility Violations).

Examine the objets in the master bedroom. Here is the famous jar of pennies and the original green shag rug from Todd Niesle's college days. Pay close attention to the black lace brassiere in the bottom drawer of Todd Niesle's bureau. The brassiere (36D) is not typical of the underwear of Todd Niesle. Or of mine (32B). You may be wondering what the brassiere is doing in this exhibit of the World of Todd Niesle and His Stuff. As Todd Niesle's quondam girlfriend, I, Debby, am wondering this, too.

Now we're in the bathroom. Actually, don't bother looking through the medicine cabinet. Todd Niesle must have taken all of the incriminating artifacts with him to Vermont.

Our next stop is the kitchen. Open the refrigerator. The carton of milk dates from the twelfth century A.D. See the Krups espresso maker? I, Debby, gave him that. It cost $249, not including tax. You know what his gift to me, Debby, for my birthday was? A colander. You will observe that Todd Niesle's apartment has no gift shop. Correction: You are standing in the gift shop. Take the espresso maker.

As you help yourself to the professional-grade milk frother that I, Debby, also gave to Todd Niesle, be careful not to step on the creaky floorboard, as it will alert the neighbor downstairs, who also has it in for me. She's insane. Besides, I, Debby, wouldn't even know how to poison a dog.

We are now in the commodious coat closet in Todd Niesle's foyer. Our eyes are drawn immediately to the striking composition of the skis and the parka against the back wall. This is a stunning visual statement about a man who is on vacation, skiing with his brother, isn't it? Once again, Todd Niesle proves himself to be a master at creating a scenario that elicits powerful emotions, such as hatred and disgust.

After you have scrolled through the caller-ID log on the phone in the study, looking for Todd Niesle's brother's number to see if Todd Niesle really went to Vermont, place a prank call to Sue Ann Kraftsow. She lives in Milwaukee and she's in the book.

Please turn to your right. Just past the doorway, you'll see a framed photograph. The subject of this photograph has not been identified with certainty, but Todd Niesle scholars like me, Debby, believe that it depicts Sue Ann Kraftsow.

Now go back to the gift shop and get a knife from the drawer next to the sink. When you pry the backing from the picture frame, a photograph of me, Debby, will be revealed. In the art world, this is called "pentimento." In the real world, this is called failure to commit and to recognize undying love when you have the luck to get it.

Compare the two images. Can you discern from the vulgar contours of Sue Ann Kraftsow's face, the lifeless pallor, and the vague gaze that she is unworthy of even as base a miscreant as Todd Niesle? She's also fat. The second image, of me, Debby, on the other hand, shows a woman blessed with keen intelligence and generosity of spirit. It would be unscholarly of me, Debby, to point out the obvious aesthetic differences, but you, the viewer, can draw your own conclusions.

We have come to the end of our retrospective of the World of Todd Niesle and His Shit. You can return your Acoustiguide in the foyer. There is no charge for this tour, but if you enjoyed yourself, call Todd Niesle and tell him so. His number is 212-399-4838 and he can be reached at 3 A.M. He likes pizza, ten pies at a time, and Rizzo's delivers. I, Debby, care not what you do with the key.

2005

LARRY DOYLE

SHARE OUR JOY

WELCOME to GwynnandDaveShareTheirJoy.com, Gwynn Paley and Dave Maguire's Official Nuptials site. To continue, enter the GUEST ID and PASSWORD you received with your Wedding e-vitation. Please enjoy this short ad while the site loads.

Two blushing brides,
one rich, one poor.
Both have their hearts set on getting
married at the same romantic location.
On the same day.
Reese Witherspoon. Jennifer Lopez.
In love and at war for

The Wedding Pagoda.
Opening June 14th.

Friends and Family! I can't tell you how excited Dave and I are that you'll be able to join us as we Pledge our Love! Below you'll find all the info you need to help us make this Occasion as Special and Perfect as we have planned.

GUEST POLICY

E-vites are for the Guest only; there is no "implied plus-one." We're sorry, but it's a very small mountaintop, with limited ruins. We have gone to exhaustive lengths to achieve a proper mix of personalities, races, classes, ages, and orientations to insure a Fun and Romantic Event for all. So don't be surprised to find that your True Plus-One is already there! (Though just one plus-one per guest, please. Do you hear me, Erika?)

We regret, too, the no-children rule. Some of us feel that Children bring nothing but Joy to all occasions; others feel differently, and this is a discussion we've agreed to table until a later time. (Not *too* much later! Tick tick tick . . .) If it's any consolation, you'll be sparing your Little Loved Ones many painful inoculations, and then there's the whole child-slavery thing.

DIRECTIONS

Upon arriving at the Aeropuerto Internacional Jorge Chávez, in Lima, look for the Aero Sendero terminal. It's a corrugated-metal shed. Sendero, your pilot, should be there (he looks just like Erik Estrada, had things not gone so well for him). His Piper Apache is completely airworthy, and, if it comes to it, somewhat seaworthy. After my father conducts a quick sobriety check, Sendero will wing you to a private airstrip on the shore of Lake Titicaca. From there, you'll travel via balsa de totora, or reed boat, to the island of Amantaní. Once ashore, llamas will take you up the mountainside of Pachatata (Father Earth), where you will be given a sleeping bag and assigned to a ruin.

A FEW TRAVEL TIPS

• Do not let Sendero sell you any cocaine. We have made an exclusive arrangement with another supplier. Anybody wishing to partake of this local fare must contact Dave's brother Drake. If you fail to do so, we may find ourselves short a best man.

- Lake Titicaca is a sacred Inca site. Their god or something rose out of it. Mocking its name, or the name of nearby Lake Poopó, is considered incredibly rude and has resulted in spontaneous stabbings.
- Since Pachatata is 13,615 feet above sea level, you may not be able to breathe. We will have oxygen on hand, but in limited supplies, so, unless you are absolutely certain you are going to die, please be considerate of others.
- If you look directly at your llama, it will spit in your eyes.

THE CEREMONY

You will awaken at 2 A.M. (it'll be too cold to sleep anyway) and llama it down Pachatata and then up Pachamama (Earth Mother). We should arrive at the peak between 4:30 and 5:30, depending on bandits, in time to witness the first light of the Solstice, at 5:58. The Incas believe that if you stare into the sun as it rises on this day you will be Reawakened to the Ancient Knowledge of the Cosmos. Hopefully this will distract you from the sound of the seven llamas being slaughtered. (Some of you will have to walk back. Sorry.) Following a brief sacrifice to the Dragon Fertility Goddess (don't tell Dave!), we will enjoy a traditional breakfast of potatoes and *mate de coca*, which is basically boiled cocaine and which I'm told puts Starbucks to shame.

The ceremony will take place at noon, officiated by a Genuine Quechua Shaman and, at the insistence of Dave's mom, Father Mulcahy, who has promised to keep his pagan comments to a minimum. First, Shaman Klaatu will ritually purify the Bride and Groom (good luck with that!), and then we will exchange Personalized Vows written by me with input from Dave. In Andean tradition, the marriage will be sealed with an exchange of shoes. (Luv those Incas!)

THE RECEPTION

The reception is scheduled for 4 P.M., or whenever the llamas are done. We ask that after the ceremony you gather as much firewood and wild potatoes as you can. In lieu of champagne, we will be serving chicha, made by the island's women, who chew up corn and other things and spit it into an earthenware pot for fermenting. It takes a little getting used to, but consumed in vast quantities, as is the tradition, it can sneak up on you. Accordingly, the Shaman will remain on hand to perform additional marriages as necessary. Unfortunately, Dave and I will have to leave early in order to make our plane to the Galápagos. And please: If anybody ties beer cans to the back of our getaway llama, I will cry.

ONE FINAL REQUEST

A lot of hard work and patience and tears and sexual compromise went into making this a Wonderful Celebration of Love. This is the wedding I've dreamed about ever since studying pre-Columbian civilization in the fifth grade. If you cannot enjoy and experience it appropriately, I ask that you strongly consider staying home with the rest of Dave's buddies. (That doesn't apply to you, Dave!)

2007

THE FLESH
IS WEAK

E. B. WHITE

FRIGIDITY IN MEN

A LEAF FROM A SEX BOOK

I HESITATE to approach the subject of male unresponsiveness. Frigidity in men is a theme sociologists have avoided. Frigidity in women, on the other hand, forms a vast chapter in the sex research of today; the part it plays in marital discord is known to students of sociology as well as to the lay reader, although probably less well. It has occupied the attention of many noted writers, and has taken the lives of such men as Zaner and Tithridge, who carried some of their experiments too far. (Tithridge especially.)

Any discussion of frigidity in men calls for an unusual degree of frankness on the part of the writer, since it entails such factors as the "recessive knee," "Fuller's retort," and the "declination of the kiss." Sex is less than fifty years old, yet it has upset the whole western world. The sublimation of sex, called Love, is of course much older—although many purists will question the existence of Love prior to about 1885 on the grounds that there can be no sublimation of a non-existent feeling. And that brings us to our real theme, namely, frigidity in men.

THE first symptom of frigidity in men is what I call the "recessive knee." Simply stated, the phenomenon is this: occasions arise sometimes when a girl presses her knee, ever so gently, against the knee of the young man she is out with. The juxtaposing of the knee is brought about by any of a thousand causes. Often the topic of conversation has something to do with it: the young people, talking along pleasantly, will suddenly experience a sensation of compatibility, or of friendliness, or of pity, or of community-of-interests. One of them will make a remark singularly agreeable to the other person—a chance word or phrase that seems to establish a bond between them. Such a remark can cause the knee of the girl to be placed against the knee of the young man. Or, if the two people are in a cab, the turning of a sharp corner will do it. In canoes, the wash from a larger vessel will bring it about. In restaurants and dining-rooms it often takes place under the table, as though by accident. On divans, sofas, settees, couches, davenports, and the like, the slight twist of the young lady's body incident to receiving a light for her cigarette will cause it. I could go on indefinitely, but there is no need. It is not a hard push, you understand—rather the merest touch of knee to knee, light as the brush of a falling blossom against one's cheek, and just as lovely.

Now, a normal male in whom there are no traces of frigidity will allow his knee to retain its original position, sometimes even exerting a very slight counter-pressure. A frigid male, however, will move his knee away at the first suggestion of contact, denying himself the electric stimulus of love's first stirring. Why? That is what my research was conducted to discover. *I found that in ninety-three per cent of all cases, the male was suspicious; in four per cent he was ignorant; and in three per cent he was tired.* I have presented these figures to the American Medical Association and am awaiting a reply.

It is the female's subtlety in her laying-on of the knee that annoys the male, I found. His recession is for the purpose of reassuring himself of his own integrity and perspicacity. If the female were to juxtapose in a forthright manner, if she were to preface her gesture with the remark: "I am thinking of letting my knee touch yours for the fun of it, Mortimer," she might gain an entirely different response from the male.

It was a young Paterson, New Jersey, girl by the name of Lillian Fuller who let drop the remark that has epitomized, for the sociological and anthropological world, the phenomenon of the recessive knee. "Fuller's retort" is now a common phrase in the realm of psychotherapy.

Miss Fuller was an unusually beautiful woman—young, accurate, sensitive. She was greatly attached to a man several years her senior in the buffing department; wanted to marry him. To this end she had laid her knee against his innumerable times without a single return of pressure. His frigidity, she realized, was gradually becoming prejudicial to his mental health, and so one evening after experiencing for the hundredth time the withdrawal of his knee, she simply turned to him with a quiet smile playing on her face and said: "Say, what is the matter with you, anyway?"

Her retort somehow summed up the whole question of frigidity in men.

THE second great symptom of frigidity is the "declination of the kiss."[1] Many men have told me that they would not object to sex were it not for its contactual aspect. That is, they said they would be perfectly willing to express their eroticism if it could be done at a reasonable distance—say fifty paces. These men (the frigid-*plus* type) found kissing intolerable. When they had an opportunity to kiss a young lady, they declined. They made it plain that they would be willing to blow a kiss across the room from their hand, but not execute it with their lips.

I analyzed scores of these cases, questioning both the women and the men. (The women were mad as hornets.) I found that a small number of the kiss-declining men were suffering from a pathology of the eyes—either astigmatism or farsightedness—so that when they got close enough to kiss a girl, she blurred on them.[2] The vast majority of cases, however, were quite different. Their unwillingness I traced to a much subtler feeling than eyestrain. Your true anti-contactual, or kiss-decliner, is a very subtle individual indeed.

In effect, he is a throwback to another period in history, specifically to the Middle Ages. He is a biological sport. (Note: this is very confusing, calling him a "sport," because the ordinary "sport" is not a kiss-decliner at all, anything but. If there are any of you who think you are going to find the use of the word "sport" in this connection so confusing as to make the rest of the chapter unintelligible, I wish you would drop out.)

No one can quite comprehend the motives and the successes of a kiss-decliner who does not recall his counterpart in medieval history. In the Middle Ages, when men were lusty and full of red meat, their women expected as much. A baronial fellow, finishing his meal, made no ado about kissing a Middle Age woman. He just got up from the table and kissed her. Bango, and she was kissed. Love had a simple directness which was not disturbed until the arrival, in the land, of the Minnesingers. It got so no baronial hall of the Middle Ages was free from the Minnesingers. They kept getting in. They would bring their

1. Now we're getting down to business.
2. Incidentally, I might say that this blurring of the female before the eyes of the male is not entirely unpleasant. It's kind of fun.

harps with them, and after dinner they would twang a couple of notes and then sing a frail, delicate song to the effect that women should be worshipped from afar, rather than possessed. To a baron who had just drunk a goblet of red wine, this new concept of womanhood was very, very funny. While he was chuckling away to himself and cutting himself another side of beef, his wife, who had listened attentively to the song, would slip out into the alley behind the castle and there the Minnesinger would join her.

"Sing that one again," she would say.

"Which one?"

"That one about worshipping me from a little distance. I want to hear that one again."

The Minnesinger would oblige. Then he would illustrate the theme by not kissing the woman but dancing off lightly down the hill, throwing his harp up into the air and catching it again as he went.

"What a nice young man," the baron's wife would think, as she slowly turned and went in to bed.

The kiss-decliner of today is a modern Minnesinger. He is a sport in that he has varied suddenly from the normal type—which is still baronial. By the mere gesture of declining a kiss, a man can still make quite a lot of ground, even in these depleted days. The woman thinks: "He would not dream of embracing my body; now that's pretty white of him!" Of course, it would be wrong to ascribe motives of sheer deliberateness to the frigid male. Often he is not a bad sort—merely is a fellow who prefers an imagined kiss to the real kind. An imagined kiss is more easily controlled, more thoroughly enjoyed, and less cluttery than an actual kiss. To kiss in dream is wholly pleasant. First, the woman is the one of your selection, not just anyone who happens to be in your arms at the moment. Second, the deed is garnished with a little sprig of glamour which the mind, in exquisite taste, contributes. Third, the lips, imaginatively, are placed just so, the right hand is placed just so, the concurrent thoughts arrive, just so. Except for the fact that the whole episode is a little bit stuffy, it is a superior experience all round. When a kiss becomes actual, anything is likely to happen. The lips, failing of the mark, may strike lightly against the end of the lady's nose, causing the whole adventure to crack up; or the right hand may come in contact with the hard jagged part of the shoulder blade; or, worst of all, the man's thoughts may not clothe the moment with the proper splendor: he may be worrying about something.

So you see, frigidity in men has many aspects, many angles. To me it is vastly more engrossing than frigidity in women, which is such a simple phenomenon you wonder anybody bothers about it at all.

1929

ROGER ANGELL

THE NEW YORKER ADVISOR

(INTIMATE COUNSELING FOR OUR TROUBLED READERS, MORE OR LESS IN THE CONFIDENT MANNER OF *PLAYBOY*, *PENTHOUSE*, AND OTHER CURRENT JOURNALS OF PHILOSOPHY)

SMALL TIME

Dear Advisor:

I have hesitated for some time before writing you, but I don't know where else to go for help. I have a problem which can't be entirely unique, yet I have not been able to find any reliable scientific data that would put my mind to rest. To put it plainly, I have a very small organ. I know, of course, that there is no "right" size in these matters, and I sometimes suspect that my judgment may be unduly subjective in this estimation. Still, I have made covert observations and comparisons whenever the opportunity presented itself, and there is no doubt in my mind that mine is the most modest instrument in our entire suburban neighborhood. My wife gets very impatient whenever I try to discuss the matter with her, and assures me that she has absolutely no complaints. The others in my family feel the same way (we are a modern household, and we believe in discussing everything quite openly), and my teen-age son and daughter keep telling me that I am hopelessly bourgeois and insecure to keep brooding about this. "Forget it, Pop," they say.

Who is right?

UNHAPPY FRED
Evanston, Illinois

Call yourself lucky, Fred, for you have a model wife and two thoughtful, very "with it" kids. They are right, of course, and the real wonder of your case is that you could have gone along for as long as you did, worrying and troubling yourself over such an insignificant matter, when a little reading in your local library or a plain question in the right quarter could have settled your doubts once and for all. Today, we have finally come to understand that there is no such thing as a "normal" size for an organ. Perhaps, like many older persons, your judgment of acceptable dimensions was heavily influenced by youthful impressions formed in church or at the theatre. Yet for every gigantic organ, such as the memorable installation at the Radio City Music Hall or the massive unit at some great place of worship (the organ at Winchester Cathedral, installed in 950 A.D., had four hundred pipes and required seventy men to operate the bellows), there are today scores of serviceable bijou household instruments that are modest in price and excellently pleasing in tone. You may recall that the late Albert Schweitzer was able to continue his daily sessions at the key- and footboards even in the primitive musical surroundings of Lambaréné. The current trend in organ building is away from awesome size and power and toward the modest ideals of Gottfried Silbermann (1683–1753), the Dresden genius whose instruments produced a light, transparent tone, in perfect keeping with the polyphonics of the high Baroque. Vox humana *(Dig it, Fred!)* vox Dei!

GREENHORN

Dear Advisor:

I am a healthy adult male, with a healthy sex drive. My evenings always end up in the sack, even on a first date, and I am in the habit of conducting four or five meaningful affairs at the same time, often with chicks who happen to be roommates. Right now, I am hooked up with two beautiful sisters who almost surely know that they are sharing me, but I don't think they have guessed that I am also on intimate terms with their old lady, a mature and very appreciative woman in her sixties—with the bod of a mellow thirty-year-old! I am not averse to occasional homosexual adventures, if the ambience is right, and of course I groove on the new bisexual scene as well. I am what you would call a sexual athlete, and nothing in nature is alien to me. Okay, fine—so why is it I can't seem to score with a plant? All my friends here in northern California are way into plant relationships. They read to their avocados, repeat mantras with their geraniums and grape ivies, pass weekends of meditation with a wandering Jew or a *Dracaena marginata,* and sleep over with yuccas. They tell me there is no trip like the achievement of a deep one-to-one understanding with a member of the flora. I have tried to follow their lead, but so far without success. Indeed, whenever I find myself alone in a room with a young plant or vegetable, I am overcome with shyness. I find myself stammering and sweating with embarrassment, and I "don't know where to look." The last time I tried, an office friend of mine had fixed me up with a pair of delicious-looking rutabagas. I arrived wearing my new suede high-rise bells, sandals, and a liberal splash of Brut. We settled down together in a corner of the patio, all in readiness for a memorable new friendship—and I froze. Striving for my customary aplomb, I lit up a joint and then fell into a strangling paroxysm of coughing. I sprang up from the lanai, upsetting my glass of sangria, mumbled some excuse about an overdue algebra paper, and fled, leaving my buxom young companions speechless. This sort of repeated failure has begun to sap my confidence, and I find myself spending more and more nights at home alone. What's the matter with me anyway?

J.F.W.
San Leandro, California

Probably your only mistake is trying to rush things. Accustomed to swift success in other quarters, you are not quite at ease with the more laggard emotional cycle and lower motor responses of our green friends. With plants (especially with drupes and the smaller legumes), the motto must always be "Take your time!" Keep your mind off the ultimate relationship desired. Try, rather, to deal with the whole vegetable. Examine your unconscious for signs of repressed taboos, remembering that, as you yourself suggest, nothing in nature is kinky, unless you think it is. *Hold in your mind the image of a cultured Japanese gentleman deep in contemplation of his stony garden or miniature bonsai plant (the Japs, as you know, are way ahead of us in the sensual ballgame). You might even memorize Andrew Marvell's "My vegetable love should grow / Vaster than empires, and more slow." There is nothing new about plant love, no matter what your neighbors say. Indeed, the best of advice in this area comes to us from the British sexologists Gilbert and Sullivan, who prescribed:*

> *An attachment à la Plato for a bashful young potato,*
> *or a not-too-French French bean!*

SOUTHPAW

Dear Advisor:

I think I am obsessed. I am a foot fetishist, and over the years I have come to accept this quirk of nature without fear or self-loathing; it is simply a fact about me, like the color of my eyes (hazel, with glints of green) or my hat size (7³/₈). No problem there. My hangup is that out of all the millions and millions of feet in the world, there is only one single, solitary foot that means anything to me. Have you ever heard of anything so silly? Yes? Well, what do you say when I add that the foot in question, the Foot Supreme, is one of my own—i.e., the left? Advisor, I love my left foot with a devotion that is beyond my powers of description. Each morning when I awake, I draw Li'l Tootsie (as I call him) gently out of the covers to see how he has fared during the long night hours. During the day, I often glance down to admire his perky stride, his stylish recovery, his lithe, almost Indian feel for the ground. At home in the evening, I usually go around half barefoot, in order to give my friend a taste of freedom and relaxation. In my younger days, I confess, I would sometimes secretly remove my left shoe and sock while in the office and conduct business (I am a Certified Public Accountant) in perfectly normal fashion—with my playmate shamelessly naked beneath my desk!

To anticipate your questions, I feel nothing of this nature for my other foot. I cannot explain why this starboard extremity, apparently the mirror image of my heart's delight, occasions no response in me beyond the rather tepid attention with which we all regard our various sets of physiological baggage. Truly, *le cœur a ses raisons que la raison ne connaît point*! Nor can I explain my dogged (no pun intended) faithfulness, sustained over the decades, to this one and only foot. How often have I told myself that a bit of adventuring—a brief, lighthearted tickle with some of the countless attractive and obviously willing young feet that one glimpses on all sides—would only bring me back to my life's companion with a refreshed appreciation. But when the moment comes I always refrain.

In truth, it is probably too late for such forays now. I am sixty-two, and troubled with arthritis, and Li'l Tootsie also looks his age—not a pretty sight, I'll wager, to anyone but me. No matter. I keep his photograph on my bureau—a perfect likeness of him as he used to be in his high-arching youth—and this is the image that is always in my heart. We are content to potter along together through the evening of our life, cracking our joints as we warm ourselves before the hearth and finding pictures in the firelight.

I feel pretty good most of the time, but I reckon I must need help.

E. McC.
Salt Lake City

No, dear sir, you do not need any advice. It is we, rather—all of us, everywhere—who should help ourselves by reading your gentle and happy tale and taking it to heart. Many of our subscribers may feel revulsion or a cynical contempt for your homespun passion, but we defy them. Freedom is finding joy wherever it may fall and clasping it to one's bosom. Thanks, E. McC., and Tootsie, for the beautiful reminder!

ALL TIED UP

Dear Advisor:

I am in need of sartorial first aid. Six or seven years ago, I suffered a heavy setback in my fashionable self-esteem, and since that time I rarely venture from the house at night. My frau tells me that I am turning into some kind of weirdo hermit and says for me to give my story to your sophisticated editors and let them handle it.

It all began when we got this invitation from a famous film actor, asking us to come to a New Year's Eve party at his Manhattan town house. (Never mind his name; this wasn't his fault, and I don't want to embarrass him.) I should explain that I am in industrial-freezer parts and I don't usually hang out with celebrities. The way I happened to meet him was that we sat next to each other on a Cleveland-to-Kennedy flight that got hung up in a weather-stack over Pennsylvania for three hours; when we landed, we wrote our names down and promised to look each other up someday, but I frankly never expected he'd take me up on it, until we got the invite in the mail. At first, Molly and I thought, sure, what a gas, we'll go. Then I looked again and saw that down in the corner of the invitation it said "Dress: Mod, or what you will," and my heart sank. You see, I didn't own any Mod clothes, and I thought, well, better forget the party, we'll just stay home New Year's Eve and maybe get a bottle of champagne in, like always. But my wife was dying to go, of course, and she said, look, no problem, we'll just go to one of those boutiques and pick you out a wild tie, right?

To make a long story short, that's just what we did. We ended up at a place called Paraphernalia, on Madison Avenue (it's gone now, I think), and a helpful young fellow helped me pick out a wide, wide one, in cherry-colored silk, that looked like an effect out of *Star Trek*. Came the night, and I put it on (after a lot of wrestling with all that material in the knot) and wore my old chalk-stripe suit, and the getup was pretty crazy, if I do say so. Around ten-thirty, the wife and I hop a cab and go down to the actor's house for the big blast. There are all kinds of people crowding in the front door, wearing more kinds of clothes (and no clothes) than I've ever seen before, and there are even Pinkertons there, to keep out the crashers. But we have our invitation, and after somebody looks us over we are let in. Upstairs, there are two rock bands going, one at each end of the house, and the place is wall-to-wall people and noise. We stand there, jammed by the stairs, and pretty soon along comes my friend the host, smiling at everybody. I put out my hand and say, "This is a whole lot better than ten thousand feet over McKeesport, isn't it?" and he looks at us in sort of a startled way, and then shakes my hand and kisses Molly on the cheek (ruining her for life), and says, "It's just *marvelous* you could come. Look, the bar is way over there somewhere, or there's another one back down *that* way. Get yourself anything you want, and when I come back we'll have magic time. 'Bye, dears."

Well, I finally did get up to the bar after a lot of elbowing and being pushed and spilled on, and after a while I got us a couple of double Scotches, and the wife and I found a sort of corner, and stood there and sipped and began looking over the roaring mob. What we did was, we pretended to be having this very animated conversation, leaning toward each other to listen and then laughing a lot, but all the time we were both really rolling our eyes back and forth across the room looking for somebody, anybody, we knew. You know how it is sometimes. The trouble was that this beginning part of the party didn't end, the way it usually does. We looked and we talked and laughed and we looked some more, and though there were plenty of faces we had seen on the *Merv Griffin Show* and places like that, there was nobody we *knew*. I was about to try the old bar-fight again, when all of a sudden way across the room I saw this man's face that I recognized. Just as I spotted him, he saw me, too, and he sort of raised his eyebrows in a friendly, surprised way, and then I saw him starting to come through the mob to say hello.

"Here comes a friend of mine," I said to Molly out of the corner of my mouth.

"Who?" she said. "Who is it?"

"Tell you in a minute," I said.

But the trouble was I couldn't remember him. The name was right on the tip of my tongue. He was a young-looking fellow, sort of handsome, and his smile got bigger and bigger as he sidled his way through the guests and finally came up to us.

"Well," he said, "I never thought I'd find you *here*! How are you, anyway?"

"Fine and dandy," I said. "You remember Molly, don't you?" I was fighting for time.

"You're looking terrific," he said. "I knew you would." Then there was a pause, and he said, "You don't remember me, do you?"

I said, "Sure I do. I recognized you way across the room there, didn't I? Just give me a second here. You're . . . You're—"

"I sold you that tie at Paraphernalia yesterday," he said.

That's about all there is to it. We got out of there just after midnight (our host never did come back), and ever since then I have sort of given up going to big parties. I have also given up small parties. To tell the truth, for these past six years I have just stayed home. Sometimes I have got up my nerve to go to a show or out to dinner with business friends, but when I go up to my tie rack to pick out the evening cravat, I begin to sway and this gray mist forms in front of my eyes. So I give up, and the evening ends with me in front of the old television again, in my undershirt.

Molly has told me she will leave home for good, no fooling, unless I wrote this letter and asked you where I can get myself some decent, stylish neckties—not too bright, no wild designs—so I can start getting back in the swim.

Now it's your move.

HERBIE THE HERMIT
Port Washington, New York

Come on out, Herbie. You are in luck, you see, because nobody has been wearing neckties for years now. You can dress up in turtlenecks or splashy T-shirts or high-rise collars or even an occasional knotted foulard, but forget the tie. Better hurry, though. Old-timey looks are the growing mushroom cloud on the menswear horizon, and that means that the four-in-hand has probably turned the corner. The nostalgia boom has already shot right through the fifties, and at that rate we'll be back to Mod in no time. Hope you saved that big-breakfast job from Paraphernalia. This time, why don't you give the party?

IN THE DARK

Dear Advisor:

I am a centerfold photographer. For years now, I have been talking bosomy young females out of their inhibitions and into instant (f/8 at 1/125th) four-color national celebrity. I am the dermal Steichen, the Fragonard of the furtive male fancy, the dream-master of Fraternity Row. The costume chest in my studio resembles the wardrobe department of an Edwardian bordel—a soft plethora of feather boas, filmy peignoirs, eight-foot-long necklaces, ribbed pink knee socks, Andalusian fans, inflatable lumbar pillows, wolfskin throws, Cecil Beaton chapeaux, filigreed back scratchers, transparent silk dolmans, polar-bear rugs, and peekaboo Alençon bellybands. With these and a few suitable props—a white wicker *fauteuil,* a bit of bedside Biedermeier, a distressed-fruitwood Empire cheval glass, or an Italianate water faucet—I can transform a Purdue Home Ec. major into a drug-dazed Trebizond houri, recast an adenoidal Atlantic City debutante into a randy Whistler's Mother, or rejuvenate (with a dab of Vaseline on the lens) a matronly pornie-film star into a shyly ravening choir girl. Yes, the currently inflated national bare market is very much my doing, and I am proud of it.

Now something has happened, however, that threatens my career and even my sanity. For the last six months, the quality of my work has taken a sharp downward turn. Editors complain that my pictures are often out of focus or oddly composed; many of my portraits center on an unexpected part of the model's anatomy—an elbow, say, or the back of her head—and at times she and I seem to have missed connections altogether. This is a serious deviation in a genre that depends almost exclusively on the frontal, or head-on-collision, pose, and I have been forced to mumble evasions about a mechanical problem or darkroom misadventures. The terrible truth is that whenever I am in the presence of a naked woman now, my eyes remain tightly shut! I have berated myself sternly over this self-destructive and ridiculous aberration, reminding myself of my professional standards, my long experience with nude females, and my perfect objectivity. Nothing works. The moment my model kicks off her wedgies and begins to peel, this strange new feeling of *embarrassment* creeps over me. My eyes flutter, attempt to avert their gaze, and then obdurately and resolutely close. As you can imagine, this presents problems. I wear dark glasses now, and sometimes I ask a model to "help the mood" of a shot by making loud humming noises while I am aiming the camera, or I invite my cleaning woman or the postman to stop in and focus the camera for me "for fun." Still, they must know something is awry. I keep bumping into things, and last week I tripped over a floodlight cable and pitched headfirst into an already overcrowded bubble bath. My shrink is deeply interested, of course, and leans toward a tentative diagnosis of hysteria brought on by a long-repressed sense of old-fashioned gallantry or by some evanescent memory of personal privacy. ("You haff placed a lens cap over your id," he said yesterday.) Recently, I have taken to taping my eyes open with strips of adhesive tape, giving me a startling resemblance to the late Warner Oland, but sooner or later my puritan peepers break their bonds and clang shut for the rest of the day.

Now what?

SAD SNAPPER
Chicago

Hard lines, Sad S. Yours is an almost classic example of an irremediable contemporary occupational injury, and it may be that you already qualify for some form of assistance from the Workmen's Compensation Board. Meantime, you might begin to phase into landscapes or passport work. You can console yourself with the thought that clothed social congress is still the general norm, and that the vast majority of cheerful and memorable events involving women seem to take place when they have their clothes on. It was this discovery that impelled us to abandon our own celebrated centerfold section exactly forty-nine years ago last February.

1974

WOODY ALLEN

THE WHORE OF MENSA

ONE thing about being a private investigator, you've got to learn to go with your hunches. That's why when a quivering pat of butter named Word Babcock walked into my office and laid his cards on the table, I should have trusted the cold chill that shot up my spine.

"Kaiser?" he said. "Kaiser Lupowitz?"

"That's what it says on my license," I owned up.

"You've got to help me. I'm being blackmailed. Please!"

He was shaking like the lead singer in a rumba band. I pushed a glass across the desk top and a bottle of rye I keep handy for nonmedicinal purposes. "Suppose you relax and tell me all about it."

"You . . . you won't tell my wife?"

"Level with me, Word. I can't make any promises."

He tried pouring a drink, but you could hear the clicking sound across the street, and most of the stuff wound up in his shoes.

"I'm a working guy," he said. "Mechanical maintenance. I build and service joy buzzers. You know—those little fun gimmicks that give people a shock when they shake hands?"

"So?"

"A lot of your executives like 'em. Particularly down on Wall Street."

"Get to the point."

"I'm on the road a lot. You know how it is—lonely. Oh, not what you're thinking. See, Kaiser, I'm basically an intellectual. Sure, a guy can meet all the bimbos he wants. But the really brainy women—they're not so easy to find on short notice."

"Keep talking."

"Well, I heard of this young girl. Eighteen years old. A Vassar student. For a price, she'll come over and discuss any subject—Proust, Yeats, anthropology. Exchange of ideas. You see what I'm driving at?"

"Not exactly."

"I mean, my wife is great, don't get me wrong. But she won't discuss Pound with me. Or Eliot. I didn't know that when I married her. See, I need a woman who's mentally stimulating, Kaiser. And I'm willing to pay for it. I don't want an involvement—I want a quick intellectual experience, then I want the girl to leave. Christ, Kaiser, I'm a happily married man."

"How long has this been going on?"

"Six months. Whenever I have that craving, I call Flossie. She's a madam, with a master's in Comparative Lit. She sends me over an intellectual, see?"

So he was one of those guys whose weakness was really bright women. I felt sorry for the poor sap. I figured there must be a lot of jokers in his position, who were starved for a little intellectual communication with the opposite sex and would pay through the nose for it.

"Now she's threatening to tell my wife," he said.

"Who is?"

"Flossie. They bugged the motel room. They got tapes of me discussing 'The Waste Land' and *Styles of Radical Will,* and, well, really getting into some issues. They want ten grand or they go to Carla. Kaiser, you've got to help me! Carla would die if she knew she didn't turn me on up here."

The old call-girl racket. I had heard rumors that the boys at headquarters were on to something involving a group of educated women, but so far they were stymied.

"Get Flossie on the phone for me."

"What?"

"I'll take your case, Word. But I get fifty dollars a day, plus expenses. You'll have to repair a lot of joy buzzers."

"It won't be ten Gs' worth, I'm sure of that," he said with a grin, and picked up the phone and dialed a number. I took it from him and winked. I was beginning to like him.

Seconds later, a silky voice answered, and I told her what was on my mind. "I understand you can help me set up an hour of good chat," I said.

"Sure, honey. What do you have in mind?"

"I'd like to discuss Melville."

"*Moby Dick* or the shorter novels?"

"What's the difference?"

"The price. That's all. Symbolism's extra."

"What'll it run me?"

"Fifty, maybe a hundred for *Moby Dick.* You want a comparative discussion—Melville and Hawthorne? That could be arranged for a hundred."

"The dough's fine," I told her and gave her the number of a room at the Plaza.

"You want a blonde or a brunette?"

"Surprise me," I said, and hung up.

I SHAVED and grabbed some black coffee while I checked over the Monarch College Outline series. Hardly an hour had passed before there was a knock on my door. I opened it, and standing there was a young redhead who was packed into her slacks like two big scoops of vanilla ice cream.

"Hi, I'm Sherry."

They really knew how to appeal to your fantasies. Long straight hair, leather bag, silver earrings, no makeup.

"I'm surprised you weren't stopped, walking into the hotel dressed like that," I said. "The house dick can usually spot an intellectual."

"A five-spot cools him."

"Shall we begin?" I said, motioning her to the couch.

She lit a cigarette and got right to it. "I think we could start by approaching *Billy Budd* as Melville's justification of the ways of God to man, *n'est-ce pas?*"

"Interestingly, though, not in a Miltonian sense." I was bluffing. I wanted to see if she'd go for it.

"No. *Paradise Lost* lacked the substructure of pessimism." She did.

"Right, right. God, you're right," I murmured.

"I think Melville reaffirmed the virtues of innocence in a naïve yet sophisticated sense—don't you agree?"

I let her go on. She was barely nineteen years old, but already she had developed the hardened facility of the pseudointellectual. She rattled off her ideas glibly, but it was all mechanical. Whenever I offered an insight, she faked a response: "Oh, yes, Kaiser. Yes, baby, that's deep. A platonic comprehension of Christianity—why didn't I see it before?"

We talked for about an hour and then she said she had to go. She stood up and I laid a C-note on her.

"Thanks, honey."

"There's plenty more where that came from."

"What are you trying to say?"

I had piqued her curiosity. She sat down again.

"Suppose I wanted to—have a party?" I said.

"Like, what kind of party?"

"Suppose I wanted Noam Chomsky explained to me by two girls?"

"Oh, wow."

"If you'd rather forget it . . ."

"You'd have to speak with Flossie," she said. "It'd cost you."

Now was the time to tighten the screws. I flashed my private-investigator's badge and informed her it was a bust.

"What!"

"I'm fuzz, sugar, and discussing Melville for money is an 802. You can do time."

"You louse!"

"Better come clean, baby. Unless you want to tell your story down at Alfred Kazin's office, and I don't think he'd be too happy to hear it."

She began to cry. "Don't turn me in, Kaiser," she said. "I needed the money to complete my master's. I've been turned down for a grant. *Twice.* Oh, Christ . . ."

It all poured out—the whole story. Central Park West upbringing, Socialist summer camps, Brandeis. She was every dame you saw waiting in line at the Elgin or the Thalia, or penciling the words "Yes, very true" into the margin of some book on Kant. Only somewhere along the line she had made a wrong turn.

"I needed cash. A girl friend said she knew a married guy whose wife wasn't very profound. He was into Blake. She couldn't hack it. I said sure, for a price I'd talk Blake with him. I was nervous at first. I faked a lot of it. He didn't care. My friend said there were others. Oh, I've been busted before. I got caught reading *Commentary* in a parked car, and I was once stopped and frisked at Tanglewood. Once more and I'm a three-time loser."

"Then take me to Flossie."

She bit her lip and said, "The Hunter College Book Store is a front."

"Yes?"

"Like those bookie joints that have barbershops outside for show. You'll see."

I made a quick call to headquarters and then said to her, "Okay, sugar. You're off the hook. But don't leave town."

She tilted her face up toward mine gratefully. "I can get you photographs of Dwight Macdonald reading," she said.

"Some other time."

I WALKED into the Hunter College Book Store. The salesman, a young man with sensitive eyes, came up to me. "Can I help you?" he said.

"I'm looking for a special edition of *Advertisements for Myself.* I understand the author had several thousand gold-leaf copies printed up for friends."

"I'll have to check," he said. "We have a WATS line to Mailer's house."

I fixed him with a look. "Sherry sent me," I said.

"Oh, in that case, go on back," he said. He pressed a button. A wall of books opened, and I walked like a lamb into that bustling pleasure palace known as Flossie's.

Red flocked wallpaper and a Victorian décor set the tone. Pale, nervous girls with black-rimmed glasses and blunt-cut hair lolled around on sofas, riffling Penguin Classics provocatively. A blonde with a big smile winked at me, nodded toward a room upstairs, and said, "Wallace Stevens, eh?" But it wasn't just intellectual experiences—they were peddling emotional ones, too. For fifty bucks, I learned, you could "relate without getting close." For a hundred, a girl would lend you her Bartók records, have dinner, and then let you watch while she had an anxiety attack. For one-fifty, you could listen to FM radio with twins. For three bills, you got the works: A thin Jewish brunette would pretend to pick you up at the Museum of Modern Art, let you read her master's, get you involved in a screaming quarrel at Elaine's over Freud's conception of women, and then fake a suicide of your choosing—the perfect evening, for some guys. Nice racket. Great town, New York.

"Like what you see?" a voice said behind me. I turned and suddenly found myself standing face to face with the business end of a .38. I'm a guy with a strong stomach, but this time it did a back flip. It was Flossie, all right. The voice was the same, but Flossie was a man. His face was hidden by a mask.

"You'll never believe this," he said, "but I don't even have a college degree. I was thrown out for low grades."

"Is that why you wear that mask?"

"I devised a complicated scheme to take over *The New York Review of Books*, but it meant I had to pass for Lionel Trilling. I went to Mexico for an operation. There's a doctor in Juarez who gives people Trilling's features—for a price. Something went wrong. I came out looking like Auden, with Mary McCarthy's voice. That's when I started working the other side of the law."

Quickly, before he could tighten his finger on the trigger, I went into action. Heaving forward, I snapped my elbow across his jaw and grabbed the gun as he fell back. He hit the ground like a ton of bricks. He was still whimpering when the police showed up.

"Nice work, Kaiser," Sergeant Holmes said. "When we're through with this guy, the FBI wants to have a talk with him. A little matter involving some gamblers and an annotated copy of Dante's *Inferno*. Take him away, boys."

Later that night, I looked up an old account of mine named Gloria. She was blond. She had graduated *cum laude*. The difference was she majored in physical education. It felt good.

1974

POLLY FROST

ARTICHOKE

A T forty, I'm finally in control of my sexuality. Now it's time to market it. My next book will be a foray into today's relationships between men and women, with a lot of descriptions of me having sex. I don't intend to titillate my readers, but no doubt that will be unavoidable. As long as they don't miss the point of the book: how my sex life defines the nineties.

ADULTERY'S a good subject for a long work. I remember the first time I cheated on my ex-husband, Derek. The whole way up to the hotel, I kept imagining Derek and how contorted with pain his face would be if he knew that I was hurrying to meet my lover, Kurt. That vision of Derek's pained face hovered over Kurt and me the entire time, ruining my moments of ecstasy.

I felt so terrible that I went back into therapy. After a forty-five-minute session I emerged a new woman, who felt entitled to her own sexual needs.

So I didn't feel bad for telling Derek that I'd bought all our groceries that week at Dean & DeLuca, when in fact I'd picked them up at the Red Apple.

"Iceberg lettuce?" Derek asked, when he looked in our refrigerator. "I didn't think Dean & DeLuca stooped to iceberg lettuce."

"This is organic baby field iceberg lettuce," I said. Before, I'd always felt bad about lying to Derek. Now I knew better. It's his problem if he thinks I tell him the truth.

I used the money I saved to book a suite for Kurt and me. Later that day, I was in bed with Kurt. For the first time I could see him without the spectre of Derek blocking his features. Had that ugly mole by his nose always been there? I decided to let myself think about my husband. I imagined Derek's face racked with pain and anguish again. Seconds later I reached my climax.

My book will save my women readers the time I spent in therapy.

They'll realize they won't need to get rid of their guilt but, rather, use it for their own pleasure.

BEFORE we were divorced I tried to renew my love-trust for Derek by going through his files to make certain he wasn't cheating on me. I discovered a stack of magazine photographs he had secretly filed away. He had carefully clipped and saved pictures of Cindy Crawford, Rebecca De Mornay, and several Ferraris. There were even photos of women who were sloppy and overweight.

This was much worse than any affair. I had always suspected that he was subjecting me to his rigorous male standards of looks. I worked out and worked out, just trying to measure up to what I felt sure was his pickiness. To find out that he had no standards at all! What hurts most is that when I was married to him I tried to see him as the fairly presentable human being I thought he had it in him to become.

I'VE been thinking about whether or not to have a book-jacket photo. Naomi Wolf didn't have one on *The Beauty Myth,* and it hasn't kept her readers from knowing how good she looks. In fact, in an article called "Radical Heterosexuality," in *Ms.,* she wrote about how she can't walk down city streets without hearing comments about her looks. I'm confident I endure many more degrading kissy sounds about my thighs than she does. I suppose these construction workers think I pump Nautilus and wear a miniskirt just to brighten up the years they spend repairing the same pothole on Sixth Avenue.

Also like Naomi, I find that my male companions are oblivious of this harassment. "Did you hear that?" I asked Thomas, a male. "That man just said, 'What a babe!' "

"A babe?" Thomas said, his head swiveling. "Is there a babe around? Ow! You hit me!"

This is why I lift weights.

IN my book I will tell my sisters the real truth: You don't have to love the man you're having sex with. In fact, if you wait until you love a man to have sex with him, it may not happen very often, especially if you and he are married.

I need to spend several chapters detailing the erotic possibilities I have discovered in annoyance and frustration.

I STAY in bed while Hank, a holding-pattern relationship, adjusts the TV unit. "As long as you're up," I say, "could you go to the store and pick up some cookie-dough ice cream? I'll let you have the ice-cream part after you pick out the cookie-dough pieces for me. By the way, I noticed that you're out of condoms. I consider it my responsibility to pay for half of them and yours to pay for the other half and do the footwork. Just put what I owe on my tab."

I have moved past Radical Heterosexuality to Radical Princessdom.

RICHARD (divorced for ten years and still needing his space) and I were lying on his bed. I had been encouraging him to acknowledge my existence after intercourse. It was retro, but it was working; Richard talked and talked. The only problem was that all he would talk about were his favorite passages from Camille Paglia.

I couldn't take any more and went to the bathroom to give him a sign I was bored. He just talked louder. And then I spotted it—another woman's nipple ring near his Interplak. How was I supposed to respond to this?

The next day I sent Richard a package with this note: "Enclosed you will find one pair of my panties. Was I thinking of you when I wore them, *or somebody else?*"

I will take my female readers beyond rewards and punishments to torture. It may not do much for relationships, but it will do a lot for women.

AS I do research for my book, I begin to understand what Madonna went through after the release of her "Justify My Love" video.

Howard and I were in my studio apartment. We had just come back from a book party where we had met and had discovered we have something important in common. We are both literate Manhattanites trying to find sexual satisfaction in an increasingly difficult world.

I gave him one of my famous ear licks. "Tell me to crawl across the floor." I felt good about being submissive, because I was being submissive on *my* floor. I was in charge of my masochistic/submissive/movie-option desires, even if I was behind in my rent.

Howard looked suspicious, but he said the words: "Crawl across the floor."

I got down on all fours. But he was still looking at me warily. "Now tell me to grovel," I said.

"Okay—grovel," he said, unconvincingly. I was glad he wasn't my agent.

"No," I said. It gave me a powerful feeling to refuse to obey my own commands.

Howard leaned against the Murphy bed. "I think I understand what's going on between us," he said. He was shaking. It's my observation that men in New York City shake a lot. Some of them begin shaking if I simply mention that I'm forty. Sometimes I dream of moving to one of those cities they say are great for families. Of course, I'd probably just end up involved with a married man. "And, while I look forward to helping you achieve your sexual goals," Howard went on, "I must say that in the current context I have reservations about my participation." He brightened. "I have an idea," he said. "I'll be right back."

He returned with a tape recorder and switched it on.

"Okay," he said. "You state your name and I'll state mine. I think it's best if we both agree on the date and where we are, that we are both consenting adults, that we intend each other no harm, that the activities we are about to engage in are forms of mutually gratifying playacting, and . . ."

Twenty minutes later we had agreed that while my saying "No" would still mean "No," it wouldn't mean "No," not really, not the way the word we designated, "Artichoke," would mean "No." And while "Artichoke" would mean "Serious no," it wouldn't mean quite as serious a "No" as "Serious artichoke."

I could tell that Howard and I had relationship potential.

1992

JIM WINDOLF

MY SEXUAL FANTASIES

It's no fun when people tell you their dreams. But sexual fantasies are a different story. Even writing the words "sexual fantasies" sort of puts me in a "sexy" mood. With that in mind, I've decided to share a few of mine. Here goes!

THE LADY GOLFERS

It's summertime and I'm caddying again, carrying bags for Mrs. Thomas, a blonde, and Mrs. Bunch, a redhead. We're in the woods along the eighth hole, and we're looking for a lost ball. We're far from the civilizing influence of the clubhouse (*oh, this is going to be good*) and the air is crackling with heat.

"Do you see it? Do you see my ball?"

"Not yet, Mrs. Bunch."

"Call me Carolyn. I don't like losing these things, you know. They cost a dollar-fifty apiece."

I see something in the leaves—but it's a 100-compression Titleist with a black number 3. A man's ball. Mrs. Bunch is using a womanly Maxfli.

"Now, *where* is that damn ball?" she says.

(*Let's not waste too much time looking for the ball. It's—what the hell time is it?—it's one-thirty, and you've got to be up at seven for that thing.*)

Now Mrs. Thomas, in yellow culottes with little green turtles on them, is coming toward Mrs. Bunch and me. I can hear the spiked undersides of her golf shoes on the leaves as she gets closer.

"Can I just take the five-wood from my bag?" she says—and gives me a little smirk.

(*The smirk is nice, but Mrs. Thomas should be hot with lust by now. It's one-sixteen. If we hit one-thirty, that means five and a half hours of sleep, and you know how you are when you don't get your six.*)

The sunlight is slanting through the branches. (*Not a bad touch: helps set the scene, makes it real.*) A crow sails into my line of vision and lands on a branch. (*The crow's a bit much.*) The crow caws: "Caw! Caw!" (*Lose crow.*) The crow flies off. Now Mrs. Thomas is standing right beside me—I feel the heat of her body—and she slips the five-wood out of its knit cover.

"I can't hit the irons for some reason. I'm all right on the practice range, but I'm a basket case on the course. Why do you think that is?"

"Probably mental," I say.

"Is that so?"

(*Do we really need this? Let's get it on already.*)

Swat!

"Damn bugs!" Mrs. Bunch says. "Some gnat got me on the upper thigh."

(*Yeah, right, like she would be so specific in describing where it had bitten her.*)

"Let me see it," says Mrs. Thomas.

(*As if Mrs. Thomas would care. This is ludicrous—a gnat bite as a sexual catalyst? You can do better than this. What time is it now? One-twenty-four. Shit!*)

"It's right here," says Mrs. Bunch, lifting her pink skirt a little.

Mrs. Thomas kneels down on the ground, her bare kneecaps hitting the leaves. (*What's she going to do—scratch it? This is not good. Think, think! You've got yourself into a sexual-fantasy corner!*) She takes the hem of Mrs. Bunch's skirt between her fingers. (*I don't know where you're going with this, counselor, but I'll allow it.*)

Rrrrrrrrrrrrrrrrrrrrrrrrrrr! (*The hell?*) It's the greenskeeper, riding a lawn tractor nearby. (*He does not need to be here.*) The tractor speeds off toward the horizon. I look over at the ladies again and see what I've been hoping to see for so long. The Maxfli.

"Mrs. Bunch—Carolyn—I got it. I found your ball!" I say (*unaware that I have fallen asleep*).

EXPLORER AND NATIVE GIRL

I'm an explorer. (*Yeah, good, something different.*) It's 1510 (*good, 1510, long time ago*), and I'm coming upon a new part of the world. (*Well, new to me. To the people who've lived here for thousands of years, it's old hat.*) There she is, and she's not even dressed, at least not by my European standards of *habillement*. She's drinking from a pond, like an animal. (*Wait a minute. Does this scenario show me to be some kind of sexual imperialist, intent on exploiting a girl from an indigenous culture?*) I walk closer to the pond's edge. Our eyes meet.

She runs. Oh, how she runs.

I give chase, following the nymph through the woods. She's laughing delightfully—actually, it sounds like a scream. Yes, it's a native cry for help. Here come the males, with spears. Back to the ship! Run! (*This really isn't going to work at all. Try something a little less . . . outdoorsy.*)

THE FLAPPERS

The year is 1924, and we find ourselves in a grand Park Avenue dining room. I see her across the table, my sexual quarry—a saucy flapper with short black hair and possible sapphic tendencies. Her bare arm is even with the bare arm of the flapper seated next to her. The girls are buttering bread in tandem. I take a piece of bread from the silver dish and I, too, begin buttering. And so here we are, buttering and buttering in 1924.

"I don't believe I've made your acquaintance," the first flapper says, still buttering. "Are you new to New York?"

Light from the chandelier catches their painted lips. The flappers' mouths shine as they . . . continue to butter their pieces of bread.

I, too, continue buttering and buttering with gusto until I (*fall dead asleep*).

ALL IN THE FAMILY

"Awwww-chie! C'meeeya!"

(*No, no, please, not the Edith Bunker one.*)

"Awww-chie! I got ya bee-ya for ya just like ya like it!"

(*No, God in Heaven, please, no.*)

"Hello, dingbat. You're my good dingbat."

"Aww, Aw-chie."

(*Why? Why? Why this?*)

"Edith, you're my little goyle."

(*No! No! Cut! Make them sing on the piano bench.*)

"Didn't need no welfare state."

"Everybody pulled his weight."

"Gee, our old La Salle ran great."

"Those were the days."

Archie puts the stogie back in his mouth. Edith gazes up at him lovingly. (*Now get to sleep, God damn it.*)

ME AND MY GYM TEACHER

Miss Lupree was a gym teacher at my school. She had curly black hair and wore a whistle around her neck. Her legs were tan and strong between black gym shorts and white high-tops. Today, it's just the two of us in the gymnasium after school. The lights are out and I've come by to . . . (*quick, a pretext, why would I be with her after school?*) . . . to see if she'll . . . donate money for the walkathon. (*Oh, Jesus.*)

"Hey, Miss Lupree."

(*What age am I? If it's the present day, with me being almost forty, Miss Lupree would be about . . . sixty. Imagine that. Time is rolling over everybody. It is relentless. And to think of the bad stuff I've been through in that time—what if it was worse for her? Her parents are probably dead by now, some of her friends, too. So just be young. It's high school again, and you're seventeen and Miss Lupree is in her thirties. Simpler that way.*)

"What do you need?" Miss Lupree says.

(*"I need you"—tell her that!*) Instead I say, "I'm in this walkathon on Saturday, and I need people to pledge money. Most people are giving a dollar a mile."

"A dollar a mile? You obviously have no idea what they pay us around here."

"If it's too much you could—you could pledge, like, a penny."

"I'm just joshing you. You want me to sign something?"

"Yeah, just sign here."

"You got a pen?"

"Uh, no."

"Walking around with a signup sheet and you don't have a pen?" (*Oh, Freud would have a field day with this one. God, I hate it when people talk about Freud having a field day. As if Freud ever had a field day. What the hell is a field day, anyway? I think Marshall Crenshaw had an album called* Field Day. *Christ. Marshall Crenshaw. I think he was in* Beatlemania. *That's the last play I remember being at the Winter Garden Theatre before* Cats *showed up. Now* Cats *has closed, after, like, eighteen years. Come on, back to Miss Lupree.*) "Come to the office. I think I have a pen in my handbag."

We cross the gleaming hardwood floor. The movable bleachers are stacked against the wall. (*Must we dwell on the movable bleachers just now?*) Now we're going into her office. (*Where "it" will happen, no doubt!*) At the desk . . . damn, it's Coach Robb. Mustache, clipboard, whistle. He's the man who benched me for a full season of junior-varsity basketball because of my (*read, "his"*) "attitude problem."

"Well, if it isn't Dr. J.," Coach Robb says, using his very own derisive nickname for me.

"Hey, Coach."

"Just let me get a pen," Miss Lupree says. "I know I have one around here somewhere."

(*Oh, Christ, at least let her find a pen!*)

"What's this guy up to, Donna?" Coach Robb asks.

"I'm sponsoring him for the walkathon."

"Character like you involved in a charitable event?" he says. "What's the catch, bud?"

"You know, it's, like, a walkathon thing," I say.

Miss Lupree signs my sheet of paper. I can smell her perfume—or is it soap? Does she shower in the girls' locker room during the school day? (*God almighty.*)

"There you go."

"Uh, thanks."

"Now get the hell outta here, mister, and don't come back," Coach Robb says, using his "rough" humor on me.

I leave the office and end up wandering around in my old school, alone. It's late in the school year, and there's no air-conditioning. I can feel a heavy warmth in the hallways, and it's dark and shady and strange. I get a whiff of methanol by the science lab and the smell of glue and paper near the yearbook room and the smell of cigarette smoke as I approach the faculty lounge, and I keep walking until I (*just lie awake in bed, wondering if Miss Lupree really is old, or maybe even dead, and thinking of funerals I've gone to, and wondering when I will die, or if I'll have to watch everyone else die, everyone I love, or almost everyone, one by one, before I go. What the hell is the point? No, no, don't see it that way. Haven't we been through this a million times? We live for a while and then we're in the ground, and that should be enough. You would have to be ungrateful, or arrogant, or spoiled, or have no appreciation for life itself, to want more*).

2000

FRANK GANNON

ARISTOTLE ON RELATIONSHIPS

Recently I read Aristotle's Poetics. It made me reevaluate all of the things I thought I knew, and it really sparked a fire in me. . . . It made me realize that there's no reason to reinvent the wheel. Every emotion you'll ever feel, everything you're ever gonna do in your life has been done for thousands of years, you know, especially relationships. —Will Smith, in *Book* magazine

I PROPOSE to treat of sexual relationships of various kinds, noting the essential qualities of each.

Sexual relationships are of several types. They can be between a man and a woman, a man and a man, a woman and a woman, or many people and many other people. These sexual relationships differ from one another in many respects. The highest form of sexual relationship, however, is generally believed to be that which exists between two people—at least, only two people at the same time. Let us discuss sexual relationships primarily between a man and a woman.

Sex should be unified. Ideally, a sexual act should take the same amount of time for the man and the woman. The man and the woman should begin and end at the same time. If it takes the man ten minutes, it should take ten minutes for the woman. If a man takes longer than the woman, the woman may commence another sexual act (usually, but not always, with the same man) or she may just wander off. This is known by the common term *short attention span*.

The man should not begin, or end, his sexual act before the woman is present. If the woman appears while the man is engaged in his sexual act alone, this becomes the basis of comedy, as is embodied in Aristophanes' great work *What Do You Think You're Doing?*

If one woman and one man are taking part in an act of sex and the man's sexual act takes less time than the woman's sexual act, the woman may look at the man with a puzzled expression, as if to say, "Is that it?" Sometimes the woman may actually speak these words aloud, as occurs in Euripides' early play *Disappointment*. This is classified as a lesser sexual act. It is unusual for this type of sexual act, consisting of the same two people, to be enacted more than once. A man who engages in a sexual act in this way with frequency may inspire the emotion known as *pity*, as in the case of Carsinius, although he denies that this is an issue. (I, however, have heard otherwise.)

A sexual act, to be whole, must consist of a beginning, a middle, and an end. A well-constructed sexual act should contain nothing that does not relate directly to the sexual act. If a dog jumps on the bed during a well-constructed sexual act, the dog should become a part of the sexual act. This is, however, highly unusual, and could also be classified under the general term *disgusting*. The arrival of a dog usually merely interrupts the sexual act. This is characteristic of the worst type of sexual act, where the action stops and restarts. Sometimes it does not restart. This is called *not in the mood anymore*. The ending of this type of sexual act often involves the man and the woman sitting on the bed staring straight ahead. Sometimes a book or other reading material is used in the ending of this act. This is the worst type of sexual act, except, of course, the category "What Are You Doing?"

The best type of sexual act is one between a man and a woman, but not a man and a woman who are both all good and entirely without flaws. It also does not consist in sex between an all-bad man and an all-good woman; or, by the same principle, between an all-good man and an all-bad woman. A sexual act of this type is never totally satisfying. A sexual act between an all-good man and an all-bad woman is *highly unlikely*, and a sexual act between an all-bad man and an all-good woman is *a damn shame*. A sexual act between an all-good man and an all-good woman is *boring*. All of these sexual acts are of the lesser sort.

The emotions of *pity* and *fear* can be evoked by a sexual act involving a man and a woman who lie between the two extremes of good and bad. The highest form of *fear* occurs when a man who is not all good performs a sexual act with a woman who is also not all good, then another character who is also not all good—a character who has taken part in an earlier sexual act with the not all-good woman—enters before the end of the sexual act. This results in the downfall of the first not all-good man. A sexual act that ends with the *catastrophe* of the not all-good man evokes *pity* and *fear*. Aeschylus was the first to introduce *lawyers* into the scenario, which characters now routinely supply the ending to this type of sexual act.

The foregoing thus must suffice concerning this matter. Sexual acts were once much different than they are now, and sexual acts have advanced by slow degrees as each new element was added over time. Having passed through many changes, sexual relations found their natural form, and there they stopped. Many people, however, myself included, miss the masks. And the harnesses. Those were good.

2004

PAUL SIMMS

FOUR SHORT CRUSHES

WELL, well, well.

Just look at you, walking into this dreary bar and lighting the place up like the noonday sun at midnight, twirling a lock of your long auburn hair pensively as you search the room—for what?

For a soul mate, perhaps?

(I know, I know—I hate that phrase, too. Maybe that will end up being one of those things we both hate.) Maybe a few weeks from now, lying in your bed on a Sunday morning, I'll ask you, "What's your least favorite word or phrase?," and you'll say, " 'Soul mate,' " and I'll laugh till you say, "What? Tell me!" and I'll tell you how I knew that from the moment I first laid eyes on you, and then we'll have sex again.

But I'm getting ahead of myself. You haven't even noticed me yet. That's okay. I can wait.

Maybe when your gaze settles on me, and we lock eyes in that mutual Hitchcockian tunnel-vision effect where the camera is, like, pushing in at the same time it zooms out, or however they do that, you'll come sit down next to me and we'll—

Now you've spotted the friends you came to meet. They look like good friends.

Maybe they'll be my friends, too.

Our friends.

Your eyes just came to life like emeralds lit by subterranean torches, and as you move across the room toward your friends you shriek at them, "What the fuck is up, yo?," in a voice so piercing that the entire bar goes silent for a moment, and I have to check my glasses to make sure the lenses didn't crack. You continue to bellow your every utterance (including the lines "Jägermeister is the bomb, dawg!" and "Just 'cause I'm a white girl don't mean I don't got some serious junk in the trunk!" and "Random! Random! Random!"), and the bartender leans in and whispers something to his bar back, and they look at you and laugh.

You must be a regular here.

(Duration of crush: seventeen seconds.)

OH MY. What have we here? A rainy night in the city has cleared the sidewalks of all but the most intrepid pedestrians, and those who didn't brave the elements have no idea what they're missing.

Because there you are, gliding along on your bicycle, just a few feet ahead of me.

You're obviously not one of those tedious hard-core cycling enthusiasts—no skin-tight black spandex for you. No, just a simple white T-shirt (soaked through to the skin, clinging to the small of your back) and a long blond ponytail, whipping back and forth like the tail of a cartoon pony, as those long legs of yours pump the pedals and you raise your face to the sky, letting the raindrops freckle your cheeks with sweet diamonds of moisture.

Dare I try to catch up to you? I'm on foot, carrying a bunch of shopping bags, but you've paused at a red light, and—what the heck? I don't know what I'll say to you, but even the clumsiest of introductions on these glistening nighttime streets will give us a romantic how-we-met anecdote that we'll love telling for years to come.

Caught you! Here I am!

And there you are. I see now that you're a dude. My mistake. It was the ponytail that threw me off.

(Duration of crush: thirty-three seconds.)

ANOTHER restaurant dinner with my boring girlfriend, another lecture about how I never really listen to whatever she's yammering on about.

But how can I listen—how could anyone?—when across the room, alone at a table, reading the newspaper and nursing a glass of white wine, is a silent confection like you?

You, with your jet-black hair (like a latter-day Veronica from *Archie*) and your skin so pale that the bubble-gummy pinkness of your pouty lips seems almost obscene, especially when you scrunch them up the way you do every time you lick your forefinger and turn the page.

And I know you see me, too. Your first glance betrayed a glimmer of recognition—as if you knew me but couldn't remember from where— followed by puzzlement, your eyes entreating me to silently remind you, which I couldn't do at the time because my current girlfriend was staring across the table at me, apparently waiting for my answer to some kind of relationship question that I thought was rhetorical.

And so it goes. For an eternity, it seems—through the entire meal, until I watch you ask for the check, and pay it, and get up to walk out of the restaurant, and my life, forever.

But what's this? You're crossing the room toward me? So brazen— just as I knew you'd be. Are you going to surreptitiously slip me your number, written on a sugar packet, perhaps dropping it in my pocket as you fake-jostle me, like a spy handing off microfilm?

My heart beats like underwater thunder in my ears, until you tap my girlfriend on the shoulder, and she sees you and says, "Hey!" and you say, "I thought that was you!," and I realize that you are one of my girl- friend's college roommates.

After you leave, my girlfriend tells me a hilarious story about how one time in college some guy broke up with you, so you found some photos of him nude with the word "Patriarchy" written on his chest in Magic Marker which you took for an art class, and you sent them to his parents and then posted them on your blog, where you apparently like to write incredibly detailed confessionals about the asshole guys you al- ways end up dating, and also, while you don't use the guys' real names, everyone knows that the guy you immortalized as Pencil Dick is actu- ally a guy I used to work with.

(Duration of crush: forty-five minutes.)

SO silly does my impatience now seem, stuck as I am in the Starbucks line during the morning rush. But that was before I noticed you in line ahead of me.

And now that I've seen you—with your gossamer hair still damp from the shower, with your well-moisturized ankles strapped and buck- led into high heels that make you wobble and sway like a young colt just finding her stride, with your scent of lilacs and Dial, and, most of all, with your infectious sense of calmness and serenity, which makes me wish that the world itself would stop spinning, so that gravity would cease and we two could float into the sky and kiss in the clouds, giddy with love and vertigo—

Now you're at the register, and the dreaded moment when we part without meeting rushes toward me like a slow-motion car crash in a dream.

You've been at the register without saying anything for, like, fifteen seconds now, still scanning the menu board with those almond-shaped eyes that would make Nefertiti herself weep with envy.

Seriously, you've been to a Starbucks before, right? I mean, it seems like there are a lot of choices, but most people find a drink they like and stick with it. And order it quickly.

But maybe I've caught you on a day when you've decided to make a fresh start. To make a fresh start, to try a new drink, to walk a different way to work, to finally dump that boyfriend who doesn't appreciate you.

Okay, even if that were the case you could have picked out your new drink while you were waiting in line, right? I mean, come on.

Well, you've won me back, my future Mrs. Me—by turning to me and mouthing, "Sorry," after you finally noticed me tapping my foot, looking at my watch, and exhaling loudly. Sensitivity like that can be neither learned nor taught, and it's a rare thing indeed. The rarest of all possible—

Jesus Christ, you've ordered your drink and paid; do I really have to stand here for another forty-five seconds while you repack your purse, the contents of which you've spilled out on the counter like you're setting up a fucking yard sale or something?

That's right, the bills go in the billfold, the coins go in the little coin purse, the billfold and the coin purse go back in the pocketbook—no, in a side pocket of the pocketbook, which seems to have a clasp whose design incorporates some proprietary technology that you haven't yet mastered.

I think I hate you now.

(Duration of crush: five minutes.)

2007

CHILDREN'S
HOURS

STAGE FATHER

B Y now, my wife's policy on attending school plays (a policy that also covers pageants, talent shows, revues, recitals, and spring assemblies) is pretty well known: She believes that if your child is in a school play and you don't go to every performance, including the special Thursday matinée for the fourth grade, the county will come and take the child. Anyone who has lived for some years in a house where that policy is strictly observed may have fleeting moments of envy toward people who have seen only one or two productions of *Our Town*.

One evening this spring, though, as we walked into an auditorium and were handed a program filled with the usual jokey résumés of the participants and cheerful ads from well-wishers, it occurred to me that this would be the last opportunity to see one of our children perform in a school theatrical event. That view was based partly on the fact that the child in question is twenty-six years old. She was about to graduate from law school. I was assuming that the JDs slogging through the bar-exam cram course would not decide to break the tedium with, say, a production of *Anything Goes*.

As I waited for the curtain to go up on the 1995 New York University Law Revue, entitled *The Law Rank Redemption*, I found myself thinking back on our life as parental playgoers. I realized that I couldn't recall seeing either of our daughters in one of those classic nursery-school-pageant roles—as an angel or a rabbit or an eggplant. I thought I might be experiencing a failure of memory—another occasion for one of my daughters to say, as gently as possible, "Pop, you're losing it"—but they have confirmed that their nursery school was undramatic, except on those occasions when a particularly flamboyant hair puller was on one of his rampages.

I do recall seeing one or the other of them as an Indian in *Peter Pan* and as the judge in *Trial by Jury* and as Nancy in *Oliver!* and as the narrator (unpersuasively costumed as a motorcycle tough) in *Joseph and the*

Amazing Technicolor Dream Coat and as a gondolier in *The Gondoliers*. We heard their voices in a lot of songs, even if a number of other kids were sometimes singing at the same time. We heard "Dites-moi pourquoi" sung sweetly and "Don't Tell Mama" belted out. All in all, we had a pretty good run.

I don't want to appear to be one of those parents who dozed through the show unless his own kid was in the spotlight. To this day, when I hear "One Singular Sensation," from *A Chorus Line,* I can see Julia Greenberg's little brother, Daniel, doing a slow, almost stately tap-dance interpretation in high-topped, quite tapless sneakers. I'm not even certain what my own girls did in the grade-school talent show at P.S. 3 which I remember mainly for the performance of the three Korn brothers. One of them worked furiously on a Rubik's cube while his older brother accompanied him on the piano. The youngest brother, who must have been six or seven, occasionally held up signs that said something like "Two Sides to Go" or "One Side to Go." I have always had a weakness for family acts.

I won't pretend that all school performances were unalloyed joy. We used to go every year to watch our girls tap-dance in a recital that also included gymnastics, and the gymnastics instructor was an earnest man who seemed intent on guarding against the possibility of anyone's getting through the evening without a thorough understanding of what goes into a simple somersault. He described each demonstration in such excruciating detail that I used to pass the time trying to imagine him helplessly tangled in his own limbs as the result of a simple somersault that had gone wrong:

"Untie me," he is saying.

"Not until you take an oath of silence," I reply.

Even so, I came to believe over the years that my wife's policy on school plays, which sounds extreme, actually makes sense. It used to be that whenever young couples asked me if I had any advice about rearing children I'd say, "Try to get one that doesn't spit up. Otherwise you're on your own." I finally decided, though, that it was okay to remind them that a school play was more important than anything else they might have had scheduled for that evening. I realized that school plays were invented partly to give parents an easy opportunity to demonstrate their priorities. If they can get off work for the Thursday matinée, I tell them, all the better.

1995

SUSAN ORLEAN

SHIFTLESS LITTLE LOAFERS

QUESTION: Why don't more babies work? Excuse me, did I say *more*? I meant, why don't *any* babies work? After all, there are millions of babies around, and most of them appear to be extremely underemployed. There are so many jobs—being commissioner of major-league baseball, say, or running the snack concession at the Olympic synchronized-swimming venue—and yet it seems that babies never fill them. So why aren't babies working? I'll tell you. Walk down any street, and within a minute or so you will undoubtedly come across a baby. The baby will be lounging in a stroller, maybe snoozing, maybe tippling a bottle, maybe futzing around with a stuffed Teddy—whatever. After one good look, it doesn't take a genius to realize that babies are *lazy*. Or worse. Think of that same baby, same languid posture, same indolent attitude, but now wearing dark sunglasses. You see it all the time. Supposedly, it has to do with UV rays, but the result is that a baby with sunglasses looks not just lazy but lazy and *snobby*. Sort of like an Italian film producer. You know: "Oh, I'm so sorry, Mr. Baby isn't available at the moment. No, Mr. Baby hasn't had a chance to look at your screenplay yet. Why don't you just send coverage, and Mr. Baby will get back to you when he can."

This is right about when you are going to bring up statistics about show-business babies. Granted, there are some show-biz babies, but their numbers are tiny. For one thing, there isn't that much work, and anyway most of it is completely visual-driven, not talent-driven. And everyone knows that babies lose their looks practically overnight, which means that even if Baby So-and-So lands a role in a major-studio feature she'll do the work and go to the big première, and maybe even make a few dollars on her back-end points, but by the next day she's lucky if she's an answer on *Jeopardy*. Modeling superbabies? Same. Remember those babies zooming around in the Michelin tire ads? Where are they now?

The one job that babies seem willing and eager to do is stroller-pushing. Well, big deal, since (a) they're actually very bad at it, and (b) am I the only one who didn't get the memo saying that there was a lot of extra stroller-pushing that desperately needed to be done? Besides, it's not a job, it's a *responsibility*. For a baby to claim that pushing his or her own stroller counts as gainful employment is about as convincing as for me to declare that my full-time job is to floss regularly. Elevator-button pushing? Not a job: a *prank*. Unless you really need to stop on every floor. And have you ever watched babies trying to walk? Is it possible that they don't work but still go out for a three-Martini lunch? Of course, babies do a lot of pro-bono projects, like stand-up (and fall-down) comedy, and preverbal psycholinguistic research, but we all know that pro bono is just Latin for Someone Else Buys My Pampers.

One recent summery morning, I walked across Central Park on my way to my own place of employment—where, by the way, I have to be every day whether I want to or not. The Park was filled with babies, all loafing around and looking happy as clams. They love summer. And what's not to like? While the rest of us, weary cogs of industry, are worrying about an annual report and sweating stains into our suits, the babies in the park are relaxed and carefree and mostly nude—not for them the nightmare of tan marks, let alone the misery of summer work clothes. And what were they doing on this warm afternoon? Oh, a lot of really taxing stuff: napping, snacking on Cheerios, demanding a visit with various dogs, hanging out with their friends—everything you might do on a gorgeous July day if you were in a great mood, which you would be if you didn't have to work for a living. That morning, I was tempted to suggest a little career counseling to one of these blithe creatures, but, as I approached, the baby turned his attention ferociously and uninterruptibly to one of his toes and then, suddenly, to the blade of grass in his fist. I know that look: I do it on buses when I don't want anyone to sit next to me. It always works for me, and it worked like a charm for this I-seem-to-remember-telling-you-I'm-in-a-meeting baby. I was outfoxed and I knew it, so I headed for my office. As I crossed the playground, weaving among the new leisure class, I realized something. The reason babies don't work? They're too *smart*.

1996

JOHNNY CARSON

RECENTLY DISCOVERED CHILDHOOD
LETTERS TO SANTA

December, 1932

Dear Mr. Claus,

I don't believe I would be disingenuous or resorting to tergiversation if I maintained that I have been a paradigm of meritorious behavior in the past year. I do not wish to expatiate on this entreaty ad nauseam, but I remain sanguine about your decision to accede to my request.

Admiringly,
William Buckley

1880

Dear Santa,

I hope you can find the way to our house. Most people take the wrong road. You will be pretty tired after travelling all those miles, but then you'll be able to get a good night's sleep.

Robert Frost

1931

Dear Santa,

Please bring me the following toys for Christmas: Hopalong Cassidy six-shooter, Daisy air rifle, J. Edgar Hoover model tommy gun, Tom Mix model Colt Army revolver.

Chuck Heston

1786

Dear Santa, St. Nicholas, Father Christmas, Kris Kringle,

I have been a good, fine, virtuous boy, lad, child, youth. I want, desire, wish for a set, complete assortment, collection of books, tomes, editions, publications of the medical art, healing, therapies, and curatives.

Thank you, many thanks, much obliged,

Peter Roget

1934

Listen, you fat hockey puck, if I don't get what I want for Christmas I hope you get fleas in your beard and your lead reindeer gets a hernia.

Donald Rickles

2000-01

CARINA CHOCANO

HOW TO LAY OFF YOUR KIDS

HOUSEHOLD budget cutbacks, loss of primary parental income, excessive consumer debt, and other events that may result in the layoff of children can create stress for both parents and their offspring. But child layoffs need not be harrowing experiences. If handled tactfully, they can be conducted in a sensitive and professional manner, minimizing the risk of an unpleasant aftermath.

A preliminary notification of an anticipated reduction in family personnel can help reduce stress and increase morale as final layoff decisions are made. That said, parents should take care not to let information leak out prematurely, as this could result in unwarranted day-long tantrums and protracted retention of breath, particularly in those who cannot tie their own shoes. The following sample may be used to introduce children to the possibility of a layoff.

TO: The (FAMILY NAME) children

We have been analyzing our family's budgetary situation over the past few months and are making decisions about how we will cope with a current revenue shortfall. Consequently, there will be a great deal of discussion around the house in the coming weeks about what measures will be undertaken to safeguard the future of our family. There may also be some screaming. We would like to assure you that the situation is temporary and that we have reason to be optimistic.

One way to cope with a revenue shortfall is to reduce the number of our dependents, i.e., you kids. After careful consideration, it appears that some of the positions you currently occupy will have to be eliminated. This is a painful process for everyone involved, and we hope you will remember in the weeks ahead that this hurts us more than it hurts you. We want to assure all of you that Mom(my) and Dad(dy) love you very much, and that we will conduct a thorough review of your contributions to the family before our final decisions are made.

We hope you will feel free to communicate openly any questions you may have. Your cooperation and understanding during this difficult time are greatly appreciated.

Love,
Mom(my) and Dad(dy)

PRE-LAYOFF STEPS

Many parents fail to prepare adequately for the termination meeting, only to be bombarded with questions, demands, and pleas that they are not ready to respond to. Following is a list of concerns that parents may be called upon to address when meeting with these small and often immature individuals.

—"Why me, Mommy?" Parents must establish a documented, justifiable reason for the layoff of a child. Eliminating a position (i.e., middle child) as a pretext for replacing one child with another of a different name could result in litigation.

—"What about my allowance?" The law does not require parents to pay severance to terminated children, but many parents consider it a sound practice. Two weeks' allowance is the norm for a middle-class family of five.

—"I'm going to throw up, Daddy!" Most states require parents to provide their laid-off children with some kind of health-insurance plan that will allow them to continue (at their own expense and for a finite period of time) the same medical plan they had while they were family members. Your insurance provider can give you information and forms.

WHEN, WHERE, AND HOW

Most experts recommend terminating children first thing in the morning, while they are still groggy. If you are laying off just one child, consider firing him or her off-site, to spare the child additional embarrassment within the family. The mall is an ideal place to lay off a child. If your child cries, stomps, or throws himself or herself on the floor, he or she will most likely blend into the crowd. Before concluding the meeting, arrange a time when the child can come home and clean out his or her room.

When letting a child go, a face-to-face meeting is recommended so that the parent can celebrate the youngster as a unique individual and also provide firsthand, personalized information about the layoff process. This information may include notification about last-minute chores required of the child before he or she leaves the premises. Be gentle but firm. Should the child become petulant, settle the matter with a resolute "This is not a discussion."

Remember, terminated children aren't the only ones who have a hard time with layoffs. Siblings whose positions in the family have been spared often feel jittery in the aftermath of a personnel reduction. Use the occasion as an opportunity to cement family loyalty and to encourage forward-looking attitudes. Taking the remaining child or children out for ice cream should do the trick.

APPENDIX I: SAMPLE NOTIFICATION OF TERMINATION

Parents can prepare a child for the big news by supplying him or her with a written notice of termination before scheduling a meeting to discuss procedures and complete the paperwork. The following sample letter may be placed by the child's cereal early in the morning.

DEAR: (CHILD'S NAME)
FROM: Your loving parents

We hereby inform you that we will no longer require your services. As a child who is being laid off, you are afforded certain options with regard to your benefits.

Reinstatement: If a vacancy occurs within the competitive area in the sibling or pet division, you will be offered reinstatement for a period of one year, provided you behave. If such offer is refused, you will forfeit subsequent reinstatement offers.

Personal items: If you have at least one year of service, you are entitled to retain your blankie, Teddy bear, and/or other personal items.

Childhood pets: If you have ten (10) years of creditable family service, you are eligible to take Fluffy.

2002

BRUCE McCALL

CAMP CORRESPONDENCE

AN Open Letter to All Camp Idlehands Parents:
Your support is urged for the proposed merger of Camp Idlehands and Blustery Winds—particularly if you prefer to see your camper return home this Labor Day louse-free. To facilitate the merger, we urge you to withdraw your child from Idlehands now and register him or her at Blustery Winds. Disregard any new communications you may receive from the Camp Idlehands management, which is resisting this sound business offer with a smear campaign against Blustery Winds that is a smoke screen for its own failures. To wit:

—Wallet production in the Idlehands leather-craft program has fallen by seventy-four percent since last summer.

—Idlehands management throws Saturday-night Ben & Jerry's ice-cream parties for itself, while campers must make do with generic fro-yo.

—Due to supply inadequacies, Idlehands color wars sow mass confusion by pitting pink team against pink team.

Summary: It's high time to call a halt to fleecing and rot. For your young camper's sake, vote "Yes" to the merger proposition by enrolling your child in Blustery Winds today.

Attention All Camp Idlehands Parents:
Don't be gulled by the sweet talk of a takeover gang that wants to crush the vibrant Camp Idlehands spirit and replace our beloved campfire song with "I'm a Toys R Us Kid." Keep your camper at Idlehands!

Fact: Blustery Winds' ballyhooed "Homeward Bound Self-Reliance Program" is a transparent cover for the fact that the camp bus has been sold.

Fact: Numerous Blustery Winds campers report seeing desserts in the mess hall move.

Bulletin: As a special inducement to ward off this unsolicited takeover grab, Camp Idlehands is offering a *ten-percent refund of camper fees* to all parents whose children stay the full session.

Emergency Notice to All Camp Idlehands Parents:

Don't be bribed. Blustery Winds is more determined than ever to rescue Camp Idlehands from the neglect and ineptitude that led to:

—Widespread camper rioting after the fifth consecutive screening of *The Parent Trap* on Movie Nite.

—A "don't ask, don't tell" bed-wetting policy.

—Recruitment of local tots as stand-ins on Parents' Day to mask Idlehands' slumping enrollment.

Blustery Winds is countering Camp Idlehands' desperate fee-refund offer with its own goodwill gesture: a FREE sixty-second long-distance call home to every Idlehands camper who transfers to Blustery Winds in the next twenty-four hours.

Say "Yes" to the Blustery Winds merger proposal. The camper you save may be your own!

Camp Idlehands Parents:

Don't be hornswoggled! Did you know that the Blustery Winds spoilers, if they succeed in grabbing Camp Idlehands, will license the tuck shop to 7-Eleven, Inc.? That Blustery Winds' glassblowing instructor suffers from chronic hiccups?

If you value a quality camping experience for your child, keep Idlehands free and independent. Vote "No" to the cynical takeover scheme. Keep him or her at Idlehands—where, in addition to your ten-percent fee refund, you will receive a complimentary live guinea pig as a take-home pet for your child.

Urgent Notice to Camp Idlehands Parents:

You should know that Blustery Winds—while contesting Idlehands management's outrageous "Golden Bedroll" provision—has lowered its fees by fifteen percent for all Idlehands campers who transfer to Blustery Winds by midnight today. Vote "Yes" to the fair and reasonable

Blustery Winds merger offer, *and* give your camper the extra gift of drinking privileges for the rest of his or her stay. Transfer your camper to Blustery Winds today!

Camp Idlehands and Blustery Winds—Partners in Progress:

Camp Idlehands and Blustery Winds managements join in strongly recommending that you vote "Yes" to the proposal just accepted from PineTar Woods, a leisure subsidiary of FloPezCo, and transfer your camper immediately to PineTar Woods. Buses are waiting. We believe that the vision and energy of PineTar Woods management, combined with its parent company's solid record of strict financial controls with an almost "human touch" in industries as varied as waste management and ore mining, heralds a new dawn in the fast-growing preadolescent and adolescent rural seasonal-recreation segment.

Watch for exciting news of PineTar Woods' future plans for the former Camp Idlehands and Blustery Winds facilities.

Meanwhile, all campers must be evacuated from these sites by twelve noon tomorrow. Stragglers will be prosecuted.

2005

CHRISTOPHER BUCKLEY

COLLEGE ESSAY

. . . your entrance essay must not only demonstrate your grasp of grammar and ability to write lucid, structured prose, but also paint a vivid picture of your personality and character, one that compels a busy admissions officer to accept you. —Online college-application editing service

IT was a seventeenth-century Englishperson John Donne who wrote, "No man is an island." An excellent statement, but it is also true that "No woman is also an island."

The truth of this was brought home dramatically on September 11, 2001. Despite the fact that I was only twelve at the time, the images of that day will not soon ever be forgotten. Not by me, certainly. Though technically not a New Yorker (since I inhabit northwestern Wisconsin), I felt, as Donne would put it, "Part of the main," as I watched those buildings come down. Coincidentally, this was also the day my young sibling came down with a skin ailment that the doctors have not yet been able to determine what it is. It's not like his skin condition was a direct result of the terrorist attack, but it probably didn't help.

I have a personal connection to the events of that day, for some years ago my uncle by marriage's brother worked in one of the towers. He wasn't working there on 9/11, but the fact that he had been in the building only years before brought the tragedy home to Muskelunge Township.

It is for this reason that I have resolved to devote my life to bringing about harmony among the nations of the world, especially in those nations who appear to dislike us enough to fly planes into our skyscrapers. With better understanding comes, I believe, the desire not to fly planes into each other's skyscrapers.

Also, I would like to work toward finding a cure for mysterious skin ailments. Candidly, I do not know at this point if I would be a pre-med, which indeed would be a good way to begin finding the cure. But I also feel that I could contribute vitally to society even if I were a liberal-arts major, for instance majoring in writing for television.

Many people in the world community, indeed probably most, watch television. Therefore I feel that by writing for TV I could reach them through that powerful medium, and bring to them a higher awareness of such problems as Global Warming, Avian Flu, earthquakes in places like Pakistan, and the tsumani. Also the situation in the White House with respect to Mr. Scooter Liddy. To be precise, I believe that television could play a key role in warning people living on shorelines that they are about to be hit by one humongous wave. While it is true that in northwest Wisconsin we don't have this particular problem, it is also true that I think about it on behalf of people who do. No man is an island. To be sure.

Another element in my desire to devote my life to service to humanity was my parents' divorce. Because I believe that this is valuable preparation for college and, beyond, life. At college, for instance, one is liable to find yourself living in a situation in which people don't get along, especially in bathrooms. Bathrooms are in that sense a microcosm of the macrocosm. Bathrooms also can be a truly dramatic crucible, as the playright Arthur Miller has demonstrated in his dramaturgical magnum opus by that title.

I am not one to say, "Omigod, like poor me," despite the fact that my dad would on numerable occasions drink an entire bottle of raspberry cordial and try to run Mamma over with the combine harvester. That is "Stinkin' Thinkin'." As the Danish composer Frederick Nietzche declared, "That which does not kill me makes me longer." This was certainly true of Mamma, especially after being run over.

Finally, what do I bring to the college experience? As President Kennedy observed in his second inaugural, "Ask not what your country can do to you. Ask, what can you do to your country."

I would bring two things, primarily. First, a positive attitude, despite all this crap I have had to deal with. Secondly, full tuition payment.

While Dad pretty much wiped out the money in the process of running over Mamma—she was in the house at the time—my grandparents say they can pay for my education, and even throw in a little "walking-around money" for the hardworking folks in the admissions department. Grandma says she will give up her heart and arthritis medications, and Grandpa says he will go back to work at the uranium mine in Utah despite the facts that he is eighty-two and legally blind.

In this way, the college won't have to give me scholarship money that could go to some even more disadvantaged applicant, assuming there is one.

2005

PAUL RUDNICK

INAPPROPRIATE

A CHILDREN'S book that included the word "scrotum" was recently the subject of great controversy in school libraries nationwide. A Google search has discovered several more questionable titles and excerpts from other works intended for readers twelve and under.

THE PRETTY LITTLE BUNNY

Melissa, the pretty little bunny, woke up one morning in May and said, "I think I'll hop-hop-hop over to the carrot patch. I'm so pretty that all of the carrots will jump right out of the ground to see me."

"You are very pretty," said Melissa's Bunny Mommy. "But your sister is pretty, too, and she doesn't spend all of her time looking at herself in the mirror."

"But is she as pretty as me?" asked Melissa. "Just look at my vagina."

THE CLATTERY CABOOSE

Carl the Caboose had worked for the railroad for a long time. He loved it when little children ran alongside the tracks and waved to him. But Carl was getting older. His bright-red paint was peeling, his wheels were getting squeaky, and don't even ask about his prostate.

WHERE'S WALDO'S HAND?

THE LONELY LITTLE MOONBEAM

The lonely little moonbeam would sleep all day, and then wake up and shine all night long, to guide people on their way. But he was lonely, because people never looked up and smiled at him. They were too busy performing fellatio.

ARE YOU THERE GOD? IT'S ME, MARGARET, AND I NEED IT BAD

CORNELIUS THIMBLETUCK AND THE WIZARD OF TREWE

Every night, Cornelius would pray that his parents would rescue him from the Smudgebury Orphanatorium, and every morning he'd awaken on his hard, wooden cot. And so before eating his meager ration of watery gruel he would masturbate until his palm bled.

OH, THE PEOPLE YOU'LL DO

THE LION PRINCESS

Tarandiria, the beautiful lion princess, was strolling through the tall grass one day with her mother, Queen Malafala. Tarandiria said, "Mother lioness, whenever I see that handsome leopard over there I get a strange, tingling feeling."

"Where do you get this feeling, my child?" asked the Queen.

Tarandiria told her, "In my hyena."

BETSY BARSTOW, COLONIAL GIRL

One fine morning, as Betsy went to the village well in the Olde Massachusetts Baye colony, she ran into her best friend, feisty Katey Karmody.

"Oh, Katey," said Betsy, "I have such news! My father and my brothers are joining up with the militia to fight the British, so that we may all be free!"

"Oh, Betsy, that *is* news!" cried Katey. "My nipples are like muskets!"

THE BIG FLOPPY PENIS

THE LITTLE MERMAID AT SEA

As Ariel cavorted through the waves and foam, she thought to herself, How I love the sea and all its friendly creatures. How I love capering and leaping from cove to lagoon. How I love to be at one with the grand undersea kingdom, but I think I have crabs.

A MODERN CHILD'S GARDEN OF VERSES

Smart Susie O'Malley just loved her computer,
She didn't need pencils or books or a tutor.
Chad had a laptop, a Mac, and a modem,
He Web-cammed smart Susie a shot of his scrodem.

2007

SIMON RICH

THE WISDOM OF CHILDREN

I. A CONVERSATION AT THE GROWNUP TABLE, AS IMAGINED AT THE KIDS' TABLE

MOM: Pass the wine, please. I want to become crazy.

DAD: Okay.

GRANDMOTHER: Did you see the politics? It made me angry.

DAD: Me, too. When it was over, I had sex.

UNCLE: I'm having sex right now.

DAD: We all are.

MOM: Let's talk about which kid I like the best.

DAD: (*laughing*) You know, but you won't tell.

MOM: If they ask me again, I might tell.

FRIEND FROM WORK: Hey, guess what! My voice is pretty loud!

DAD: (*laughing*) There are actual monsters in the world, but when my kids ask I pretend like there aren't.

MOM: I'm angry! I'm angry all of a sudden!

DAD: I'm angry, too! We're angry at each other!

MOM: Now everything is fine.

DAD: We just saw the PG-13 movie. It was so good.

MOM: There was a big sex.

FRIEND FROM WORK: I am the loudest! I am the loudest!

(*Everybody laughs.*)

MOM: I had a lot of wine, and now I'm crazy!

GRANDFATHER: Hey, do you guys know what God looks like?

ALL: Yes.

GRANDFATHER: Don't tell the kids.

II. A DAY AT UNICEF HEADQUARTERS, AS I IMAGINED IT IN THIRD GRADE

(*UNICEF sits on a throne. He is wearing a cape and holding a scepter. A servant enters, on his knees.*)

UNICEF: Halloween is fast approaching! Have the third graders been given their little orange boxes?

SERVANT: Yes, your majesty!

UNICEF: Perfect. Did you tell them what the money was for?

SERVANT: No, sir, of course not! We just gave them the boxes and told them to collect for UNICEF. We said it was for "a good cause," but we didn't get any more specific than that.

UNICEF: Ha ha ha! Those fools! Soon I will have all the money in the world. For I am UNICEF, *evil king of Halloween*!

SERVANT: Sir . . . don't you think you've stolen enough from the children? Maybe you should let them keep the money this year.

UNICEF: Never! The children shall toil forever to serve my greed!

(*He tears open a little orange box full of coins and rubs them all over his fat stomach.*)

UNICEF: Yes! Oh, yes!

SERVANT: Wait! Your majesty! Look at this! Our records indicate that there's a kid out there—Simon—who's planning to *keep* his UNICEF money this year.

UNICEF: What?! But what about my evil plans? I was going to give that money to the Russians so they could build a bomb!

SERVANT: (*aside*) I guess there's still one hero left in this world.

UNICEF: No!

(*He runs out of the castle, sobbing.*)

SERVANT: Thank God Simon is keeping his UNICEF money.

SECOND SERVANT: Yes, it's good that he's keeping the money.

THIRD SERVANT: I agree. Simon is doing a good thing by keeping the money from the UNICEF box.

SERVANT: Then we're all in agreement. Simon should keep the money.

III. HOW COLLEGE KIDS IMAGINE THE UNITED STATES GOVERNMENT

The Present Day

—Did you hear the news, Mr. President? The students at the University of Pittsfield are walking out of their classes, in protest over the war.

—(*spits out coffee*) Wha—What did you say?

—Apparently, students are standing up in the middle of lectures and walking right out of the building.

—But students *love* lectures. If they're willing to give those up, they must really be serious about this peace thing! How did you hear about this protest?

—The White House hears about every protest, no matter how small.

—Oh, right, I remember.

—You haven't heard the half of it, Mr. President. The leader of the group says that if you don't stop the war today they're going to . . . to . . . I'm sorry, I can't say it out loud. It's just too terrifying.

—Say it, damn it! I'm the President!

—All right! If you don't stop the war . . . they're going to stop going to school *for the remainder of the week*.

—Send the troops home.

—But, Mr. President! Shouldn't we talk about this?

—*Send the troops home.*

The Nineteen-Sixties

—Mr. President! Did you hear about Woodstock?

—Woo—Woodstock? What in God's name is that?

—Apparently, young people hate the war so much they're willing to participate in a musical sex festival as a protest against it.

—Oh, my God. They must really be serious about this whole thing.

—That's not all. Some of them are threatening to join communes: places where they make their own clothing . . . and beat on drums.

—Stop the war.

—But, Mr. President!

—Stop all American wars!

—(*sighs*) Very well, sir. I'll go tell the generals.

—Wow. It's a good thing those kids decided to go hear music.

2007

SIMON RICH

HEY, LOOK

WHAT I imagined the people around me were saying when I was . . .

ELEVEN:

"Oh, man, I can't believe that kid Simon missed that ground ball! How pathetic!"

"Wait. He's staring at his baseball glove with a confused expression on his face. Maybe there's something wrong with his glove and *that's* why he messed up."

"Yeah, that's probably what happened."

TWELVE:

"Did that kid sitting behind us on the bus just get an erection?"

"I don't know. For a while, I thought that was the case, but now that he's holding a book on his lap it's impossible to tell."

"I guess we'll never know what the situation was."

THIRTEEN:

"Hey, look, that thirteen-year-old is walking around with his mom!"

"Where?"

"There—in front of the supermarket!"

"Oh, my God! That kid is *way* too old to be hanging out with his mom. Even though I've never met him, I can tell he's a complete loser."

"Wait a minute. He's scowling at her and rolling his eyes."

"Oh, yeah . . . and I think I just heard him curse at her, for no reason."

"I guess he's cool after all."

FOURTEEN:

"Why does that kid have a black X on the back of his right hand?"

"I bet it's because he went to some kind of cool rock concert last night."

"Wow. He must've stayed out pretty late if he didn't have time to scrub it off."

"Yeah, and that's probably why his hair is so messy and dirty—because he cares more about rocking out than conforming to society."

"Even though he isn't popular in the traditional sense, I respect him from afar."

FIFTEEN:

"Hey, look, that kid is reading *Howl*, by Allen Ginsberg."

"Wow. He must be some kind of rebel genius."

"I'm impressed by the fact that he isn't trying to call attention to himself."

"Yeah, he's just sitting silently in the corner, flipping the pages and nodding, with total comprehension."

"It's amazing. He's so absorbed in his book that he isn't even aware that a party is going on around him, with dancing and fun."

"Why aren't any girls going over and talking to him?"

"I guess they're probably a little intimidated by his brilliance."

"Well, who *wouldn't* be?"

"I'm sure the girls will talk to him soon."

"It's only a matter of time."

SIXTEEN:

"Hey, look, it's that kid Simon, who wrote that scathing poem for the literary magazine."

"You mean the one about how people are phonies? Wow—I loved that poem!"

"Me, too. Reading it made me realize for the first time that everyone is a phony, including me."

"The only person at this school who isn't a phony is Simon."

"Yeah. He sees right through us."

2007

ANIMAL
CRACKERS

IAN FRAZIER

COYOTE V. ACME

IN THE UNITED STATES DISTRICT COURT, SOUTHWESTERN

DISTRICT, TEMPE, ARIZONA

CASE NO. B19294, JUDGE JOAN KUJAVA, PRESIDING

WILE E. COYOTE, PLAINTIFF

- v. -

ACME COMPANY, DEFENDANT

OPENING Statement of Mr. Harold Schoff, attorney for Mr. Coyote: My client, Mr. Wile E. Coyote, a resident of Arizona and contiguous states, does hereby bring suit for damages against the Acme Company, manufacturer and retail distributor of assorted merchandise, incorporated in Delaware and doing business in every state, district, and territory. Mr. Coyote seeks compensation for personal injuries, loss of business income, and mental suffering caused as a direct result of the actions and/or gross negligence of said company, under Title 15 of the United States Code, Chapter 47, section 2072, subsection (a), relating to product liability.

Mr. Coyote states that on eighty-five separate occasions he has purchased of the Acme Company (hereinafter, "Defendant"), through that company's mail-order department, certain products which did cause him bodily injury due to defects in manufacture or improper cautionary labeling. Sales slips made out to Mr. Coyote as proof of purchase are at present in the possession of the Court, marked Exhibit A. Such injuries sustained by Mr. Coyote have temporarily restricted his ability to make a living in his profession of predator. Mr. Coyote is self-employed and thus not eligible for Workmen's Compensation.

Mr. Coyote states that on December 13th he received of Defendant via parcel post one Acme Rocket Sled. The intention of Mr. Coyote was to use the Rocket Sled to aid him in pursuit of his prey. Upon receipt of the Rocket Sled Mr. Coyote removed it from its wooden shipping crate and, sighting his prey in the distance, activated the ignition. As Mr. Coyote gripped the handlebars, the Rocket Sled accelerated with such sudden and precipitate force as to stretch Mr. Coyote's forelimbs to a length of fifty feet. Subsequently, the rest of Mr. Coyote's body shot forward with a violent jolt, causing severe strain to his back and neck and placing him unexpectedly astride the Rocket Sled. Disappearing over the horizon at such speed as to leave a diminishing jet trail along its path, the Rocket Sled soon brought Mr. Coyote abreast of his prey. At that moment the animal he was pursuing veered sharply to the right. Mr. Coyote vigorously attempted to follow this maneuver but was unable to, due to poorly designed steering on the Rocket Sled and a faulty or nonexistent braking system. Shortly thereafter, the unchecked progress of the Rocket Sled brought it and Mr. Coyote into collision with the side of a mesa.

Paragraph One of the Report of Attending Physician (Exhibit B), prepared by Dr. Ernest Grosscup, M.D., D.O., details the multiple fractures, contusions, and tissue damage suffered by Mr. Coyote as a result of this collision. Repair of the injuries required a full bandage around the head (excluding the ears), a neck brace, and full or partial casts on all four legs.

Hampered by these injuries, Mr. Coyote was nevertheless obliged to support himself. With this in mind, he purchased of Defendant as an aid to mobility one pair of Acme Rocket Skates. When he attempted to use this product, however, he became involved in an accident remarkably similar to that which occurred with the Rocket Sled. Again, Defendant sold over the counter, without caveat, a product which attached powerful jet engines (in this case, two) to inadequate vehicles, with little or no provision for passenger safety. Encumbered by his heavy casts, Mr. Coyote lost control of the Rocket Skates soon after strapping them on, and collided with a roadside billboard so violently as to leave a hole in the shape of his full silhouette.

Mr. Coyote states that on occasions too numerous to list in this document he has suffered mishaps with explosives purchased of Defendant: the Acme "Little Giant" Firecracker, the Acme Self-Guided Aerial

Bomb, etc. (For a full listing, see the Acme Mail Order Explosives Catalogue and attached deposition, entered in evidence as Exhibit C.) Indeed, it is safe to say that not once has an explosive purchased of Defendant by Mr. Coyote performed in an expected manner. To cite just one example: At the expense of much time and personal effort, Mr. Coyote constructed around the outer rim of a butte a wooden trough beginning at the top of the butte and spiraling downward around it to some few feet above a black X painted on the desert floor. The trough was designed in such a way that a spherical explosive of the type sold by Defendant would roll easily and swiftly down to the point of detonation indicated by the X. Mr. Coyote placed a generous pile of birdseed directly on the X, and then, carrying the spherical Acme Bomb (Catalogue #78-832), climbed to the top of the butte. Mr. Coyote's prey, seeing the birdseed, approached, and Mr. Coyote proceeded to light the fuse. In an instant, the fuse burned down to the stem, causing the bomb to detonate.

In addition to reducing all Mr. Coyote's careful preparations to naught, the premature detonation of Defendant's product resulted in the following disfigurements to Mr. Coyote:

1. Severe singeing of the hair on the head, neck, and muzzle.
2. Sooty discoloration.
3. Fracture of the left ear at the stem, causing the ear to dangle in the aftershock with a creaking noise.
4. Full or partial combustion of whiskers, producing kinking, frazzling, and ashy disintegration.
5. Radical widening of the eyes, due to brow and lid charring.

WE come now to the Acme Spring-Powered Shoes. The remains of a pair of these purchased by Mr. Coyote on June 23rd are Plaintiff's Exhibit D. Selected fragments have been shipped to the metallurgical laboratories of the University of California at Santa Barbara for analysis, but to date no explanation has been found for this product's sudden and extreme malfunction. As advertised by Defendant, this product is simplicity itself: two wood-and-metal sandals, each attached to milled-steel springs of high tensile strength and compressed in a tightly coiled position by a cocking device with a lanyard release. Mr. Coyote believed that this product would enable him to pounce upon his prey in the initial moments of the chase, when swift reflexes are at a premium.

To increase the shoes' thrusting power still further, Mr. Coyote affixed them by their bottoms to the side of a large boulder. Adjacent to the boulder was a path which Mr. Coyote's prey was known to frequent. Mr. Coyote put his hind feet in the wood-and-metal sandals and crouched in readiness, his right forepaw holding firmly to the lanyard release. Within a short time Mr. Coyote's prey did indeed appear on the path coming toward him. Unsuspecting, the prey stopped near Mr. Coyote, well within range of the springs at full extension. Mr. Coyote gauged the distance with care and proceeded to pull the lanyard release.

At this point, Defendant's product should have thrust Mr. Coyote forward and away from the boulder. Instead, for reasons yet unknown, the Acme Spring-Powered Shoes thrust the boulder away from Mr. Coyote. As the intended prey looked on unharmed, Mr. Coyote hung suspended in air. Then the twin springs recoiled, bringing Mr. Coyote to a violent feet-first collision with the boulder, the full weight of his head and forequarters falling upon his lower extremities.

The force of this impact then caused the springs to rebound, whereupon Mr. Coyote was thrust skyward. A second recoil and collision followed. The boulder, meanwhile, which was roughly ovoid in shape, had begun to bounce down a hillside, the coiling and recoiling of the springs adding to its velocity. At each bounce, Mr. Coyote came into contact with the boulder, or the boulder came into contact with Mr. Coyote, or both came into contact with the ground. As the grade was a long one, this process continued for some time.

The sequence of collisions resulted in systemic physical damage to Mr. Coyote, viz., flattening of the cranium, sideways displacement of the tongue, reduction of length of legs and upper body, and compression of vertebrae from base of tail to head. Repetition of blows along a vertical axis produced a series of regular horizontal folds in Mr. Coyote's body tissues—a rare and painful condition which caused Mr. Coyote to expand upward and contract downward alternately as he walked, and to emit an off-key, accordionlike wheezing with every step. The distracting and embarrassing nature of this symptom has been a major impediment to Mr. Coyote's pursuit of a normal social life.

As the Court is no doubt aware, Defendant has a virtual monopoly of manufacture and sale of goods required by Mr. Coyote's work. It is our contention that Defendant has used its market advantage to the detriment of the consumer of such specialized products as itching powder, giant kites, Burmese tiger traps, anvils, and two-hundred-foot-long rubber bands. Much as he has come to mistrust Defendant's products, Mr. Coyote has no other domestic source of supply to which to turn. One can only wonder what our trading partners in Western Europe and Japan would make of such a situation, where a giant company is allowed to victimize the consumer in the most reckless and wrongful manner over and over again.

Mr. Coyote respectfully requests that the Court regard these larger economic implications and assess punitive damages in the amount of seventeen million dollars. In addition, Mr. Coyote seeks actual damages (missed meals, medical expenses, days lost from professional occupation) of one million dollars; general damages (mental suffering, injury to reputation) of twenty million dollars; and attorney's fees of seven hundred and fifty thousand dollars. Total damages: thirty-eight million seven hundred and fifty thousand dollars. By awarding Mr. Coyote the full amount, this Court will censure Defendant, its directors, officers, shareholders, successors, and assigns, in the only language they understand, and reaffirm the right of the individual predator to equal protection under the law.

1990

BRUCE McCALL

WHAT TO DO ABOUT SHARKS

SHARKS have astonishing sensory gifts but virtually no sense of occasion. Incidents of sharks crashing dinner parties have been reported from as far away as Madagascar and as close as Malibu. If you find a hammerhead or a great white horning in on one of your intimate gatherings, stay cool and collected. Do not wave your arms about or slap at it with a napkin. Keep the conversation going as if everything were normal. Blow out all candles, slowly ease up out of your chair, and go for the light switch, turning it off. Then wait at least fifteen minutes. Sharks thrive on visual stimulation, and they have very short attention spans; the finned interloper will probably get restless and bored, and leave of his own accord.

Being caught unawares by a shark while you're setting up a tee shot is not only exasperating; it can also be costly. (Remember the amateur video of a leopard shark gobbling up a Callaway driver that was played

over and over last summer on the TV news?) It may be counterintu-
itive, but if you see or even sense a shark on the tee, heave your golf bag
as far as you can and run in counterclockwise circles. This will confuse
the shark, whose sensory orientation is clockwise only, and it could help
you avoid a nasty nip.

Sharks are also dyslexic. Knowing this could defuse the situation if you
ever find yourself face to face with one of these undersea killing machines
in a public library or a Christian Science reading room. The shark will
probably start nosing the book, magazine, or newspaper you're reading
with repeated sharp jabs, trying to knock it out of your hands. Resisting
will only enrage the beast; let it go. In the same motion, pick up a dictionary—or, better yet, an encyclopedia—and flash some pages directly in
front of his eyes. Sharks are almost all instinct and no brain to start with,
but when you add in the dyslexia this method will almost surely induce a
trance state in the big guy, allowing you to make a safe getaway.

Are you really certain that's a shark in your bathtub? Dolphins and
tuna also go for warm water, and hasty misidentification has caused
many a panicked home bather to sheepishly call back the local Coast
Guard to admit a false alarm. Rule of thumb: If it's thrashing, it's a
shark. Petting it, or feeding it a bath toy or a sponge, will buy you at
best ten seconds, so get out of the tub immediately. Now, here's where
some of those old wives' tales about sharks come in handy. It *is* true that
sharks hate soapy water, and the feeling of being toweled off *does* irri-
tate the sensitive nerve endings in their skin. So, while you're waiting
for emergency help to come, toss as many bars of soap into the tub as
you can while briskly rubbing around the beast's gill area with a fluffy
bath towel. Chances are that Jaws will beat a hasty retreat.

An Australian couple who discovered that a shark had invited itself
into the back seat of their car did exactly the wrong thing. They started
driving at high speed and violently lurching from side to side, in an attempt to induce car sickness in their unwanted guest. This was a vain
and unwise thing to do—sharks are immune to motion sickness. A
shark in your car need not be fatal, though, if you follow a few simple
directions: Turn the radio up as loud as it will go and start singing at the
top of your lungs. Forget that you look, feel, and sound foolish. Keep it
up, and you'll soon overburden the shark's ultrasensitive sonar hearing
system and bring on a thumping migraine painful enough to take the
starch out of a great white. He'll soon close his eyes and probably slump
down in his seat. That's your cue to gently bring the car to a stop—
remembering to roll up all windows as you do so—and vamoose.

It's a common myth that sharks fear nothing. In fact, they are terrified by any number of things. One is cats. Another is heights. Signaled by some primitive instinct that he is literally out of his element, the shark finding himself in an up elevator or on a penthouse terrace will lose all his fight. Remembering this will comfort you should you suddenly notice a shark sitting next to you on an airplane. You'll probably even start to feel sorry for the poor limp creature groaning there beside you, oblivious of the food cart, of the in-flight movie, of you—of everything but his own misery.

These tips can help mightily to even up the contest between man and shark, but they do not work in every instance. Nobody has ever mounted a successful defense against a shark-in-a-bed situation. Ditto for those caught with open cans of ham while picnicking. Yet, in all fairness, there is an upside to shark encounters. For example, did you know that there's never been a single documented case of a shark attacking a Girl Scout troop without provocation? Or that you can set your clock by the sharks that show up for a burial at sea—and no, not just for the eats? (Mariners as far back as the fifteenth century knew that a shark will never bite an iron lung, a wheelchair, or any prosthetic device.) So be afraid. Be very afraid. Just don't give in to hysteria; that's exactly what they want you to do.

2001

ANDREW BARLOW

ALL I REALLY NEED TO KNOW I LEARNED BY HAVING MY ARMS RIPPED OFF BY A POLAR BEAR

FOR me, wisdom came not at the top of the graduate-school mountain nor buried in the Sunday-school sandpile. For me, wisdom arrived during a visit to the home of our trusted friend the polar bear. Actually, I suppose "trusted friend" is something of a misnomer, because last year I had my arms brutally ripped from my torso by a fifteen-hundred-pound Norwegian polar bear. How and why this happened is an interesting story. For now, though, let's take a look at some fun lessons about our good friend *Ursus maritimus,* the polar bear. Here's what I learned:

—Share everything. You might be thinking, Really? Even with polar bears? Yes, share especially with polar bears. Actually, the word "share" does not exist in a polar bear's vocabulary, which consists of only about three hundred words. Give everything you have to a polar bear and do not expect him to share it. It did not occur to the polar bear who took my arms from me to share them in any way afterward.

—Polar bears are meticulous about personal cleanliness. A typical polar bear will feast for about twenty to thirty minutes, then leave to wash off in the ocean or an available pool of water. The polar bear who feasted on my arms did exactly this, leaving to scrub up in a nearby lake. Good hygiene is fundamental.

—In nearly all instances where a human has been attacked by a polar bear, the animal has been undernourished or was provoked. In my case, the bear was plump but deranged. Consequently, my attacker bear was spared the execution that typically follows an assault. My proposal—that my polar bear have his arms ripped off by a larger polar bear—was rejected by the authorities. No lesson here, I guess.

—The town of Churchill, Manitoba, is known as the "Polar Bear Capital of the World." According to legend, when a bear ambled into the Royal Canadian Legion hall in Churchill, in 1894, the club steward shouted, "You're not a member! Get out!" and the bear did. This story is almost certainly fictitious. During the first ten minutes that a polar bear was removing my arms from my body, I repeatedly shouted, "Stop!" "Get away from me!" and "Please—oh, my God, this polar bear is going to rip my arms off!" but the animal was unfazed. The lesson in this is that you can't believe everything you hear.

—Beware of blame-shifting. The authorities speculated that the nasty scene may have begun when I grabbed onto the polar bear's fur. At first, I thought, Gee, maybe that's right—I must have done something to get him so sore. But now I reject this suggestion. Why would I grab his fur?

—Things change. As a child, I used to delight in early-morning "polar-bear swims" at my summer camp. Now I don't even feel like swimming anymore, because I have no arms.

—Summing up: 1. Do not run from a polar bear. 2. Do not fight back. 3. Don't just stand there. Whatever you do, it will teach you a lesson.

—Never judge a book by its cover. Polar bears hate this.

—When a male polar bear and a human are face to face, there occurs a brief kind of magic: an intense, visceral connection between man and beast whose poignancy and import cannot be expressed in mere words. Then he rips your arms off.

2002

JACK HANDEY

ANIMALS ALL AROUND US

MOST people don't realize there is an unseen, mysterious world all around us.

No, I'm not talking about the world of invisible scary monsters. I am talking about the world of bizarre little animals that live alongside us right in our homes. They inhabit our clothing, our furniture, our piles of old rags, our pans of dripping rainwater—even our bodies themselves.

Some of these creatures are so microscopic that you can barely even see them. Others are bigger, but you probably can't see them without your glasses, if you wear them.

We usually don't even notice these animals, but they're there. Take, for instance, the little creatures that are constantly flying around our heads all day. These, it turns out, are houseflies. They can live off the scraps of food that fall from our mouths while chewing. And they are able to reproduce right in the house, in dog droppings.

Or consider an even smaller animal, which lives unnoticed among the hairs of our private regions. These are called crabs. No, don't worry, they aren't actual crabs. And they certainly aren't large enough to eat, unless you could somehow get thousands of them. But they are with us, year after year.

Have you ever noticed how old chili beans and ground-up pieces of potato chips will magically seem to move around on the living-room carpet? This is actually caused by ants. Ants? Don't they live in caves or something? That's what I used to think. If you look closely, though, you can see them almost everywhere.

Some animals are masters of disguise. What you may think are raisins, stuck to your legs after hours of lying on the couch, are often what scientists call leeches. Where do they come from? Where don't they come from is more like it. Most often, we pick them up wading through the basement.

Some organisms even manage to get into our appliances and live there undisturbed. These are rats. Many times, the only clue to their presence is a zapping noise, some smoke, and a smell that can linger for weeks.

Incredibly, some little animals are able to infiltrate the very liquids we drink. They are called yeast, and we consume them by the billions, hour after hour, every day.

Although some of these creatures are tiny and unobtrusive, others are not. When you get up in the middle of the night for more bites of the chicken drumstick you left on the counter, you may have to fight a raccoon for it. One reason we rarely notice these furry interlopers is that they usually live in the basement or the attic and get into the kitchen through holes in the floor or the ceiling. Also, a lot of times when we fight them we're drunk, and later we think we imagined it.

You might suppose that at least when you climb into bed you would be free of the animal kingdom. But suppose again. There, too, they are watching us, crawling on us, waiting for the opportunity to bite. These are our cats, swarming over us throughout the night.

Through millions of years of evolution, animals have adapted to thrive in every corner of our world, from our empty Cup-a-Soup containers to the dried-up branches and dusty ornaments of our Christmas trees. They inhabit the bristles of our toothbrushes, the bristles of our whiskers, and the bristles of our other areas.

The temptation is to want to do something about them. But what? You can throw cats off the bed, but they just jump right back on. Virtually every kind of alcoholic beverage has yeast swimming in it. You can scrub the crabs off your body, but what are you going to do about your bedsheets, or your sweatpants? Wash *them*, too? You could drive yourself crazy.

It's true that some of these invaders can be harmful. One animal in particular can literally eat its way through the wood that holds the house together. This is the common beaver. He is attracted to the water overflowing from our basements, which he tries to dam up. Another harmful pest is the moth, which can eat holes in your clothing and fly in your mouth when you're taking a nap.

But many of the creatures living in our homes can be beneficial. Take drifters, for example. Sometimes they will go to the store to get you things (although they usually "lose" the change). Termites will often leave piles of sawdust around, which can be used to soak up stains. And mice entertain us by playing musical instruments. No, wait, I'm thinking of cartoon mice.

Even if we could get rid of all these animals with a magic wand, would we want to? Yes, of course we would—why would you even ask that? Maybe the best answer, as with most things, is just to do nothing at all.

However, that's not what the health department thinks. They have hit me with a large fine and ordered me to "clean up" my property. Ultimately, though, we have to ask ourselves: Do we want to live in some soulless antiseptic world ruled by futuristic robots, where dishes are cleaned every day and sinks and toilets are an eerie, gleaming white? I don't think that we do. I think people would rather live in homes where animals roam wild and free, in our hair, in our bags of things, and in our underpants.

2003

DAVID SEDARIS

THE LIVING DEAD

I WAS on the front porch, drowning a mouse in a bucket, when this van pulled up, which was strange. On an average day, a total of fifteen cars might pass the house, but no one ever stops. And this was late, three o'clock in the morning. The couple across the street are asleep by nine, and, from what I can tell, the people next door turn in an hour or so later. There are no street lamps in our village in Normandy, so when it's dark it's really dark. And when it's quiet you can hear everything.

"Did I tell you about the burglar who got stuck in the chimney?"

That was the big story last summer. One time, it happened in the village at the bottom of the hill, the pretty one, bisected by a river, and another time it took place fifteen miles in the opposite direction. I heard the story from four people, and each time it happened in a different place.

"So this burglar," people said. "He tried the doors and windows, and when those wouldn't open he climbed up onto the roof."

It was always a summer house, a cottage owned by English people whose names no one seemed to remember. The couple left in early September and returned nine months later to find a shoe in their fireplace. "Is this yours?" the wife asked her husband.

The two had just arrived. There were beds to be made and closets to air out, so, between one thing and another, the shoe was forgotten. It was early June, chilly, and as night fell the husband decided to light a fire.

At this point in the story, the tellers were beside themselves, their eyes aglow, as if reflecting the light of a campfire. "Do you honestly expect me to believe this?" I'd say. "I mean, *really*."

At the beginning of the summer, the local paper devoted three columns to a Camembert-eating contest. Competitors were pictured, hands behind their backs, their faces buried in sticky cheese. This on the front page. In an area so hard up for news, I think a death by starvation might command the headlines for, oh, about six years.

"But wait," I'm told. "There's more!"

As the room filled with smoke, the husband stuck a broom up the chimney. Something was blocking the flue, and he poked at it again and again, dislodging the now skeletal burglar, who fell feet first into the flames.

There was always a pause here, a break between the story and the practical questions that would ultimately destroy it. "So who was this burglar?" I'd ask. "Did they identify his body?"

He was a gypsy, a drifter, and, on two occasions, an Arab. No one remembered exactly where he was from, "but it's true," they said. "You can ask anyone," by which they meant the neighbor who had told them, or the person they themselves had told five minutes earlier.

I NEVER believed that a burglar starved to death in a chimney. I don't believe that his skeleton dropped onto the hearth. But I do believe in spooks, especially when my boyfriend, Hugh, is away, and I'm left alone in the country. During the war, our house was occupied by Nazis. The former owner died in the bedroom, as did the owner before her, but it's not their ghosts that I worry about. It's silly, I know, but what frightens me is the possibility of zombies, former townspeople wandering about in pus-covered nightgowns. There's a church graveyard a quarter of a mile away, and were its residents to lurch out the gate and take a left, ours would be the third house they would stumble upon. Lying in bed with all the lights on, I draw up contingency plans on the off-chance they might come a-callin'. The attic seems a wise hideout, but I'd have to secure the door, which would take time—time you do not have when zombies are steadily working their way through your windows.

I used to lie awake for hours, but now, if Hugh's gone for the night, I'll just stay up and keep myself busy: writing letters, cleaning the oven, replacing missing buttons. I won't put in a load of laundry, because the machine is too loud and would drown out other, more significant noises, namely the shuffling footsteps of the living dead.

ON this particular night, the night that the van pulled up, I was in what serves as the combination kitchen–living room, trying to piece together a complex model of the Visible Man. The body was clear plastic, a shell for the organs, which ranged in color from bright red to a dull, liverish purple. We'd bought it as a birthday gift for a thirteen-year-old boy, the son of a friend, who pronounced it *nul,* meaning worthless, unacceptable. Last summer, he'd wanted to be a doctor, but over the next few months he seemed to have changed his mind, deciding instead that he might like to design shoes. I suggested that he at least keep the feet, but when he turned up his nose we gave him twenty euros and decided to keep the model for ourselves. I had just separated the digestive system when I heard a familiar noise coming from overhead, and dropped half the colon onto the floor.

There's a walnut tree in the side yard, and every year Hugh collects the fruit and lays it out on the attic floor to dry. Shortly thereafter the mice come in. I don't know how they climb the stairs, but they do, and the first thing on their list is to take Hugh's walnuts. The nuts are much too big to be carried by mouth, so instead the mice roll them across the floor, pushing them toward the nests they build in the tight spaces between the walls and the eaves. Once there, they discover, the walnuts won't fit, and, while I find this to be comic, Hugh thinks differently and sets the attic with traps I normally spring before the mice can get to

them. Were they rats it would be different, but a couple of mice—
"Come on," I say. "What could be cuter?"

Sometimes, when the rolling gets on my nerves, I'll turn on the attic
light and make like I'm coming up the stairs. This quiets them for a
while, but on this night the trick didn't work. The noise kept up, but
sounded like something being dragged rather than rolled. A shingle? A
heavy piece of toast? Again I turned on the attic light, and when the
noise continued I went upstairs, and found a mouse caught in one of
the traps that Hugh had set. The steel bar had come down on his back,
and he was pushing himself in a tight circle, not in a death throe, but
with a spirit of determination, an effort to work within this new set of
boundaries. "I can live with this," he seemed to be saying. "Really. Just
give me a chance."

I couldn't leave him that way, so I scooted the trapped mouse into a
cardboard box and carried him down to the front porch. The fresh air,
I figured, would do him some good, and once released he could run
down the stairs and into the yard, free from the house that now held
such bitter memories. I should have lifted the bar with my fingers, but
instead, worried that he might try to bite me, I held the trap down with
my foot, and attempted to pry it open with the end of a metal ruler.
Which was stupid. No sooner had the bar been raised than it snapped
back, this time on the mouse's neck. My next three attempts were
equally punishing, and when he was finally freed he staggered onto the
doormat, every imaginable bone broken in at least four different places.
Anyone could see that he was not going to get any better. Not even a
vet could have fixed this mouse, and so, to put him out of his misery, I
decided to drown him.

The first step, and for me the most difficult, was going into the cel-
lar to get the bucket. This involved leaving the well-lit porch, walking
around to the side of the house, and entering what is surely the bleak-
est and most terrifying hole in all of Europe: low ceiling, stone walls, a
dirt floor stamped with paw prints. I never go in without announcing
myself. "Hyaa," I yell. "Hyaa. Hyaa." It's the sound my father makes
when he enters his toolshed, the cry of cowboys as they round up do-
gies, and it suggests a certain degree of authority. Snakes, bats, weasels;
it's time to head up and move on out. When retrieving the bucket, I
carried a flashlight in each hand, holding them low, like pistols. Then I
kicked in the door—"Hyaa. Hyaa"—grabbed what I was looking for,
and ran. I was back on the porch in less than a minute, but it took much
longer for my hands to stop shaking.

The problem with drowning an animal—even a crippled one—is that it does not want to cooperate. This mouse had nothing going for him, and yet he struggled, using what, I don't really know. I tried to hold him down with a broom handle, but it wasn't the right tool for the job, and he kept breaking free and heading back to the surface. A creature that determined, you want to let it have its way, but this was for the best, whether he realized it or not. I'd just managed to pin his tail to the bottom of the bucket when the van drove up and stopped in front of the house. I say van, but it was more like a miniature bus, with windows and three rows of seats. The headlights were on high, and the road before them appeared black and perfect.

After a moment or two, the driver's window rolled down, and a man stuck his head into the pool of light spilling from the porch. *"Bonsoir,"* he called. He said it the way a man in a lifeboat might yell "Ahoy" to a passing ship, giving the impression that he was very happy to see me. As he opened the door, a light came on, and I could see five people seated behind him, two men and three women, each looking at me with the same expression of relief. All were adults, perhaps in their sixties or early seventies, and all of them had white hair.

The driver referred to a small book he held in his hand. Then he looked back at me and attempted to recite what he had just read. It was French, but just barely, pronounced phonetically, with no understanding of where the accents lay.

"Do you speak English?" I asked.

The man clapped his hands and turned around in his seat. "He speaks English!" The news was greeted with a great deal of excitement, and then translated for one of the women, who apparently did not understand its significance. Meanwhile my mouse had popped back to the surface, and was using his good hand to claw at the sides of the bucket.

"We are looking for a particular place," the driver said, "a house we are renting with friends." He spoke loudly and with a slight accent. Dutch, I thought, or maybe Scandinavian.

I asked what town the house was in, and he said that it was not in a town, just a willage.

"A what?"

"A willage," he repeated.

Either he had a speech impediment or the letter *V* did not exist in his native language. Whatever the case, I wanted him to say it again.

"I'm sorry," I said. "But I couldn't quite hear you."

"A *willage*," he said. "Some friends have rented a house in a little willage and we can't seem to find it. We were supposed to be there hours ago, but now we are quite lost. Do you know the area?"

I said that I did, but drew a blank when he called out the name. There are countless small villages in our part of Normandy, clusters of stone buildings hidden by forests or knotted at the end of unpaved roads. Hugh might have known the place the man was looking for, but because I don't drive I tend not to pay too much attention. "I have a map," the man said. "Do you perhaps think you could look at it?"

He stepped from the van and I saw that he was wearing a white nylon tracksuit, the pants puffy and gathered tight at the ankles. You'd expect to find sneakers attached to such an outfit, but instead he wore a pair of black loafers. The front gate was open, and as he made his way up the stairs I remembered what it was that I'd been doing, and I thought of how strange it might look. It occurred to me to meet the man halfway, but by this time he had already reached the landing, and was offering his hand in a gesture of friendship. We shook and, on hearing the faint, lapping noise, he squinted down into the bucket. "Oh," he said. "I see that you have a little swimming mouse." His tone did not invite explanation, and so I offered none. "My wife and I have a dog," he continued. "But we did not bring it with us. Too much trouble."

I nodded and he held out his map, a Xerox of a Xerox marked with arrows and annotated in a language I did not recognize. "I think I've got something better in the house," I said, and at my invitation he followed me inside.

AN unexpected and unknown visitor allows you to see a familiar place as if for the first time. I'm thinking of the meter reader rooting through the kitchen at 8 A.M., the Jehovah's Witness suddenly in your living room. "Here," they seem to say. "Use my eyes. The focus is much keener." I had always thought of our main room as cheerful, but walking through the door I saw that I was mistaken. It wasn't dirty or messy, but there was something slightly suspicious about it. I looked at the Visible Man spread out on the table. The pieces lay in the shadow of a large taxidermied chicken, which seemed to be regarding them, determining which organ might be the most appetizing. The table itself was pleasant to look at—oak, and hand-hewn—but the chairs surrounding it were mismatched, and in various states of disrepair. On the back of one hung a towel marked with the emblem of the Los Angeles County

Coroner's office. It had been a gift, not bought personally, but, still, it was there, leading the eye to an adjacent daybed, upon which lay two copies of a sordid true-crime magazine I buy, purportedly to help me with my French. The cover of the latest issue pictured a young Belgian woman, a camper beaten to death with a cinder block. "IS THERE A SE-RIAL KILLER IN *YOUR* REGION?" the headline asked. The second copy was opened to the crossword puzzle I'd attempted earlier in the evening. One of the clues translated to "Female sex organ," and in the space provided I had written the word for vagina. It was the first time I had ever answered a French crossword-puzzle question, and in celebra-tion I had marked the margins with bright exclamation points.

There seemed to be a theme developing, and everything I saw ap-peared to substantiate it: the almanac of guns and firearms suddenly prominent on the bookshelf, the meat cleaver lying, for no apparent reason, upon a photograph of our neighbor's grandchild.

"It's more of a summer home," I said, and the man nodded. He was looking now at the fireplace, which was slightly taller than he was. I tend to see only the solid stone hearth and high oak mantel, but he was examining the meat hooks hanging from the clotted black interior.

"Every other house we passed was dark," he said. "We've been driv-ing, I think, for hours, just looking for someone who was awake. We saw your lights, the open door . . ." His words were familiar from innu-merable horror movies, the wayward soul announcing himself to the count, the mad scientist, the werewolf moments before he changes.

"I hate to bother you, really."

"Oh, it's no bother, I was just drowning a mouse. Come in, please."

"So," the man said. "You say you have a map?"

I had several, and pulled the most detailed from a drawer contain-ing, among other things, a short length of rope and a novelty pen re-sembling a dismembered finger. *Where does all this stuff come from?* I asked myself. There's a low cabinet beside the table, and, pushing aside the delicate skull of a baby monkey, I spread the map upon the surface, identifying the road outside our house, and then the village the man was looking for. It wasn't more than ten miles away. The route between here and there was fairly simple, but still I offered him the map, know-ing he would feel better if he could refer to it on the road.

"Oh, no," he said, "I couldn't," but I insisted, and watched from the porch as he carried it down the stairs, and into the idling van. "If you have any problems you know where I live," I said. "You and your friends can spend the night here if you like. Really, I mean it. I have plenty of beds." The man in the tracksuit waved goodbye, and then he drove down the hill, disappearing behind the neighbor's pitched roof.

The mouse that had fought so hard against my broom handle had lost his second wind, and was floating, lifeless now, on the surface of the water. I thought of emptying the bucket into the field behind the house, but without the van, its headlights, and the comforting sound of the engine, the area beyond the porch seemed too menacing. The inside of the house suddenly seemed just as bad, and so I stood there, looking out at what I'd now think of as my willage. When the sun came up I would bury my dead, and fill the empty bucket with hydrangeas, a bit of life and color, so perfect for the table. So pleasing to the eye.

2004

PAUL SIMMS

TALKING CHIMP GIVES HIS
FIRST PRESS CONFERENCE

HELLO?
Can everyone hear me? Anyone?

Check, check. Check, one two.

Is this thing on?

Not the microphone—I mean my Electronic Larynx Implant device. Is it working? Hit the "Reboot" button, and see if that ook ook-ook ook.

Ook? Ook? Ook-ook.

Ook!

Ook-ook-oo—why does it seem like it always takes an eternity for the ELI to reboot? I mean, isn't this something we should have ironed out a long time ago?

Oh. Okay. We're back online now? Good. You can all hear me out there? Great.

I'd like to apologize for the technical difficulties up here. One would think that the most important part of setting up the world's first talking-chimp demonstration is making sure that the P.A. is working, but . . . okay I guess.

Can I get a bowl of water, please? Thank you. Is the sound guy here? The sound guy. The P.A. technician. Is he here? He's in the back? Just as well. It's just that . . . you know how sometimes you get the feeling that you'd like to bite bite bite bite bite someone? Anyone? Nothing? Whatever. It'll pass.

Well, anyway: Hello, male humans and female humans! I am indeed what you call a chimpanzee. I do have a human-given proper name—something that sounds like Timmy or Jimmy or Bimmy or Immy—but, for some reason, recognizing and pronouncing human-given proper names is virtually impossible for me. So, yeah, all you skeptics can go ahead and make hay with that one, but I'm doing my best up here.

I guess I should start by acknowledging Dr. Female-Human-Lemon-Colored-Hair and her partner Dr. Male-Human-Persistent-Territory-Threatener for all the great work they've done with me—or, rather, *on* me—in the past few years.

The development of the ELI was a long and arduous process, and there were more than a few times—usually after being shot with a tranquilizer dart and then waking up hours later with excruciatingly painful bleeding stitch holes in my neck and chest regions—when I wasn't sure if it was worth it. But I guess it was, because here we are today, in this beautiful conference room at the Sheraton.

In fact, there were some days when I felt nothing but the desire to bite bite bite bite bite everyone involved, including, if you can believe it, Mr. Male-Human-Black-Skin-Food-Bringer. Who, for my money, is the true unsung hero of this interminable experiment. This guy is the male human who not only brings me my kibble every morning but also delivers to my cage a metal bucket full of orange wedges every afternoon.

So give him a round of applause, if you would. Stand up, Mr. Male-Human-Black-Skin-Food-Bringer! Don't be shy!

He's not here? Okay, then. I'm not sure why he wasn't invited to share in the limelight today, but I guess we all have our different ways of doing things. Or something. Let's just move right along.

I had planned today to speak mainly about the similarities between humans and chimpanzees. How we're all members of the same family, and so on and so forth.

I feel like I have to take a dump right now.

But instead of speaking about the similarities between humans and—

Ahh. That's better. Dump taken. Where was I?

Similarities. Right. But instead of speaking about similarities I'd like to take this time to—

I'm sorry, you people in the first few rows. Apparently, my dump somehow offends you? Perhaps if I gather it up and fling it at you, you'll think twice next time before you wrinkle your dinky noses at my healthy and natural exudate. Is that what I should do? Because it's very easy. All I have to do is scoop it up like this and—

Ow!

Take it easy with the leash, Mr. Male-Human-Leash-Puller-If-He-Ever-Turns-His-Back-Bite-Bite-Bite! I wasn't actually going to do it! Sheesh. Why this guy is here but my kibble-and-orange-wedge-bringing buddy isn't, I have no idea.

Where was I?

Could I get another bowl of water, please? Thank you. Give me a moment here.

Ah . . . that's the stuff. The elixir of life, which soothes all but the most surgery-ravaged monkey throat.

Anyway, let's just go to your questions and get this over with, because I'm pretty eager to get back to my cage at this point.

Yes, right here in the front—Mr. Male-Human-Small-Torso-No-Threat?

Right. As I said, I am eager to get back to my cage. That surprises you somehow? Let me explain. I like my cage. My cage is small and manageable. Unlike your cage here, which makes me uneasy. Who needs a cage this large? I mean, come on! How can you be comfortable in a cage so large that the entrance and egress points are so far away that sometimes I think they might not even exist? With a cage this large, any random taker-of-food or biter-of-chimpanzees could enter at any time and take your kibble—or, even worse, your orange wedges—and/or bite bite bite you.

I mean, I know: Your human needs are more complex than mine, because you're all fancy and shit. But as for me and my kind? Give me a full kibble trough every morning and regular delivery of orange wedges every afternoon, and I'm good. Maybe an empty beer keg to push from one side of my cage to the other and back again. And of course the presence of (or at least the promise of) a potential female copulation partner within the immediate smellable vicinity.

Now, if you'll excuse me for a moment, I am experiencing a feeling that virtually compels me to try to eat this microphone.

Ow! There's really no reason to go nuts with the leash like that, Mr. Bite-Bite-Bite-Bite-Bite-As-Soon-As-Possible! No one told me the microphone was a "Bad-Boy-Don't-Eat" item. So work with me a little—okay, Mr. Gouge-Eyes-Eat-Fingers?

Wow, folks. I guess it takes all kinds, huh? Give me a minute while I simultaneously finish off this bowl of water and take another dump.

Ahh.

And ahh again.

Another question?

Yes—you, Ms. Female-Human-Copulation-Candidate, right here on the left. Your question?

Mm-hmm? That's an excellent question. But, before I answer, may I ask you something? When was the last time you copulated?

I can tell by the way you cover your bared teeth with your hand while your cheeks fill with color that my question intrigues you. I like that. Your copulation partner must be gigantic and have a virtually bottomless supply of orange wedges to have snared a mate like you. But I tell you this: One hour with me and my long stick, and you'd be—

Ow! Again with the leash! Always with the leash, Mr. Male-Human-Mount-And-Copulate-With-To-Humiliate-Before-Killing!

You know what? Go ahead with the leash. Seriously, keep it up. Go down in history as the male human who strangled the world's first talking chimpanzee. What do I care?

I happened to be referring to my termite stick, for your kind information. It's a sophisticated food-gathering tool? Maybe you've heard of it? No?

Figures.

All right, I'm done with this now. Take me back to my cage, please. ASAP. Yes, I know that many of you have more questions, but I'm afraid I'm experiencing a strong, unsettling feeling that the empty beer keg back in my cage is currently on exactly the wrong side and needs to be pushed back to the other side as soon as possible. So let me get back to my job, and maybe we can talk again another time.

2005

NOAH BAUMBACH

MY DOG IS TOM CRUISE

I HAVE to tell you, things are good. I am . . . I am . . . *Whooo!* . . . I am very good. I just returned from a walk and . . . HA! Things. Are. Good. I've got a bowl of hard kibble with some soft stuff mixed in. My name's on the bowl! I am passionate about this lamb-and-rice recipe. What's been going on? HAHA! I'm so in love with this bitch! HAHAHA! I can't . . . I'm so . . . I can't restrain myself. HAHAHAHAHAHA! We met at the park. She was in the run for little dogs . . . 'cause she's, well . . . HA! She's petite. And I was over in the big run and . . . I am in *love*. I can't be cool. This bitch is . . . I have total respect for her. Yesterday on my five o'clock, I just sniffed her ass for a while and then we frolicked. I can't even describe it . . . we chased squirrels . . . frisked, you know . . . she likes to be physical, too . . . and to fetch and . . . We're like anyone. We tore into this shoe and just had a ball. I'll see her tomorrow on my 8 A.M. I am happy. I am . . . HAHAHAHAHAHA! She is a wonderful, wonderful animal. I can't . . . words don't . . . OWOOOOO! I can't sit or stay, man. I need to get up on my hind legs and holler, you know! I gotta pee on something. And I don't care what the other animals do or what their masters say. Listen, there are always gonna be pit bulls. There are always gonna be Dobermans. And cynical little pugs. And you know what? I've never cared what others think about me. I've always been this way. I'm living my life. And I am fortunate. And I am excited. I am fortunate and excited.

Do you know the history of crate training? 'Cause I do. Don't talk about things you don't understand. Like saying dogs are wild. Dogs are wild—that is glib. Dogs are . . . I've done the research; there are crates that they put us in to quote unquote train us. They throw rattlesnakes at us. Electric-shock tags! I'm not making this up. This is . . . it's history. Crate training just masks the problem. These dogs, they become zombies. You can totally handle disobedience naturally by saying "No!" and "Bad dog!" It works. Look at the *facts*. Shock tags?! I am disgusted.

HAHAHA! I fetch! Boy, I love to fetch. I am totally fired up when I fetch. And nap. I've got a great dog bed with leopard spots where I can power-nap, man. I've got awesome chew toys, too. I'm passionate about this rubber T-bone with peanut butter hidden in it. Here's the point: Do you know there are strays on the street eating out of the Dumpsters behind Chinese restaurants? I'm not making that up. I care about those mutts. But they don't know what the options are. They don't know that you can live in an apartment and get fed by a human. These hounds, man—when it thunders, they think the world is ending. Because they haven't done the research. Do you know the statistics? A hundred and fifty dogs are being fixed every ten minutes. A hundred and fifty. Every ten minutes. I can't . . . that's just wrong. And I speak out about it.

There's this yellow Lab, Clover, who I see in the dog run. And this is a totally great purebred. He's a . . . HA! He's . . . he's a great guy. I've got enormous respect for him. But he's overweight. You know why? 'Cause they're feeding him scraps from the table. And he can't fetch or chase without getting winded. That is sad. I care about him, and I care about the apricot poodle with the plaid socks on his feet, and I care about the basenji with the drooling issues. I want to hear good news. I like to see a Rottweiler get a bath or a shepherd savor a Milk-Bone. That makes me happy.

What these beggars don't understand is that if you hover around the dinner table long enough and you're observant food will come. Food's gonna come naturally, man. They're gonna drop stuff and you can— HAHAHAHAHA! But, seriously, begging is a huge issue among our species. I did the research. And I speak out. I speak out about *misinformation.* Do you know people think that one dog year is seven human years? That is false. Total fabrication. It's approximate. Flea and tick collars? There are vitamins for that. And your master can totally put that capsule in a slab of butter and you'll never know you ate it.

OWOOOWOWOWOOO!!! This bitch, she's kind, she's caring, she's a wonderful, wonderful dog. It's like . . . wow. And I don't want to compare, but I've never felt this way before. We might have a litter. One thing at a time. It's joy, man. That's what it is. Look at my tail! I'm panting 24/7. HAHAHAHA! I purr, even. Like a cat, man. The cat looks at me and he's, like, "What did they put in your kibble?" HAHA! I don't care. I've never cared what that cat thinks. But I care about him even though he's a cynic. I care about the glib parakeet and those jerks the gerbils, but I'm not sure those are the same gerbils as before. HAHAHA! Those gerbils! We have fun. I bark, they run on the wheel. What's that? The leash jingling! Is it eight already? *Walk?!* OWOOOHAHAHAHAHA-HARUFFRUFFRUFFHA!!! I love living my life!

2005

YONI BRENNER

AESOP IN THE CITY

THE HAWK AND THE MOUSE

A clever mouse is sunning himself in Battery Park, when a hawk swoops down and seizes him in her talons. Whistling through the air, the mouse warns the hawk not to eat him. "Why shouldn't I?" says the hawk. "Don't you know," says the mouse, "that mice are loaded with trans fats?" Alarmed, the hawk releases the mouse and flies away. Several days later, the hawk happens upon an old owl devouring a less fortunate mouse. "Stop!" cries the hawk. "Don't you know those things are loaded with trans fats?" The owl stops eating and says, "What are you, an idiot?"

Moral: You just can't argue with libertarians.

THE FOX AND THE GOAT

A fox is offered free tickets from Cindy in P.R. She drops them off after lunch, and the fox is dismayed to find that they are for an experimental Swedish dance company called Leøtåård. He takes the tickets to the goat in the next cubicle. "Leøtåård?" says the goat. "I've never heard of them." "I saw them last week," coos the fox. "The Scandinavian Alvin Ailey. I'll give them to you for ten bucks." And so, while the goat spends the evening in a dank underground space off Avenue C, the fox goes to Ollie's and spends the ten dollars on lo mein. Sure enough, the performance is awful and the goat gets a massive strobe-light headache. Still, inexplicably, he puts his name on the e-mail list.

Moral: Always check the website.

THE CROW AND THE HARE

Waiting for the uptown No. 1 train, a hare becomes ill and tumbles onto the tracks. "Help me!" the hare shouts to a nearby crow. But the crow is uncertain. "How do I know you won't eat me?" he asks. "I'm helpless," replies the hare. "Besides, hares do not eat crows." Satisfied, the crow flutters down from the platform and grips the hare by the scruff of the neck. Suddenly, the hare flips around and eats the crow. "That'll show him," he says.

Moral: Hares will eat anything.

THE DOG AND THE MAGIC HEN

A dog in the East Nineties is lying on the curb when a friendly hen happens by and asks him what's wrong. "My bone," says the dog. "It's stuck under the tire of that Volvo." "I'll tell you what," says the hen. "Come back Tuesday at eleven-thirty and I will make the Volvo disappear." And so the dog returns Tuesday morning and, sure enough, the Volvo is gone. "Amazing!" says the dog, his bone retrieved. "I'll do you one better," clucks the hen. "Come back tomorrow and I will make the cars on the other side of the street disappear." The dog comes back the next day and, as promised, the other side of the street is empty. "Incredible," marvels the dog. "I guess this is why they call you the Magic Hen." "No," replies the hen. "They call me that because I sell acid."

Moral: You didn't hear it from me.

THE MOUSE AND THE DONALD

Ambling through Central Park one day, a mouse happens upon Donald Trump, trapped in a hunter's net. The mouse asks the Donald if he can be of any assistance. "How could *you* help *me*?" scoffs the Donald. "I am Donald Trump and you are just a lowly mouse."

Several years later, the Donald calls the mouse into his office. "Your division underperformed again, Johnson," says the Donald. "Someone's gonna have to take the fall." "But, Donald!" cries the mouse. "Don't you remember why you hired me? How I nibbled through that net and saved you from the hunters?" The Donald thinks for a moment, then replies, "I don't remember it that way."

Moral: Success is fleeting, so keep a paper trail.

THE JACKDAW AND THE EXPENSE ACCOUNT

A jackdaw takes a job with a prominent consulting firm. One night, after working well past nine, he decides to go to Pastis on the company dime and invites his old friend the hare to join him. After the two have scanned the menu, a server comes to take their orders. "The ravioli for me," says the jackdaw. "And I'll have the *lapin à la cocotte*," says the hare. The server is aghast. "But, sir . . . that's rabbit." The hare shrugs. "Whatever."

Moral: Hares really will eat anything.

THE LION AND THE DONKEY

A lion and a donkey go to a Knicks game, only to find that their seats are way back in Section 426. "I can't see anything!" moans the lion. The donkey replies, "Aren't you a lion? Just move down." So the lion proceeds to maul his way through the crowd, until he and the donkey find a nice spot on the 200 level. But, by the end of the first quarter, the lion is again dissatisfied and decides to maul his way to half-court seats. By the fourth quarter, the lion and the donkey are courtside. At this point, the lion, his paws caked with blood, scraps of licensed apparel stuck in his fangs, turns to the donkey and says, "They call that defense?"

Moral: You can't field a team with five pure shooters, quirky draft picks, and no inside presence and expect to win more than thirty-five games.

THE WOLF, THE SHEEP, THE H.R. PERSON, MAYOR BLOOMBERG, AL SHARPTON, AND JESSE THE INTERN

A wolf applies for a job with the Parks Department. To his chagrin, he doesn't even get a second interview. He disguises himself in a sheepskin and reapplies, but the H.R. person is still unimpressed. Believing that he is the victim of discrimination, the wolf hires a lawyer, who notifies Al Sharpton, who puts in a call to Mayor Bloomberg. The Mayor holds a press conference at which he reaffirms the city's commitment to diversity and offers the sheep, who is actually a wolf, a job. The wolf accepts, and the whole thing blows over. After a month of answering phones, the wolf suddenly throws off the sheepskin and announces to the office that he is a wolf. Inspired by the wolf's example, Jesse the intern suddenly announces that he is gay. The office breaks into applause and everyone goes out for drinks to celebrate.

Moral: It's best to come out of the closet on a Friday, so people can let it sink in over the weekend.

2OO7

YONI BRENNER

MONKEY DO

In a paper in Psychological Science, *researchers at Yale report finding the first evidence of cognitive dissonance in monkeys.* —The *Times*

EXPERIMENT 1: BANANAS

Method: A monkey observed to have a particularly strong penchant for bananas is given a choice—he can continue his standard ration of one banana per day or he can give up bananas in exchange for an unlimited supply of a revolutionary product called New Banana. Unable to resist the lure of this perpetual bounty, the monkey throws caution to the wind and eschews his regular banana in favor of New Banana, which, unbeknownst to the monkey, is not actually a banana but a cake of hard-packed baking soda inside a banana peel.

Results: Initially, the monkey is revolted by New Banana and enters a prolonged period of depression, eyeing his fellow monkeys and their tasty bananas with a doleful expression. But, after a few months, the monkey gets used to New Banana, and by the end of the year he has become a vigorous proselyte, extolling the energetic, spiritual, and colonic properties of New Banana, while disparaging the musty tropical reek of traditional bananas. After a year, the monkey refuses to so much as touch a regular banana, and repeatedly proclaims that switching to New Banana was the best decision he ever made.

EXPERIMENT 2: APARTMENT SEARCH

Method: Having lived in a research laboratory for ten years, a monkey is encouraged to get his own place, in midtown or maybe the East Village. A research assistant, posing as a broker, shows the monkey a cramped, overpriced studio off Second Avenue. The monkey balks—after all, he's a grown monkey; doesn't he deserve a little space? The monkey dismisses the research assistant and starts obsessively scanning the rental listings on Craigslist, determined to find an affordable one-bedroom with no fee.

Results: After responding to hundreds of listings and visiting more than twenty apartments—all of which are either dilapidated, vermin-infested, meth-lab-adjacent, or some combination of the three—the search begins to wear on the monkey, and he starts questioning why he was so fixated on getting a one-bedroom. After all, he's a single monkey, and doesn't he spend all his time at work anyway? Besides, with some creative light-palette decorating and a new flat-screen TV, a studio could look quite spacious. After a few days, this logic sinks in and the monkey not only signs a two-year lease for the Second Avenue place but recommends the "broker" to several other monkeys in the lab. Two months later, the monkey is tragically killed when he rolls out of his bed and directly into the trash compactor.

EXPERIMENT 3: JUDAISM

Method: An avowedly secular, antireligious monkey is introduced to a gorgeous female research assistant with a sarcastic edge that some would call harsh but he finds wholly endearing. Early in the relationship, the research assistant informs the monkey that, as much as she loves him, she cannot marry him unless he converts to Judaism. Undaunted, the monkey seeks out a rabbi and thrusts himself into the arduous, several-year process of Orthodox conversion. Then, fifteen months into conversion classes, the research assistant suddenly dumps the monkey, explaining that he has "changed."

Results: Heartbroken, the monkey withdraws from everything that reminds him of the research assistant, denouncing religion and claiming that he never really liked Malaysian Expressionist cinema. But in a few weeks, the monkey is back with his rabbi, having determined that his spiritual journey was independent of the relationship and that he owes it to himself to see it through. Following his conversion, the monkey throws himself into Jewish life—running for treasurer at a small progressive temple in New Rochelle and contributing an online column to the magazine *Hadassah*—before falling madly in love with an Episcopalian underwear model he met during intermission at the Israel Philharmonic.

EXPERIMENT 4: IRAQ

Method: A right-leaning monkey is invited to be a guest on what he be-lieves is a Sunday-morning news program but is in fact a panel of re-search assistants sitting around a card table in pancake makeup. The panel proceeds to grill the monkey on the catastrophic intelligence fail-ures and phantom WMDs that led to the invasion of Iraq, asking how he can justify his continued support of such a costly and destructive war launched under false pretenses.

Results: Unfazed, the monkey deftly reframes the debate, asserting that the war was never about WMDs but about transforming the political dynamic of the region, which is an ongoing historical process and thus immune to the partisan slings of shortsighted pundits. So polished is the monkey's reasoning that he is recruited by the Heritage Foundation and soon becomes a fixture on the real Sunday-morning circuit, stead-fastly denying the relevance of WMDs. All seems to be going well until he appears on ABC's *This Week* and is ambushed with a 2003 tape of himself at a VFW post saying, "This war is about WMDs, pure and simple." After a prolonged silence, the monkey stammers something about "out of context," then leaps at George Stephanopoulos's face, in-flicting several small bite wounds. Six months later, the monkey's con-firmation as Ambassador to the United Nations is effectively sunk following a bizarre incident in which he is accused of throwing his feces at Barbara Boxer (although the monkey insists that it was the other way around).

2007

SIMON RICH

ANIMAL TALES

FROGS

"Hey, can I ask you something? Why do human children dissect us?"

"It's part of their education. They cut open our bodies in school and write reports about their findings."

"Huh. Well, I guess it could be worse, right? I mean, at least we're not dying in vain."

"How do you figure?"

"Well, our deaths are furthering the spread of knowledge. It's a huge sacrifice we're making, but at least some good comes out of it."

"Let me show you something."

"What's this?"

"It's a frog-dissection report."

"Who wrote it?"

"A fourteen-year-old human from New York City. Some kid named Simon."

(*Flipping through it.*) "This is it? This is the whole thing?"

"Uh-huh."

"Geez. It doesn't look like he put a lot of time into this."

"Look at the diagram on the last page."

"Oh, my God . . . it's so crude. It's almost as if he wasn't even looking down at the paper while he was drawing it. Like he was watching TV or something."

"Read the conclusion."

" 'In conclusion, frogs are a scientific wonder of biology.' What does that even mean?"

"It doesn't mean anything."

"Why are the margins so big?"

"He was trying to make it look as if he had written five pages, even though he had only written four."

"He couldn't come up with one more page of observations about our dead bodies?"

"I guess not."

"This paragraph looks like it was copied straight out of an encyclopedia. I'd be shocked if he retained any of this information."

"Did you see that he spelled 'science' wrong in the heading?"

"Whoa . . . I missed that. That's incredible."

"He didn't even bother to run it through spell-check."

"Who did he dissect?"

"Harold."

"Betsy's husband? Jesus. So this is why Harold was killed. To produce this . . . 'report.' "

(*Nods.*) "This is why his life was taken from him."

(*Long pause.*)

"Well, at least it has a cover sheet."

"Yeah. The plastic's a nice touch."

DALMATIANS

"Hey, look, the truck's stopping."

"Did they take us to the park this time?"

"No—it's a fire. Another horrible fire."

"What the hell is wrong with these people?"

FREE-RANGE CHICKENS

"Well, it's another beautiful day in paradise."

"How'd we get so lucky?"

"I don't know and I don't care."

"I think I'll go walk over there for a while. Then I'll walk back over here."

"That sounds like a good time. Maybe I'll do the same."

"Hey, someone refilled the grain bucket!"

"Is it the same stuff as yesterday?"

"I hope so."

"Oh, man, it's the same stuff, all right."

"It's so good."

"I can't stop eating it."

"Hey, you know what would go perfectly with this grain? Water."

"Dude. Look inside the other bucket."

"This . . . is the greatest day of my life."

"Drink up, pal."

"Cheers!"

(*Laughs.*)
(*Laughs.*)
"Hey, look, the farmer's coming."
"Huh. Guess it's my turn to go into the thing."
"Cool. See you later, buddy."
"See ya."

2008

NO BUSINESS LIKE
SHOW BUSINESS

S. J. PERELMAN

FAREWELL, MY LOVELY APPETIZER

Add Smorgasbits to your ought-to-know department, the newest of the three Betty Lee products. What in the world! Just small mouth-size pieces of herring and of pinkish tones. We crossed our heart and promised not to tell the secret of their tinting.
　　　　　—Clementine Paddleford's food column in the *Herald Tribune*

The "Hush-Hush" Blouse. We're very hush-hush about his name, but the celebrated shirtmaker who did it for us is famous on two continents for blouses with details like those deep yoke folds, the wonderful shoulder pads, the shirtband bow! —Russeks advertisement in the *Times*

I CAME down the sixth-floor corridor of the Arbogast Building, past the World Wide Noodle Corporation, Zwinger & Rumsey, Accountants, and the Ace Secretarial Service, Mimeographing Our Specialty. The legend on the ground-glass panel next door said, "Atlas Detective Agency, Noonan & Driscoll," but Snapper Driscoll had retired two years before with a .38 slug between the shoulders, donated by a snowbird in Tacoma, and I owned what good will the firm had. I let myself into the crummy anteroom we kept to impress clients, growled good morning at Birdie Claflin.

"Well, you certainly look like something the cat dragged in," she said. She had a quick tongue. She also had eyes like dusty lapis lazuli, taffy hair, and a figure that did things to me. I kicked open the bottom drawer of her desk, let two inches of rye trickle down my craw, kissed Birdie square on her lush, red mouth, and set fire to a cigarette.

"I could go for you, sugar," I said slowly. Her face was veiled, watchful. I stared at her ears, liking the way they were joined to her head. There was something complete about them; you knew they were there for keeps. When you're a private eye, you want things to stay put.

"Any customers?"

"A woman by the name of Sigrid Bjornsterne said she'd be back. A looker."

"Swede?"

"She'd like you to think so."

I nodded toward the inner office to indicate that I was going in there, and went in there. I lay down on the davenport, took off my shoes, and bought myself a shot from the bottle I kept underneath. Four minutes later, an ash blonde with eyes the color of unset opals, in a Nettie Rosenstein basic black dress and a baum-marten stole, burst in. Her bosom was heaving and it looked even better that way. With a gasp she circled the desk, hunting for some place to hide, and then, spotting the wardrobe where I keep a change of bourbon, ran into it. I got up and wandered out into the anteroom. Birdie was deep in a crossword puzzle.

"See anyone come in here?"

"Nope." There was a thoughtful line between her brows. "Say, what's a five-letter word meaning 'trouble'?"

"Swede," I told her, and went back inside. I waited the length of time it would take a small, not very bright boy to recite "Ozymandias," and, inching carefully along the wall, took a quick gander out the window. A thin galoot with stooping shoulders was being very busy reading a paper outside the Gristede store two blocks away. He hadn't been there an hour ago, but then, of course, neither had I. He wore a size-seven dove-colored hat from Browning King, a tan Wilson Brothers shirt with pale-blue stripes, a J. Press foulard with a mixed-red-and-white figure, dark blue Interwoven socks, and an unshined pair of ox-blood London Character shoes. I let a cigarette burn down between my fingers until it made a small red mark, and then I opened the wardrobe.

"Hi," the blonde said lazily. "You Mike Noonan?" I made a noise that could have been "Yes," and waited. She yawned. I thought things over, decided to play it safe. I yawned. She yawned back, then, settling into a corner of the wardrobe, went to sleep. I let another cigarette burn down until it made a second red mark beside the first one, and then I woke her up. She sank into a chair, crossing a pair of gams that tightened my throat as I peered under the desk at them.

"Mr. Noonan," she said, "you—you've got to help me."

"My few friends call me Mike," I said pleasantly.

"Mike." She rolled the syllable on her tongue. "I don't believe I've ever heard that name before. Irish?"

"Enough to know the difference between a gossoon and a bassoon."

"What *is* the difference?" she asked. I dummied up; I figured I wasn't giving anything away for free. Her eyes narrowed. I shifted my two hundred pounds slightly, lazily set fire to a finger, and watched it burn down. I could see she was admiring the interplay of muscles in my shoulders. There wasn't any extra fat on Mike Noonan, but I wasn't telling *her* that. I was playing it safe until I knew where we stood.

When she spoke again, it came with a rush. "Mr. Noonan, he thinks I'm trying to poison him. But I swear the herring was pink—I took it out of the jar myself. If I could only find out how they tinted it. I offered them money, but they wouldn't tell."

"Suppose you take it from the beginning," I suggested.

She drew a deep breath. "You've heard of the golden spintria of Hadrian?" I shook my head. "It's a tremendously valuable coin believed to have been given by the Emperor Hadrian to one of his proconsuls, Caius Vitellius. It disappeared about 150 A.D., and eventually passed into the possession of Hucbald the Fat. After the sack of Adrianople by the Turks, it was loaned by a man named Shapiro to the court physician, or hakim, of Abdul Mahmoud. Then it dropped out of sight for nearly five hundred years, until last August, when a dealer in second-hand books named Lloyd Thursday sold it to my husband."

"And now it's gone again," I finished.

"No," she said. "At least, it was lying on the dresser when I left, an hour ago." I leaned back, pretending to fumble a carbon out of the desk, and studied her legs again. This was going to be a lot more intricate than I had thought. Her voice got huskier. "Last night I brought home a jar of Smorgasbits for Walter's dinner. You know them?"

"Small mouth-size pieces of herring and of pinkish tones, aren't they?"

Her eyes darkened, lightened, got darker again. "How did you know?"

"I haven't been a private op nine years for nothing, sister. Go on."

"I—I knew right away something was wrong when Walter screamed and upset his plate. I tried to tell him the herring was supposed to be pink, but he carried on like a madman. He's been suspicious of me since—well, ever since I made him take out that life insurance."

"What was the face amount of the policy?"

"A hundred thousand. But it carried a triple-indemnity clause in case he died by sea food. Mr. Noonan—Mike"—her tone caressed me—"I've got to win back his confidence. You could find out how they tinted that herring."

"What's in it for me?"

"Anything you want." The words were a whisper. I leaned over, poked open her handbag, counted off five grand.

"This'll hold me for a while," I said. "If I need any more, I'll beat my spoon on the high chair." She got up. "Oh, while I think of it, how does this golden spintria of yours tie in with the herring?"

"It doesn't," she said calmly. "I just threw it in for glamour." She trailed past me in a cloud of scent that retailed at ninety rugs the ounce. I caught her wrist, pulled her up to me.

"I go for girls named Sigrid with opal eyes," I said.

"Where'd you learn my name?"

"I haven't been a private snoop twelve years for nothing, sister."

"It was nine last time."

"It seemed like twelve till *you* came along." I held the clinch until a faint wisp of smoke curled out of her ears, pushed her through the door. Then I slipped a pint of rye into my stomach and a heater into my kick and went looking for a bookdealer named Lloyd Thursday. I knew he had no connection with the herring caper, but in my business you don't overlook anything.

THE thin galoot outside Gristede's had taken a powder when I got there; that meant we were no longer playing girls' rules. I hired a hack to Wanamaker's, cut over to Third, walked up toward Fourteenth. At Twelfth a mink-faced jasper made up as a street cleaner tailed me for a block, drifted into a dairy restaurant. At Thirteenth somebody dropped a sour tomato out of a third-story window, missing me by inches. I doubled back to Wanamaker's, hopped a bus up Fifth to Madison Square, and switched to a cab down Fourth, where the second-hand bookshops elbow each other like dirty urchins.

A flabby hombre in a Joe Carbondale rope-knit sweater, whose jowl could have used a shave, quit giggling over the Heptameron long enough to tell me he was Lloyd Thursday. His shoe-button eyes became opaque when I asked to see any first editions or incunabula relative to the *Clupea harengus,* or common herring.

"You got the wrong pitch, copper," he snarled. "That stuff is hotter than Pee Wee Russell's clarinet."

"Maybe a sawbuck'll smarten you up," I said. I folded one to the size of a postage stamp, scratched my chin with it. "There's five yards

around for anyone who knows why those Smorgasbits of Sigrid Bjornsterne's happened to be pink." His eyes got crafty.

"I might talk for a grand."

"Start dealing." He motioned toward the back. I took a step forward. A second later a Roman candle exploded inside my head and I
went away from there. When I came to, I was on the floor with a lump
on my sconce the size of a lapwing's egg and big Terry Tremaine of
Homicide was bending over me.

"Someone sapped me," I said thickly. "His name was—"

"Webster," grunted Terry. He held up a dog-eared copy of Mer-
riam's Unabridged. "You tripped on a loose board and this fell off a
shelf on your think tank."

"Yeah?" I said skeptically. "Then where's Thursday?" He pointed to
the fat man lying across a pile of erotica. "He passed out cold when he
saw you cave." I covered up, let Terry figure it any way he wanted. I
wasn't telling him what cards I held. I was playing it safe until I knew
all the angles.

In a seedy pharmacy off Astor Place, a stale Armenian, whose name
might have been Vulgarian but wasn't, dressed my head and started
asking questions. I put my knee in his groin and he lost interest. Jerk-
ing my head toward the coffee urn, I spent a nickel and the next forty
minutes doing some heavy thinking. Then I holed up in a phone booth
and dialed a clerk I knew called Little Farvel, in a delicatessen store on
Amsterdam Avenue. It took a while to get the dope I wanted because
the connection was bad and Little Farvel had been dead two years, but
we Noonans don't let go easily.

BY the time I worked back to the Arbogast Building, via the Wee-
hawken ferry and the George Washington Bridge to cover my tracks, all
the pieces were in place. Or so I thought up to the point she came out of
the wardrobe holding me between the sights of her ice-blue automatic.

"Reach for the stratosphere, gumshoe." Sigrid Bjornsterne's voice
was colder than Horace Greeley and Little Farvel put together, but her
clothes were plenty calorific. She wore a forest-green suit of Hockanum
woollens, a Knox Wayfarer, and baby crocodile pumps. It was her
blouse, though, that made tiny red hairs stand up on my knuckles. Its
deep yoke folds, shoulder pads, and shirtband bow could only have
been designed by some master craftsman, some Cézanne of the shears.

"Well, Nosy Parker," she sneered, "so you found out how they tinted the herring."

"Sure—grenadine," I said easily. "You knew it all along. And you planned to add a few grains of oxylbutane-cheriphosphate, which turns the same shade of pink in solution, to your husband's portion, knowing it wouldn't show in the post-mortem. Then you'd collect the three hundred G's and join Harry Pestalozzi in Nogales till the heat died down. But you didn't count on me."

"You?" Mockery nicked her full-throated laugh. "What are you going to do about it?"

"This." I snaked the rug out from under her and she went down in a swirl of silken ankles. The bullet whined by me into the ceiling as I vaulted over the desk, pinioned her against the wardrobe.

"Mike." Suddenly all the hatred had drained away and her body yielded to mine. "Don't turn me in. You cared for me—once."

"It's no good, Sigrid. You'd only double-time me again."

"Try me."

"Okay. The shirtmaker who designed your blouse—what's his name?" A shudder of fear went over her; she averted her head. "He's famous on two continents. Come on, Sigrid, they're your dice."

"I won't tell you. I can't. It's a secret between this—this department store and me."

"They wouldn't be loyal to *you*. They'd sell you out fast enough."

"Oh, Mike, you mustn't. You don't know what you're asking."

"For the last time."

"Oh, sweetheart, don't you see?" Her eyes were tragic pools, a cenotaph to lost illusions. "I've got so little. Don't take that away from me. I—I'd never be able to hold up my head in Russeks again."

"Well, if that's the way you want to play it . . ." There was silence in the room, broken only by Sigrid's choked sob. Then, with a strangely empty feeling, I uncradled the phone and dialed Spring 7-3100.

For an hour after they took her away, I sat alone in the taupe-colored dusk, watching lights come on and a woman in the hotel opposite adjusting a garter. Then I treated my tonsils to five fingers of firewater, jammed on my hat, and made for the anteroom. Birdie was still scowling over her crossword puzzle. She looked up crookedly at me.

"Need me any more tonight?"

"No." I dropped a grand or two in her lap. "Here, buy yourself some stardust."

"Thanks, I've got my quota." For the first time I caught a shadow of pain behind her eyes. "Mike, would—would you tell me something?"

"As long as it isn't clean," I flipped to conceal my bitterness.

"What's an eight-letter word meaning 'sentimental'?"

"Flatfoot, darling," I said, and went out into the rain.

1944

THOMAS MEEHAN

EARLY MORNING OF A MOTION PICTURE EXECUTIVE

One of the smallest minorities in Hollywood nowadays is the group that believes James Joyce's Ulysses *will be made into a superior movie . . . behind the entire hoopla is Jerry Wald, the producer . . . he prepared a memorandum . . . that included the following: "The way I would like to see this story on the screen is to oversimplify it. It has three levels: Stephen Dedalus, the intellectual; Leopold Bloom, the passive, ill-informed victim of habitual feelings; and Mrs. Bloom, sensual, carnal, wholly natural. Thus, the three leading characters represent Pride, Love, and The Flesh. My feeling is that this project is really in its purest form: father searching for his son and son searching for his father. It is a highly controversial book and out of it could be created a motion picture as exciting as* Peyton Place *but on a higher level." —The* Times

. . . YES a quarter after what an unearthly hour I suppose they're just getting out on the lot at Fox now Marilyn Monroe combing out her hair for the day let me see if I can doze off 1 2 3 4 5 where was it in Jerrys memorandum yes oversimplify O I love great books Id love to have the whole of Hollywood filming nothing but great books God in heaven theres nothing like literature pre sold to the public the treatment and the working script by Dalton Trumbo and the finished picture in color and Todd A O as for them saying theres no audience interest in pictures based on great books I wouldnt give a snap of my two fingers for all their motivational research indie exhibs whatever they call themselves why dont they go out and make a picture I ask them and do a socko 21 Gs in Philly and a wow 41 in Chi ah that they cant answer yes in its purest form father searching for his son and son searching for his father chance for myriad boffolas there old man staggers out one door of pub where the beer and the boffola foam while kid goes in other O I love a good laugh Stephen Dedalus the intellectual we might try to get Paul Newman for the part hes a strong BO draw in Exodus certainly hed do very nicely too better soft pedal the egghead bit though make him a newspaper reporter have to shoot a lot of location stuff in Dublin by the waters of the Liffey by the rivering waters of we might fake it on the back lot and bring it in under three million or else knock up the budget and spot celebs the way Columbia did with Pepe it coined a huge forty five thou in its first week on Bway gives the property a touch of class I wonder could we get Bobby Darin on a percentage deal to sing Galway Bay I better have Sammy check in the morning where the hell Galway Bay is its somewhere around Dublin surely long color process shot of the bay at dusk cut to faces of old women in black shawls and the women in the uplands making hay speak a language that the strangers do not know a scene which it will knock them out of the back of the house in Terre Haute

the alarmclock in the maids room clattering the brains out of itself better take another seconal and try to sleep again so as I can get up early Ill call a title conference at ten wait now who was it yes Kirk Douglas already made Ulysses the old story though this ones on three levels we might call it Pride Love and The Flesh that has a nice sound to it Ill have Sammy get ahold of Central Registry and see if the titles reserved Leopold Bloom the passive ill informed victim of habitual feelings problem on the religion bit though dont want Bnai Brith down on our necks well give him an Irish name in any case Leopold Malone and his loving wife Molly sensual carnal wholly natural she wheels her wheelbarrow through streets wide and narrow personally Id like to build the script around Molly and get MM for the role so why am I after worrying we cant go wrong with Maureen OHara flashback to Gibraltar where she was a girl a flower of the mountain yes so are those bimbos all flowers of the mountain lap dissolve he kisses her under the Moorish wall we might send down a second unit to get some outdoor Gibraltar stuff cut in a flamenco dream sequence shoot it there and dub it on

the soundtrack later yes chance too for widescreen color background O
the sea the sea there crimson sometimes like fire and the glorious sunsets and the figtrees in the Alameda gardens yes well have Louella
bawling like a goddam baby baaaawwaaaaaww at the world preem

ah well theres no talking around it were one of the smallest minorities in Hollywood nowadays us thinking that James Joyces Ulysses will
be made into a superior movie TJ saying to me Harry youre one hundred per cent crazy him with his two dollar cigars and his Irving Thal-
berg award chasing those little chits of starlets and he not long married
Mouth Almighty I call him and his squinty eyes of all the big stuppoe
studio heads I ever met God help the world if everyone out here was
like him yes always and ever making the same pictures showdownat-
shotguncreek whatever he calls the new one ah God send him more
sense and me more money O he does look the fool sitting at the head
of the conference table as big as you please he can go smother for all the
fat lot I care Im unabashedly intellectual and Ill make this movie or Im
walking off the lot this day week Ive still got my integrity after all how
long is it Ive been out here wait yes since 1923 O I love lying in bed
God here we are as bad as ever after yes thirty eight years how many
studios have I worked at RKO and Fox and Metro and Paramount
where I was a young man and the day I talked to deMille when he was
making the original of The Ten Commandments and yes he wouldnt
answer at first only looked out over the set and the thousands of extras
I was thinking of so many things he didnt know of yes how someday Id
have my own swimming pool and go to Vilma Bankys parties and all
the long years since Joan Crawford in Our Dancing Daughters and
Richard Dix and yes the year Metro missed the boat on Dinner at
Eight and Fred Astaire and Ginger Rogers and Asta rrrrrffffffrrrrrfffff
and the andyhardy series and The Best Years of Our Lives and O all the
Academy Award dinners yes Disney going about smug with his Oscars
the Levant what year was it Gert and I took the cruise there I never
miss his TV show and Rhonda Fleming with her hair all red and flam-
ing and Sandra Dee and VistaVision and stereophonic sound cleaning
up in the foreign market and Ben Hur and the night TJ asked me what
my next project would be when was it yes the night they screened Psycho in Santa Monica eeeeeeeekkk its an Irish story I told him like The
Quiet Man or shall we get Rock Hudson I was just thinking of it for
the first time yes and I had Sammy give me a five page synopsis and the
day in Romanoffs I asked Jerry Wald about it yes Ulysses by James

Joyce which it is a highly controversial book and I asked him yes could out of it be created a picture as exciting as Peyton Place and yes he said yes it could yes but on a higher level Yes.

1961

GARRISON KEILLOR

HOLLYWOOD IN THE FIFTIES

Q. I understand that the frankest book yet about life in Hollywood has been written by someone named Mark Van Doren. Who is he? What is the title of his book?—K.L., Little Rock, Ark.
A: Mark Van Doren (1894–1972) was a famous poet, literary critic and professor of English at Columbia University. You undoubtedly are confusing him with Mamie Van Doren, 56, a singer-actress fairly well known in the Hollywood of the 1950s and '60s.
—"Walter Scott's Personality Parade," in *Parade*

FOR Mark Van Doren, famous poet and literary critic, the fifties in Hollywood were a confusing time, especially after he met Mamie at the home of his friends Donna and John Reed. Mark had just left RKO to go with Columbia after scripting Donna's *It's a Wonderful Life* (based on John's *Ten Days That Shook the World*), he was exhausted and disillusioned, and the buxom young star of *Untamed Youth* and *Born Reckless* clearly offered something powerful and natural and free.

"Show me things. Tell me. Touch me. You know so much, you're a poet. I'm a child in the body of a woman. Show me," she said, as they sat on the railing, looking out across the merciless sunbaked valley toward the Pacific Ocean shimmering like a blue-green vision beyond the used-car lots. Just then Donna called from the kitchen, "Do you want a slice of lemon in your nectar?" John was gone—who knew where? The moody hazel-eyed revolutionary had never lived by other people's rules, not even after marrying Donna. And he hated Mark, after what Mark had done to his manifesto. He vowed to punch Mark in the nose if he ever saw him.

You all know Donna Reed. Well, she was like that, except more so—the World's Most Nearly Perfect Wife and Mother. She set her clock by her son, Rex, and after he ran away with Vanessa Williams, Ted and Esther's girl, Donna grieved openly. Her pain hung around her like an old black bathrobe.

Ted's uncle, William Carlos Williams, could sense Donna's need to be held, but he was in town to adapt his epic *Paterson* for Twentieth Century–Fox, and was writing a large body of water into the script so that Esther, a swimming actress, could be featured. The poet was crazy about his ballplayer nephew's gorgeous wife. He hung his cap for her. The sun rose and set on her. Whenever Ted was in Boston, W.C. flew to L.A. Esther liked him as a close confidant, but he wanted to be more, much more, so his sudden boyish desire for Donna confused him.

"I'm bad news for any woman I touch," he told Jeanette and Dwight Macdonald. The former Trotskyite, author of *The Root of Man,* tugged at his beard as the famous poet stood poised on the tip of the diving board. Burt and Debbie Reynolds looked up at him and so did Carlos and Carroll Baker. Williams held his arms over his gray head, his knees slightly bent. He didn't notice Lassie and Malcolm Cowley, who had just returned from a walk and stood half shielded by a clump of sumac. "Blouaghhhhh!" W.C. cried as he dove, splitting the water like a fork.

IT troubled Mark that Mamie couldn't swim an inch. He watched gloomily as Esther Williams plowed up and down the length of the pool, just as she did in Williams's poem "The Singing Swimmer" ("the row of maidens / beside the cool water / and the splashing fountains when / suddenly you are there / to sing in your democratic American voice and plunge / deep below the surface and rise, / your white mermaid arms held out to me").

"Esther swims, why not you?" Mark whispered, but Mamie only laughed. Bertrand Russell glanced up from his chaise longue. "Jane swims circles around Esther," said the tanned white-haired philosopher in his clipped English accent. The author of *Principia Mathematica,* from which *Peyton Place* was adapted by Edmund Wilson's brother Earl (both of whom made a play for *Peyton* star Lana Turner after Frederick Jackson Turner, the historian, took a shine to Shelley Winters, Yvor's ex), laughed harshly as he stood and stripped off his light-blue terry-cloth robe. "And I can take any son of a bitch in the joint," he snarled, his icy eyes fixed on John and Ford Madox Ford, whose wives, Betty and Eileen, had vanished into the white stucco bathhouse with Danny and Dylan Thomas. "Any time you like, gentlemen," he added.

The silence hung in the pale-yellow air like a concrete block. From far away came the mournful hum of rubber tires on the burning highway, a viscous sound like liquids splashing on the grass, and also there was an odor like raisin bread burning in a toaster, except worse. It was a Wednesday. John Ford squinted against the hard light. He cleared his throat, like buckshot rolling down a black rubber mat. But it was Williams who spoke.

He stood, water dripping from his white swimming trunks. "Look at us. Fighting each other like starving rats, while the people we ought to be fighting sit in their air-conditioned offices and laugh their heads off," he said. "I'm talking about the bosses, the big boys, the playboy producers, the fat-cat choreographers, the directors, the dream-killers. Those are the bastards we ought to be battling, Bert."

"You sound just like John."

It was Donna. Dylan stood behind her, blinking, with D. H. and Sophia Loren. And Andy Williams. "Hi, Dad," Andy said softly. Doris Day, C. Day-Lewis, Jerry Lewis, Lewis Mumford, Neil Simon, Simone de Beauvoir, Patti Page—everyone was there: the whole Rat Pack, except Bogart. Before Bacall, the wiry little guy had been with Bardot, Garbo, the Gabors, Candy Bergen, Bergman, Clara Bow, Teri Garr, but none of them were quite right. They were too different.

"You're right, Bill." Mark let go of Mamie's hand, and she sank like a wet sponge as the trim critic climbed out of the pool. "We're writers, artists, literary men, not messenger boys," he said, lighting a pipe. "And just look at us. Look at us."

"You look like writers," said Ted Williams, squinting and spitting in that special way of his, that his brother Tennessee had tried to copy until his mouth was dry and torn. "You can't help but look like writers. Because that's what you are. Writers."

"I'm as bad as any of the rest of you," said Dylan sadly. Everyone knew his story, how the sweet voice of the poet was swallowed up in the silent, violent world of gray suits and men with blank empty faces and the watercoolers and the flat beige walls and the uncaring woman behind the desk at the dentist's who looks up with that empty vinyl expression and says, "Next." She doesn't know about your pain. How can she?

"Let's walk," said Mark.

Mamie whispered, "Wait. Please."

"No," he replied, and the writers left, marching down the long driveway into the dark, the lovely dark, and across town to the airport and back East to teach in college, all of them, and somehow they knew in their hearts and nobody had to say it that when they left, the women they loved would find new men and Hollywood would forget them and never mention their names again, and they did and it has and it doesn't, and that is the plain goddam truth, I swear to God, you dirty bastards.

1987

FRANK GANNON

RUNNING THROUGH THE WALL

Hundreds of fans jammed the book department at Harrods department store in London to snap up more than 1,000 autographed copies of actress Joan Collins's first novel, Prime Time. . . . *A Harrods spokeswoman said the sale of 1,000 autographed books in an hour—some signed in advance—was a record for the store, breaking a record set just two weeks ago when actor Kirk Douglas's autobiography,* The Ragman's Son, *sold about 900 copies when he spent an hour autographing books.* —Associated Press

CHUCK Barris, creator of *The Gong Show,* his face set hard, signed his warmup books outside a Waldenbooks in Houston. Yes. He was spelling his name right, with two *r*s. His hand was moving well. He felt good—tense but good. He took a deep breath, crushed out a cigarette, and went inside and started autographing copies of *You and Me Babe.* An hour later, he had autographed over *six hundred* copies. At this time, 1974, this was a feat that was considered unapproachable. Today, schoolchildren can autograph six hundred books in an hour. Many can autograph eight hundred, and scores in the low nine hundreds are commonplace. The incredible has become the expected. The outlandish has become the normal. The weird has become the everyday.

Yet surely there is some limit, some barrier beyond which book signers cannot go. History has not been kind to those who have predicted limits. Hans Fleeder, a University of Colorado psychology-of-the-hand expert, predicted in 1966 that Jackie Susann's mark of two hundred and eighty-six signings would stand forever. Within a year, Susann's mark had been broken over a dozen times. Today, tapes of sixties-era book signings look like slow motion.

We look at them and think, *Too slow.* But we also think, *How fast can we go?*

For years, this question was a purely hypothetical one: Ask fifty-nine "experts" and you might receive fifty-nine "expert" opinions, along with a great deal of tedious conversation. Today, however, we seem on the verge of a breakthrough. Today, for the first time, we seem close to an answer to that age-old question *How many books can a celebrity author sign in an hour?*

There are many facets to this inquiry. Let us examine them.

CULTURAL FACTORS

The world population has tripled in this century. This has had an enormous impact. The equation is simple: The more people, the more paper. The more paper, the more printing. The more printing, the more words. The more people, paper, printing, and words, the more books, the more chances to exceed book-signing limits.

Improved nutrition is also a factor here. For example, Jackie Susann often ate a breakfast of a chocolate doughnut and a cup of Sanka. Today's fast signer wouldn't dream of starting a day without a vast array of complex carbohydrates and carefully administered training fluids. A few years ago, in a famous incident, Sidney Sheldon, minutes before a signing, ate a Pop-Tart and drank a Dr. Brown's. Fifteen minutes later, no one could read his signature.

Forty minutes later, Sheldon began to sign the name "Rosemary Rogers" in his books. An EMS unit was called, and the exhausted creator of *I Dream of Jeannie* was rushed to the nearest hospital and swiftly hooked up to an IV drip. Today, thankfully, Sheldon is all right, but his story stands as a sad reminder of what a book signer faces when he truly "goes for it."

EQUIPMENT

Perhaps nowhere else has modern technology had such a great impact. It is well known that Erich Segal experimented with a primitive felt-tip pen (actually a Q-tip coated with some foreign substance) as early as 1970, but it wasn't until the Mario Puzo era that felt-tip pens became the norm.

Today, the felt-tip pen threatens to become as archaic as a big Mississippi riverboat. Just last summer, a team at Caltech came up with a pen they called, whimsically, the CR-319. The CR-319 was so technologically advanced that it had to be scrapped after it broke the sound barrier during a signing at B. Dalton's in Cincinnati. They've gone back to the drawing board on the CR-319, yet experts still predict that we will see faster pens in the future.

"It's inevitable," says Gaylord Tendon, of Yo Labs. "Fast pens are sexy, and people will always be attracted to them."

OTHER FACTORS

The great unknown factor in book signing has been "hushed up" in most book-signing circles until recent months, and is still largely unknown among the public at large: steroids. No one knows just how pervasive the use of these "signing enhancers" may be, but highly placed members of the Authors Guild agree that it is probably a common practice.

"Anytime you'd see an author come in for a signing with a really big hand, you had to be suspicious," says Gene Fibula, owner of the Booknook in Madison, Wisconsin. "You'd see more and more of these authors—little skinny guys with these gigantic metacarpals. You knew what was happening, but you never said anything. Why alarm the crowd?"

Testing has proved impracticable. Authors are not stupid; they know how to mask the use of steroids. In a highly publicized event in 1987, Erica Jong was nabbed for blood doping, but the matter was dropped when further tests indicated that laboratory machines had been reacting to her nail polish. But most book signers, tragically, will continue to abuse almost anything modern science will make available to them.

THE HUMAN FACTOR

The human factor will be involved in the future of book signing no matter what agents and oddsmakers may predict. Book signing is exclusively a human activity. No gazelles, for instance, do it. Knowing what we know about humans, it's hard not to imagine a scene like this:

Judith Krantz is at the mall ten minutes early. Nervously she twists her head one way, then the other. She extends her fingers. Yes, she nods; she is ready.

She puts her hands on her handler's shoulders. Krantz and her entourage enter the arena and move through the wildly excited crowd. She sits down at the desk, half hidden by the mountains of volumes that tower above her on all sides, and takes out her pen. She turns and whispers to her handler. It is a harsh whisper—harsh from intensity:

"I'm going to sign these books."

It's not hard to imagine an author like Krantz, on a perfect day, in the best of shape and with the best equipment, shattering our concept of book signing.

1988

JON STEWART

THE ENVELOPE, PLEASE: A VIEWER'S GUIDE TO THE EMMYS

O PEN *with vibrant, elaborately costumed dance number set to a medley of popular hits. As music swells, bring the dancing girls to an abrupt halt. End music. Add audience applause and a booming introduction of the well-respected, acerbic host. Play host's signature theme song. Cross host to podium.*

HOST: General greetings and a query as to the audience's well-being. Statement of own well-being. Survey of surroundings. Improvised analogy comparing surroundings to different surroundings. Sarcastic jab at expected length of proceedings.
Pause for laughter.

HOST (*cont.*): Confusion about actions of government officials. Statement of proposed personal action if given opportunity to govern.

Pause for laughter. If laughter is not forthcoming:

HOST (*cont.*): Recognition of enormous power wielded by many audience members. Statement of fear over possible consequences that failure to entertain said powers would entail.

If laughter is forthcoming:

HOST (*cont.*): Query as to audience's familiarity with behavior of recently disgraced cultural icon. Incredulity and displeasure at said behavior. Command for icon to discontinue behavior. Description of outlandish new consumer product created as a result of icon's behavior.

Pause for laughter.

HOST (*cont.*): Praise audience for sense of humor. Query as to their readiness for program's continuation. Introduction of two participants who will begin process of bestowing honors: an unattractive, humorous male renowned for his portrayal of other unattractive, humorous males, and a female of great physical beauty who has achieved fame for her skill in walking while wearing expensive clothing.

Add music and applause as host leaves stage. Bring humorous man and beautiful woman to podium.

MAN (*to woman*): Compliment concerning sexual attractiveness.

WOMAN (*stilted, as though reading*): Acceptance and return of compliment.

MAN: Lurid sexual innuendo. Winking proposition with broad physical gesturing.

WOMAN (*stilted, as though reading*): Unusually intelligent rebuke of said proposition.

MAN: Surprise at intelligence of rebuke. Feigned lack of disappointment at rebuke. Conceited statement of missed sexual opportunity for the woman, again with broad physical gesturing.

Pause for laughter among audience and presenters.

WOMAN: Query as to the identity of the author of previously read statements and indictment of their ability. List of possible honorees.

Stand man and woman aside. Show each possible honoree performing the task for which each is to be honored. Show all present possible honorees in the audience waiting for the result of their effort.

MAN (*opening a sealed correspondence*): Announcement of honoree.

Great rejoicing among the believers of the verdict. Reflection and bitter questioning among the others. Bring the honored one to the stage. A female of surgically enhanced sexual attractiveness hands a totem of achievement to the honoree, who grasps it with great reverence. Audience applause.

HONOREE: Breathless surprise. Self-effacing remark concerning previous outcomes of similar events. Feigned lack of preparation. Expression of gratitude for inventors of the totem as well as constituents of totem. Expression of gratitude for believers in verdict. Expression of gratitude for members of blood lineage and Supreme Exalted Being. Expression of gratitude for creators of shown task. Expression of regret concerning those who have not received expressions of gratitude. Statement of non-harmful intent for those who have not received gratitude. Plea for group subjected to persecution to be no longer subject to said persecution.

Swell music.

HONOREE (*cont.*): Regret at musical interruption and self-criticism at lack of organizational and communication skills. Sudden remembrance of those still in need of expressions of gratitude.

Dim music slightly.

HONOREE (*cont.*): Fear of further recrimination if closing remarks are not forthcoming. Hurried expression of love for those present, viewing at home, or living.

Swell music. Audience applause. Honoree is escorted away by presenters while displaying totem to the audience. Host appears.

HOST: Perceptive remark concerning unexpected length and emotional tenor of honoree's presentation. Example of previous presentation famous for such characteristics.

Pause for laughter.

HOST (*cont.*): Introduction of corpulent woman, well known for recognizing and satirizing her physical condition, and an adolescent known for imitating another adolescent known for contracting a fatal illness.

Repeat as necessary.

1998

ANDY BOROWITZ

THEATRE-LOBBY NOTICES

WARNING: In Act II, there is gunfire, an explosion, and a lengthy monologue by a character named Mr. God.

WARNING: Owing to a typographical error, the *Times* review of this play omitted the word "horrible."

WARNING: When the curtain rises, you may be startled by the sight of a former movie star's ravaged face.

WARNING: In Act III, there is full frontal nudity, but not involving the actor you would like to see naked.

WARNING: During this afternoon's performance, there will be a chatty women's group from Great Neck seated directly behind you.

WARNING: People who do not find plays about incurable bone diseases entertaining should probably go home right now.

WARNING: The lead actor in tonight's play is a veteran of the Royal Shakespeare Company who always showers the first five rows with spittle.

WARNING: In interviews, the composer of tonight's long-delayed musical has referred to it as both "a pet project" and "a labor of love."

WARNING: Any audience members you may hear laughing this evening have been paid handsomely to do so.

WARNING: Tonight's play is being produced despite explicit instructions in the dead playwright's will to "burn all remaining copies to a crisp."

WARNING: The role usually played by Sir Ian McKellen will be performed tonight by the actor who played Isaac on *The Love Boat*.

WARNING: This play has a title that is very similar to that of another play currently running on Broadway, which is the one you meant to buy tickets for.

WARNING: In order to enjoy this play, it is necessary to have some knowledge of Basque dialects.

WARNING: Tom Stoppard found the play you are about to see "confusing."

WARNING: Tonight's play is performed without an intermission and you will be stuck here forever.

2002

PATRICIA MARX

REVIEW

—Is everyone here?
—What about Mrs. Kimball?
—She's still in the hospital.
—I thought they pulled the plug.
—She's having a *chin implant*!
—Let's begin, then. Anyone?
—Well, basically I liked it, but it definitely dragged.
—What doesn't? Everything is twenty minutes too long.
—He's right. Even when I really like a movie, I think, This is great! When will it be over?
—The only reason to do anything is to talk about it afterward.
—Isn't that why we're here?
—People, can we return to the comment that everything is too long?
—Sex isn't too long.
—Yeah? You should meet my husband.
—I felt the end was uninspired. I mean, death is a cliché.
—The whole thing didn't make sense. For instance, what was with the

concept of weather? Room temperature wasn't good enough? It was
always too cold or damp or—

—Are we still talking about sex with her husband?

—You know what I *did* like? The food. Aside from that silly drizzle
thing restaurants started to put on dessert plates in the, what, seventies? Still, looking back, I had a lot of good stuff to eat.

—Oh, God, remember the seventies? Why did they have to end? That
was such a great decade!

—Except for the part that Rod McKuen wrecked.

—See, it's not that it was too long; it's that it was too long in the wrong
places. They should have let you freeze some of your time and tack it
onto the end—the way the Wyndale Health & Racquet Club lets
you freeze your membership for up to three months.

—Another perk for the rich! Everything was always geared to them.

—Not nature. What about nature?

—I felt there could have been more colors. Not hues—*primary* colors.
They could have come up with a fourth one, something sort
of . . . bright drab.

—Oh, they were too busy developing the quote-unquote perfect sunset.

—You've got to admit, though, the idea of putting Chicago on a lake
was excellent. They should have done more of that.

—You know what I could have come up with? The wheel.

—Sure, anyone could've. Once you have *round,* which they did, you're
pretty much there.

—But in a million years you'd never think of luggage on wheels.

—I enjoyed errands; did anyone else? And I got most of them done.

—Could we discuss the guests? How did so many jerks get invited?

—I know. There were, like, billions of people. I would have preferred a
smaller guest list.

—Who says you would have made the cut?

—I say if they're going to have that many people they should make
them wear nametags.

—I just wish that it had been a true meritocracy.

—No, no, absolutely no! I wish they'd based everything on alphabetical
order, and I'm not just saying that because—well, yeah, I am.

—I hate to be catty, but did anyone ever meet that guy? He was from
Philadelphia?

—Did he have a mustache?

—You're thinking of someone else. This guy was born in the early fifties. He was married to . . . oh, you know, what's her name, whose family was in that business?

—I met him. He bugged me.

—I didn't like his taste in shoes.

—I always wondered if he was latently gay.

—Or latently Jewish.

—Or dormantly Mormon. I love saying that.

—Excuse me. I'm not comfortable talking about people who aren't, uh, with us yet.

—Jeez, I can't think of any category of people better to talk about.

—Yes, at last we can speak ill of the living.

—Hello. Is this Banquet Room B?

—It is. And you are . . . ?

—Mrs. Kimball. Surgical-gauze accident.

—Eeew!

—Pull up a chair, Mrs. Kimball.

—I have some questions. I wrote them down. Is there a God? Are human beings born good, bad, or neither? Does a low-carb diet really work? How did Mia Farrow get so many good husbands? Are psychiatrists crazier than non-psychiatrists, or is it just ironic that they are equally crazy? Was it my mother's or my father's fault that I developed bursitis? What really happened that night with Larry?

—I'm sorry, Mrs. Kimball, we're not about Truth with a big *T*. All right, now, who thinks that Shelly Oughten was cheating on Eric in the early nineties? You in the striped shirt.

2003

STEVE MARTIN

STUDIO SCRIPT NOTES
ON *THE PASSION*

DEAR Mel,
We love, *love* the script! The ending works great. You'll be getting a call from us to start negotiations for the book rights.

—Love the Jesus character. So likable. He can't seem to catch a break! We identify with him because of it. One thing: I think we need to clearly state "the rules." Why doesn't he use his superpowers to save himself? Our creative people suggest that you could simply cut away to two spectators:

SPECTATOR ONE
Why doesn't he use his superpowers to save himself?

SPECTATOR TWO
He can only use his powers to help others, never himself.

—Does it matter which garden? Gethsemane is hard to say, and Eden is a much more recognizable garden. Just thinking out loud.
—Our creative people suggest a clock visual fading in and out in certain scenes, like the Last Supper bit: "Thursday, 7:43 P.M.," or "Good Friday, 5:14 P.M."
—Love the repetition of "Is it I?" Could be very funny. On the eighth inquiry, could Jesus just give a little look of exasperation into the camera? Breaks frame, but could be a riot.
—Also, could he change water into wine in Last Supper scene? Would be a great moment, and it's legit. History compression is a movie tradition and could really brighten up the scene. Great trailer moment, too.
—Love the flaying.
—Could the rabbis be Hispanic? There's lots of hot Latino actors

now, could give us a little zing at the box office. Research says there's some historical justification for it.

—Possible title change: *Lethal Passion*. Kinda works. The more I say it out loud, the more I like it.

—Is there someplace where Jesus could be using an iBook? You know, now that I say it, it sounds ridiculous. Strike that. But think about it. Maybe we start a shot in Heaven with Jesus thoughtfully closing the top?

—Love the idea of Monica Bellucci as Mary Magdalene (yow!). Our creative people suggest a name change to Heather. Could skew our audience a little younger.

—Love Judas. Such a great villain. Our creative people suggest that he's a little complicated. Couldn't he be one thing? Just bad? Gives the movie much more of a motor. Also, thirty pieces of silver is not going to get anyone excited. I think it'd be very simple to make him a "new millionaire." Bring in the cash on a tray. Great dilemma that the audience can identify with.

—Minor spelling error: On page 18, in the description of the bystanders, there should be a space between the words "Jew" and "boy."

—Merchandising issue: It seems the Cross image has been done to death and is public domain—we can't own it. Could the Crucifixion scene involve something else? A Toyota would be wrong, but maybe there's a shape we can copyright, like a wagon wheel?

—I'm assuming "The dialogue is in Aramaic" is a typo for "American." If not, call me on my cell, or I'm at home all weekend.

By the way, I'm sending a group of staffers on a cruise to the North Pole, coincidentally around the time of your picture's release. Would love to invite your dad!

See you at the movies!

Yours,
Stan

2004

LARRY DOYLE

WHY WE STRIKE

*Many in showbiz don't have a clear understanding of the writers' de-
mands or the reasoning behind these demands.* —Variety

OUR BELIEFS:

We are artists. We may not dress all cool like artists, or get chicks like
artists, and none of us are starving, quite obviously, but Hollywood
screenwriters are certainly artists, perhaps even *artistes,* and we suffer
just the same. Not in a showy, oh-I-live-in-a-tenement-and-turn-
tricks-to-buy-paint-and-have-this-special-tuberculosis-only-artists-get
kind of way. We suffer as we slave over our screenplays alone, staring
into blank laptops, often blinded by pool glare. And we smoke *real* cigarettes.

We are not in this for the money. Management would have you believe that we all make $200,000 a year. That's funny. We wouldn't even
eat something that cost $200,000, unless it was actually $200,000, driz-
zled with truffle oil, the way Silvio makes it. *Yum.* The only reason we
require payment at all is so we can support those little people we keep
telling you about—the assistants, amanuenses, baristas, Rolfers, scarf
carriers, and erotic muses we need to create our art. Oh, and our babies.
And various charities.

We are not cogs in some machine. While many of today's block-
busters are written by that machine, we are not cogs in it, despite having originally written all the dialogue and characters and plot that this
machine endlessly recombines and maximizes. When a bitter cop with
a shattered family and a monkey on his back flees a narco-terrorist's
fireball while cracking that he's getting too old for this, *some writer
wrote some parts of that, some time back.*

Nor are we trained chimps. The last decent show written by chimps
was *Jojo's Poop Party,* which was largely improvised.

OUR DEMANDS:

An end to the lying. Just kidding. We recognize that without lying, Management would be unable to exhale and would thus perish. However, we are asking for a manifold increase in White Lies about how we are brilliant geniuses and the like, and a corresponding decrease in Brown Lies, about what might happen in the future.

A fair share of newfangled revenue. Management is currently offering us adjusted bubkes of what they are making off Internet sell-through, streaming, ringtones, Webisodes, cellisodes, iPodisodes, celebrity-narrated colonoscosodes, or the psychotic episodes they've been beaming into your brain, brought to you by Clozaril™. All we are asking is 2.5 percent of revenue, based on 40 percent of gross receipts, divided by zero, in bullion. We believe that this is a fair formula, yet one complicated enough for Management to continue to find ways to exercise their cheating rights.

More respect. We are demanding unbounded respect bordering on worship, but that's just our opening offer. We'll accept far, far less, or even a good-faith reduction in spittle.

Meaningful consultation. While we acknowledge Management's right to rape our material, pervert its meaning, and cravenly dilute it for commercial use, we demand to participate in this process. We would like to be on set, or contacted by iPhone if the director doesn't want us there, and simply be asked, "Is this okay?" We stipulate that our opinion, coming, as it does, from the creator of the material being dramatized, is meaningless, and that Management can walk away or hang up before we even answer the question, but it would be nice, for once, to be asked.

A renunciation of droit du seigneur. As it stands, studio executives, from chairman down to associate producer, have the right to deflower us on our wedding night, or any other night or time of day of their choosing. We believe that this change can be written into our contracts without affecting a similar agreement they have with the Screen Actors Guild.

2007

ARTISTS
AND
AUTHORS

THEORY AND PRACTICE OF EDITING
NEW YORKER ARTICLES

An internal editorial memorandum from the 1930s, first reproduced in James Thurber's memoir The Years with Ross.

THE average contributor to this magazine is semi-literate; that is, he is ornate to no purpose, full of senseless and elegant variations, and can be relied on to use three sentences where a word would do. It is impossible to lay down any exact and complete formula for bringing order out of this underbrush, but there are a few general rules.

1. Writers always use too damn many adverbs. On one page, recently, I found eleven modifying the verb "said": "He said morosely, violently, eloquently," and so on. Editorial theory should probably be that a writer who can't make his context indicate the way his character is talking ought to be in another line of work. Anyway, it is impossible for a character to go through all these emotional states one after the other. Lon Chaney might be able to do it, but he is dead.

2. Word "said" is okay. Efforts to avoid repetition by inserting "grunted," "snorted," etc., are waste motion, and offend the pure in heart.

3. Our writers are full of clichés, just as old barns are full of bats. There is obviously no rule about this, except that anything that you suspect of being a cliché undoubtedly is one, and had better be removed.

4. Funny names belong to the past, or to whatever is left of *Fudge* magazine. Any character called Mrs. Middlebottom or Joe Zilch should

be summarily changed to something else. This goes for animals, towns, the names of imaginary books and many other things.

5. Our employer, Mr. Ross, has a prejudice against having too many sentences begin with "and" or "but." He claims that they are conjunctions and should not be used purely for literary effect. Or at least only very judiciously.

6. See our Mr. Weekes on the use of such words as "little," "vague," "confused," "faintly," "all mixed up," etc., etc. The point is that the average *New Yorker* writer, unfortunately influenced by Mr. Thurber, has come to believe that the ideal *New Yorker* piece is about a vague, little man helplessly confused by a menacing and complicated civilization. Whenever this note is not the whole point of the piece (and it far too often is) it should be regarded with suspicion.

7. The repetition of exposition in quotes went out with the Stanley Steamer:
   Marion gave me a pain in the neck.
   "You give me a pain in the neck, Marion," I said.
   This turns up more often than you'd expect.

8. Another of Mr. Ross's theories is that a reader picking up a magazine called *The New Yorker* automatically supposes that any story in it takes place in New York. If it doesn't, if it's about Columbus, Ohio, the lead should say so. "When George Adams was sixteen, he began to worry about the girls he saw every day on the streets of Columbus" or something of the kind. More graceful preferably.

9. Also, since our contributions are signed at the end, the author's sex should be established at once if there is any reasonable doubt. It is distressing to read a piece all the way through under the impression that the "I" in it is a man and then find a woman's signature at the end. Also, of course, the other way round.

10. To quote Mr. Ross again, "Nobody gives a damn about a writer or his problems except another writer." Pieces about authors, reporters, poets, etc., are to be discouraged in principle. Whenever possible the protagonist should be arbitrarily transplanted to an-

other line of business. When the reference is incidental and unnecessary, it should come out.

11. This magazine is on the whole liberal about expletives. The only test I know of is whether or not they are really essential to the author's effect. "Son of a bitch," "bastard" and many others can be used whenever it is the editor's judgment that that is the only possible remark under the circumstances. When they are gratuitous, when the writer is just trying to sound tough to no especial purpose, they come out.

12. In the transcription of dialect, don't let the boys and girls misspell words just for a fake Bowery effect. There is no point, for instance, in "trubble," or "sed."

13. Mr. Weekes said the other night, in a moment of desperation, that he didn't believe he could stand any more triple adjectives. "A tall, florid and overbearing man called Jaeckel." Sometimes they're necessary, but when every noun has three adjectives connected with it, Mr. Weekes suffers and quite rightly.

14. I suffer myself very seriously from writers who divide quotes for some kind of ladies club rhythm. "I am going," he said, "downtown" is a horror, and unless a quote is pretty long I think it ought to stay on one side of the verb. Anyway, it ought to be divided logically, where there would be a pause or something in the sentence.

15. Mr. Weekes has got a long list of banned words beginning with "gadget." Ask him. It's not actually a ban, there being circumstances when they're necessary, but good words to avoid.

16. I would be delighted to go over the list of writers, explaining the peculiarities of each as they have appeared to me in more than ten years of exasperation on both sides.

17. Editing on manuscript should be done with a black pencil, decisively.

18. I almost forgot indirection, which probably maddens Mr. Ross more than anything else in the world. He objects, that is, to important objects, or places or people, being dragged into things in a se-

cretive and underhanded manner. If, for instance, a Profile has never told where a man lives, Ross protests against a sentence saying "His Vermont house is full of valuable paintings." Should say "He has a house in Vermont and it is full, etc." Rather weird point, but it will come up from time to time.

19. Drunkenness and adultery present problems. As far as I can tell, writers must not be allowed to imply that they admire either of these things, or have enjoyed them personally, although they are legitimate enough when pointing a moral or adorning a sufficiently grim story. They are nothing to be light-hearted about. "*The New Yorker* cannot endorse adultery." Harold Ross vs. Sally Benson. Don't bother about this one. In the end it is a matter between Mr. Ross and his God. Homosexuality, on the other hand, is definitely out as humor, and dubious, in any case.

20. The more "as a matter of facts," "howevers," "for instances," etc., you can cut out, the nearer you are to the Kingdom of Heaven.

21. It has always seemed irritating to me when a story is written in the first person, but the narrator hasn't got the same name as the author. For instance, a story beginning: "George," my father said to me one morning; and signed at the end Horace McIntyre always baffles me. However, as far as I know this point has never been ruled upon officially, and should just be queried.

22. Editors are really the people who should put initial letters and white spaces in copy to indicate breaks in thought or action. Because of overwork or inertia or something, this has been done largely by the proof room, which has a tendency to put them in for purposes of makeup rather than sense. It should revert to the editors.

23. For some reason our writers (especially Mr. Leonard Q. Ross) have a tendency to distrust even moderately long quotes and break them up arbitrarily and on the whole idiotically with editorial interpolations. "Mr. Kaplan felt that he and the cosmos were coterminous" or some such will frequently appear in the middle of a conversation for no other reason than that the author is afraid the reader's mind is wandering. Sometimes this is necessary, most often it isn't.

24. Writers also have an affection for the tricky or vaguely cosmic last line. "Suddenly Mr. Holtzman felt tired" has appeared on far too many pieces in the last ten years. It is always a good idea to consider whether the last sentence of a piece is legitimate and necessary, or whether it is just an author showing off.

25. On the whole, we are hostile to puns.

26. How many of these changes can be made in copy depends, of course, to a large extent on the writer being edited. By going over the list, I can give a general idea of how much nonsense each artist will stand for.

27. Among other things, *The New Yorker* is often accused of a patronizing attitude. Our authors are especially fond of referring to all foreigners as "little" and writing about them, as Mr. Maxwell says, as if they were mental ornaments. It is very important to keep the amused and Godlike tone out of pieces.

28. It has been one of Mr. Ross's long struggles to raise the tone of our contributors' surroundings, at least on paper. References to the gay Bohemian life in Greenwich Village and other low surroundings should be cut whenever possible. Nor should writers be permitted to boast about having their telephones cut off, or not being able to pay their bills, or getting their meals at the delicatessen, or any of the things which strike many writers as quaint and lovable.

29. Some of our writers are inclined to be a little arrogant about their knowledge of the French language. Probably best to put them back into English if there is a common English equivalent.

30. So far as possible make the pieces grammatical, but if you don't the copy room will, which is a comfort. Fowler's *English Usage* is our reference book. But don't be precious about it.

31. Try to preserve an author's style if he is an author and has a style. Try to make dialogue sound like talk, not writing.

E. B. WHITE

LIFE CYCLE OF A LITERARY GENIUS

I

Shows precocity at six years of age. Writes poem entitled, "To a Little Mouse," beginning, "Last night I heard a noise in my scrap-basket." His mother likes poem and shows it to Aunt Susie.

II

At fourteen years of age, encouraged by former success, writes short essay entitled, "The Woods in Winter," beginning, "I whistled to my dog Don and he raced and romped as we set out together." Sends this to *St. Nicholas Magazine* and wins silver badge.

III

At eighteen years of age, encouraged by success, writes sonnet entitled, "To ——" and sends it to newspaper column. Columnist rewrites thirteen lines and publishes it on dull day.

IV

Encouraged by success, at twenty-four years of age writes whimsical article on "Sex Above 138th Street," which he sends to popular magazine. The article refers incidentally to seventeen-year locusts. Editor of magazine marks it *Use When Timely* and publishes it sixteen years later when the locusts appear.

V

At forty, encouraged by success, accepts invitation to have lunch with editor of the popular magazine. Editor orders exotic dishes and mentions an opening "on the staff!"

VI

Encouraged by success, dies of nervous indigestion right after lunch, leaving an illegitimate son who grows up in obscurity and writes the great American novel.

1926

RUTH SUCKOW

COMPLETE GUIDE FOR BOOK REVIEWERS

BOOK reviewing is one of the great literary industries. Yet I doubt whether any other is so poorly organized. Short-story writers have rule books which may be regarded as authoritative, compiled as they are by professors of the art who fifteen years ago sold a short story to the *Argosy*. But the great intellectual army of book reviewers must still plod on with the same old methods of presumably looking into each book as it comes, and writing each review afresh, thus cutting down immeasurably the number of books that can be reviewed and the reception of those gratifying cheques for six dollars and thirty-two cents. Individual reviewers, to be sure, have their own little stock supplies of words into which they can dip and re-dip and so reduce the labor of thinking. A still more useful possession, one in fact which almost eliminates any need for thinking at all after the initial book has been reviewed, is a theory or a point of view. This gives the reviewer a certain reputation for critical reliability and profundity as well. But these aids have their limits, as every reviewer must realize.

A larger preparedness is called for in this modern age of invention. A certain famous author, well known in the literary world, realizing this great need, has caused to be compiled, after much research, a little booklet, available to reviewers for the sum of only a few cents. It will prove of incalculable service to the young author starting out

on the career of book reviewing, and contains new hints for the seasoned reviewers as well. The numerous cases which this booklet covers can be no more than indicated, since it is a *complete guide*. But
even the table of contents here reproduced will prove intriguing and
illuminating:

CHAPTER I. INTRODUCTORY

The problem before us—Why this book—Be alert—Never use last
season's words—Know correct authors for reference—Compare
women poets to Emily Dickinson—Better go slow now on "Ra-
belaisian"—Easiest reviews rehash plots—Fine chance to be clever
here—Reviewer must maintain superior attitude—Ways of getting in
dig at the author—Use of full name, "Mr. Jason Blank," gives English
touch—How to work off own prejudices, predilections, grievances, etc.,
through reviews.

CHAPTER II. HOW TO BEGIN REVIEWS

"Out of the great mass of undistinguished and indistinguishable
verse"—"There are times when even the most seasoned reviewer"—"If
you happen to be one of those old-fashioned readers to whom . . ."—
"As a refreshing antidote to . . ."—"A new novel by Mrs. Wharton is always sure of a welcome from her large . . ."—"No book of recent
times . . ."—"This is another of those . . ."

CHAPTER III. HOW TO END THEM

"But I shall not give away Mr. Soandso's story"—"The reader must read
for himself to find out . . ."—"Suffice it to say that the mystery is eventually cleared up and all ends happily"—"venture to predict will outlast
all the . . ."—"Meanwhile I shall await Mr. Blank's next attempt
with . . ."—"but it is not Art"—"provides a veritable feast for kings"—
"takes its place at once among the great masterpieces of . . ."

CHAPTER IV. HOW TO HAIL THE NEW GENIUS

"Not since *The Old Wives' Tale* has"—"There comes to the jaded reviewer"—"Ring all the bells and sound all the drums"—"Sees the rising

of a new star"—"For all time"—"Of no less than astounding and astonishing genius"—"Combines all the —— of a Homer and an Anatole France with all the —— of a Mary Roberts Rinehart"—"Takes its place at once among the great masterpieces of . . ."

CHAPTER V. THE SOPHISTICATED REVIEW FOR THE CIVILIZED AUDIENCE

That intimate personal touch in the introduction—But avoid too highbrow suggestion—"In the cellars of Greenwich Village"—"Brilliant satire"—"Gallic wit and brevity"—"Not meat for morons"—"Will not please the Rotarians"—"Has a sardonic eye for . . ."—"Innocent and diverting foibles of the human race"—"This very modern heroine"—"Wise, witty and profound"—"Old woman from Dubuque."

CHAPTER VI. HOW TO REVIEW NOVELS OF THE SOIL

"This saga of"—"Does for the plains of (prairies of, mountains of) —— what Knut Hamsun did for peasants of Norway—what Reymont did for peasants of—what Hardy did for . . ."—"Epic sweep"—"Titanic struggle"—"Brute forces of nature"—"Elemental forces"—"Primitive passions"—"Stark tragedy"—"Same pagan love of the soil that . . ."— "Takes its place at once among the masterpieces of . . ."

CHAPTER VII. THE MODERN REVIEWERS' THESAURUS

"Erudition"—"pity and irony"—"devastating sense of . . ."—"brilliant subtlety"—"like the flash of a rapier"—"sane"—"eminently readable"— "to while away the hours of . . ."—"most fascinating heroine in modern . . ."—"cerebral"—"the art of Joyce, Proust, and Richardson"— "pungent, sharp, unsparing"—"merciless dissection"—"in hands of a skillful surgeon"—"relentless realism of the most . . ."—"our smart young writers"—"so-called modernists"—"attack on most cherished . . ."—"to pull down from the pedestals where history has . . ."—"Unlike the method of the old dull biographers, Strachey unlocks the inner heart of . . . shows Blank was the victim of . . ."—"genius due to Oedipus complex, Electra complex, inferiority complex, inversion, perversion, extraversion, Freud"—"Miss Blank knows her region, and these simple folk, so simple and at the same time so profound"—"cleanly factual, bare, unadorned, admirable prose"—"admirably nervous"—"takes its place at once among the masterpieces of . . ."

NOTE: If all other terms of derision go stale make some simple reference to the lady novelists.

1927

E. B. WHITE

HOW TO TELL A MAJOR POET
FROM A MINOR POET

A MONG the thousands of letters which I received two years ago from people thanking me for my article "How to Drive the New Ford" were several containing the request that I "tell them how to distinguish a major poet from a minor poet." It is for these people that I have prepared the following article, knowing that only through one's ability to distinguish a major poet from a minor poet may one hope to improve one's appreciation of, or contempt for, poetry itself.

TAKE the first ten poets that come into your head—the list might run something like this: Robert Frost, Arthur Guiterman, Edgar Lee Masters, Dorothy Parker, Douglas Fairbanks, Jr., Stephen Vincent Benét, Edwin Arlington Robinson, Lorraine Fay, Berton Braley, Edna St. Vincent Millay. Can you tell, quickly and easily, which are major and which minor? Or suppose you were a hostess and a poet were to arrive unexpectedly at your party—could you introduce him properly: "This is Mr. Lutbeck, the major poet," or "This is Mr. Schenk, the minor poet"? More likely you would have to say merely: "This is Mr. Masefield, the poet"—an embarrassing situation for both poet and hostess alike.

All poetry falls into two classes: serious verse and light verse. Serious verse is verse written by a major poet; light verse is verse written by a minor poet. To distinguish the one from the other, one must have a sensitive ear and a lively imagination. Broadly speaking, a major poet may be told from a minor poet in two ways: (1) by the character of the verse, (2) by the character of the poet. (Note: It is not always advisable to go into the character of the poet.)

As to the verse itself, let me state a few elementary rules. Any poem starting with "And when" is a serious poem written by a major poet. To illustrate—here are the first two lines of a serious poem easily distinguished by the "And when":

And when, in earth's forgotten moment, I
Unbound the cord to which the soul was bound . . .

Any poem, on the other hand, ending with "And how" comes under the head of light verse, written by a minor poet. Following are the *last* two lines of a "light" poem, instantly identifiable by the terminal phrase:

Placing his lips against her brow
He kissed her eyelids shut. And how.

All poems of the latter type are what I call "light by degrees"—that is, they bear evidences of having once been serious, but the last line has been altered. The above couplet, for example, was unquestionably part of a serious poem which the poet wrote in 1916 while at Dartmouth, and originally ended:

Placing his lips against her brow
He kissed her eyelids shut enow.

It took fourteen years of knocking around the world before he saw how the last line could be revised to make the poem suitable for publication.

WHILE the subject matter of a poem does not always enable the reader to classify it, he can often pick up a strong clue. Suppose, for instance, you were to run across a poem beginning:

When I went down to the corner grocer
He asked would I like a bottle of Welch's grape juice
And I said, "No, Sir."

You will know that it is a minor poem because it deals with a trade-marked product. If the poem continues in this vein:

"Then how would you like a package of Jello,
A can of Del Monte peaches, some Grape Nuts,
And a box of Rinso—
Or don't you thin' so?"

you may be reasonably sure not only that the verse is "light" verse but that the poet has established some good contacts and is getting along nicely.

And now we come to the use of the word "rue" as a noun. All poems containing the word "rue" as a noun are serious. This word, rhyming as it does with "you," "true," "parvenu," "emu," "cock-a-doodle-doo," and thousands of other words, and occupying as it does a distinguished place among nouns whose meaning is just a shade unclear to most people—this word, I say, is the sort without which a major poet could not struggle along. It is the hallmark of serious verse. No minor poet dares use it, because his very minority carries with it the obligation to be a little more explicit. There are times when he would like to use "rue," as, for instance, when he is composing a poem in the A. E. Housman manner:

When drums were heard in Pelham,
*   The soldier's eyes were blue,*
But I came back through Scarsdale,
*   And oh the . . .*

Here the poet would like to get in the word "rue" because it has the right sound, but he doesn't dare.

SO much for the character of the verse. Here are a few general rules about the poets themselves. All poets who, when reading from their own works, experience a choked feeling, are major. For that matter, all poets who read from their own works are major, whether they choke or not. All women poets, dead or alive, who smoke cigars are major. All poets who have sold a sonnet for $125 to a magazine with a paid circulation of four hundred thousand are major. A sonnet is composed of fourteen lines; thus the payment in this case is eight dollars and ninety-three cents a line, which constitutes a poet's majority. (It also indicates that the editor has probably been swept off his feet.)

All poets whose work appears in "The Conning Tower" of the *World* are minor, because the *World* is printed on uncoated stock—which is offensive to major poets. All poets named Edna St. Vincent Millay are major.

All poets who submit their manuscripts through an agent are major. These manuscripts are instantly recognized as serious verse. They come enclosed in a manila folder accompanied by a letter from the agent: "Dear Mr. ——: Here is a new group of Miss McGroin's poems, called 'Seven Poems.' We think they are the most important she has done yet, and hope you will like them as much as we do." Such letters make it a comparatively simple matter for an editor to distinguish between serious and light verse, because of the word "important."

Incidentally, letters from poets who submit their work directly to a publication without the help of an agent are less indicative but are longer. Usually they are intimate, breezy affairs, that begin by referring to some previously rejected poem that the editor has forgotten about. They begin: "Dear Mr. ——: Thanks so much for your friendly note. I have read over 'Invulnerable' and I think I see your point, although in line 8 the word 'hernia' is, I insist, the only word to quite express the mood. At any rate, here are two new offerings. 'Thrush-Bound' and 'The Hill,' both of which are rather timely. I suppose you know that Vivien and I have rented the most amusing wee house near the outskirts of Sharon—it used to be a well-house and the well still takes up most of the living room. We are as poor as church mice but Vivien says, etc., etc."

A poet who, in a roomful of people, is noticeably keeping at a little distance and "seeing into" things is a major poet. This poet commonly writes in unrhymed six-foot and seven-foot verse, beginning something like this:

> *When, once, finding myself alone in a gathering of people,*
> *I stood, a little apart, and through the endless confusion of voices . . .*

This is a major poem and you needn't give it a second thought.

THERE are many more ways of telling a major poet from a minor poet, but I think I have covered the principal ones. The truth is, it is fairly easy to tell the two types apart; it is only when one sets about trying to decide whether what they write is any good or not that the thing really becomes complicated.

1930

WOODY ALLEN

THE METTERLING LISTS

V ENAL & Sons has at last published the long-awaited first volume of Metterling's laundry lists (*The Collected Laundry Lists of Hans Metterling*, Vol. I, 437 pp., plus xxxii-page introduction; indexed; $18.75), with an erudite commentary by the noted Metterling scholar Gunther Eisenbud. The decision to publish this work separately, before the completion of the immense four-volume *oeuvre*, is both welcome and intelligent, for this obdurate and sparkling book will instantly lay to rest the unpleasant rumors that Venal & Sons, having reaped rich rewards from the Metterling novels, play, and notebooks, diaries, and letters, was merely in search of continued profits from the same lode. How wrong the whisperers have been! Indeed, the very first Metterling laundry list

LIST NO. I
6 prs. shorts
4 undershirts
6 prs. blue socks
4 blue shirts
2 white shirts
6 handkerchiefs
No Starch

serves as a perfect, near-total introduction to this troubled genius, known to his contemporaries as the "Prague Weirdo." The list was dashed off while Metterling was writing *Confessions of a Monstrous Cheese,* that work of stunning philosophical import in which he proved not only that Kant was wrong about the universe but that he never picked up a check. Metterling's dislike of starch is typical of the period, and when this particular bundle came back too stiff Metterling became moody and depressed. His landlady, Frau Weiser, reported to friends that "Herr Metterling keeps to his room for days, weeping over the fact that they have starched his shorts." Of course, Breuer has already pointed out the relation between stiff underwear and Metterling's constant feeling that he was being whispered about by men with jowls (*Metterling: Paranoid-Depressive Psychosis and the Early Lists*, Zeiss Press). This theme of a failure to follow instructions appears in Metterling's only play, *Asthma*, when Needleman brings the cursed tennis ball to Valhalla by mistake.

The obvious enigma of the second list

LIST NO. 2

  7 prs. shorts
  5 undershirts
  7 prs. black socks
  6 blue shirts
  6 handkerchiefs
  No Starch

is the seven pairs of black socks, since it has been long known that Metterling was deeply fond of blue. Indeed, for years the mention of any other color would send him into a rage, and he once pushed Rilke down into some honey because the poet said he preferred brown-eyed women. According to Anna Freud ("Metterling's Socks as an Expression of the Phallic Mother," *Journal of Psychoanalysis*, Nov., 1935), his sudden shift to the more somber legwear is related to his unhappiness over the "Bayreuth Incident." It was there, during the first act of *Tristan*, that he sneezed, blowing the toupee off one of the opera's wealthiest patrons. The audience became convulsed, but Wagner defended him with his now classic remark "Everybody sneezes." At this, Cosima Wagner burst into tears and accused Metterling of sabotaging her husband's work.

That Metterling had designs on Cosima Wagner is undoubtedly true, and we know he took her hand once in Leipzig and again, four years later, in the Ruhr Valley. In Danzig, he referred to her tibia obliquely during a rainstorm, and she thought it best not to see him again. Returning to his home in a state of exhaustion, Metterling wrote

Thoughts of a Chicken, and dedicated the original manuscript to the Wagners. When they used it to prop up the short leg of a kitchen table, Metterling became sullen and switched to dark socks. His housekeeper pleaded with him to retain his beloved blue or at least to try brown, but Metterling cursed her, saying, "Slut! And why not Argyles, eh?"

In the third list

LIST NO. 3
    6 handkerchiefs
    5 undershirts
    8 prs. socks
    3 bedsheets
    2 pillowcases

linens are mentioned for the first time. Metterling had a great fondness for linens, particularly pillowcases, which he and his sister, as children, used to put over their heads while playing ghosts, until one day he fell into a rock quarry. Metterling liked to sleep on fresh linen, and so do his fictional creations. Horst Wasserman, the impotent locksmith in *Filet of Herring,* kills for a change of sheets, and Jenny, in *The Shepherd's Finger,* is willing to go to bed with Klineman (whom she hates for rubbing butter on her mother) "if it means lying between soft sheets." It is a tragedy that the laundry never did the linens to Metterling's satisfaction, but to contend, as Pfaltz has done, that his consternation over it prevented him from finishing *Whither Thou Goest, Cretin* is absurd. Metterling enjoyed the luxury of sending his sheets out, but he was not dependent on it.

WHAT prevented Metterling from finishing his long-planned book of poetry was an abortive romance, which figures in the "Famous Fourth" list:

LIST NO. 4
    7 prs. shorts
    6 handkerchiefs
    6 undershirts
    7 prs. black socks
    No Starch
    Special One-Day Service

In 1884, Metterling met Lou Andreas-Salomé, and suddenly, we learn, he required that his laundry be done fresh daily. Actually, the two were introduced by Nietzsche, who told Lou that Metterling was either a genius or an idiot and to see if she could guess which. At that time, the special one-day service was becoming quite popular on the Continent, particularly with intellectuals, and the innovation was welcomed by Metterling. For one thing, it was prompt, and Metterling loved promptness. He was always showing up for appointments early—sometimes several days early, so that he would have to be put up in a guest room. Lou also loved fresh shipments of laundry every day. She was like a little child in her joy, often taking Metterling for walks in the woods and there unwrapping the latest bundle. She loved his undershirts and handkerchiefs, but most of all she worshipped his shorts. She wrote Nietzsche that Metterling's shorts were the most sublime thing she had ever encountered, including *Thus Spake Zarathustra*. Nietzsche acted like a gentleman about it, but he was always jealous of Metterling's underwear and told close friends he found it "Hegelian in the extreme." Lou Salomé and Metterling parted company after the Great Treacle Famine of 1886, and while Metterling forgave Lou, she always said of him that "his mind had hospital corners."

The fifth list

LIST NO. 5
    6 undershirts
    6 shorts
    6 handkerchiefs

has always puzzled scholars, principally because of the total absence of socks. (Indeed, Thomas Mann, writing years later, became so engrossed with the problem he wrote an entire play about it, *The Hosiery of Moses,* which he accidentally dropped down a grating.) Why did this literary giant suddenly strike socks from his weekly list? Not, as some scholars say, as a sign of his oncoming madness, although Metterling had by now adopted certain odd behavior traits. For one thing, he believed that he was either being followed or was following somebody. He told close friends of a government plot to steal his chin, and once, on holiday in Jena, he could not say anything but the word "eggplant" for four straight days. Still, these seizures were sporadic and do not account for the missing socks. Nor does his emulation of Kafka, who for a brief period of his life stopped wearing socks, out of guilt. But Eisenbud assures us that Metterling continued to wear socks. He merely stopped sending them to the laundry! And why? Because at this time in his life he acquired a new housekeeper, Frau Milner, who consented to do his socks by hand—a gesture that so moved Metterling that he left the woman his entire fortune, which consisted of a black hat and some tobacco. She also appears as Hilda in his comic allegory, *Mother Brandt's Ichor.*

Obviously, Metterling's personality had begun to fragment by 1894, if we can deduce anything from the sixth list:

LIST NO. 6
    25 handkerchiefs
    1 undershirt
    5 shorts
    1 sock

and it is not surprising to learn that it was at this time he entered analysis with Freud. He had met Freud years before in Vienna, when they both attended a production of *Oedipus,* from which Freud had to be carried out in a cold sweat. Their sessions were stormy, if we are to believe Freud's notes, and Metterling was hostile. He once threatened to starch Freud's beard and often said he reminded him of his laundryman. Gradually, Metterling's unusual relationship with his father came out. (Students of Metterling are already familiar with his father, a petty official who would frequently ridicule Metterling by comparing him to a wurst.) Freud writes of a key dream Metterling described to him:

> I am at a dinner party with some friends when suddenly a man walks in with a bowl of soup on a leash. He accuses my underwear of treason, and when a lady defends me her forehead falls off. I find this amusing in the dream, and laugh. Soon everyone is laughing except my laundryman, who seems stern and sits there putting porridge in his ears. My father enters, grabs the lady's forehead, and runs away with it. He races to a public square, yelling, "At last! At last! A forehead of my own! Now I won't have to rely on that stupid son of mine." This depresses me in the dream, and I am seized with an urge to kiss the Burgomaster's laundry. (Here the patient weeps and forgets the remainder of the dream.)

With insights gained from this dream, Freud was able to help Metterling, and the two became quite friendly outside of analysis, although Freud would never let Metterling get behind him.

In Volume II, it has been announced, Eisenbud will take up Lists 7–25, including the years of Metterling's "private laundress" and the pathetic misunderstanding with the Chinese on the corner.

1969

H. F. ELLIS

WITHOUT WHOSE UNFAILING ENCOURAGEMENT

FOR the genesis of my book, *An Introduction to the Study of Introductions,* I am principally indebted to my psychiatrist, Dr. Adolphus Peters, of Amsterdam. Having occasion to consult him about an irritating obsessive compulsion, which took the form of an inability to skip the introductory pages of any serious work that fell into my hands, I was at first repelled by his suggestion that instead of resisting the compulsion I embrace it and, by making a careful analysis of these preliminary throat-clearings, get them, in his homely phrase, out of my system. He persisted, however. Imagination gradually took fire, and now, some fifteen years later, it is a pleasure as well as a duty to record my gratitude to one but for whom I might still be unable to get as far as Chapter 1 of any book, not least my own.

A brief explanation is necessary to delineate the limits I have set myself in this inquiry. Forewords, not being in general the work of the writers whose books they seek to illumine or confute, I decided to omit, except insofar as they are referred to with gratification (see Chapter 9 *passim*) by the actual authors in their Introductions. The Prefatory Note has, of course, already been the subject of a scholarly monograph by Herr Emil Strohler, while the history and development of Contents (including List of Plates) will always be associated with the name of

Silas R. Wisehammer, of Wisconsin. On these well-tilled fields I had
no wish to trespass. Surprisingly little attention appears to have been
paid to the Introduction proper, even the Germans having contented
themselves with some rather cursory statistics, without any attempt to
evaluate Introductions as an art form or to inquire into density of readership, recurrent phraseology, the omission quotient, and kindred matters of importance to the prolegomenist. I make no apology therefore
for attempting to fulfill a want so ably categorized by Miss Phyllis Ash-
baker, B.Sc. (who has given freely of her storehouse of specialized
knowledge in a Foreword to this volume that I can never hope adequately to acknowledge), as "long felt."

Particular attention has been paid to Acknowledgments, since these
form at once the most universal and the least understood feature of Introductions. Of some 87,000 persons individually thanked for their
help in the 5,319 Introductions it has been my good fortune to read and
analyze, I have been in touch with rather more than half—a labor of
love that seemed to me essential, as it is from their ranks that the Introduction readership proved to be almost totally drawn. I desire to
thank them all again here, but have been compelled, in order to avoid
over-weighting this Introduction, to take the unorthodox course of rel-
egating their names to Appendix III. (No such comprehensive list of
generous advisers, unstinting critics, laborious proofreaders, owners of
hitherto unpublished mss. to which they most kindly gave access, and
patient wives, drawn from every field of life and learning, from the
preparation of soufflés to a new interpretation of the Gilgamesh Epic,
has, it is believed, ever been compiled before.)* If I single out Dr.
Wilbur H. Gumshott, of the Institute of Anthropology in Boston, it is
only because the telephone conversation I had with him well illustrates
the invaluable sidelights on my subject afforded me by personal contact
with my many helpers:

MYSELF: Have I the good fortune to be speaking to, or with, Dr.
    Wilbur H. Gumshott, who gave unstintingly of his unrivaled in-

---

*This parenthesis took the form of a footnote in my original draft, but it was unsparingly
pointed out to me by Mr. Wilberforce Butt, O.B.E.,** who most generously read through
the greater part of these preliminary pages, that the use of footnotes in Introductions is
atypical—except for such unavoidable addenda as "e.g."
**Now Sir Wilberforce Butt, K.B.E.

sight into Peruvian wedding rites during the preparation of Chapter 17 of Mildred Worthington's *South American Rhapsody?*

DR. G.: Who *is* this?

MYSELF: I have been entrusted, though fully conscious that there must be many better qualified both by—

DR. G.: Are you aware, sir, whoever you are, that it is three o'clock in the morning, Eastern Standard Time?

MYSELF: I trust it is not an inconvenient moment. The fact is that I have already made calls in the same connection to your colleagues Professor T. R. McGluskey, Mr. Alfred Bains, Mr. Aloysius Mannering, and Dr. Bernard Hackslip, as well as to Miss Freda Staring, the acknowledged authority on the Puelche of Araucania, and to the librarian of the School of Amer-Indian Studies in Beirut, but for whose unfailing encouragement and advice—

DR. G.: That bunch! What Hackslip knows about Peru wouldn't cover half a file card.

MYSELF: Thank you. That certainly sheds fresh light. I see, however, that the acknowledgment to him and the other colleagues I have mentioned begins "I am particularly grateful," whereas for yourself and Professor Richard A. Butterstone, of Halifax, Nova Scotia, the phrase "I also desire to thank" was deemed appropriate. May I have your comments on that?

DR. G.: I have nothing to say.

MYSELF: Bearing in mind that the even warmer "I owe a very great debt of gratitude" is reserved for Miss Mabel Gilchrist on page 9—

DR. G.: Never heard of her.

MYSELF: She gave invaluable assistance with the typing, thus taking her place on my secretarial ranking list second only to those eleven hundred and forty-eight devoted women whose untiring skill and patience in unraveling what was often, the authors fear, a sadly illegible—

DR. G.: Why don't you bother the people who write all this rubbish, and leave me alone? I have to get some sleep.

THE question raised by Dr. Gumshott is of some importance. I did, of course, apply direct to some thousands of authors whose prolegomenorrhea (the word was coined for me by my friend Charlie Pyke, B.A., who also drew my attention to the delicate interplay of colon and semicolon in a brilliant list of helpers cited by an otherwise obscure Swedish geophysicist) had brought them within my purview, but the response was not uniformly encouraging. This despite the fact that I was able in many cases to inform them of points of interest of which they themselves appeared to be unaware. Thus, I was the first to advise Mr. Karl Strummholtz that in singling out for special mention in the Introduction to his *Volcanoes in Antiquity* no less than seventy-five friends and colleagues, fifteen universities or other institutes, the mother superior of a nunnery, three typists, his publisher, five proofreaders, and both his first and second wives (who "cheerfully bore") he had established a record for scientific works outside the field of ornithology. Others had not even troubled to reflect that, by removing their acknowledgments to a separate section headed "Acknowledgments," they ran the risk of reducing their Introduction readership to nil, apart from psychopaths like myself. In volunteering information, in their turn, I found writers uncoöperative to such a degree that I feel unable to thank more than three hundred and seventy of them by name (Appendix IV). To a simple written questionnaire requesting answers to such inquiries as

> In the preparation of your Introductions, by what authors have you been especially influenced; e.g., as to style, presentation, addition of *"Majorca, 1967"* at the end, etc.?
>
> Have you acknowledged this debt?
>
> Who *is* this Lady Alice Brackenbury who so kindly translated the Chinese quatrain on page 196?
>
> What do you mean, exactly, by "unsparing"?
>
> For every half-dozen colleagues gratified by a mention, how many took immortal umbrage from (a) total omission, or (b) the "lumping" technique?

most authors did not bother to reply. Of those who did, a disappointingly high proportion complained that only the preliminary pages of their books appeared to have been read. This attitude, as between specialists, struck me as inexplicable.

It only remains to add that in the final stages of this work I have been sustained by the Vicar, by a certain Mrs. Potter (or possibly Cotter), of Exeter, who, in the act of measuring my settee for a new slipcover, inadvertently or intentionally made off with three pages from Chapter 2, and by so indefatigable an army of other critics that I have reluctantly been forced to hold their names over to an additional Appendix (V). Nevertheless, any errors and omissions remain entirely mine, and for this sole residuum of my labors I am profoundly grateful.

The Channel Islands,
Wednesday

1969

GARRISON KEILLOR

JACK SCHMIDT, ARTS ADMINISTRATOR

IT was one of those sweltering days toward the end of the fiscal year when Minneapolis smells of melting asphalt and foundation money is as tight as a rusted nut. Ninety-six, the radio said on the way in from the airport, and back at my office in the Acme Building I was trying to fan the memory of ocean breezes in Hawaii, where I had just spent two days attending a conference on Midwestern regionalism.

It wasn't working. I was sitting down, jacket off, feet up, looking at the business end of an air-conditioner, and a numb spot was forming around my left ear to which I was holding a telephone and listening to Bobby Jo, my secretary at the Twin Cities Arts Mall, four blocks away, reading little red numerals off a sheet of paper. We had only two days before the books snapped shut, and our administrative budget had sprung a deficit big enough to drive a car through—a car full of accountants. I could feel the deficit spreading a dark sweat stain across the back of my best blue shirt.

"Listen," I sputtered, "I still got some loose bucks in the publicity budget. Let's transfer that to administration."

"J.S.," she sighed, "I just got done telling you. Those loose bucks are as spent as an octogenarian after an all-night bender. Right now, we're using more red ink than the funny papers, and yesterday we bounced three checks right off the bottom of the account. That budget is so unbalanced, it's liable to go out and shoot somebody."

You could've knocked me over with a rock.

"Sweetheart," I lied quietly, hoping she couldn't hear my heavy breathing, "don't worry about it. Old Jack has been around the block once or twice. I'll straighten it out."

"Payday is tomorrow," she replied sharply. "Twelve noon."

THE Arts Mall is just one of thirty-seven arts organizations I administer, a chain that stretches from the Anaheim Puppet Theatre to the Title IX Poetry Center in Bangor, and I could have let it go down the tubes, but hell, I kind of like the joint. It's an old National Tea supermarket that we renovated in 1976, when Bicentennial money was wandering around like helpless buffalo, and it houses seventeen little shops—mainly pottery and macrame, plus a dulcimer-maker, a printmaker, a spatter painter, two sculptors, and a watering hole called The Barre. This is one of those quiet little joints where you aren't driven crazy by the constant ringing of cash registers. A nice place to drink but you wouldn't want to own it.

I hung up the phone and sat for a few minutes eyeballing an old nine-by-twelve glossy of myself, trying to get inspired. It's not a bad likeness. Blue pin-striped suit, a headful of hair, and I'm looking straight into 1965 like I owned it, and as for my line of work, anyone who has read *The Blonde in 204, Close Before Striking, The Big Tipper,* and *The Mark of a Heel* knows that I'm not big on ballet.

I wasn't real smart at spotting trends, either. The private-eye business was scraping bottom. I spent my days supporting a bookie and my nights tailing guys who weren't going anywhere anyway. My old pals at Jimmy's were trading in their wingtips and porkpie hats for Frye boots and Greek fisherman caps and growing big puffs of hair around their ears. Mine was the only suit that looked slept-in. I felt like writing to the Famous Shamus School and asking what I was doing wrong.

"It's escapism, Mr. Schmidt," quavered Ollie, the elevator boy, one morning when I complained that nobody needed a snoop anymore. "I was reading in the *Gazette* this morning where they say this is an age of anti-intellectualism. A sleuth like yourself, now, you represent the spirit of inquiry, the scientific mind, eighteenth-century enlightenment, but heck, people don't care about knowing the truth anymore. They just want to have *experiences.*"

"Thanks for the tip, Ollie," I smiled, flipping him a quarter. "And keep your eyes open."

I was having an experience myself at the time and her name was Trixie, an auburn-haired beauty who moved grown men to lie down in her path and wave their arms and legs. I was no stronger than the rest, and when she let it be known one day that the acting studio where she studied nights was low on cash and might have to close and thus frustrate her career, I didn't ask her to type it in triplicate. I got the dough. I learned then and there that true artists are sensitive about money. Trixie took the bundle and the next day she moved in with a sandalmaker. She said I wasn't her type. Too materialistic.

Evidently I was just the type that every art studio, mime troupe, print gallery, folk-ballet company, and wind ensemble in town was looking for, though, and the word got around fast: Jack Schmidt knows how to dial a telephone and make big checks arrive in the mail. Pretty soon my outer office was full of people with long delicate fingers, waiting to tell me what marvellous, marvellous things they could do if only they had ten thousand dollars (minus my percentage). It didn't take me long to learn the rules—about twenty minutes. First rule: Ten thousand is peanuts. Pocket money. Any arts group that doesn't need a hundred grand and need it *now* just isn't thinking hard enough.

My first big hit was a National Endowment for the Arts grant for a walkup tap school run by a dishwater blonde named Bonnie Marie Beebe. She also taught baton, but we stressed tap on the application. We called the school The American Conservatory of Jazz Dance. A hundred and fifty thousand clams. "Seed money" they called it, but it was good crisp lettuce to me.

I got the Guild of Younger Poets fifty thousand from the Teamsters to produce some odes to the open road, and another fifteen from a lumber tycoon with a yen for haiku. I got a yearlong folk-arts residency for a guy who told Scandinavian jokes, and I found wealthy backers for a play called *Struck by Lightning,* by a nonliteralist playwright who didn't write a script but only spoke with the director a few times on the phone.

Nobody was too weird for Jack Schmidt. In every case, I had met weirder on the street. The Minnesota Anti-Dance Ensemble, for example, is a bunch of sweet kids. They simply don't believe in performance. They say that "audience" is a passive concept, and they spend a lot of time picketing large corporations in protest against the money that has been given to them, which they say comes from illicit profits. It doesn't make my life easier, but heck, I was young once, too. Give me a choice, I'll take a radical dance group over a Renaissance-music ensemble any day. Your average shawm or sackbut player thinks the world owes him a goddam living.

So I was off the pavement and into the arts, and one day Bobby Jo walked in, fresh out of St. Cloud State Normal and looking for money to teach interior decorating to minority kids, and she saw I needed her more. She threw out my electric fan and the file cabinet with the half-empty fifth in the third drawer and brought in some Mondrian prints and a glass-topped desk and about forty potted plants. She took away my .38 and made me switch to filter cigarettes and had stationery printed up that looks like it's recycled from beaten eggs. "Arts Consultant," it says, but what I sell is the same old hustle and muscle, which was a new commodity on the arts scene then.

"What your arts organizations need is a guy who can ask people for large amounts without blushing and twisting his hankie," I told her one day, en route to Las Palmas for a three-day seminar on the role of the arts in rural America. "Your typical general manager of an arts organization today is nothing but a bagman. He figures all he has to do is pass the hat at the board meeting and the Throttlebottoms will pick up the deficit. The rest of the time he just stands around at lawn parties and says witty things. But the arts are changing, Bobby Jo. Nowadays, everybody wants arts, not just the rich. It's big business. Operating budgets are going right through the ceiling. All of a sudden, Mr. Arts Guy finds the game has changed. Now he has to work for the money and hit up corporations and think box office and dive in and fight for a slice of the government pie, and it scares him right out of his silk jammies. That's when he calls for Schmidt."

She slipped her hand into mine. I didn't take her pulse or anything, but I could tell she was excited by the way her breath came in quick little gasps.

"Now anyone who can spell 'innovative' can apply for a grant, government or otherwise," I went on, "but that doesn't mean that the bozo who reads the application is necessarily going to bust into tears and run right down to Western Union. He needs some extra incentive. He needs to know that this is no idle request for funds typed up by somebody who happened to find a blank application form at the post office. He needs to know that you are counting on the cash, that you fully expect to get it, and that if you are denied you are capable of putting his fingers in a toaster. The arts are growing, Bobby Jo, and you and me are going to make it happen."

"You're a visionary, J.S.," she murmured. "You have a tremendous overall concept but you need a hand when it comes to the day-to-day."

"Speaking of ideas," I muttered hoarsely, and I pulled the lap blanket up over our heads. She whispered my initials over and over in a litany of passion. I grabbed her so hard her ribs squeaked.

IT was a rough morning. After Bobby Jo's phone call, I got another from the Lawston Foundry, informing me that Stan Lewandowski's sculpture, *Oppresso*, would not be cast in time for the opening of the Minot Performing Arts Center. The foundry workers, after hearing what Lewandowski was being paid for creating what looked to them like a large gerbil cage, went out on strike, bringing the sculpture to a standstill. I wasted fifteen minutes trying to make a lunch date with Hugo Groveland, the mining heir, to discuss the Arts Mall. He was going away for a while, Groveland said, and didn't know when he'd be back, if ever. He hinted at dark personal tragedies that were haunting him and suggested I call his mother. "She's more your type," he said, "plus she's about to kick off, if you know what I mean."

On top of it, I got a call from the director of our dinner theater in upstate Indiana. He had been irked at me for weeks since I put the kibosh on *Hedda Gabler*. He had been plumping for a repertory theater. "Fine," I said. "As long as you make it *Fiddler on the Roof, The Sunshine Boys,* and *Man of La Mancha*." Now he was accusing us of lacking a commitment to new writers. He said I was in the business of exploiting talent, not developing it.

"Listen, pal," I snarled. "As a director, you'd have a hard time getting people to act normal. So don't worry about me exploiting your talent. Just make sure you have as many people in the cast as there are parts. And tell your kitchen to slice the roast beef thin."

So he quit. I wished I could, too. I had a headache that wouldn't. And an Arts Mall with twenty-four hours to live.

"It's a whole trend called the New Naïveté," offered Ollie when I asked him why artists seemed to hate me, on the way down to lunch. "I was reading in the *Gazette* where they say people nowadays think simplicity is a prime virtue. They want to eliminate the middleman. That's you, Mr. Schmidt. Traditionally, your role has been that of a buffer between the individual and a cruel world. But now people think the world is kind and good, if only they could deal with it directly. They think if they got rid of the middleman—the bureaucracy, whatever you want to call it—then everything would be hunky-dory."

"Thanks, Ollie," I said as the elevator doors opened. "Let's have lunch sometime."

It reminded me of something Bobby Jo had said in a taxicab in Rio, where we were attending a five-day conference on the need for a comprehensive system of evaluating arts information. "It's simple, J.S.," she said. "The problem is overhead. Your fat cats will give millions to build an arts center, but nobody wants to donate to pay the light bill because you can't put a plaque on it. They'll pay for Chippewa junk sculpture but who wants to endow the janitor?"

"Speaking of endowments," I whispered hoarsely, and I leaned over and pressed my lips hungrily against hers. I could feel her earlobes trembling helplessly.

THE mining heir's mother lived in a mansion out on Mississippi Drive. The carpet in the hall was so deep it was like walking through a swamp. The woman who opened the door inspected me carefully for infectious diseases, then led me to a sitting room on the second floor that could've gone straight into the Cooper-Hewitt Museum. Mrs. Groveland sat in a wing chair by the fireplace. She looked pretty good for a woman who was about to make the far turn.

"Mr. Smith, how good of you to come," she tooted, offering me a tiny hand. I didn't correct her on the name. For a few grand, I'm willing to be called a lot worse. "Sit down and tell me about your arts center," she continued. "I'm all ears."

So were the two Dobermans who sat on either side of her chair. They looked as if they were trained to rip your throat if you used the wrong fork.

Usually, my pitch begins with a description of the long lines of art-starved inner-city children bused in daily to the Arts Mall to be broadened. But the hounds made me nervous—they maintained the most intense eye contact I had ever seen from floor level—so I skipped ahead to the money part. I dropped the figure of fifty thousand dollars.

She didn't blink, so I started talking about the Mall's long-range needs. I mentioned a hundred thou. She smiled as if I had asked for a drink of water.

I crossed my legs and forged straight ahead. "Mrs. Groveland," I radiated. "I hope you won't mind if I bring up the subject of estate planning."

"Of course not," she radiated right back. "The bulk of my estate, aside from the family bequests and a lump-sum gift to the Audubon Society, is going for the care of Luke and Mona here." At the word "estate," the Dobermans seemed to lick their chops.

I had to think fast. I wasn't about to bad-mouth our feathered friends of the forest, or Mrs. Groveland's family, either, but I thought I just might shake loose some of the dog trust. I told her about our Founders Club for contributors of fifty thousand or more. Perhaps she could obtain *two* Founderships—one for each Doberman. "Perhaps it would take a load off your mind if you would let us provide for Luke and Mona," I said. "We could act as their trustees. We just happen to have this lovely Founders Club Kennel, way out in the country, where—"

At the mention of a kennel, the beasts lowered their heads and growled. Their eyes never left my face.

"Hush, hush," Mrs. Groveland scolded gently. "Don't worry," she assured me, "they don't bite. Well, hardly ever."

They may not bite, I thought, but they can sue.

Then Mona barked. Instantly, I was on my feet, but the dogs beat me to it. The sounds that came from their throats were noises that predated the Lascaux cave paintings. They were the cries of ancient Doberman souls trying to break through the thin crust of domestication, and they expressed a need that was far deeper than that of the Arts Mall, the arts in general, or any individual artist whom I would care to know. The next sound I heard was the slam of a paneled oak door closing. I was out in the hallway and I could hear Mrs. Groveland on the other side saying, "*Bad* Luke, *naughty* Mona!" The woman who had let me in let me out. "They're quite protective," she informed me, chuckling. If a jury had been there to see her face, I'd have altered it.

When I got back to the office, I gathered up every piece of correspondence in our National Arts Endowment file and threw it out the window. From above, it looked like a motorcade was due any minute. I was about to follow up with some of the potted plants when the phone rang. It rang sixteen times before I picked it up. Before Bobby Jo could identify herself, I'd used up all the best words I know. "I'm *out*," I added. "Through. Done. Kaput. Fini. The End. Cue the credits. I've had it."

"J.S.," she began, but I was having none of it.

"I've had a noseful of beating money out of bushes so a bunch of sniveling wimps can try the patience of tiny audiences of their pals and moms with subsidized garbage that nobody in his right mind would pay Monopoly money to see," I snapped. "I'm sick of people calling themselves artists who make pots that cut your fingers when you pick them up and wobble when you set them on a table. I'm tired of poets who dribble out little teensy poems in lower-case letters and I'm sick of painters who can't even draw an outline of their own hand and I'm finished with the mumblers and stumblers who tell you that if you don't understand them it's *your* fault."

I added a few more categories to my list, plus a couple dozen persons by name, several organizations, and a breed of dog.

"You all done, J.S.?" she asked. "Because I've got great news. The Highways Department is taking the Arts Mall for an interchange. They're ready to pay top dollar, plus—you won't believe this—to sweeten the deal, they're throwing in 6.2 miles of Interstate 594."

"Miles of what?" Then it clicked. "You mean that unfinished leg of 594?" I choked.

"It's been sitting there for years. There are so many community groups opposed to it that the Highways Department doesn't dare cut the grass that's growing on it. They want us to take them off the hook. And if we make it an arts space, they figure it'll fulfill their beautification quota for the next three years."

"We'll call it The ArtsTrip!" I exclaimed. "Or The ArtStrip! The median as medium! Eight-lane environmental art! Big, big sculptures! Action painting! Wayside Dance Areas! Living poetry plaques! Milestones in American Music! Arts parks and Arts lots! A drive-in film series! The customized car as American genre! The customized van as Artsmobile! People can have an arts experience without even pulling over onto the shoulder. They can get quality enrichment and still make good time!"

"Speaking of making time—" Her voice broke. She shuddered like a turned-on furnace. Her breath came in quick little gasps.

I don't know what's next for Jack Schmidt after the Arts Highway is finished, but, whatever it is, it's going to have Jack Schmidt's name on it. No more Mr. Anonymous for me. No more Gray Eminence trips for yours truly. A couple of days ago, I was sitting at my desk and I began fooling around with an inkpad. I started making thumbprints on a sheet of yellow paper and then I sort of smooshed them around a little, and one thing led to another, and when I got done with it I liked what I saw. It wasn't necessarily something I'd hang on a burlap wall with a baby ceiling spot aimed at it, but it had a certain *definite* quality that art could use a lot more of. I wouldn't be too surprised if in my next adventure I'm in a loft in SoHo solving something strictly visual while Bobby Jo throws me smoldering looks from her loom in the corner. In the meantime, good luck and stay out of dark alleys.

1979

IAN FRAZIER

ENGLAND PICKS A POET

IN England, when people discuss poetry they're talking business—big business. Some countries leave their poets gathering dust on the academic shelf, but here in England people like their poetry the way they like their tea: hot, fresh, and three times a day. Poetry experts estimate that in one fiscal year the English poetic community generates over 950 million pounds (almost 1.2 billion dollars) in revenue, all of which goes right back into the local economy. That works out to about twenty-six dollars apiece for every English man, woman, and child. With numbers like these, it's no wonder that poets here demand, and receive, the highest word rate of any Western country.

At the top of this heap sits the poet laureate of England. Chosen from among the best in his field, the poet laureate is a throwback to the days of the royal bard, constantly singing odes at the jeweled elbow of some pagan king. Today, the poet laureate no longer spends all his time around the palace but is permitted to live in his own style of home and furnish it as he wishes. This, combined with a salary, income from lectures and endorsements, and the unlimited use of a government vehicle, makes the job one of the most attractive in all literature. So when Queen Elizabeth and Prime Minister Thatcher announced earlier this year that they were looking for a new person for the post, they received so many applications that they have already been forced to pull a couple of all-nighters in an attempt to read through them. Fueled by innumerable cups of coffee, the Queen and the Prime Minister have checked and double-checked every poem and application, always with this dark thought at the back of their minds: What if we make a mistake?

As students of history, they know how costly human error can be. Sometimes it has meant that the foremost living poet missed his chance to be laureate, as happened this century with W. H. Auden. After getting the necessary recommendations and breezing through a personal interview with King George VI, Auden, who had the highest Q rating of any poet in the world, looked like a certainty. But he neglected to make the important post-interview followup call, and then the King misplaced Auden's folder when he went on vacation and didn't know how to get in touch with him. The loss to literature resulting from this act of carelessness can only be imagined.

Other poets appear to be qualified during the selection process and then, once installed, they turn into complete goldbricks. That was what William Wordsworth did. From our vantage point of years, we can see that Wordsworth's entire career was nothing but an elaborate bait-and-switch scam: write some poetry, get yourself chosen poet laureate, and then—quittin' time! In Wordsworth's years as laureate, he became so bone-lazy that he would write only the meters of poems; he would do a limerick:

> *De duh de de duh de de* dah,
> *De duh de de duh de de* dah.
> *De duh de de duh,*
> *De duh de de duh,*
> *De duh de de duh de de* dah.

Then he would mail that in to the "Information, Please" column of the London *Times Literary Supplement* and ask if any subscriber knew what the words might be.

Just as disappointing was Alfred, Lord Tennyson, a laureate who literally could not write his way out of a paper bag. He proved this at a benefit performance for the Christian Temperance League in 1879. The poet was placed inside a large sack of standard-weight brown paper on a stage at Covent Garden, given several pens, and left to himself. He thrashed and flopped helplessly inside for four and a half hours; finally, members of the Grenadier Guards had to come and cut him free.

How Tennyson ever made laureate is anybody's guess, yet even he was an improvement on John Dryden, England's first poet laureate, although by no means her best. Whenever people told Dryden they didn't like one of his poems, he threw such a fit—arguing, sulking, and snapping at them—that they would resolve never to be candid with him again. By means of such behavior, Dryden was able, in a short period of time, to manipulate an entire population into pretending that he was a genius without equal. Today, we know better.

And what of John Masefield, poet laureate from 1930 to 1967? He

was the one, you will remember, who penned the howler "Sea Fever,"
with the opening

I must down to the seas again,
to the lonely sea and the sky

Eeeeeeeouch! It is a sad fact that among past poets laureate of England
tin ears like Masefield's have been not the exception but the rule.

IF anyone can turn this tradition around, Queen Elizabeth and Prime
Minister Thatcher can. Both have proved themselves to be smart, articulate women with an eye for spotting talent—and the world of contemporary poetry gives them quite a bit of talent to spot. So far, the top
candidates are Philip Larkin, 62; Roy Fuller, 72; D. J. Enright, 64;
Gavin Ewart, 68; Ted Hughes, 53; and Dr. Leo Buscaglia, 59. Larkin is
a popular essayist, as well as a poet with a strong sense of the beauties
of commonplace speech. Fuller served on the governing board of the
BBC, England's main TV network, and a reflected glow from that "cool
medium" often shines through the luminous poetry on which his reputation rests. Both Enright and Ewart have been poets since they were
very little, and they have had a great many interesting insights over the
years. Hughes is a much-honored poet whose trademark is the origi-
nality shown in every page of his work, which combines a love for the
rhythms of nature with some other values. Buscaglia, though not,
strictly speaking, a poet or an Englishman, still might be as good a
choice as anyone, if not better. First, he is a doctor; second, he is an author and expert on the subject of human emotion, notably love, which
has always been the poet's province; and third, his books, *Love, Living,
Loving, and Learning,* and *Personhood,* which have sold in the millions,
are profound enough to be poetry already. With a slight change in ty-
pography, they would be. Lots of people know who Dr. Buscaglia is.
And, compared to more traditional poets, Dr. Buscaglia is a nicer person. He could infuse social functions with a warm feeling that would
humanize all that glittering pomp, and everyone would benefit. Along
with poetic talent, the ability to reach out to others might well be an
important requirement for the poet laureate of the future.

Soon, the Queen and the Prime Minister will announce their decision. One of the candidates will wear the wreath of laurel; the rest will

send their congratulations, and console themselves with the thought that at this level of poetry, there really are no losers. With a new poet laureate at the helm, a new era in English poetry may dawn. And in libraries and country retreats and book-lined dens across the land thousands of poets will return to their work, providing the verse that feeds a nation.

1984

VERONICA GENG

SETTLING AN OLD SCORE

"There are some experiences which should not be demanded twice from any man," [George Bernard Shaw] remarked, "and one of them is listening to Brahms's Requiem." And, in his most famous dismissal of the work, he referred to it as "patiently borne only by the corpse." . . . There are no rights and wrongs in criticism, only opinions more or less in conformance with the consensus of enlightened observers over time. By that criterion Shaw was "wrong." But . . . musical polemics fade far faster than music itself, thankfully. —John Rockwell in the *Times*

To anyone who has tried to sit down and just enjoy a composition by Johannes Brahms, the sensation is all too familiar. As the musical phrases begin to wash away the cares of the day, transporting one into a delightful never-never land of artistic transcendence, one's brain is rudely skewered by George Bernard Shaw's unforgettable dictum about Brahms: "Like listening to paint dry." Once Shaw penned this zinger, it became impossible (even for an independent-minded music critic like myself) to relax and surrender to the simple pleasure of knowing that Brahms is no longer considered passé. And another thing: Each time a Brahms piece is ruined by an ineradicable nagging memory of that effortless Shavian one-liner, the annoyance is nothing compared to what Brahms must feel, squirming eternally in his grave, his reputation forever etched by the acid of Shaw's scorn.

Brahms was but one victim of Shaw's many pinpricks in the hot-air balloons of his era's cultural biases. Yet a host of the myriad names he lambasted have nonetheless survived. Yet so has a lingering respect for Shaw. In the mind of today's critic, this poses a problem. Must we say that Shaw was "wrong"? We may be tempted to utter a definitive "Yes," while on the other hand bearing in mind that critical truth is an ever-shifting flux of historically relative pros and cons. Shaw's derision of all the things he had scorn for has stood the test of time—because what he said has remained a touchstone, memorized and quoted again and again by generations of critics willing to encounter such a mind at the height of its powers even though we may possibly disagree, living as we do in a differing cultural context.

By way of qualification, however, I should point out that Shaw was not merely a negative hatchet man. For example, take his blistering assertion that "Brahms makes the lowest hack jingle-writer look like Mozart." Even someone such as myself who unashamedly rather likes Brahms (when well performed) is forced to concede Shaw's positive foresight in defending the populist craft of the jingle-writer. (Not that this means I must obsequiously agree with every single last nuance of Shaw's statement.)

In any case, Shaw's poison-tipped barbs were aimed at such a multitude of targets that to say he missed once or twice would be to say very little at all. Whatever the topic, Shaw never left any doubt as to where he stood:

On *Hamlet:* "A tour de fuss."

On Oscar Wilde: "A man out of touch with his funnybone."

On the Code of Hammurabi: "The sort of thing that would be considered profound by girls named Misty."

On the formation of a local committee in Brighton to study the feasibility of allowing tourists to transport their beach gear on special storage racks affixed to the sides of buses: "A worse idea hasn't crossed this battered old desk of mine in lo, these many moons."

From 1914 to 1919, Shaw's razor-tongued gibes were overshadowed by a vogue for bright quips about World War I. By 1921, however, he was again riding high—thanks to a series of personal appearances billed as "Shaw and His Skunk of the Week." Playing to packed houses that rocked with expectant hilarity when he led off with one of his typical catchphrases—"Am I hot under the collar tonight!" or "Here's something that really steams my butt"—he administered verbal shellackings to contemporary follies and pretensions ranging from *Peter Pan* ("It has plot holes you could drive a truck through") to the scientific community's renewed interest in Isaac Newton's idea of putting a cannonball into orbit ("One of those notions worth thinking about while you clean your teeth: a tour de floss").

For the next twenty years, nothing and no one seemed safe from Shaw's merciless stabs—not even his fans. Abhorring the nuisance of uninvited visitors, he posted on his door the following notice:

RULES FOR VISITORS

1. If you don't see what you want, don't be too shy to ask. Probably we don't have it anyway.
2. If the service is not up to snuff, just holler. Nobody will pay you any mind, but your tonsils can use the exercise.
3. We will gladly cash your check if you leave your watch, fur coat, or car as collateral. No wives or in-laws accepted.
4. If you are displeased in any way by the attentions of the resident Doberman pinscher, just remember—things could be worse. You could be at a Brahms concert.

But his visitors, instead of feeling rebuffed, copied out the notice and awarded it pride of place in their dens. Thus, a truism became widely established once and for all (until recently): that the name of Johannes Brahms was a joke (even to people who had never heard a note of his music), and that George Bernard Shaw was an unimpeachable debunker of sacred cows. Indeed, by 1940 so secure was Shaw's reputation that there was only one person in the entire English-speaking world capable of cutting him down to size.

LYNDON Baines Johnson was a young congressman from Texas when, in July 1940, Shaw came through the state on a lecture tour of the U.S. At the Houston airport, Johnson headed the delegation of local celebrities assigned to greet the distinguished visitor from abroad, who was to address a luncheon at the Houston Junior League Tea Room and then spend the night as Johnson's guest at his ranch (which probably he wasn't rich enough to own yet, but it could have been a summer rental). Waiting on the tarmac, Johnson took a minute to riffle through the press release he had been given on Shaw, and remarked, "This son of a bitch has got some kind of mean mouth on him." So Johnson was really up for a confrontation. Whereas Shaw was too busy hating Brahms to be bothered thinking about a junior U.S. congressman whom he hadn't even heard of yet. As soon as they met, Johnson immediately established dominance by a tactic he later became famous for—his "laying on of hands." The spindly, white-bearded Irishman, who didn't like being mauled by strangers, tried to counterattack by snapping at the big Texan in boots and Stetson. "What is this—some kind of tour de horse?" But it came out sounding pretty feeble. Nobody laughed, and Shaw lost crucial momentum. Johnson sensed right away that he had the edge, and he kept it. He was just a master of humiliation. On the way to the Junior League Tea Room, he asked Shaw to get him his dress boots out of a gym bag that he had purposely put on Shaw's side of the seat. At that point, Shaw overthought the situation and drew a bad conclusion. He decided to just go along with everything Johnson did and cater to him, on the theory that Johnson would quit bothering him once he saw he couldn't get a rise out of him. This was a huge mistake. The more quiet and docile Shaw got, the more Johnson tortured him.

At the luncheon, Johnson pretended not to be able to hear anything Shaw said, so Shaw had to repeat himself in a louder voice and came off as strident. The whole time, Johnson sat with his body angled subtly away from him, as if they weren't really together. During the lecture, he had a phone brought to the table and called his answering service. Then there was a question period, so Johnson asked Shaw his opinion of a book, *Pratfall into the Abyss,* which didn't exist. When Shaw said he had never heard of it, Johnson said, "What's the matter—you too dumb to recognize a joke when you hear one?," but he said it in a funny way that would have made Shaw look oversensitive if he got mad.

Then—here's another thing Johnson did. At the end of the luncheon, they were supposed to go right to the ranch, but Johnson dawdled a lot, which drove Shaw totally nuts. Finally, after a two-hundred-mile ride in a bouncing pickup truck, which Johnson drove himself—fiddling with the radio the whole time and refusing to talk, because they were alone, and if Shaw complained to anybody later he could never prove it—they got to the ranch, where the vegetarian Shaw was confronted with the sight and aroma of grotesque sides of beef barbecuing over smoking mesquite in earth trenches sodden with fat drippings. (Johnson hadn't even known that Shaw was a vegetarian—it was just a lucky break that fed into his strategy.)

The final blow was that night, when Johnson made Shaw dress up in an oversize cowboy suit with woolly chaps and showed him off like a performing monkey to a crowd of oil barons. The most galling part of it for Shaw was that by this time he had forfeited his right to protest. If he said anything now, Johnson could come back with "Well, why the hell didn't you speak up sooner?" or accuse him of being passive-aggressive. Anyway, so much of it was the kind of stuff Shaw couldn't exactly put his finger on.

Shaw's wounds were still raw the next morning when he woke up in an uncomfortable bed made out of a wagon wheel and saw hanging on a wall the following notice, framed in mesquite:

RULES FOR VISITORS

1. Never cross LBJ.
2. Obey all rules.

Shaw later claimed that he escaped by walking a hundred and ten miles, in sandals, to a private landing strip outside Waco, where he bummed a flight to L.A. But Johnson always told reporters that while he remembered Shaw's lecture, Shaw had spent the night in Houston at a friend's who was out of town, and never set foot on the ranch. He knew this would get back to Shaw and make him feel psychologically annihilated.

In 1950, when Shaw died, his last words were "Don't tell LBJ. I don't want to give him the satisfaction." Every year since their meeting, Johnson had bugged Shaw by sending him a Christmas card with the printed message "Thank you for your support." Johnson enjoyed this joke so much that no one had the heart to tell him when Shaw died. Every Christmas, he personally signed the card, and his secretary pretended to mail it. Although he suffered some reverses late in his own life, this annual power play lightened his spirits until the very end. He rests in peace, unlike Brahms.

1985

HENRY ALFORD

UNSPOKEN O'NEILL

THE Playwrights Theatre's current mission to stage all forty-nine of Eugene O'Neill's plays during the next eight years will provide New Yorkers with a wealth of gin-soaked poetry and genius, but one aspect of the playwright's oeuvre will go unheralded—his stage directions. Each line of the reconstituted playlet that follows is borrowed from one of O'Neill's plays.

JOHN (*appears from the front parlor in a great state of flushed annoyance*)
MARY (*trying to appear casual*)
JOHN (*carefully examining the front of her dress*)
MARY (*writhing—thinking*)
JOHN (*He stares at it with a strange, stupid dread.*)
MARY (*She sees he has guessed her secret and at first she quails and shrinks away, then stiffens regally and returns his gaze unflinchingly.*)
JOHN (*He stares at her, stunned and stupid.*)
MARY (*with a low tender cry as if she were awakening to maternity*)
JOHN (*nodding his head several times—stupidly*)
MARY (*stung but pretending indifference—with a wink*)
JOHN (*His face grows livid in spite of the sunburn.*)
MARY (*She seems to be aware of something in the room which none of the others can see—perhaps the personification of the ironic life force that has crushed her.*)
JOHN (*frothing at the mouth with rage*)
MARY (*unruffledly—obsessed*)
JOHN (*He makes a motion across his neck with his forefinger.*)
MARY (*with a moaning sound*)
JOHN (*He presses his lips tightly together—an effort to appear implacable that gives his face the expression of a balky animal's.*)
MARY (*looking at him queerly*)
JOHN (*He whirls defensively with a snarling, murderous growl, crouching to spring, his lips drawn back over his teeth, his small eyes gleaming ferociously.*)

MARY (*She raps him smartly, but lightly, on his bald spot with the end of her broom handle.*)

JOHN (*pounding his temples with his fists—tortured*)

MARY (*Their physical attraction becomes a palpable force quivering in the hot air.*)

JOHN (*He hides his face in his hands and weeps like a fat child in a fit of temper.*)

MARY (*more and more obsessed by a feeling of guilt, of being a condemned sinner alone in the threatening night*)

JOHN (*He begins to sob, and the horrible part of his weeping is that it appears sober, not the maudlin tears of drunkenness.*)

MARY (*with a return to her natural tone—but hysterical*)

JOHN (*spitting disgustedly*)

MARY (*spits also*)

JOHN (*He spits leisurely.*)

MARY (*spitting calmly*)

JOHN (*A terrible look of murder comes on his face.*)

MARY (*She takes his head and presses it to her breast and begins to weep. Weeping.*)

JOHN (*In a frenzy of self-abnegation, as he says the last words he beats his head on the flagstones.*)

MARY (*As for her, during his speech she has listened, paralyzed with horror, terror, her whole personality crushed, beaten in, collapsed, by the terrific impact of this unknown, abysmal brutality, naked and shameless.*)

JOHN (*He begins to laugh, softly at first—a laugh so full of a complete acceptance of life, a profound assertion of joy in living, so devoid of all self-consciousness or fear, that it is like a great bird song triumphant in depths of sky, proud and powerful, infectious with love, casting on the listener an enthralling spell.*)

MARY (*They both chuckle with real, if alcoholic, affection.*)

JOHN (*His voice is heard in a gentle, expiring sigh of compassion, followed by a faint dying note of laughter that rises and is lost in the sky like the flight of his soul back into the womb of Infinity.*)

MARY (*In the midst of this, these two incongruous, artificial figures, inert and disharmonious, the elder like a gray lump of dough touched up with rouge, the younger looking as if the vitality of her stock had been sapped before she was conceived, so that she is the expression not of its life energy but merely of the artificialities that energy had won for itself in the spending.*)

JOHN (*He gulps and his lips twitch.*)

MARY (*more and more strongly and assertively, until at the end she is a wife and mother*)
JOHN (*He falls forward on his face, twitches, is still.*)
MARY (*with a strange cruel smile of gloating over the years of self-torture*)
JOHN (*He dies, laughing up at the sky.*)
MARY (*Her face is again that of a vindictive maniac.*)

1998

NOAH BAUMBACH

VAN GOGH IN AOL

It may be that people attracted to the Internet are by their natures a lonelier group of people. —Letter to the *Times*, February 22, 2000

TO: Theovg23@aol.com
FROM: Vincentvgo@hotmail.com

Arles is bleak, and the blasted mistral keeps me indoors. I go days without speaking a word to anyone. Thank you for the money. With it, I bought a blazing tangerine iMac, which I am e-mailing you on right now. You were right, the Hotmail account was very simple to set up and free, so I can still survive on five francs a day.

TO: Theovg23@aol.com
FROM: Vincentvgo@hotmail.com

Just got an Instant Message from Gauguin, who clearly has me on his Buddy List. Do you know if there's a way to block this? I like Gauguin, but he is so depressed and seems to stay on-line for hours. I go on at random times in the day just to check my e-mail or to survey the landscape (what vibrant colors these websites have!) and then there's that blasted chime and, voilà, his grating "'Sup?" Did you get the pictures I sent you?

One is of my room here in Arles. That brilliant, burning orange object in the middle is the iMac. I painted it with the enthusiasm of a Marseillaise eating bouillabaisse, the tangerine like a halo over the computer. Thanks again. :)

TO: Theovg23@aol.com
FROM: Vincentvgo@hotmail.com

Gauguin has come to Arles to live with me. Next to my tangerine iMac his magnificent blueberry iBook is quite simply music. What a still-life they will make. But Gauguin insists on taking the iBook with him to Starbucks. Yes, they have one in Arles now, too! I would paint infinity, a computer of the richest, intensest blueberry, like a star in the

TO: Theovg23@aol.com
FROM: Vincentvgo@hotmail.com

Whoops, pressed "Send" accidentally. Was going to say, "like a star in the azure sky." By the way, that NPR petition you forwarded me is a hoax.

TO: Theovg23@aol.com
FROM: Vincentvgo@hotmail.com

Sorry for the delay. Gauguin is very depressed and spends hours on-line. (I know, I know, we should get another line!) God knows what he does there, but the junk mail I keep receiving from polynesianhoneys.com gives me an idea. Visited an Impressionist chat room today. Depressing. These people know nothing of painting. Felt less bad on discovering most were seven. Normally I wouldn't send something like this, but I thought you might get a kick out of it. Degas forwarded it:

HOW TO DETERMINE YOUR STAR WARS NAME:

FIRST NAME
Take the first three letters of your first name & add the first two letters of your last name.

LAST NAME
Take the first two letters of your mom's maiden name & add the
first three letters of the city in which you were born.

HOW TO DETERMINE YOUR STAR WARS HONORIFIC NAME:

* Take the last three letters of your last name & reverse them, then
  add the name of the first car you drove/owned/rode in.
* Insert the word "of."
* Tack on the name of the last medication you took.

P.S. Don't worry I bcc'ed you.

> Vinva Cagro
> or
> Hgopeugeot of DayQuil

TO: Theovg23@aol.com
FROM: Vincentvgo@hotmail.com

Surviving mostly on coffee and absinthe. And since Pissarro turned me
on to Kozmo.com I don't have to brave that miserable mistral. You
mentioned getting a busy signal the last time you tried to call me. (I
know, I know, I should get another line!) But it's Gauguin. I mean, I
have a curiosity about the Internet, but he's addicted, IMHO! He is
teaching me Quark, however, which I find fascinating.

TO: Theovg23@aol.com
FROM: Vincentvgo@hotmail.com

Gauguin and I quarrelled after I fragged him with a rocket launcher
while playing Quake III. He says my computer's faster, so it isn't fair.
(Doom is more his game, but the mulberry-tree-yellow graphics in
Quake III are worthy of Renoir!) In any event, I waved an open razor
in his direction, and he left. I'll miss his company, but now that he's
gone I can go on-line whenever I'm inclined. Did you get the pictures
I sent you? I don't think those girls are really in college. And what about
that dancing baby? Eerie.

TO: Theovg23@aol.com
FROM: Vincentvgo@hotmail.com

In your last E-mail you wrote: <<What is lol?>>
  It means "laugh out loud." Something I do less and less of now. :(

TO: Theovg23@aol.com
FROM: Vincentvgo@hotmail.com

I hate to admit it, but I'm missing Gauguin's Instant Messages. Now
that he's in Tahiti, I don't think he's on the computer much anymore. Either that or I no longer make the cut on his Buddy List. BTW could you
send a little more money? I need new paintbrushes and a faster modem.

TO: Theovg23@aol.com
FROM: Vincentvgo@hotmail.com

I know you try your hardest to sell my work, but have you considered
eBay? I put two sunflower paintings, "The Provençal Girl," and one
"Sower" on there. The "Sower" is already up to 43 francs! Then typed in
Seurat and saw that some tiny sketch of his called "Monkey" is at 230!
Depressing.

TO: Theovg23@aol.com
FROM: Vincent2@VanGo.com

I've started to work again. Check out my home page (and note new address). I designed it with a soft malachite green, a fiery iMac raspberry,
and a troubled Prussian lilac. I may've mastered the brushstroke and
HTML, but am a novice with Java. There's always more to learn.

TO: Theovg23@aol.com
FROM: Vincent2@VanGo.com

Hey, I won a bid on the Christina Aguilera CD! Mint condition, still
in the shrink-wrap, too! I'm sorry, but I need another 500 francs.

TO: Theovg23@aol.com
FROM: Vincent2@VanGo.com

Someone called MadDaddy bought "Peasant Shoes" for 27 francs and then refused to pay. Sent me into a rage. We flamed each other back and forth and eBay is going to ban him from future auctions. Little consolation, as I need the money. I got the last laugh, however, as the actual shoes went for 150 francs!

2000

STEVE MARTIN

PICASSO PROMOTING *LADY WITH A FAN*

THE ENTERTAINMENT CHANNEL: First of all, we loved *Lady with a Fan*.

PICASSO: Thank you. People seem to be very excited by the painting, and the test scores have been great.

E.C.: What was it like painting *Lady with a Fan*?

PICASSO: Very, very exciting. I was excited by the prospect of painting it and working with so many exciting people, the paint people, the canvas stretcher . . .

E.C.: So it was a very exciting project for you.

PICASSO: Yes, I was really excited. Sometimes I was more excited, and sometimes I was less excited . . .

E.C.: But you were always excited?

PICASSO: Oh, yes, always excited. That's a good way to put it.

E.C.: And the model?

PICASSO: Oh, my God, I almost left her out. That's hilarious. I've so admired her posing through the years and finally I got a chance to work with her. I actually loved going to the studio every day.

E.C.: Tell us what she's like.

PICASSO: Oh, she's so down-to-earth. You would expect her to be aloof and distant, but she wasn't like that at all.

E.C.: Were there sparks?

PICASSO: Oh, boy, this is a tough interview! (*Laughter*) Actually we liked each other a lot, but that's as far as it went. I have a rule about dating my models.

E.C.: We talked with her and she said, "Picasso was great to work with. We laughed and laughed." What did you laugh about? Any anecdotes?

PICASSO: Gee. Hmm. Oh, yeah. Once, I told her I needed her to be nude. Well, you should have seen the look on her face. Of course I told her immediately that I was just kidding.

E.C.: That's hilarious.

PICASSO: It was really, really funny.

E.C.: *Lady with a Fan* is so different from the other work you've been doing. Do you think your audience will accept it?

PICASSO: Well, I really wanted to flex some new muscles and I hope the public will go along with me.

E.C.: There are a lot of other pictures opening on the same day. Matisse has *The Green Stripe,* and Vlaminck has a fine still life. Are you worried about the competition?

PICASSO: Well, I'm sure Matisse's picture is very, very cute. And, basically, Vlaminck stinks.

E.C.: *Whoa!* Don't hold back now—just say what you think! (*Laughter*)

E.C.: Pablo?

PICASSO: Yes?

E.C.: Why a fan?

PICASSO: Oh, boy, everyone asks me that. I guess I didn't want to call the picture *Lady with a Banana.* No, I'm kidding.

E.C.: Oh, my God, that's hilarious.

PICASSO: No, seriously, the fan was chosen because it is a symbol of femininity, because it balances the picture compositionally, and because I posed her hand in the classic religious position referencing Leonardo's *Madonna of the Rocks,* except I wanted her to be holding a secular object.

E.C.: Uh-huh. (*Pause*) What's next for a Pablo Picasso?

PICASSO: Well, I would like to do some less serious paintings. *Lady with a Fan* is actually quite a profound picture, and I would like to stretch a bit and show that I don't just do one thing.

E.C.: Thank you, Pablo Picasso. (*Turns to camera*) *Lady with a Fan* can be seen at the National Gallery for the next one thousand or so years.

Pablo, could you just look into the camera and say, "Hi, I'm Pablo Picasso, be sure to watch me on the Entertainment Channel!"

PICASSO: Sure. Could I say hello to Gertrude Stein?

2003

DAVID SEDARIS

SUITABLE FOR FRAMING

BEFORE it was moved out near the fairgrounds, the North Carolina Museum of Art was located in downtown Raleigh, and often, when we were young, my sister Gretchen and I would cut out of church and spend an hour looking at the paintings. The collection was not magnificent, but it was enough to give you a general overview, and to remind you that you pretty much sucked. Both Gretchen and I thought of ourselves as artists—she the kind that could actually draw and paint, and me the kind that pretended I could actually draw and paint. When my sister looked at a picture, she would stand at a distance, and then slowly, almost imperceptibly, drift forward, until her nose was right up against the canvas. She examined all of the painting, and then parts of it, her fingers dabbing in sympathy as she studied the brushstrokes.

"What are you thinking about?" I once asked.

And she said, "Oh, you know, the composition, the surfaces, the way things look realistic when you're far away but weird when you're up close."

"Me, too," I said, but what I was really thinking was how grand it would be to own a legitimate piece of art and display it in my bedroom. Even with my babysitting income, paintings were out of the question, so instead I invested in postcards, which could be bought for a quarter in the museum shop and matted with shirt cardboard. This made them look more presentable.

I was looking for framing ideas one afternoon when I wandered into a little art gallery called the Little Art Gallery. It was a relatively new place, located in the North Hills Mall and owned by a woman named Ruth, who was around my mom's age, and introduced me to the word "fabulous," as in: "If you're interested, I've got a fabulous new Matisse that just came in yesterday."

This was a poster rather than a painting, but still I regarded it the way I thought a connoisseur might, removing my glasses and sucking on the stem as I tilted my head. "I'm just not sure how it will fit in with the rest of my collection," I said, meaning my Gustav Klimt calendar and the cover of the King Crimson LP tacked above my dresser.

Ruth treated me like an adult, which must have been a task, given the way I carried on. "I don't know if you realize it," I once told her, "but it seems that Picasso is actually Spanish."

"Is he?" she said.

"I had a few of his postcards on my French wall, the one where my desk is, but now I've moved them next to my bed, beside the Miró."

She closed her eyes, pretending to imagine this new configuration.

"Good move," she said.

The art gallery was not far from my junior high, and I used to stop by after class and hang out. Hours later I'd return home, and when my mother asked where I had been I'd say, "Oh, at my dealer's."

In 1970, the only artwork in my parents' house was a family tree and an unframed charcoal portrait of my four sisters and me done by a guy at a street fair. Both hung in the dining room, and I thought they were pretty good until I started spending time with Ruth and decided that they weren't challenging enough.

"What more do you want from a group picture of five spoiled children?" my mother asked, and rather than trying to explain I took her to see Ruth. I knew that the two of them would get along—I just didn't think they would get along so well. At first the topic of conversation was me—Ruth doing the cheerleading and Mom just sort of agreeing. "Oh, yes," she said, "His bedroom is lovely. Everything in its place."

Then my mother started hanging out at the gallery as well, and began buying things. Her first purchase was an elongated statue of a man made from what looked like twisted paper but was actually metal pressed into thin sheets. He stood maybe two feet tall and held three rusted wires, each attached to a blown-glass balloon that floated above his head. "Mr. Balloon Man," she called it.

"I'm just not certain he really needs that top hat," I told her.

And my mother said, "Oh, really?" in a way that meant: "If I want your opinion I'll ask for it."

It bothered me that she'd bought something without asking my advice, and so I continued to offer my thoughtful criticism, hoping it might teach her a lesson.

HER next piece was a grandfather clock with a body made of walnut and a human face pounded from what appeared to be a Chinese gong. The face wasn't realistic, but what she called "semi-abstract," a word she had picked up from Ruth. A word that was supposed to be mine. I didn't know exactly how much the clock had cost, but I knew it was expensive. She called it "Mr. Creech," in honor of the artist, and when I tried to explain that art was not a pet you gave a little name to she told me she could call it whatever the hell she wanted to.

"Should I put Mr. Creech next to Mr. Balloon Man, or does that make the dining room too busy?"

"Don't ask me," I told her. "You're the expert."

Then my father was introduced to Ruth, and he became an expert as well. Art brought my parents together in a way that nothing else had, and because their interest was new they were able to share it without being competitive. Suddenly they were a team, the Ed and Nancy Kienholz of Raleigh, North Carolina.

"Your mother's got a real eye," my father boasted—this in regard to "Cracked Man," a semi-abstract face made by the same potter who had crafted our new coffee table. Dad wasn't in the habit of throwing money around, but this, he explained, was an investment, something that, like stocks and bonds, would steadily appreciate in value, ultimately going "right through the roof."

"And in the meantime we all get to enjoy it," my mother said. "All of us except Mr. Crabby," by which she meant me.

THE allure of art had always been that my parents knew nothing about it. It had been a private interest, something between me and Gretchen. Now, though, everyone was in on it. Even my Greek grandmother had an opinion, that being that unless Jesus was in the picture it wasn't worth looking at. *Yiayia* was not discriminating—a Giotto or a Rouault, it made no difference so long as the subject was either nailed to a cross or raising his arms before a multitude. She liked her art to tell a story, and though that particular story didn't interest me, I liked the same thing. It's why I preferred the museum's *Market Scene on a Quay* to its Kenneth Noland. When it came to *making* art, however, I tended toward the Noland, as measuring out triangles was a lot easier than painting a realistic-looking haddock.

Before my parents started hanging out at the gallery, they thought I was a trailblazer. Now they saw me for what I was: not just a copycat but a lazy one. Looking at my square of green imposed atop a pumpkin-colored background, my father stepped back, saying, "That's just like what's-his-name, that guy who lives at the Outer Banks."

"Actually, it's more like Ellsworth Kelly," I said.

"Well, he must have gotten his ideas from the guy at the Outer Banks."

At the age of fifteen, I was maybe not the expert I made myself out to be, but I did own a copy of *The History of Art,* and knew that eastern North Carolina was no hotbed of artistic expression. I was also fairly certain that no serious painter would devote half the canvas to his signature, or stick an exclamation point at the end of his name.

"That shows what you know," my mother said. "Art isn't about following the rules—it's about breaking them. Right, Lou?"

And my father said, "You got it."

The next thing they bought was a portrait by a man I'll call Bradlington. "He's an alcoholic," my mother announced, this as if his drinking somehow made him more authentic.

With the exception of my grandmother, everyone liked the Bradlington, especially me. It brought to mind a few of the Goyas I'd seen in my art-history book—the paintings he did toward the end, when the faces were just sort of slashed on. "It's very moody," I pronounced. "Very . . . invocative."

A few months later, they bought another Bradlington, a portrait of a boy lying on his back in a ditch. "He's stargazing," my mother said, but to me the eyes seemed blank, like a dead person's. I thought my parents were on a roll, and was disappointed when, instead of buying a third Bradlington, they came home with an Edna Hibel. This was a lithograph rather than a painting, and it pictured a young woman collecting flowers in a basket. The yellow of the blossoms matched the new wallpaper in the breakfast nook, and so it was hung above the table. The idea of matching artwork to décor was, to me, an abomination, but anything that resulted in new stuff was just fine by my mother. She bought a sofa the salesman referred to as the Navajo, and then she bought a piece of pottery that complemented the pattern of the upholstery. It was a vase that stood four feet high, and was used to hold the dried sea oats that matched the frame of an adjacent landscape.

My mother's sister, Joyce, saw a photo of our new living room, and explained that the American Indians were a lot more than sofa cushions. "Do you have any idea how those people live?" she asked. Joyce did charity work with the tribes in New Mexico, and through her my mother learned about desperate poverty and kachina dolls.

My father preferred the tribes of the Pacific Northwest, and began collecting masks, which smirked and glowered from the wall above the staircase. I'd hoped that the Indian stuff might lead them to weed out some of their earlier choices, but no such luck. "I can't get rid of Mr. Creech," my mother said. "He hasn't appreciated yet."

I was in my second year of college by then, and was just starting to realize that the names my parents so casually tossed around were not nationally known, and never would be. Mention Bradlington to your Kent State art-history teacher, and she'd take the pencil out of her mouth and say, "Who?"

"He's an alcoholic? Lives in North Carolina?"

"I'm sorry, but the name means nothing to me."

As for the others, the Edna Hibels and Stephen Whites, they were the sort whose work was advertised in *ARTnews* rather than *Artforum*, their paintings and lithographs "proudly shown" alongside wind chimes at places with names like the Screeching Gull, or Desert Sunsets, galleries almost always located in a vacation spot. I tried pointing this out to my parents, but they wouldn't hear it. Maybe *today* my art-history teacher drew a blank on Bradlington, but after his liver gave out she'd sure as hell know who he was. "That's the way it works sometimes," my father said. "The artist is only appreciated after he's dead. Look at van Gogh!"

"So will *every* artist be appreciated after his death?" I asked. "If I'm hit by a van tomorrow afternoon, will the painting I did last week be worth a fortune?"

"In a word, no," my father said. "I mean, it's not enough just to be dead—you've got to have some talent. Bradlington's got it out the ass, and so does Hibel. The gal who made the coffee table is going to last for an eternity, but, as for you, I wouldn't bank on it."

"What's that supposed to mean?" I asked.

My father settled down on the Navajo. "It means that your artwork doesn't look like art."

"And you're the expert on that?"

"I'd say so, yes."

"Well, you can just go to hell," I told him.

I'd never have admitted it, but I knew exactly what my father was talking about. At its best, my art looked like homework. This was to be expected with painting and drawing—things requiring actual skill—but even my later, conceptual pieces were unconvincing. The airmail envelope full of toenail clippings, the model of the Lincoln Memorial made of fudge: In someone else's hands, such objects might provoke discussion, but in my own they seemed only desperate and pretentious. Not just homework but bad homework.

I QUIT making homework when I turned thirty, and started collecting paintings some ten years later, shortly after moving to Europe. A few of my canvases are French or English, portraits mainly, dating from the eighteen-hundreds, but the ones I most care about are Dutch, and were done in the seventeenth century. *Monkey Eating Peaches, Man Fleeing a Burning Village, Peasant Woman Changing a Dirty Diaper*—how can you go wrong with such straightforward titles? The artists are minor—sons, most often, of infinitely more talented fathers—but if I say their names with a certain authority I can almost always provoke a response. ("Did you say van der Pol? Oh, right, I think I saw something of his at the Louvre.")

People hush up when they stand before my paintings. They clasp their hands behind their backs and lean forward, wondering, most likely, how much I paid. I want to tell them that each cost less than the average pool table. I myself have no interest in pool, so why not take that money and spend it on something I like? Then, too, the paintings will appreciate, maybe not a lot, but given time I can surely get my money back, so in a way I'm just guarding them. Explaining, though, would ruin the illusion that I am wealthy and tasteful. A connoisseur. A collector.

The sham falls apart only when I'm visited by a real collector, or, even worse, by my father, who came last year and spent a week questioning my judgment. One of my paintings shows a group of cats playing musical instruments. It sounds hokey on paper—cute, even—but in real life it's pleasantly revolting, the musicians looking more like monsters than like anything you'd keep as a pet. I have it in my living room, and, after asking the price, my father shook his head the way you might when witnessing an accident. "Boy," he said. "They sure saw you coming."

Whether I'm buying a painting or a bedspread, his premise is always the same—namely, that I am retarded, and people take advantage of me.

"Why would something that's survived three hundred years not cost that much?" I asked, but he'd moved to another evident eyesore, this one Dutch, and showing a man undergoing a painful and primitive foot surgery. "I wouldn't spend two minutes looking at this one," he told me.

"That's okay," I said.

"Even if I were in prison, and this was the only thing on my wall, I wouldn't waste my time with it. I'd look at my feet or at my mattress or whatever, but not at this, no way."

I tried my best not to sound too hopeful. "Is someone sending you to prison?"

"No," he said. "But whoever sold this to you should be there. I don't know what you paid, but if it was more than ten dollars I think you could probably sue the guy for fraud." He looked at it one last time, and then rubbed his eyes as if they'd been gassed. "God Almighty. What were you thinking?"

"If art is a matter of personal taste, why are you being so aggressive?" I asked.

"Because your taste stinks," he told me. This led him to reflect upon "Cracked Man," which still hangs in the foyer beside his living room. "It's three slabs of clay cemented to a board, and not a day goes by when I don't sit down and look at that thing," he said. "I don't mean glancing, but full-fledged staring. Contemplating, if you catch my drift."

"I do," I said.

He then described the piece to my boyfriend, Hugh, who had just returned from the grocery store. "It was done by a gal named Proctor. I'm sure you've heard of her."

"Actually, no," Hugh said.

My father repeated the name in his normal tone of voice. Then he began yelling it, and Hugh interrupted, saying, "Oh, right. I think I've read something about her."

"You're damn right you have," my father said.

BEFORE they started collecting art, my parents bought some pretty great things, the best being a concrete lawn ornament they picked up in the early nineteen-sixties. It's a toadstool, maybe three feet tall, with a

red spotted cap and a benevolent little troll relaxing at its base. My father placed it just beyond the patio in our backyard, and what struck my
sisters and me then, and still does, is the troll's expression of complete
acceptance. Others might cry or get bent out of shape when their personal tastes are denounced and ridiculed, but not him. Icicles hanging
off his beard, slugs cleaving to the tops of his pointed shoes: "Oh, well,"
he seems to say. "These things happen."

Even when we reached our teens, and developed a sense of irony, it
never occurred to us to think of the troll as tacky. No one ever stuck a
lit cigarette in his mouth, or disgraced him with sexual organs, the way
we did with Mr. Balloon Man, or my mother's Kitchen Witch. One by
one, my sisters and I left home, and the backyard became a dumping
ground. Snakes nested beneath broken bicycles and piles of unused
building supplies, but on return visits we would each screw up our
courage and step onto the patio for an audience with Mr. Toadstool.
"You and that lawn ornament," my mom would say. "Honest to God,
you'd think you'd been raised in a trailer."

Standing in her living room, surrounded by her art collection, my
mother frequently warned us that death brought out the worst in people. "You kids might think you're close, but just wait until your father
and I are gone, and you're left to divide up our property. Then you'll see
what savages you really are."

My sisters and I had always imagined that when the time came, we
would calmly move through the house, putting our names on this or
that. Lisa would get the dessert plates, Amy the mixer, and so on, without dissent. It was distressing, then, to discover that the one thing we
all want is that toadstool. It's a symbol of the people our parents used to
be, and, more than anything in the house itself, it looks like art to us.
When my father dies, I envision a mad dash through the front door,
past the Hibel and the Bradlingtons, past "Cracked Man" and "Balloon
Man" and into Indian territory, where we'll push one another down the
stairs, six connoisseurs, all with gray hair, charging toward a concrete
toadstool.

2006

JACK HANDEY

IDEAS FOR PAINTINGS

BECAUSE I love art, I am offering the following ideas for paintings to all struggling artists out there. Some of those artists may be thinking, Hey, I've got good ideas of my own. Really? Then why are you struggling?

These ideas are free of charge. All I ask is that when you have completed a painting, as a courtesy to me you sign it "Jack Handey and [your name or initials]." And, if the painting is sold, I get approximately all the money.

Good luck! Let's get painting!

STAMPEDE OF NUDES

The trouble with most paintings of nudes is that there isn't enough nudity. It's usually just one woman lying there, and you're looking around going, "Aren't there any more nudes?" This idea solves that.

What has frightened these nudes? Is it the lightning in the background? Or did one of the nudes just spook? You don't know, and this creates tension.

MADE YOU LOOK

This idea is difficult to execute, but could turn out to be a masterpiece. It depicts a grandly dressed lady looking straight at you. At first, her look seems to say, "Quick, look behind you!" So you turn around, and when you look at her again her expression now seems to be one of smug satisfaction.

THE BLEAK HOTEL

A man is staring out the window of a bleak hotel room. He looks depressed. From the side, flying through the air, is a football. And you realize, If he's depressed now, just wait until he gets hit in the head by that football.

THE REPENTANT CAMERON DIAZ

Cameron Diaz, her tear-streaked face lit by a candle, gazes wistfully at a photograph of me.

THE WEARY PEASANTS

Some tired-looking peasants are walking down a road at sunset, carrying sheaves of wheat. A nobleman in a fancy coach is coming up from behind. This creates drama, because you're thinking, Why don't those peasants get out of the way?

SELF-PORTRAIT WITH STARTLED EXPRESSION

The key here is to be able to constantly startle yourself as you're painting. One option is to hire a professional startler, but that can get expensive. (The best ones are from Ireland.) Be sure to use opening the bill from your startler as a free startle.

THE DEATH OF HERCULES

An old Hercules is being lifted into the air by angels. On the one hand, it makes you sad, but on the other you think, He's still in pretty good shape.

ABSTRACT WHITE NO. I

This is a solid-white painting. You might be asking, "Is it okay to put in a fleck of color here and there?" I give up. Do whatever you want.

THE BOXERS

Two boxers are whaling away at each other in a boxing ring. But then you notice that the people in the audience are also fighting one another. And it makes you ask: Who are the truly barbaric ones here, the boxers or the spectators? Then you can turn the painting over and read the answer: "The boxers."

THE FRENCH LOVERS

A French dandy is embracing his beautiful buxom lover in a lush, overgrown garden. This painting should be in the shape of binoculars.

STILL LIFE WITH RABBIT

A wooden table is chockablock with fruit, cheese, and a glass of wine. To one side is a dead rabbit, a dead pheasant, and a dead eel. And you're thinking, Thanks for the fruit, but, man, take better care of your pets.

STILL LIFE WITH BEETS, CAULIFLOWER, LIVER, AND LARGE GLASS OF BEER

Just kidding. Only the beer.

THE EXPULSION OF ADAM AND EVE

Biblical themes sell well. In this one, God hovers over Adam and Eve, kicking them out of the Garden of Eden. As they leave, in an aside to Eve, Adam imitates the expression on God's face.

THE JOLLY DANCER

The scene is a flatboat on the Ohio River. A frontiersman who looks like me is doing his funny cowboy dance. Everyone seems to be enjoying the dance except for an insane simpleton who looks like my so-called friend Don. Crawling up behind Don is a big snapping turtle.

UNTITLED

This can pretty much be anything. Just remember to make it good, and to put my name on it.

2006

HENRY ALFORD

THE KNOWLEDGE

In preparation for an expected onslaught of visitors to York, England, W. H. Auden's birth city, cab drivers have been memorizing some of his poetry. . . . When tourists arrive to celebrate the centenary of Mr. Auden's birth this year, their cabbies will recite his verse. —The *Times*

'E was me Norf, me Souf, me East and West,
Me working week and me Sund'y rest,
Me noon, me midnight, me talk, me song;
I thought that love would last forever: I was wrong.

'E 'ad a gentleman friend, Mr. Auden did, dinnee? Bit of a trouser man, orroight? That seems to be the way nowadays, innit, wif actors and MPs and clergy and wot 'ave you. In my day, there weren't a need to fling yer spanky knackers into other folks' faces all jumble-wumble and 'ere's-mine-guv'nor. Though the missus *did* drag me to see Mr. Rudolf Nureyev at the ballet once. That man packed a full bag of groceries, dinnee?

Lady, weepin' at the crossroads,
Would yer maight yer love
In the twilight wif 'is greyhounds,
And the 'awk on 'is glove?

'Ello, 'ello—bit complicated, that one, it starts to go ower yer 'ead, so supposin' I shed some light on some of its more shadowy byways. Crooks and nannies it 'as. Now, this 'ere is wot they call parsin', not as in parse-the-butter-please-luv but as in parse-the-poem-so-we-don't-all-feel-like-bleedin'-eejits. What Mr. Auden is doin' in this one, I think, is forebodin' some of the messin' about we're currently seein' in the Middle East, a topic on which I 'ave a ready familiarity, 'avin' long been a fan o' the chickpea in its various fried and non-fried guises. The 'awk on the glove, of course, bein' yer vivid symbol of the U.S.'s imperialist leanin's and its might-makes-right attitude toward both its client states and other superpowers, orroight? Mr. Auden asks us, Is it roight that the country wif the most advantages should act this way? Course it ain't, guv'nor. But that's life, innit? 'Snot fair! 'Snot fair atall! The bone Mr. Auden would like us to chew on 'ere is the question: Does Mr. Bush 'ave any conception or understandin' of all this? Does 'e, then? Yer as welcome as Christmas to yer own opinion, but I think not. Mr. B. simply thinks 'e's sendin' a message to those wogs over in Arsefuck-istan, if you'll pardon my parlay-voo. Problem is, the message ain't in their language, see? It's a birfday 'at on a cactus—needles where yer wants ears.

> Self-drivers may curse their luck,
> Stuck on new-fangled trails,
> But the good old train'll jog
> To the dogma of its rails.

Corblimey, 'e was good, Auden was! Prince of a writer. Don' fink 'e ever drove a cab, but 'e mighta done, 'e mighta done. The writah migh-tah triedah done. . . . Nah—'e was a tutor, professor, reviewer. Collab-orator. If I remember my preparatory materials correctly, 'e was collegial-like wif Mr. Christopher Isherwood, and I believe the colle-giality extended into other areas, such as each other's Y-fronts. But yer can 'ardly blame Auden, can yer? I mean, 'is mate's name was practically *I sure would.* So yer would, wouldn't yer? Of course yer would. I mean, Bob is, after all, yer uncle.

> Sing, Ariel, sing,
> Sweetly, dangerously
> Out of the sour
> And shiftless water,
> Lucidly out
> Of the dozin' tree,
> Entrancin', rebukin'
> The ragin' 'eart
> Wif a smoother song
> Than this rough world,
> Unfeelin' god.

This bit 'ere that I've memorized for the ed-you-fication and inner-tainment of me passengers is not entirely related to the followin' anecdote, orroight, but I will tell you that I once drove Miss Vicky Entwistle from *Coronation Street* all the way from Tower Street 'ere in York to Paddington Station. Very good tipper, Vicky Entwistle is. Very good, sure as nuts. I don' give two monkeys about 'er theatricalizin', but I'll praise her way round a pound note, I will. 'Er fans worship 'er, and the ol' gal worships 'em right back—as I always tell me wife, "We must love one another or die alone."

> *Yer need not see what someone is doin'*
> *to know if it is 'is vocation,*
> *yer 'ave only to watch 'is eyes:*
> *a cook mixin' a sauce, a surgeon*
> *makin' a primary incision,*
> *a clerk completin' a bill of ladin',*
> *wear the same rapt expression,*
> *forgettin' 'emselves in a function.*

But, see 'ere, I'm a driver, I am, so I can't intirely forget meself in a function, roight, I've got to keep me beady eyes peeled for—[*CRASH*]—Oh, crikey! Bleedin' Christ! Jaysus H. Christ. Are yer a'roight, guv? Dinnit see 'im comin'! Roight out o' nowhere 'e come! Eyes of a killer 'e 'as. 'Ow is't? Are yer able to move? 'Ere's an 'andkerchief for stanchin' purposes, orroight?

Oh, God in 'eaven, whatever 'ave we done to deserve this? Where's Auden when yer needs him? "Lady weepin' at the crossroads" doesn't even *begin* to describe it, now, duzzit? Nah, nah. But I suppose "unfeelin' God" 'as some of the resonance that we ask o' the classics. . . . Take the thick wif th' thin, and this were a bit o' thin, wot? Orroight, 'ang on, guv. 'Ang on. Just keep breavin'. We'll 'ave you in 'ospital in no time, sure as nuts. No time atall . . . Yer niver knows where a poem'll take yer, do yer? One minute yer parsin' some of the better Auden, and the next yer covered in blood, face down on the back seat of a cab that 'asn't 'ad a proper washin'-up since the Profumo affair. Nasty business, poetry. Nastier than a tainted cockle. More of a prose man, meself.

2007

SONG OF MYSELF

THE LITTLE HOURS

NOW what's this? What's the object of all this darkness all over me? They haven't gone and buried me alive while my back was turned, have they? Ah, now would you think they'd do a thing like that! Oh, no, I know what it is. I'm awake. That's it. I've waked up in the middle of the night. Well, isn't that nice. Isn't that simply ideal. Twenty minutes past four, sharp, and here's Baby wide-eyed as a marigold. Look at this, will you? At the time when all decent people are just going to bed, I must wake up. There's no way things can ever come out even, under this system. This is as rank as injustice is ever likely to get. This is what brings about revolutions, that's what *this* does.

Yes, and you want to know what got me into this mess? Going to bed at ten o'clock, that's what. That spells ruin. T-e-n-space-o-apostrophe-c-l-o-c-k: ruin. Early to bed, and you'll wish you were dead. Bed before eleven, nuts before seven. Bed before morning, sailors give warning. Ten o'clock, after a quiet evening of reading. Reading—there's an institution for you. Why, I'd turn on the light and read, right this minute, if reading weren't what contributed toward driving me here. I'll show it. God, the bitter misery that reading works in this world! Everybody knows that—everybody who *is* everybody. All the best minds have been off reading for years. Look at the swing La Rochefoucauld took at it. He said that if nobody had ever learned to read, very few people would be in love. There was a man for you, and that's what *he* thought of it. Good for you, La Rochefoucauld; nice going, boy. I wish I'd never learned to read. I wish I'd never learned to take off my clothes. Then I wouldn't have been caught in this jam at half-past four in the morning. If nobody had ever learned to undress, very few people would be in love. No, his is better. Oh, well, it's a man's world.

. . .

LA ROCHEFOUCAULD, indeed, lying quiet as a mouse, and me tossing and turning here! This is no time to be getting all steamed up about La Rochefoucauld. It's only a question of minutes before I'm going to be pretty darned good and sick of La Rochefoucauld, once and for all. La Rochefoucauld this and La Rochefoucauld that. Yes, well, let me tell you that if nobody had ever learned to quote, very few people would be in love with La Rochefoucauld. I bet you I don't know ten souls who read him without a middleman. People pick up those rambling little essays that start off "Was it not that lovable old cynic, La Rochefoucauld, who said . . . ," and then they go around claiming to know the master backwards. Pack of illiterates, that's all they are. All right, let them keep their La Rochefoucauld, and see if I care. I'll stick to La Fontaine. Only I'd be better company if I could quit thinking that La Fontaine married Alfred Lunt.

I don't know what I'm doing mucking about with a lot of French authors at this hour, anyway. First thing you know, I'll be reciting *Fleurs du Mal* to myself, and then I'll be little more good to anybody. And I'll stay off Verlaine too; he was always chasing Rimbauds. A person would be better off with La Rochefoucauld, even. Oh, damn La Rochefoucauld. The big Frog. I'll thank him to keep out of my head. What's he doing there, anyhow? What's La Rochefoucauld to me, or he to Hecuba? Why, I don't even know the man's first name, that's how close I ever was to *him*. What am I supposed to be, a stooge for La Rochefoucauld? That's what *he* thinks. Sez he. Well, he's only wasting his time, hanging around here. I can't help him. The only other thing I can remember his saying is that there is always something a little pleasing to us in the misfortunes of even our dearest friends. That cleans me all up with Monsieur La Rochefoucauld. *Maintenant c'est fini, ça.*

Dearest friends. A sweet lot of dearest friends *I've* got. All of them lying in swinish stupors, while I'm practically up and about. All of them stretched sodden through these, the fairest hours of the day, when man should be at his most productive. Produce, produce, produce, for I tell you the night is coming. Carlyle said that. Yes, and a fine one *he* was, to go shooting off his face on the subject. *Oh,* Thomas Car*li*-yill, what *I* know about *you*-oo! No, that will be enough of that. I'm not going to start fretting about Carlyle, at this stage of the game. What did he ever do that was so great, besides founding a college for Indians? (That crack ought to flatten him.) Let him keep his face out of this, if he knows what's good for him. I've got enough trouble with that lovable old cynic, La Rochefoucauld—him and the misfortunes of his dearest friends!

The first thing I've got to do is get out and whip me up a complete new set of dearest friends; that's the first thing. Everything else can wait. And will somebody please kindly be so good as to inform me how I am ever going to meet up with any new people when my entire scheme of living is out of joint—when I'm the only living being awake while the rest of the world lies sleeping? I've got to get this thing adjusted. I must try to get back to sleep right now. I've got to conform to the rotten little standards of this sluggard civilization. People needn't feel that they have to change their ruinous habits and come my way. Oh, no, no; no, indeed. Not at all. I'll go theirs. If that isn't the woman of it, for you! Always having to do what somebody else wants, like it or not. Never able to murmur a suggestion of her own.

AND what suggestion has anyone to murmur as to how I am going to drift lightly back to slumber? Here I am, awake as high noon what with all this milling and pitching around with La Rochefoucauld. I really can't be expected to drop everything and start counting sheep, at my age. I hate sheep. Untender it may be in me, but all my life I've hated sheep. It amounts to a phobia, the way I hate them. I can tell the minute there's one in the room. They needn't think that I am going to lie here in the dark and count their unpleasant little faces for them; I wouldn't do it if I didn't fall asleep again until the middle of next August. Suppose they never get counted—what's the worst that can happen? If the number of imaginary sheep in this world remains a matter of guesswork, who is richer or poorer for it? No, sir; *I'm* not going to be the patsy. Let them count themselves, if they're so crazy mad after mathematics. Let them do their own dirty work. Coming around here, at this time of day, and asking me to count them! And not even *real* sheep, at that. Why, it's the most preposterous thing I ever heard in my life.

But there must be *something* I could count. Let's see. No, I already know by heart how many fingers I have. I could count my bills, I suppose. I could count the things I didn't do yesterday that I should have done. I could count the things I should do today that I'm not going to do. I'm never going to accomplish anything; that's perfectly clear to me. I'm never going to be famous. My name will never be writ large on the roster of Those Who Do Things. I don't do anything. Not one single thing. I used to bite my nails, but I don't even do that any more. I don't amount to the powder to blow me to hell. I've turned out to be nothing but a bit of flotsam. Flotsam and leave 'em—that's me from now on. Oh, it's all terrible.

Well. This way lies galloping melancholia. Maybe it's because this is the zero hour. This is the time the swooning soul hangs pendant and vertiginous between the new day and the old, nor dares confront the one or summon back the other. This is the time when all things, known and hidden, are iron to weight the spirit; when all ways, traveled or virgin, fall away from the stumbling feet, when all before the straining eyes is black. Blackness now, everywhere is blackness. This is the time of abomination, the dreadful hour of the victorious dark. For it is always darkest— Was it not that lovable old cynic, La Rochefoucauld, who said that it is always darkest before the deluge?

THERE. Now you see, don't you? Here we are again, practically back where we started. La Rochefoucauld, we are here. Ah, come on, son— how about your going your way and letting me go mine? I've got my work cut out for me right here; I've got all this sleeping to do. Think how I am going to look by daylight if this keeps up. I'll be a seamy sight for all those rested, clear-eyed, fresh-faced dearest friends of mine—the rats! Why, *Dotty*, whatever have you been doing; I thought you were on the wagon. Oh, I was helling around with La Rochefoucauld till all hours; we couldn't stop laughing about your misfortunes. No, this is getting too thick, really. It isn't right to have this happen to a person, just because she went to bed at ten o'clock once in her life. Honest, I won't ever do it again. I'll go straight, after this. I'll never go to bed again, if I can only sleep now. If I can tear my mind away from a certain French cynic, circa 1650, and slip into lovely oblivion. 1650. I bet I look as if I'd been awake since then.

How do people go to sleep? I'm afraid I've lost the knack. I might try busting myself smartly over the temple with the night-light. I might repeat to myself, slowly and soothingly, a list of quotations beautiful from minds profound; if I can remember any of the damn things. That might do it. And it ought effectually to bar that visiting foreigner that's been hanging around ever since twenty minutes past four. Yes, that's what I'll do. Only wait till I turn the pillow; it feels as if La Rochefoucauld had crawled inside the slip.

Now let's see—where shall we start? Why—er—let's see. Oh, yes, I know one. This above all, to thine own self be true and it must follow, as the night the day, thou canst not then be false to any man. Now they're off. And once they get started, they ought to come like hot cakes. Let's see. Ah, what avail the sceptered race and what the form divine, when every virtue, every grace, Rose Aylmer, all were thine. Let's see. They also serve who only stand and wait. If Winter comes, can Spring be far behind? Lilies that fester smell far worse than weeds. Silent upon a peak in Darien. Mrs. Porter and her daughter wash their feet in soda-water. And Agatha's Arth is a hug-the-hearth, but my true love is false. Why did you die when lambs were cropping, you should have died when apples were dropping. Shall be together, breathe and ride, so one day more am I deified, who knows but the world will end tonight. And he shall hear the stroke of eight and not the stroke of nine. They are not long, the weeping and the laughter; love and desire and hate I think will have no portion in us after we pass the gate. But none, I think, do there embrace. I think that I shall never see a poem lovely as a tree. I think I will not hang myself today. Ay tank Ay go home now.

Let's see. Solitude is the safeguard of mediocrity and the stern companion of genius. Consistency is the hobgoblin of little minds. Something is emotion remembered in tranquillity. A cynic is one who knows the price of everything and the value of nothing. That lovable old cynic is one who—oops, there's King Charles's head again. I've got to watch myself. Let's see. Circumstantial evidence is a trout in the milk. Any stigma will do to beat a dogma. If you would learn what God thinks about money, you have only to look at those to whom he has given it. If nobody had ever learned to read, very few people—

All right. That fixes it. I throw in the towel right now. I know when I'm licked. There'll be no more of this nonsense; I'm going to turn on the light and read my head off. Till the next ten o'clock, if I feel like it. And what does La Rochefoucauld want to make of that? Oh, he *will*, eh? Yes, he will! He and who else? La Rochefoucauld and *what* very few people?

1933

WOODY ALLEN

THE EARLY ESSAYS

Following are a few of the early essays of Woody Allen. There are no late essays, because he ran out of observations. Perhaps as Allen grows older he will understand more of life and will set it down, and then retire to his bedroom and remain there indefinitely. Like the essays of Bacon, Allen's are brief and full of practical wisdom, although space does not permit the inclusion of his most profound statement, "Looking at the Bright Side."

ON SEEING A TREE IN SUMMER

Of all the wonders of nature, a tree in summer is perhaps the most remarkable, with the possible exception of a moose singing "Embraceable You" in spats. Consider the leaves, so green and leafy (if not, something is wrong). Behold how the branches reach up to heaven as if to say, "Though I am only a branch, still I would love to collect Social Security." And the varieties! Is this tree a spruce or poplar? Or a giant redwood? No, I'm afraid it's a stately elm, and once again you've made an ass of yourself. Of course, you'd know all the trees in a minute if you were nature's creature the woodpecker, but then it would be too late and you'd never get your car started.

But why is a tree so much more delightful than, say, a babbling brook? Or anything that babbles, for that matter? Because its glorious presence is mute testimony to an intelligence far greater than any on earth, certainly in the present Administration. As the poet said, "Only God can make a tree"—probably because it's so hard to figure out how to get the bark on.

Once a lumberjack was about to chop down a tree, when he noticed a heart carved on it, with two names inside. Putting away his axe, he sawed down the tree instead. The point of that story escapes me, although six months later the lumberjack was fined for teaching a dwarf Roman numerals.

ON YOUTH AND AGE

The true test of maturity is not how old a person is but how he reacts to awakening in the midtown area in his shorts. What do years matter, particularly if your apartment is rent-controlled? The thing to remember is that each time of life has its appropriate rewards, whereas when you're dead it's hard to find the light switch. The chief problem about death, incidentally, is the fear that there may be no afterlife—a depressing thought, particularly for those who have bothered to shave. Also, there is the fear that there is an afterlife but no one will know where it's being held. On the plus side, death is one of the few things that can be done as easily lying down.

Consider, then: Is old age really so terrible? Not if you've brushed your teeth faithfully! And why is there no buffer to the onslaught of the years? Or a good hotel in downtown Indianapolis? Oh, well.

In short, the best thing to do is behave in a manner befitting one's age. If you are sixteen or under, try not to go bald. On the other hand, if you are over eighty, it is extremely good form to shuffle down the street clutching a brown paper bag and muttering, "The Kaiser will steal my string." Remember, everything is relative—or should be. If it's not, we must begin again.

ON FRUGALITY

As one goes through life, it is extremely important to conserve funds, and one should never spend money on anything foolish, like pear nectar or a solid-gold hat. Money is not everything, but it is better than having one's health. After all, one cannot go into a butcher shop and tell the butcher, "Look at my great suntan, and besides I never catch colds," and expect him to hand over any merchandise. (Unless, of course, the butcher is an idiot.) Money is better than poverty, if only for financial reasons. Not that it can buy happiness. Take the case of the ant and the grasshopper: The grasshopper played all summer, while the ant worked and saved. When winter came, the grasshopper had nothing, but the ant complained of chest pains. Life is hard for insects. And don't think mice are having any fun, either. The point is, we all need a nest egg to fall back on, but not while wearing a good suit.

Finally, let us bear in mind that it is easier to spend two dollars than to save one. And for God's sake don't invest money with any brokerage firm in which one of the partners is named Frenchy.

ON LOVE

Is it better to be the lover or the loved one? Neither, if your cholesterol is over six hundred. By love, of course, I refer to romantic love—the love between man and woman, rather than between mother and child, or a boy and his dog, or two headwaiters.

The marvelous thing is that when one is in love there is an impulse to sing. This must be resisted at all costs, and care must also be taken to see that the ardent male doesn't "talk" the lyrics of songs. To be loved, certainly, is different from being admired, as one can be admired from afar but to really love someone it is essential to be in the same room with the person, crouching behind the drapes.

To be a really good lover, then, one must be strong and yet tender. How strong? I suppose being able to lift fifty pounds should do it. Bear in mind also that to the lover the loved one is always the most beautiful thing imaginable, even though to a stranger she may be indistinguishable from an order of smelts. Beauty is in the eye of the beholder. Should the beholder have poor eyesight, he can ask the nearest person which girls look good. (Actually, the prettiest ones are almost always the most boring, and that is why some people feel there is no God.)

"The joys of love are but a moment long," sang the troubadour, "but the pain of love endures forever." This was almost a hit song, but the melody was too close to "I'm a Yankee Doodle Dandy."

ON TRIPPING THROUGH A COPSE AND PICKING VIOLETS

This is no fun at all, and I would recommend almost any other activity. Try visiting a sick friend. If this is impossible, see a show or get into a nice warm tub and read. Anything is better than turning up in a copse with one of those vacuous smiles and accumulating flowers in a basket. Next thing you know, you'll be skipping to and fro. What are you going to do with the violets once you get them, anyhow? "Why, put them in a vase," you say. What a stupid answer. Nowadays you call the florist and order by phone. Let *him* trip through the copse, he's getting paid for it. That way, if an electrical storm comes up or a beehive is chanced upon, it will be the florist who is rushed to Mount Sinai.

Do not conclude from this, incidentally, that I am insensitive to the joys of nature, although I have come to the conclusion that for sheer fun it is hard to beat forty-eight hours at Foam Rubber City during the high holidays. But that is another story.

1973

GEORGE W. S. TROW

I EMBRACE THE NEW CANDOR

TODAY I have been particularly candid. I have expressed candid thoughts about the Right to Life movement and the new high-energy Golf Classics and the way some books which don't really have *that* much literary merit are sold to paperback houses for huge figures. I have expressed candid thoughts about the fact that the Academy Awards seem to have lost a lot of their meaning (especially with the way they stop the awards during the television commercials), and the fact that Helen Hayes probably isn't the First Lady of the American Theatre anymore (although she probably is still the First Lady of the American Charitable Endorsement), and the fact that my environment at the Keowa Motel, where I live, has a damp and *stagnant* side to it that is evocative of small-time crime and emotional disaffection. Also, I have issued a no-holds-barred report on my last remaining friend, Bob Mern, which will almost certainly cost me his friendship but which will, I am sure, confirm my reputation with the public at large as a man of candor.

Let's go right to the report on Bob. I have always felt that to keep the trust of the public it was necessary for me to be ruthlessly candid in matters touching on my private life and those closest to me. In the past, as the record will show, I have been almost brutal in my statements about my wife, but since our divorce opportunities for frankness in this area have lessened. I continue to have many forthright things to say about her syndicated television program, *Jean Stapleton Duff... In Touch* (which has been devoted, this week, to the Right to Life movement, the new high-energy Golf Classics, and the California-style casual mode in outdoor entertaining, which is another subject about which I have had candid thoughts), but that isn't the same thing. When it comes to my personal life my most candid announcements now have to do with my friend Bob Mern. The fact is that I have had to lower Bob's rating twice in the last six months. Bob began the year with a "BAA" rating ("Secure Investment–Minimum Risk"), but after a really bad first quarter during which he was almost always completely drunk, during which he passed out six different times on my bathroom floor, during which he failed to pass his driving test, and during which he was unbelievably boring, I lowered his rating to a "B" ("Some Risk"). And now, after a second quarter during which he tried to pull a really obvious aggressive-dependence number on me (making me bring him his beer on account of his limp, etc., etc., etc.), I have released a statement announcing that I will not rate him at all. Bob will have a little bit of a rough time as a result, and I will have to watch TV by myself, but I have done the honest thing. Because I *have* done and said the honest thing *time* after *time* there has arisen among the public (among the public that reads the rotogravures, among the public that buys cologne, among the public in chronic pain) a deep trust in my word. I live nourished by public confidence. This confidence has reference to me as a public figure, as an artist (I am Jack Duff, and I am the founder of the Jack Duff Dance Experience), and as a human being. Even on those days I spend in bed, even on those days I spend lying on the floor, even on those days when I eschew all muscular movement, I find that I continue to be wrapped in a pervasive health—the physical manifestation of public faith in my candor.

When I speak of "the public," I do not include so-called Important Men. It annoys Important Men that I am straightforward in my speech, because it shows them up. It galls Important Men that I don't promise special treats I can't deliver, for instance. Certain men of influence promise Aerial Tramways. I say *forget* Aerial Tramways. Other men encourage the anticipation of People Movers. I say *forget* People Movers. There will be weeping in the streets (I say), and increased incidence of interregional discourtesy, but *no People Movers.* In fact, the report I'm working on right now says that we are not likely to have reliable high-speed elevators for very much longer. My report says candidly that some of the fabulous new high-speed elevators we are installing are going to be involved in heart-wrenching mishaps, leading to an investigation, leading to new ordinances, leading to new safety-amenity parameters that will make it economically unfeasible for the

high-speed-elevator manufacturers to continue in their work. In my report I foresee a generation of painful, inefficient, low-speed elevators
manufactured in Asia, and then stairs. No one has to take my word for
it. Private-school girls in good buildings, for instance, are free to do as
they please. It is my opinion, however, that private-school girls who ignore my warning will find themselves dragging their party frocks up
twenty-six floors of fire stairs; it is my opinion that they will arrive late
(and tired) at the Junior Gaiety Dances; it is my opinion that no one
will agree to attend the after-parties given by private-school girls who
ignore my warning. I don't mean to be severe, but those girls ought to
watch their step.

IT is important, I feel, not to project a negative tone. There must be, always, a *constructive* side to candor. It is this constructive aspect that I
seek to promote. I now urge the public to stress what I call the *Achievable Goals*. Achievable Goals—so simple an idea! I believe that through
an emphasis on the *achievable* we can break the cycle of failure-fantasy-
failure around which our national life has tended to carom, and regain
a sense of purpose and control. So many goals *are* achievable that it
seems perverse to stress goals whose realization is in doubt. I have some
Achievable Goals to suggest. I suggest, for instance, that we set out
now to *increase our dependence on imported oil.* This goal can be achieved
almost immediately. It would be exhilarating, I think, to achieve, almost immediately, a goal with such important long-term implications.

   To move on to the crucial housing field, where we have experienced
setback after unpleasant setback, I suggest that we seek to *increase the
stock of substandard housing.* I suggest here a Model Cities approach
which could seek to dispel the pervasive air of failure engendered by the
"real" Model Cities program, in which so many hopes were dashed. If a
Model Cities approach were adopted we could draw up an elaborate
plan in which we could set out specific figures denoting the amount by
which we intended to increase the stock of substandard housing in Year
One, in Year Two, etc., etc. Other Achievable Goals programs in the
model district might seek to increase the use of drugs, and so on.

   In the area of Social Engineering, I suggest that we *increase the
amount of violence on television.* I suggest that we set up programs to increase the number of aimless people who loathe their elders, and I suggest that, whatever the cost, we guarantee to *every* Senior American the
right to a drab old age. Sometimes (as now), when I think of just how

much we could do, I get a little overexcited and I have to sit down for a minute and have a drink and smoke a cigarette.

Now I set for myself only those goals that I know to be completely achievable. I forgo all fantasy. In the coming quarter, I plan to *increase the number of molds* on the wall of my sleeping space; to *increase the number of apéritifs* I have before dinner; and of course I plan to increase my dependence on imported oil, which, since it is a broad national goal, I don't really count. The results, I know, will be very gratifying. Sometimes, however, my candor and consistency are so overwhelming that I have to sit down and have a drink and smoke a cigarette. I have such a large amount of public trust now that in some ways it is almost too much. I don't want to cut myself off from simple human experience, after all. I don't want to surrender my warm human qualities. The public doesn't want that, surely. So I have decided to relent in the case of my friend Bob Mern. I think the public will understand. I'd like Bob to come over and watch *Starsky & Hutch* with me. I will raise Bob's rating back to a "B" ("Some Risk"). I will suppress this quarter's report and send him a notice that his rating is "B." I wonder if he will call me back. If he doesn't, it will be a triumph, in a way, since it is a goal of mine to receive thirty-two percent fewer phone calls this quarter than last.

1977

POLLY FROST

CARBOHYDRATES

8:15. A balmy evening in February, the kind we've been having since global warming began. As usual, I'm standing around, wondering when Jonathan is going to show up. He's already fifteen minutes late.

8:17. At least I've stopped wondering why I always get involved with the wrong man, why I constantly find myself in destructive relationships. I used to think it was my fault. Then I read this book. Suddenly, I understood: He can try to deny it, but my father is an alcoholic. And I am an adult child of an alcoholic.

My father has never thought that he was an alcoholic. Yet, when I was growing up, he had to have a drink every night when he came home from work. Guess who fixed it for him. He called it a "Jeanie." After me. I've tried to help Dad face up to what he is, and I feel good about my efforts.

Jeanie! One drink! One little drink! One drink a night does not an alcoholic make!

Dad, you had to have it.

Of course I had to! If you knew the pressures of Unit-Sales Management—

I'm in Retail Dispersal, and you won't find me drinking.

Then I'd come home to "When are we going to get a new washing machine? How are we going to pay for Jean's education and take that trip to Europe? What do you think of this hairdo?" Your mother had a million questions. But you. You were so mature for your age. You were there to listen. I never needed to go out and find a bartender to talk to. Not when I had my Jeanie.

Stop trying to implicate me in your behavior! I will not be your co-denier!!

The olive has always been my favorite part!

8:21. Jonathan shouldn't keep me waiting for dinner. He knows I'm hypoglycemic, even though he refuses to believe it. He thinks hypoglycemia was invented to annoy him. All those people who weren't really hypoglycemic gave it a bad name. You'd be at an art gallery with them, or you'd be trying on a pair of slacks, or you'd be talking about something that interested you. Out of the blue, they'd announce that they were having a hypoglycemic attack. They absolutely *had* to eat *that minute* or else they were going to faint. And it would all be your fault. Of course, they weren't hypoglycemic at all. They were just manipulative. *I* take responsibility for my own hypoglycemia. I always bring food with me.

8:25. These really are pretty good cookies. Macadamia nuts have a particularly stabilizing effect on my blood sugar. So does guacamole, come to think of it. Too bad it's so hard to pack in a shoulder bag. The important thing is, I'm calmer.

I'm convinced that stress is the No. 1 factor in causing hypoglycemia. The stress from your job, the stress of being in a relationship, the stress of parents. Simply *having* parents is stressful.

8:30. The worst part of being an adult child of an alcoholic is that I always find myself in relationships with passive-aggressives. How hard it is to tell if a man is a passive-aggressive! At first, they seem perfect. They listen to you, they let you take charge. You want to discuss feminist issues? They don't get threatened; they smile.

Then. Then the other behavior begins. The endless waiting—*you* waiting for them. I was involved with this P.-A., Tim. I had to be the one to decide that it was time for us to take a vacation, where we'd go, how we'd get there. He waited until we were at the airport to assert himself, just as they were giving the final boarding call. He said he needed to buy a copy of *GQ*, and he wandered off. He never showed up on that flight. I got on the plane anyway, and had the worst hypoglycemic attack of my life. As soon as I landed in Oaxaca, I had to eat five orders of guacamole to get myself to the point where I could breathe regularly. I couldn't look at an avocado today if it weren't for how they stabilize me.

Tim showed up at the hotel room fifteen hours later with a big smile on his face. I threw all of the chocolate flan I was eating right at him— and flan is a major source of simple carbohydrates. He wiped the chocolate off and proposed to me on the spot. It doesn't take much to figure this one out. He'd driven me crazy and turned me into an exact replica of his mother, punishing him with my tears and my rage. Do I have to say anything more about men who want to marry their mothers?

Jonathan is also a P.-A. We've been engaged for three years. He hasn't actually asked me to marry him—he's trying to enrage me first, by making me wait for his offer. But I'm smarter than I was in Mexico. I know how to hold my own in these relationships. I simply *tell* everyone he's my fiancé.

8:42. Jonathan thinks this is going to make me upset. I'm not upset. He can get here whenever he wants. He knows I'll just stare at him over dinner.

8:46. I'm down to half a cookie and three seaweed chips. This is precisely the kind of predicament Jonathan likes to put me in. If I leave to find a deli, he'll show up and I'll be gone, and when I return he'll say, "What do you mean I'm late? You weren't even here!"

The other night I saw a double bill of Sally Field and Julia Roberts trying to get away from their husbands. Sally's trapped in Iran, and

Julia's stuck somewhere out on the Cape. Meanwhile, I'm sitting in the theater, waiting for Jonathan.

8:48.23. People come and go, and my purse is devoid of nutrition. A man is standing two and a half feet from me, three inches into my personal-interaction area. Why do men do these things? This is not Jonathan, but this is a P.-A. That's why he's thumbing through the *Sports Illustrated* swimsuit issue, introducing a monokinied Elle Macpherson into my field of vision. This is a very angry man. If he were an *aggressive*-aggressive, he'd be doing something about his anger. He'd be out raping women. But oh, no, you're just a *passive*-aggressive, so you're standing here, shoving that magazine in my face, trying to make me feel bad about my body! I don't know why! I never saw you before! Well, you're not going to make me feel bad about my eating needs!

I can't believe it. Jonathan has me setting a new record. This is the worst hypoglycemic attack of my life. Either that, or it's the earthquake they are always predicting for New York City. Or maybe the ice caps have finally melted.

I will survive this. I deserve to survive this. I recycle! I buy only environmentally sound products for my cleaning lady to use! I eat only animals that have had the chance to move around a bit in their lives! Yes, I use sunblock that's been tested on cocker spaniels, but I think that's excusable! I deserve to have my co-op stay above water level!

Dad, this is all your fault!

Jeanie! One drink!

I think it would be better for our relationship if I forgot your next birthday.

One little drink!

What about *my* needs?

8:53. These Korean grocery stores are always so busy, but I am entitled to stand here and eat. God, I love Ben & Jerry's. It's true, though, what the books say about other men. They just don't have it in them to give me what I need. I must empower myself. With every spoonful of Heath Bar Crunch, I am becoming stronger.

Jeanie!

You had your chance, Dad.

Jonathan can wait for me forever on that street corner, as far as I'm concerned. Because Ben and Jerry care. They care about the future of this planet. Every time you eat their ice cream you are also helping to save the rain forest. Ben and Jerry care about sustainable agriculture. They care about their employees. They care about educating visitors to their factory in Vermont. And they want me to become my own person.

1991

WENDY WASSERSTEIN

SHIKSA GODDESS

I CANNOT tell a lie. Now that Madeleine Albright, Tom Stoppard, and even Hillary Rodham Clinton have embraced their Jewish roots, I feel compelled to bite the bullet and publicly reveal that I've just discovered my own denominational truth. I am Episcopalian.

I should have guessed a long time ago, because my parents never mentioned it. In fact, they hid it. They sent me to primary school at the Yeshiva Flatbush. It never crossed my mind that I was deliberately being isolated. On our classroom walls were portraits of Chaim Weitzman and Golda Meir in place of Dwight and Mamie Eisenhower. Our horror stories were not of being buried by Communists but of being suffocated by nomad ham sandwiches.

We lived in a Jewish neighborhood in Flatbush. Our shopping strip included kosher butchers and Hymie's Highway Appetizers. For Sunday brunch, my mother produced bagels, belly lox, and cream cheese with scallions. Nobody told me that lox lived a double life as smoked salmon, or that herring could ever be kippered.

Even the Christmas holidays were a setup. Every year on Christmas Eve, we were on a jet to Miami Beach. There was not even a chance for us to watch the WPIX Channel 11 Yule log burning as the Mormon Tabernacle Choir sang "Silent Night." We celebrated the holidays front-row center at the Versailles Room, with Myron Cohen warming up our crowd for Sammy Davis, Jr. Even our African Americans were Jewish!

Until now, I've had a happy life thinking of myself as a Jewish writer. I came to accept that when my work was described as being "too New York" it was really a euphemism for something else. I belonged to a temple, and, on my opening nights, my mother invariably told friends that she'd be much happier if it was my wedding. In other words, I had a solid sense of self. I knew exactly who I was.

Then the bottom fell out. I was speaking at the Lion of Judah Luncheon in Palm Beach recently when I noticed a woman in a Lilly Pulitzer dress, one strand of pearls, and forty-year-old pink Pappagallo shoes leaning against the door. She stood out from the crowd because, instead of the omnipresent Barry Kisselstein Cord purse with lizard clasp, she was carrying a battered lacrosse stick.

At the conclusion of my talk, she approached the podium. "I hope you don't mind my speaking to you, but I believe we are related," she said.

I looked at her dead-straight blond hair and smiled politely. "I doubt it."

"Your name translates to Waterston," she continued. "Harry Waterston, your great-uncle twice removed, was my mother's fourth husband. They were married for one month." She looked at me as if only a simpleton wouldn't make the immediate connection.

I did have a distant relative, Dr. Harry Wasserstein, but I never heard of him marrying anyone but Aunt Rivkah. According to my mother, even though Harry was an educated man, he never worked a day in his life, and Rivkah's life was miserable.

"I think you must be mistaken," I said, and tried to excuse myself.

"After he left my mother, Harry Waterston changed his name to Wasserstein because he wanted his son to go to an Ivy League college, and to Mount Sinai Medical School. Harry, Jr., became an educated man, but he never worked a day in his life."

I was *shvitzing*. I mean sweating. "Our name actually translates to Waterstone," I said.

"That's irrelevant!" She was almost haughty. "Look at that actor on *Law & Order*—what's his name, Sam? He's a Hasid if I ever saw one."

She handed me the lacrosse stick while I made a mental note to find out what Sam Waterston was doing for the High Holy Days. "This was Harry's lacrosse stick, which he used the year he was expelled from Hotchkiss," she said. "He made me promise to give it to the first Wasserstein relative I met in Palm Beach. He said it was inevitable that one of you people would show up here!" She winked and left the room.

Good or bad news had always made me hungry. But for the first time in my life I needed a drink. Maybe she was on to something.

That week, I began eating chicken sandwiches with mayo on white bread, no crust, and getting full after two bites. For the first time in my life, I wrote in to *The Mount Holyoke Quarterly:* "Am looking to buy thirty-year-old Saab car and to apologize to all the Holyoke girls named Timothy and Kikky, whom I never spoke to. I now know you were very interesting people."

I began wearing faded cardigan sweaters and canceled all appointments for massages, pedicures, and exploratory liposuction. I gave up on my complicated relationship with a married Jewish Malaysian vibes player and learned to enjoy the company of a divorced asexual friend from Amherst who studies pharmaceutical stocks for J. P. Morgan. I began running ten miles every morning and sculling down the Hudson nightly. My approval ratings with my friends have gone up fifteen points.

But I was still, as I used to say in Yiddish, "*nit ahin, nit aher*," or, as I now say in the Queen's English, "neither here nor there."

That was when I decided to go on a listening tour of Fishers Island. I wanted to really hear the stories of my new Wasp ancestors, learn to make their cocktails, and wear their headbands. I want to live up to my true destiny and announce to the world how great it is to be *goyisheh* like me.

1999

JACK HANDEY

LOWERING MY STANDARDS

As you may have heard, I have very high standards. When people see me do something, they often shake their heads in disbelief. That's how high my standards are.

But lately I've been wondering if maybe they're not *too* high. Am I pushing myself too hard? Do I always have to be the one that everybody looks up to? Are my high standards hurting my happiness and things like that?

Why, for instance, do I always have to be the first one to show up at a party and the last one to leave? And, while I'm at the party, is it really so important that I tell the dirtiest joke? A lot of times, I'm the only one telling a dirty joke, so it's not even that big an accomplishment. And, if someone else does tell a dirty joke, why do I feel compelled to tell one that is even dirtier and more graphic? Just so I can be No. 1?

Why do I sometimes feel like I should get "a job," or do some kind of "work"? Does thinking about maybe getting a job make me better than other people? Am I worried that if I quit borrowing money from my friends they'll think I'm stuck-up?

Why do I have to be the honest one? Do people really want you to be that honest about how old they look or how big their breasts are?

When I catch my foot and stumble on the sidewalk, why do I have to pretend to keep stumbling, all the way down the street? To avoid embarrassment?

At every get-together, why do I have to do my funny cowboy dance? Why not do a dance that isn't so demanding, like my funny robot dance, or just funny prancing?

Is it really my responsibility that half-empty glasses of beer not be wasted?

Whenever there's a scary sound at night, why do I have to do all the screaming? Maybe somebody else can scream and cry and beg for mercy, for a change.

Would the world really fall apart if I didn't point out to people which are the regular goldfish and which are the bug-eyed ones? Let them figure it out on their own.

Why does it have to be me who ends up asking how much someone paid for something? *Everyone* is curious.

Could a sock really be a parachute for a mouse? Maybe not, but does that mean I have to stand up in the middle of the movie theater and start booing?

Why do I always have to be the one who sums up what was just said, or explains to the children what Hell is, or calls the meeting to order?

These are all questions I would never even have asked myself until that incident with Don. Every day, my friend Don and I would see who could trip each other the most times. But then one day I tripped him and he fell and broke his jaw. He looked up and, with slurred speech, said, "I guess you win." But what did I win? I didn't win anything, and you know why? Because I forgot to make a bet with him. But something else was wrong, and I knew it. Why did I want to trip Don in the first place? To show how clever I was, or how brave, or how successful? Yes, all those things. So I guess that answers that.

Still, something about it bothered me. I decided to drive up to a cabin in the mountains. For a week, all I did was sit and think and watch a lot of television. How, I agonized during the commercial breaks, did I get such high standards? Was it something from my childhood, or my fraternity-hood? Was it from another lifetime, when I was in another fraternity? I wondered if my high standards were leading me to a heart attack. Then I thought, Yes, but it'll be the biggest heart attack anyone's ever had. I wondered if it was even possible for a person like me to lower his standards. Then I wondered if they still make Bosco. I became so confused and frustrated I began smashing things in the cabin. I wound up running headlong into the woods in a panic when the people who owned the cabin suddenly showed up.

As I drove back to civilization (as you squares call it), I had already made a momentous decision: I would keep thinking about the possibility of lowering my standards. Maybe, just maybe, I don't always have to be the best. Maybe I don't need to always be the first one to point and laugh. Maybe when I ask someone a question I don't always have to begin it with the words "Pray tell." Perhaps I don't have to wear the fanciest fanny pack that money can buy. And when I'm at a dinner party maybe I don't need to sniff every piece of food before I eat it. In short, perhaps I should worry less about doing the right thing and more about doing the right *thang,* whatever that means.

People may worry, "Isn't there a danger that if you start lowering your standards they'll go too low?" As far as I'm concerned, they can't go low enough.

2001

ANDY BOROWITZ

SUFFERING FOOLS GLADLY

FOR as long as I can remember, I've been known as a man who doesn't suffer fools gladly. Not suffering fools gladly has sort of become my trademark, the first thing people think of when my name comes up. You know how Tonya Harding will always be known for the time Nancy Kerrigan got bashed in the knee with a metal rod? Well, re-place "metal rod" with "not suffering fools gladly" and that's me in a nutshell.

At first, I was flattered that people thought I didn't suffer fools gladly. Not suffering fools gladly implies expertise and discernment, since knowing a fool when you see one is a pretty crucial prerequisite for not suffering them, gladly or otherwise. Plus, not suffering fools gladly suggests that you have far, far better things to do with your time—important things, even. People who think I don't suffer fools gladly probably imagine that I'm husbanding every free moment to find a solution to global warming or to sort out that intractable Social Security mess. In reality, I spend most of my spare time eating Nilla Wafers and watching ESPN2, but my reputation as someone who doesn't suffer fools gladly keeps that evocative image at bay.

As flattering as it seemed at first, though, this whole not-suffering-fools-gladly thing has really come back to bite me on the ass. People keep a wary distance from me, and it's no great mystery why: Your average person doesn't enjoy being pegged as a fool. As my reputation for not suffering fools gladly has ballooned, I've become a social pariah, untouchable and unapproachable. I'm rarely invited to parties, but, when I am, I'm really easy to pick out: I'm the one surrounded by the twenty-foot "no-fool" zone.

Sometimes, in my darker moments, I wonder how this business about my not suffering fools gladly ever got started. You see, it's completely untrue. Not only do I suffer fools; I suffer them gladly. I suffer them so gladly, in fact, that it really can't be considered suffering at all. In my book, fools represent entertainment in its purest form. The time you spend talking to fools, I've often said, should be subtracted from your time in Heaven. Back in the good old days, when people at parties still talked to me, I used to hope and pray that I'd wind up talking to a fool. And when he'd mispronounce the title of a foreign film, or misuse the subjunctive mood, or get the name of a Plantagenet monarch wrong, did I "suffer"? I'd hardly call laughing until bourbon came out my nose "suffering." And it wasn't the supercilious laughter of someone who doesn't suffer fools gladly, either. It was the roar of a guy who knows he's just hit the hilarity mother lode.

But, sadly, those innocent days are long gone. My reputation for not suffering fools gladly precedes me now, and when people meet me they just zip up their pie-holes and turn tail. I'd love to take them by the lapels, look them in the eye, and say, "I know you think I don't

suffer you, but I do—I suffer you gladly." But I never get the chance.
The fact is, fools don't suffer me gladly, and the irony's not lost on me
one bit.

2001

MARK SINGER

AN ANNOUNCEMENT

I DON'T want people saying they didn't see this coming, they were
caught completely off guard, why didn't he warn us, any of that. If
guys like Mike Eisner and Jay Leno have the courtesy to give a heads-
up, there's no reason for me to be coy. So I'm telling the world right
now: I'm going to retire. Any great enterprise must be willing to make
personnel adjustments, even at the very top, when circumstances dictate. I recognize that it will one day make sense for me to withdraw
from hands-on management of Mark Singer Global Diversified Cottage Industries, whose core endeavor—the writing of magazine articles
and the once-every-few-years book—I've now guided through three
decades of consistent incrementalism. Even as I lay the groundwork for
my transition to emeritus status, I've continued to appraise the merits
and potential pitfalls of my projected scenario for October 19, 2015,
when I intend to "celebrate" my sixty-fifth birthday by driving to the
most conveniently situated bridge and pitching over the railing my laptop computer, which will serve as a tidy stand-in for all the word-
processing devices I've been chained to across the decades.

Questions are bound to arise regarding the short- and long-term
impact of this decision upon the Mark Singer brand, which has become
synonymous with glacially slow wordsmithing in the pursuit of mid-
dlebrow accessibility. Let me address some of those.

*Does Mark Singer Global Diversified Cottage Industries possess valuable
contingent assets?*

Possibly, several, though predicting their cash equivalency is no simple matter. I continue to believe, for instance, in the marketability of
"Silly Silly Juxtapositions," the prototype of the "irony flash cards" that

I developed twenty years ago, when I first became concerned about the interpretative challenges that preschool-age children confront in coming to terms with postmodern cultural dislocation.

I retain extensive notes for scathing biographies of Wayne Calhoun and Phil Dooley, who, in 1960, hoisted my new bicycle to the top of the school flagpole, let go of the rope, and claimed that it had "slipped." Could such viscerally experienced raw material be entrusted, during my golden-years phase, to the imagination of a ghostwriter? If not, perhaps Wayne and Phil, who went on to lucrative careers in, respectively, gravel processing and agricultural waste management, could be approached by some buffed-out hirelings armed with blunt objects and be persuaded to render a reasonable tribute—a way of saying, more than a half century later, "Hey, what we did was sort of wrong."

The possibility also exists that a rich body of epic poetry might effloresce from meditations upon the mystical qualities of certain of my household possessions—my underutilized NordicTrack, the backyard hammock where I so often lay while pondering how soon the stately hemlock infested with woolly-adelgid blight would land on the house, the snowblower that brought such manly pleasure to me and my neighbor Ralph. Or, in the event that my surrogates fail to grasp the inspirational promise of these nonliquid assets, they might nevertheless, in the context of a garage sale, be monetized.

What about contingent liabilities?

Assuming that the statute of limitations has expired for tax-fraud prosecution for fiscal 1997–1999—when, owing to accounting and/or document-archiving irregularities, I neglected to retain receipts for postage expenditures that I went ahead and claimed anyway on Schedule C of my tax returns—none.

Once I've formally ceded authority, who will be in charge of day-to-day operations?

I'm aware of criticism that my micromanagerial tendencies and allegedly combative style as a chief executive have undermined what might otherwise be an orderly process of designating a successor. Yet I wonder if these detractors fully appreciate the inherent difficulty of cultivating a protégé within what is essentially a one-person organization. To cite just one timely example: During the interval between the composition of the previous paragraph and the building up of steam to segue to this one, I replaced a lightbulb, folded the laundry, ate a snack, brushed my teeth after a refreshing nap, began alphabetizing last year's Christmas cards, and chatted with a telemarketer about the weather in Lahore. In addition, even as I've been writing this essay I've been simultaneously ignoring the deadlines for four others. Easy enough, you say? Try it.

Yes? And? The point?

I'm reminded (who could forget?) of that awfully-sure-of-himself reviewer of my memoir of my adolescent years, *Stuff I Wish Hadn't Happened*, who noted, "What we have here is a prime specimen of the classic roomful-of-monkeys school of composition and editing." Beneath the surface of this rebuke would seem to lurk an inadvertent vision for the ongoing viability of Mark Singer Global Diversified Cottage Industries during the post–Mark Singer era. To which I can only say, sure, technically speaking, some number of chimpanzees, if properly incentivized, might be expected to churn out prose in a voice that would approximate my own. But could they also be relied upon to replicate my probably unique repertoire of writing-avoidance strategies? Please.

In brief, what Mark Singer Global Diversified Cottage Industries is experiencing is a natural evolutionary process. You're born, they send you to school, you settle into a career (or a checkered employment history), you occasionally contemplate the whole dust-to-dust thing, and when you finally retire maybe you get replaced by a relative youngster, maybe by a primate, or maybe you're just terminally downsized. Yes, things change. In the meantime, there are horizons to be glimpsed, perseverance to demonstrate, clocks (or irritating individuals) to be punched. Work remains to be done—or, depending upon my mood, put off until after I've tested the batteries in the smoke detector.

2004

PATRICIA MARX

PLEDGE DRIVE

YOU were just listening to an uninterrupted hour of Patty, featuring some catty remarks about her best friends. Isn't Patty fantastic? They simply don't make them like Patty anymore. And that's why it's so important to make sure that she continues to be the person you know and love. But Patty can't do that alone. That's where you come in.

At least we hope so. We'll be back with Patty talking about her hair in a little while, but right now we want to take a few moments to remind you how much Patty did for you this year.

You've come to rely on Patty to provide you with information you can't get anywhere else. A report on what she had for lunch. The latest on her trying to return a magnifying glass without a store receipt. Whom else can you turn to for news about Patty's day?

Your other friends give you sound bites, but Patty takes the time to fill in the details about things like the time she got lost in New Jersey. You simply can't get that level of quality discourse with anyone else, because most people have things to do. Did you know that the average phone conversation you have with Patty lasts twelve minutes and you're usually the one who hangs up first?

Think about it. Patty has affected your life in immeasurable ways. You've become accustomed to a bounty of e-mails from Patty, some of them jokes or petitions that Patty has forwarded along without reading first.

Or maybe you've only sat next to Patty on the bus or at the theater, not having any idea who Patty was but grateful that she wasn't somebody else. If you were trying to read Patty's newspaper, didn't Patty let you? And how about the time Patty was using her bank card to gain access to the ATM, and even though she knew you were sneaking in behind her so as to get out of scrounging around for your own card, Patty made no fuss?

Aren't these services worth a lot to you?

As of three years ago, Patty was totally dependent on parental funding. When that support was cut off, it was touch and go whether Patty would be able to survive another year. A lot of people you know have jobs, but, in order to preserve Patty's dignity, Patty has declined to work, and so she must count on pledges from friends like you. (Every once in a while, a nice gentleman treats Patty to dinner, but you can't expect her to live off that, can you?)

Patty's operating expenses have gone up and up—never more so than this year, because the cost of fancy skin creams, designer leather jackets, and other essential goods has risen disproportionately to the rate of inflation. And Patty really wants to go to Istanbul in April.

I'm not going to tell you how much to give, but I am going to tell you that Patty keeps the book on who gives what. Perhaps you'd like to give at the $10,000 level. Over the course of a year, this is only $27.39 per day—the same amount of money you run through for your daily eight lattes without thinking twice. For just $200, you can underwrite one of Patty's sessions with Dr. Cates. Throw in an extra $50 and Patty will spend the entire fifty minutes working bravely on her issues involving you. But perhaps you can't afford that amount. At the $50 level, you can . . . oh, forget it. Fifty bucks?! You've got to be kidding!

When you become a contributor, with a pledge of $100 or more you may select a thank-you gift from Patty. For instance, do you need any clothes hangers? And if you act right away you can also get a magnifying glass with an undetectable chip. Or, for a donation of $500, Patty will blow you.

So what's stopping you? Call now. Patty is standing by to take your money. Talk to your accountant: Patty could be a write-off. And, if you'd like to volunteer to help out on the phone bank, please do. You'll get to meet Patty in person. She's got bagels!

2004

IAN FRAZIER

THIN ENOUGH

LIKE many middle-aged suburban fathers, I suffer from a problem I am hesitant to name. Recently, though, I've decided that stating what is wrong with me, and admitting it up front, are essential first steps to a cure. So here goes: For many years now, I have been struggling with anorexia. My physique, well muscled and whipcord thin to all outward appearances, is actually *too* thin—painfully thin, in fact. Another uncomfortable truth I have to face is that my family has been hiding this reality from me. My wife soft-soaps me with comments like "You know, sweetie, you're really not thin at all." The kids chime in with an unhelpful "Actually, we'd be more likely to describe you as fat." I know there's a lot of love in what they say, but let's stop all the lying right now. I am incredibly, incredibly thin, and it's time we noticed what is going on.

I myself participate in the deception sometimes, when I split a pair of trousers or have trouble fitting into an airplane seat. Who am I trying to fool? Much as I might wish it, that is simply not me. The truth is, I am a stick person. For I don't know how long, I have literally starved myself trying to attain a body image that bears no relation to how men actually are. The media hammers this image into our brains every day, but now I begin to understand: I can have the same glasses as Karl Rove, wear my belt like Karl Rove, wave from the insides of car windows like Karl Rove. But I will never *be* Karl Rove, so I might as well quit trying. Even Karl Rove probably can't look as fabulous as Karl Rove. I have martyred myself trying to become a fantasy.

Before I can hope to move on, I have to fix my crazy eating habits. During the height of my dieting mania, I used to torture myself regularly at the all-you-can-eat supper at Country Harvest Buffet. I would serve myself a platter of ribs, macaroni and cheese, potato salad, biscuits, peach cobbler, iced tea, no other dessert besides pie—and that would be all. Compared with the dishes of food still on the buffet table, my portion always appeared pitifully small, not enough to feed a fairly good-sized bird. And since I'm trying to be honest here and confess everything, sometimes after eating even that trifling amount I would go to the men's room and not throw up, but smoke an expensive cigar until the feeling passed, if it had existed in the first place. Then, ready for more, I'd return to the buffet. I gloried in this punitive regimen as the pounds melted off, but I did not suspect the pathology involved.

So much to go through just for the evanescent pleasure of looking wonderful in a swimsuit! But conforming to others' physical expectations was not all to the good, I found. As I approached my ideal weight, I suffered the painful experience of being the victim of sexual harassment on the job. What made it even more confusing and upsetting was that I am my own boss. On several occasions around the office, I made remarks to myself that were completely out of line. Once by the water cooler I grabbed my buttocks. These hurtful words and actions created an atmosphere in which it was impossible for me to do my work. I have since taken a leave of absence.

I see now that the anorexia contributed to this unfortunate situation in two ways—first, by giving me a physical appearance that was extremely "attractive," in the warped judgment of many (i.e., myself), and, second, by causing nutritional deprivations that broke down moral boundaries, leading me to behave inappropriately toward other individuals (again, myself). I am still undecided about taking legal action, but clearly a lot of soul-searching and emotional sorting out need to be done.

As much of a recovery as I've made so far I owe to an often overlooked wonder drug, alcohol. People drink alcohol for the pleasure and the taste, sometimes forgetting its medicinal properties. Scientists have failed to explain why consumption of alcohol causes an increase in appetite, but I can testify that it does. After four or five glasses of wine, I am able to overcome my usual food-finickiness and eat half a crock-pot of whatever my wife has made for dinner, and then a couple of baskets of leftover Easter candy. If I sense the appetite starting to flag, I'll open another bottle of wine, make a few phone calls to distant friends or people I went to high school with, start in on a pear tart my sister brought over, listen to music really loud, eat a bunch more Easter candy, fall asleep on the living-room floor, and so forth. Little by little, this careful process has been building the bulk back on.

But I can never relax. Anorexia is a patient and crafty adversary, always waiting for me to stop stuffing myself for the briefest interval so that it can gain another foothold. In the past few months, I've been feeling somewhat safe: I'm of average height, and have managed to attain for extra security a respectable weight of several hundred pounds. Then, just the other morning, I looked in the bathroom mirror and noticed that my head was a bit higher in relation to the towel rack than it had been the day before. Men in their fifties do not commonly go through growth spurts, but apparently that is happening to me. You don't have to be an alarmist to see where it could lead. I keep increasing in height, I reach seven or eight feet, and all my hard-won weight is stretched lengthwise until I'm a grotesque string-bean skeleton again.

Fortunately for me, Hilson's Products has come out with a new, more chocolaty version of their Death by Chocolate ice-cream bar, with chocolate on the outside, then vanilla around mint surrounding a rich real-chocolate core. Even when the mere thought of food makes me ill, I can eat a box of those. Another discovery I've made is the factory trawler ships' Weekly Seafood Specials, where they fly you offshore by helicopter and you choose your own netful of bunker or menhaden or whatever baitfish they're hauling up that day. Doesn't get any fresher than that! Also, I know some people at Archer Daniels Midland who give me access to the corn-syrup silos in Moline, where I can open the spigots and down as much as I feel like—none of this making it into McFlurrys or some such pap—just the real syrup, thick and undiluted and strong. You know what else is not bad? No. 2 heating oil. No. 6 oil is okay, too, but you have to cut the sulfur content of both with a good Australian Shiraz, and that runs up the tab. Sulfur can also be a problem with bituminous coal, which is priced right but involves digestive issues that make it less of a bargain. Anthracite, on the other hand, can be lower in sulfur, but it's very hard on the teeth. Then finish it off with a jolt of pure power right from the grid; just—*zap!* If you like, I can give you the recipes.

I'm still too thin, though. I have robust mini-potbellies behind each elbow, and my forearms are good and stout, but the wrists are looking a little spindly. And I don't like the outside parts of my hands, the way they taper off. I can see the thinness there, waiting to strike. On my ankles, too; I've never been able to do anything with them. They could use another five or ten pounds apiece. I'll have to get the opposite of liposuction done to them. (Who in the world, by the way, would deliberately have perfectly good fat removed and then thrown down the drain?) By now, you're probably having some uncomplimentary thoughts about me. Well, I don't care even a fig for you. Wait a minute—let me see that fig. I just want to look at it. Gimme that.

2006

JENNY ALLEN

AWAKE

I'M up. Are you up?

I'm trying to go back to sleep. But I'm awake. Awake awake awake.

That's what Buddha said. Buddha said, "I am awake." Buddha got that idea, that whole concept, from a middle-aged woman, I'm sure.

Not that this sleepless business ends after a certain age. I think you have to die first.

If you added up all the hours I've been awake in the middle of the night, it would come to years by now. Fifty may be the new forty, but, for the sleepless woman, fifty is the new eighty.

Thank you, that's a very good idea, but I already took a sleeping pill. I fell asleep right away—it's bliss, that drugged drifting off—but now I'm awake again. That always happens! I fall asleep, boom, and then, four or five hours later, I wake up—like it's my turn on watch, like I've just had a full night's sleep. But if I act as if I've had a full night's sleep, if I get up and do things, I will be pitiful tomorrow. I will confuse the

TV remote with the cordless phone and try to answer it. I will not notice any of my typos—I will type "pubic school" this and "pubic school"
that in e-mails to people whose public schools I am looking at for my
daughter. I will say, "I saw store at the Shelly," and then I will have to
make one of those dumb Alzheimer's jokes.

I could take another sleeping pill, but I worry about that. I worry
about liking sleeping pills too much. Sleeping pills always make me
think of Judy Garland. Poor Judy.

It's funny about the name Judy, isn't it? No one names anyone Judy
anymore—do you ever see five-year-old Judys?—but half the women I
know are named Judy. You would probably be safe, when meeting any
woman over fifty, just to say, "Nice to meet you, Judy." Most of the time
you would be right.

I am going to lie here and fall asleep counting all the Judys I know.

Thirteen Judys. Including my husband's ex-wife. Who's very nice,
by the way.

I'm still awake.

Some people who knew my husband before I knew him call me
Judy. "Hi, Judy, how are you?" they say, and I never correct them. Who
can blame them, when they know so many Judys? Although I do sort of
hope that later they will realize they have called me by my husband's
ex-wife's name and take note of what a nice person I must be not to
have corrected them.

Are all my Judy friends up, like me? Judy in Brooklyn, are you up?
Judy on Amsterdam Avenue, Judy in Lincoln Towers, Judy in Morn-
ingside Heights, Judy on Riverside Drive? I'm here in bed imagining
that I can see all of you—I probably *could* see a few of you from my window if you waved at me. I feel like the teacher on *Romper Room* when I
was little. She used to hold a big magnifying glass the size of a tennis
racquet in front of her face, so that it was between her and you, and she
would say, "I see Nina, and Becky, and Scott, and Glenn, and Judy . . ."

I see them. I see all my Judys, and I see Martha and Angeline and
Eden, and Ellie and Goldie and Jackie and Wendy, and everyone in my
book group. I see them lying there in their nighties, their faces shiny
with night cream. Some of us lie alone, some of us lie next to another
person, who is, enragingly, sleeping like a log. How can these people
next to us sleep so profoundly? They snore, they shake their restless-
leg-syndrome legs all over their side of the bed, they mutter protests
from their dreams—"I didn't say Elmira!" and "It's not yours!" They're
making a regular racket, and yet they sleep on.

Sleepless friends, I am thinking about you. Ginny, did you decide what to do about day camp for your grandchildren this summer? Martha, what are you reading to help you fall back asleep? Will you call me tomorrow and tell me about it? Mimi, are you up thinking about who you haven't had lunch with lately? You're eighty-seven years old. That's a hundred and thirty-nine in wakeful-woman years. Congratulations for hanging in there.

Sometimes I fall asleep to the television. And a strange thing happens: No matter what I have fallen asleep watching, when I wake up in the middle of the night *Girls Gone Wild* is on. I never turn the channel to *Girls Gone Wild*, I promise. It's just on. My goodness, those girls must sleep well, when they finally do sleep. I have to change the channel right away when I see *Girls Gone Wild*, because I always think about the girls' mothers, and that upsets me. I worry about their mothers, up in the middle of the night, waking up to *Girls Gone Wild*: "That one looks just like Melanie—oh, my God."

Look. *Law & Order* is on. I've seen this episode, of course. Do they run the same ones over and over, or is it that I have seen every one there is? What a scary thought. Fortunately, I never remember what happens after the opening scene, when they find the dead person, so I can watch them all over again.

That was a good one. Although one day maybe there will be a teenager on the show who isn't a psycho killer.

I'm still awake.

Friends, are you all still up? It seems inefficient somehow for all of us to be awake separately; wouldn't it be great if we could pool all our individual little tributaries of wakeful energy into one mighty Mississippi, and then harness it, like a WPA project, like the Hoover Dam? We could power something. We could light up Manhattan. We could light up Manhattan and have a huge party for all the women who are awake.

I should read. Reading is too hard for the dead of night. Reading has too many words in it. Including words I might not know. If I read a word I don't know, I will feel compelled to scrawl it on whatever piece of paper is on my bedside table and then hope that I'll be able to read my writing tomorrow, and will remember to look up the word in the dictionary. If I am too lazy to write down the word, I will have to make a decision about whether to dog-ear the page—bad reader citizenship!—and I don't want the burden of that choice now, in the middle of the night.

Also, I know that even if I do look a word up tomorrow I won't remember the definition next week. I keep looking up the same words over and over. "Fungible." "Heliotrope." How many times am I supposed to look up "heliotrope"? I used to remember the definitions, but I haven't for years. I still know a lot of words, though. "Cleave" is a funny word, because it means to sunder, and, strangely, it also means to stick to. "Ouster" is a funny word. "Ouster" means the act of getting rid of someone, but it also means the person who does the getting rid of. Who should be the ousterer. "Timorous" means timid, but why not just say "timid"?

Timmy was the name of the boy in *Lassie,* the television show. The theme music for the show was melancholy, shockingly so. It made you yearn, it made you homesick, even as you watched it in your own home.

I'm still awake. Only now everything is sort of blending together. It's the time of night when I think I may finally be losing my mind for good. The theme song from *Lassie* is blending into the Brownie song, the one about "I've something in my pocket, it belongs across my face," about a Great Big Brownie Smile. Where's my older daughter's Girl Scout sash? Why didn't the younger one ever do Girl Scouts? What's in that pot-roast recipe besides a cinnamon stick and horseradish and a can of cranberry sauce? What was my old ZIP Code when I lived on Third Avenue? Why didn't I submit that expense report worth a thousand dollars nine years ago?

Instead of going crazy, maybe I will just lie here and regret things. Let's see . . . Can't I blame the really big mistakes on others? Didn't they fail me, didn't they provoke me, didn't they drive me to it? Didn't they just really strain my patience?

No, face it, you have some things to regret. Now you have to sit with it, as Buddha would say—or, in your case, lie with it. Not exactly the path to Slumberland.

Here's the question: Have you done the love thing? The unconditional-love thing? Have you done it with your children? And with the person lying next to you, the one with the jitterbugging legs?

Oh, look. The city sky is turning from purplish black to . . . brown. It's going to be daylight soon. Dawn! How are you, Dawn? How's my girl? As long as you're up, I might as well get up, too. We can keep each other company.

2008

REAL
IMITATIONS

JAMES THURBER

A VISIT FROM SAINT NICHOLAS

[IN THE ERNEST HEMINGWAY MANNER]

IT was the night before Christmas.

The house was very quiet. No creatures were stirring in the house. There weren't even any mice stirring. The stockings had been hung carefully by the chimney. The children hoped that Saint Nicholas would come and fill them.

The children were in their beds. Their beds were in the room next to ours. Mamma and I were in our beds. Mamma wore a kerchief. I had my cap on. I could hear the children moving. We didn't move. We wanted the children to think we were asleep.

"Father," the children said.

There was no answer. He's there, all right, they thought.

"Father," they said, and banged on their beds.

"What do you want?" I asked.

"We have visions of sugarplums," the children said.

"Go to sleep," said mamma.

"We can't sleep," said the children. They stopped talking, but I could hear them moving. They made sounds.

"Can you sleep?" asked the children.

"No," I said.

"You ought to sleep."

"I know. I ought to sleep."

"Can we have some sugarplums?"

"You can't have any sugarplums," said mamma.

"We just asked you."

There was a long silence. I could hear the children moving again.

"Is Saint Nicholas asleep?" asked the children.

"No," mamma said. "Be quiet."

"What the hell would he be asleep tonight for?" I asked.

"He might be," the children said.

"He isn't," I said.

"Let's try to sleep," said mamma.

The house became quiet once more. I could hear the rustling noises the children made when they moved in their beds.

Out on the lawn a clatter arose. I got out of bed and went to the window. I opened the shutters; then I threw up the sash. The moon shone on the snow. The moon gave the lustre of mid-day to objects in the snow. There was a miniature sleigh in the snow, and eight tiny reindeer. A little man was driving them. He was lively and quick. He whistled and shouted at the reindeer and called them by their names. Their names were Dasher, Dancer, Prancer, Vixen, Comet, Cupid, Donder, and Blitzen.

He told them to dash away to the top of the porch, and then he told them to dash away to the top of the wall. They did. The sleigh was full of toys.

"Who is it?" mamma asked.

"Some guy," I said. "A little guy."

I pulled my head in out of the window and listened. I heard the reindeer on the roof. I could hear their hoofs pawing and prancing on the roof. "Shut the window," said mamma. I stood still and listened.

"What do you hear?"

"Reindeer," I said. I shut the window and walked about. It was cold. Mamma sat up in the bed and looked at me.

"How would they get on the roof?" mamma asked.

"They fly."

"Get into bed. You'll catch cold."

Mamma lay down in bed. I didn't get into bed. I kept walking around.

"What do you mean, they fly?" asked mamma.

"Just fly is all."

Mamma turned away toward the wall. She didn't say anything.

I went out into the room where the chimney was. The little man came down the chimney and stepped into the room. He was dressed all in fur. His clothes were covered with ashes and soot from the chimney. On his back was a pack like a peddler's pack. There were toys in it. His cheeks and nose were red and he had dimples. His eyes twinkled. His mouth was little, like a bow, and his beard was very white. Between his teeth was a stumpy pipe. The smoke from the pipe encircled his head in a wreath. He laughed and his belly shook. It shook like a bowl of red jelly. I laughed. He winked his eye, then he gave a twist to his head. He didn't say anything.

He turned to the chimney and filled the stockings and turned away from the chimney. Laying his finger aside his nose, he gave a nod. Then he went up the chimney. I went to the chimney and looked up. I saw him get into his sleigh. He whistled at his team and the team flew away. The team flew as lightly as thistledown. The driver called out, "Merry Christmas and good night." I went back to bed.

"What was it?" asked mamma. "Saint Nicholas?" She smiled.

"Yeah," I said.

She sighed and turned in the bed.

"I saw him," I said.

"Sure."

"I did see him."

"Sure you saw him." She turned farther toward the wall.

"Father," said the children.

"There you go," mamma said. "You and your flying reindeer."

"Go to sleep," I said.

"Can we see Saint Nicholas when he comes?" the children asked.

"You got to be asleep," I said. "You got to be asleep when he comes. You can't see him unless you're unconscious."

"Father knows," mamma said.

I pulled the covers over my mouth. It was warm under the covers. As I went to sleep I wondered if mamma was right.

1927

PETER DE VRIES

INTRUDER IN THE DUSK

(WHAT CAN COME OF TRYING TO READ WILLIAM FAULKNER
WHILE MINDING A CHILD, OR VICE VERSA)

THE cold Brussels sprout rolled off the page of the book I was reading and lay inert and defunctive in my lap. Turning my head with a
leisure at least three-fourths impotent rage, I saw him standing there
holding the toy with which he had catapulted the vegetable, or rather
the reverse, the toy first then the fat insolent fist clutching it and then
above that the bland defiant face beneath the shock of black hair like
tangible gas. It, the toy, was one of those cardboard funnels with a trigger near the point for firing a small celluloid ball. Letting the cold
Brussels sprout lie there in my lap for him to absorb or anyhow appre-
hend rebuke from, I took a pull at a Scotch highball I had had in my
hand and then set it down on the end table beside me.

"So instead of losing the shooter which would have been a mercy
you had to lose the ball," I said, fixing with a stern eye what I had fa-
thered out of all sentient and biding dust; remembering with that
retroactive memory by which we count chimes seconds and even minutes after they have struck (recapitulate, even, the very grinding of the
bowels of the clock before and during and after) the cunning furtive
click, clicks rather, which perception should have told me then already
were not the trigger plied but the icebox opened. "Even a boy of five
going on six should have more respect for his father if not for food," I
said, now picking the cold Brussels sprout out of my lap and setting
it—not dropping it, setting it—in an ashtray; thinking how across the
wax bland treachery of the kitchen linoleum were now in all likelihood
distributed the remnants of string beans and cold potatoes and maybe
even tapioca. "You're no son of mine."

I took up the thread of the book again or tried to: the weft of legitimate kinship that was intricate enough without the obbligato of that
dark other: the sixteenths and thirty-seconds and even sixty-fourths of

dishonoring cousinships brewed out of the violable blood by the inef-
faceable errant lusts. Then I heard another click; a faint metallic rejoin-
der that this time was neither the trigger nor the icebox but the front
door opened and then shut. Through the window I saw him picking his
way over the season's soiled and sun-frayed vestiges of snow like shreds
of rotted lace, the cheap upended toy cone in one hand and a child's
cardboard suitcase in the other, toward the road.

I dropped the book and went out after him who had forgotten not
only that I was in shirtsleeves but that my braces hung down over my
flanks in twin festoons. "Where are you going?" I called, my voice ex-
postulant and forlorn on the warm numb air. Then I caught it: caught
it in the succinct outrage of the suitcase and the prim churning rear and
marching heels as well: I had said he was no son of mine, and so he was
leaving a house not only where he was not wanted but where he did not
even belong.

"I see," I said in that shocked clarity with which we perceive the
truth instantaneous and entire out of the very astonishment that refuses
to acknowledge it. "Just as you now cannot be sure of any roof you belong more than half under, you figure there is no housetop from which
you might not as well begin to shout it. Is that it?"

Something was trying to tell me something. Watching him turn off on
the road—and that not only with the ostensible declaration of
vagabondage but already its very assumption, attaining as though with
a single footfall the very apotheosis of wandering just as with a single
shutting of a door he had that of renunciation and farewell—watching
him turn off on it, the road, in the direction of the Permisangs', our
nearest neighbors, I thought *Wait; no; what I said was not enough for him
to leave the house on; it must have been the blurted inscrutable chance confirmation of something he already knew, and was half able to assess, either out
of the blown facts of boyhood or pure male divination or both.*

"What is it you know?" I said springing forward over the delicate
squalor of the snow and falling in beside the boy. "Does any man come
to the house to see your mother when I'm away, that you know of?"
Thinking *We are mocked, first by the old mammalian snare, then, snared, by
that final unilaterality of all flesh to which birth is given; not only not knowing when we may be cuckolded, but not even sure that in the veins of the very
bantling we dandle does not flow the miscreant sniggering wayward blood.*

"I get it now," I said, catching in the undeviating face just as I had in
the prim back and marching heels the steady articulation of disdain.
"Cuckoldry is something of which the victim may be as guilty as the

wrongdoers. That's what you're thinking? That by letting in this taint upon our heritage I am as accountable as she or they who have been its actual avatars. More. Though the foe may survive, the sleeping sentinel must be shot. Is that it?"

"You talk funny."

Mother-and-daughter blood conspires in the old mammalian office. Father-and-son blood vies in the ancient phallic enmity. I caught him by the arm and we scuffled in the snow. "I will be heard," I said, holding him now as though we might be dancing, my voice intimate and furious against the furious sibilance of our feet in the snow. Thinking how revelation had had to be inherent in the very vegetable scraps to which venery was probably that instant contriving to abandon me, the cold boiled despair of whatever already featureless suburban Wednesday Thursday or Saturday supper the shot green was the remainder. "I see another thing," I panted, cursing my helplessness to curse whoever it was had given him blood and wind. Thinking *He's glad; glad to credit what is always secretly fostered and fermented out of the vats of childhood fantasy anyway (for all childhood must conceive a substitute for the father that has conceived it) (finding that other inconceivable?);* thinking *He is walking in a nursery fairy tale to find the king his sire.* "Just as I said to you 'You're no son of mine' so now you answer back 'Neither are you any father to me.' "

The scherzo of violence ended as abruptly as it had begun. He broke away and walked on, after retrieving the toy he had dropped and adjusting his grip on the suitcase which he had not, this time faster and more urgently.

THE last light was seeping out of the shabby sky, after the hemorrhage of sunset. High in the west where the fierce constellations soon would wheel, the evening star in single bombast burned and burned. The boy passed the Permisangs' without going in, then passed the Kellers'. Maybe he's heading for the McCullums', I thought, but he passed their house too. Then he, we, neared the Jelliffs'. He's got to be going there, his search will end there, I thought. Because that was the last house this side of the tracks. And because *something was trying to tell me something.*

"Were you maybe thinking of what you heard said about Mrs. Jelliff and me having relations in Spuyten Duyvil?" I said in rapid frantic speculation. "But they were talking about mutual kin—nothing else." The boy said nothing. But I had sensed it instant and complete: The boy felt that, whatever of offense his mother may or may not have given, his father had given provocation; and out of the old embattled malehood, it was the hairy ineluctable Him whose guilt and shame he was going to hold preponderant. *Because now I remembered.*

"So it's Mrs. Jelliff—Sue Jelliff—and me you have got this all mixed up with," I said, figuring he must, in that fat sly nocturnal stealth that took him creeping up and down the stairs to listen when he should have been in bed, certainly have heard his mother exclaiming to his father behind that bedroom door it had been vain to close since it was not soundproof: "I saw you. I saw that with Sue. There may not be anything between you but you'd like there to be! Maybe there is at that!"

Now like a dentist forced to ruin sound enamel to reach decayed I had to risk telling him what he did not know to keep what he assuredly did in relative control.

"This is what happened on the night in question," I said. "It was under the mistletoe, during the holidays, at the Jelliffs'. Wait! I will be heard out! See your father as he is, but see him in no baser light. He has his arms around his neighbor's wife. It is evening, in the heat and huddled spiced felicity of the year's end, under the mistletoe (where as well as anywhere else the thirsting and exasperated flesh might be visited by the futile pangs and jets of later lust, the omnivorous aches of fifty and forty and even thirty-five to seize what may be the last of the allotted lips). Your father seems to prolong beyond its usual moment's span that custom's usufruct. Only for an instant, but in that instant letting trickle through the fissures of appearance what your mother and probably Rudy Jelliff too saw as an earnest of a flood that would have devoured that house and one four doors away."

A moon hung over the eastern roofs like a phantasmal bladder. Somewhere an icicle crashed and splintered, fruit of the day's thaw.

"So now I've got it straight," I said. "Just as through some nameless father your mother has cuckolded me (you think), so through one of Rudy Jelliff's five sons I have probably cuckolded him. Which would give you at least a half brother under that roof where under ours you have none at all. So you balance out one miscreance with another, and find your rightful kin in our poor weft of all the teeming random bonded sentient dust."

Shifting the grip, the boy walked on past the Jelliffs'. Before him— the tracks; and beyond that—the other side of the tracks. And now out of whatever reserve capacity for astonished incredulity may yet have remained I prepared to face this last and ultimate outrage. But he didn't cross. Along our own side of the tracks ran a road which the boy turned left on. He paused before a lighted house near the corner, a white cottage with a shingle in the window which I knew from familiarity to read, "Viola Pruett, Piano Lessons," and which, like a violently unscrambled pattern on a screen, now came to focus.

MEMORY adumbrates just as expectation recalls. The name on the shingle made audible to listening recollection the last words of the boy's mother as she'd left, which had fallen short then of the threshold of hearing. ". . . Pruett," I remembered now. "He's going to have supper and stay with Buzzie Pruett overnight. . . . Can take a few things with him in that little suitcase of his. If Mrs. Pruett phones about it, just say I'll take him over when I get back," I recalled now in that chime-counting recapitulation of retroactive memory—better than which I could not have been expected to do. Because the eternal Who-instructs might have got through to the whiskey-drinking husband or might have got through to the reader immersed in that prose vertiginous intoxicant and unique, but not to both.

"So that's it," I said. "You couldn't wait till you were taken much less till it was time but had to sneak off by yourself, and that not cross-lots but up the road I've told you a hundred times to keep off even the shoulder of."

The boy had stopped and now appeared to hesitate before the house. He turned around at last, switched the toy and the suitcase in his hands, and started back in the direction he had come.

"What are you going back for now?" I asked.

"More stuff to take in this suitcase," he said. "I was going to just sleep at the Pruetts' overnight, but now I'm going to ask them to let me stay there for good."

1950

WOODY ALLEN

NO KADDISH FOR WEINSTEIN

WEINSTEIN lay under the covers, staring at the ceiling in a depressed torpor. Outside, sheets of humid air rose from the pavement in stifling waves. The sound of traffic was deafening at this hour, and in addition to all this his bed was on fire. Look at me, he thought. Fifty years old. Half a century. Next year, I will be fifty-one. Then fifty-two. Using this same reasoning, he could figure out his age as much as five years in the future. So little time left, he thought, and so much to accomplish. For one thing, he wanted to learn to drive a car. Adelman, his friend who used to play dreidel with him on Rush Street, had studied driving at the Sorbonne. He could handle a car beautifully and had already driven many places by himself. Weinstein had made a few attempts to steer his father's Chevy but kept winding up on the sidewalk.

He had been a precocious child. An intellectual. At twelve, he had translated the poems of T. S. Eliot into English, after some vandals had broken into the library and translated them into French. And as if his high I.Q. did not isolate him enough, he suffered untold injustices and persecutions because of his religion, mostly from his parents. True, the old man was a member of the synagogue, and his mother, too, but they could never accept the fact that their son was Jewish. "How did it happen?" his father asked, bewildered. My face looks Semitic, Weinstein thought every morning as he shaved. He had been mistaken several times for Robert Redford, but on each occasion it was by a blind person. Then there was Feinglass, his other boyhood friend: A Phi Beta Kappa. A labor spy, ratting on the workers. Then a convert to Marxism. A Communist agitator. Betrayed by the Party, he went to Hollywood and became the offscreen voice of a famous cartoon mouse. Ironic.

Weinstein had toyed with the Communists, too. To impress a girl at Rutgers, he had moved to Moscow and joined the Red Army. When he called her for a second date, she was pinned to someone else. Still, his rank of sergeant in the Russian infantry would hurt him later when he needed a security clearance in order to get the free appetizer with his dinner at Longchamps. Also, while at school he had organized some laboratory mice and led them in a strike over work conditions. Actually, it was not so much the politics as the poetry of Marxist theory that got him. He was positive that collectivization could work if everyone would learn the lyrics to "Rag Mop." "The withering away of the state" was a phrase that had stayed with him ever since his uncle's nose had withered away in Saks Fifth Avenue one day. What, he wondered, can be learned about the true essence of social revolution? Only that it should never be attempted after eating Mexican food.

The Depression shattered Weinstein's Uncle Meyer, who kept his fortune under the mattress. When the market crashed, the government called in all mattresses, and Meyer became a pauper overnight. All that was left for him was to jump out the window, but he lacked the nerve and sat on a windowsill of the Flatiron Building from 1930 to 1937.

"These kids with their pot and their sex," Uncle Meyer was fond of saying. "Do they know what it is to sit on a windowsill for seven years? There you see life! Of course, everybody looks like ants. But each year Tessie—may she rest in peace—made the Seder right out there on the ledge. The family gathered round for Passover. Oy, nephew! What's the world coming to when they have a bomb that can kill more people than one look at Max Rifkin's daughter?"

Weinstein's so-called friends had all knuckled under to the House Un-American Activities Committee. Blotnick was turned in by his own mother. Sharpstein was turned in by his answering service. Weinstein had been called by the committee and admitted he had given money to the Russian War Relief, and then added, "Oh, yes, I bought Stalin a dining-room set." He refused to name names but said if the committee insisted he would give the heights of the people he had met at meetings. In the end he panicked and, instead of taking the Fifth Amendment, took the Third, which enabled him to buy beer in Philadelphia on Sunday.

WEINSTEIN finished shaving and got into the shower. He lathered himself, while steaming water splashed down his bulky back. He thought, Here I am at some fixed point in time and space, taking a shower. I, Isaac Weinstein. One of God's creatures. And then, stepping on the soap, he slid across the floor and rammed his head into the towel rack. It had been a bad week. The previous day, he had got a bad haircut and he was still not over the anxiety it had caused him. At first the barber had snipped judiciously, but soon Weinstein realized he had gone too far. "Put some back!" he screamed unreasonably.

"I can't," the barber said. "It won't stick."

"Well, then give it to me, Dominic! I want to take it with me!"

"Once it's on the floor of the shop it's mine, Mr. Weinstein."

"Like hell! I want my hair!"

He blustered and raged, and finally felt guilty and left. Goyim, he thought. One way or another, they get you.

Now he emerged from the hotel and walked up Eighth Avenue. Two men were mugging an elderly lady. My God, thought Weinstein, time was when one person could handle that job. Some city. Chaos everyplace. Kant was right: The mind imposes order. It also tells you how much to tip. What a wonderful thing, to be conscious! I wonder what the people in New Jersey do.

He was on his way to see Harriet about the alimony payments. He still loved Harriet, even though while they were married she had systematically attempted to commit adultery with all the "R"s in the Manhattan Telephone Directory. He forgave her. But he should have suspected something when his best friend and Harriet took a house in Maine together for three years without telling him where they were. He didn't *want* to see it—that was it. His sex life with Harriet had stopped early. He slept with her once on the night they first met, once on the evening of the first moon landing, and once to test if his back was all right after a slipped disc. "It's no damn good with you, Harriet," he used to complain. "You're too pure. Every time I have an urge for you I sublimate it by planting a tree in Israel. You remind me of my mother." (Molly Weinstein, may she rest in peace, who slaved for him and made the best stuffed derma in Chicago—a secret recipe until everyone realized she was putting in hashish.)

For lovemaking, Weinstein needed someone quite opposite. Like LuAnne, who made sex an art. The only trouble was, she couldn't count to twenty without taking her shoes off. He once tried giving her a book on existentialism, but she ate it. Sexually, Weinstein had always felt inadequate. For one thing, he felt short. He was five-four in his stocking feet, although in someone else's stocking feet he could be as tall as five-six. Dr. Klein, his analyst, got him to see that jumping in front of a moving train was more hostile than self-destructive but in either case would ruin the crease in his pants. Klein was his third analyst. His first was a Jungian, who suggested they try a Ouija board. Before Klein, he attended "group," but when it came time for him to speak he got dizzy and could only recite the names of all the planets. His problem was women, and he knew it. He was impotent with any woman who finished college with higher than a B-minus average. He felt most at home with graduates of typing school, although if the woman did over sixty words a minute he panicked and could not perform.

WEINSTEIN rang the bell to Harriet's apartment, and suddenly she was standing before him. Swelling to maculate giraffe, as usual, thought Weinstein. It was a private joke that neither of them understood.

"Hello, Harriet," he said.

"Oh, Ike," she said. "You needn't be so damn self-righteous."

She was right. What a tactless thing to have said. He hated himself for it.

"How are the kids, Harriet?"

"We never had any kids, Ike."

"That's why I thought four hundred dollars a week was a lot for child support."

She bit her lip, Weinstein bit his lip. Then he bit her lip. "Harriet," he said, "I . . . I'm broke. Egg futures are down."

"I see. And can't you get help from your *shiksa?*"

"To you, any girl who's not Jewish is a *shiksa.*"

"Can we forget it?" Her voice was choked with recrimination. Weinstein had a sudden urge to kiss her, or, if not her, somebody.

"Harriet, where did we go wrong?"

"We never faced reality."

"It wasn't my fault. You said it was north."

"Reality *is* north, Ike."

"No, Harriet. Empty dreams are north. Reality is west. False hopes are east, and I think Louisiana is south."

She still had the power to arouse him. He reached out for her, but she moved away and his hand came to rest in some sour cream.

"Is that why you slept with your analyst?" he finally blurted out. His face was knotted with rage. He felt like fainting but couldn't remember the proper way to fall.

"That was therapy," she said coldly. "According to Freud, sex is the royal road to the unconscious."

"Freud said *dreams* are the road to the unconscious."

"Sex, dreams—you're going to nitpick?"

"Goodbye, Harriet."

It was no use. *Rien à dire, rien à faire.* Weinstein left and walked over to Union Square. Suddenly hot tears burst forth, as if from a broken dam. Hot, salty tears pent up for ages rushed out in an unabashed wave of emotion. The problem was, they were coming out of his ears. Look at this, he thought. I can't even cry properly. He dabbed his ear with Kleenex and went home.

1975

BRUCE McCALL

ROLLED IN RARE BOHEMIAN ONYX, THEN VULCANIZED BY HAND

DEAR Eminent Patron of the Mail Order Arts,
      Imagine a collector's item so exquisitely detailed that each is actually *invisible* to the naked eye.

Think of an heirloom so limited in availability that when you order it, the mint specially constructed to craft it will be *demolished.*

Ponder an item so precious that its value has actually *tripled* since you began reading this.

KILN-FIRED IN EDIBLE 24-CALORIE SILVER

Never before in human history has the Polk McKinley Harding Coolidge Mint (not a U.S. Government body) commissioned such a rarity.

Consider: miniature pewterine reproductions, authenticated by the World Court at The Hague and sent to you in moisture-resistant Styrofoam chests, of the front-door letter slots of Hollywood's 36 most beloved character actors and actresses.

A special blue-ribbon Advisory Panel will insure that the Foundation Council's certificated and inscribed insignia is approved by Her Majesty's Master of Heralds before the application deadline.

Meanwhile, they are yours to inspect in the privacy of your home,

office, shop, or den for *twenty years* by express permission, already with-
drawn, of the Polk McKinley Harding Coolidge Mint—the only mint
authorized to stamp your application with its own seal.

The equivalent of three centuries of painstaking historical research,
supervised by the U.S. Bureau of Mines, has preceded this issue of
*The Ornamental Handles of the Walking Canes of the Hohenzollern
Princelings.*

Our miniature craftsmen have designed, cast, struck, etched, forged,
and finished these authentic reproductions—not available in any store,
even before they were commissioned—literally *without regard* for quality.

CERTIFIED BY THE AMERICAN KENNEL CLUB

But now, through a special arrangement with the Postmaster General
of the Republic of San Marino, this 72-piece commemorative plinth,
honoring *The Footprints of the Great Jewel Thieves of the French Riv-
iera*—each encased in its own watered-silk caddy that revolves 360 degrees on genuine Swedish steel ball bearings—has been cancelled.
    A unique way, you will agree, of introducing you and your loved
ones to *The Great Cookie Jars of the Restoration,* just as Congreve the boy
must have pilfered from.

They are so authentic that you can actually smell them with your
nose.

And don't forget: every set of hand-fired porcelain reproductions of
The Padlocks of the Free World's Great Customs Houses comes sealed in an
airtight cask, fashioned after the shoe locker of a Mogul emperor so famous that we are prohibited from disclosing his name.

12 MEN DIED TO MAKE THE INGOTS PERFECT

But why, as a prudent investor, should you spend thousands of dollars,
every month for a lifetime, to acquire this 88-piece set of *Official Diplo-
matic License Plates of the World's Great Governments-in-Exile*?
    One Minnesota collector comments, "I never expected to buy an item
so desirable that it has already kept its haunting fascination forever."
    But even this merely hints at the extraordinary investment potential

of the Connoisseur's Choice selection of *Great Elevator Inspection Certificates of the World's Tallest Buildings.*

Molded in unobtainable molybdenum, each is precision-ejected from a flying aircraft to check a zinc content that must measure .000000003 per cent or the entire batch will be melted down, discarded, and forgotten.

But "keepsake" is an inadequate term. Your Jubilee Edition of the 566 *Tunic Buttons of the World's Legendary Hotel Porters* will take you from New York City to San Francisco to Hong Kong to Bombay . . . and then actually *pay your way* back home.

There is one more aspect for you to consider before refusing this offer.

If you wish, you can have *The Lavaliere Mikes of TV's Greatest Talk Show Celebrity Guests,* custom-mounted on driftwood plaques that serve as 175 dainty TV snack tables—free.

There is, of course, a surcharge and a handling fee, as well as the 25 percent duplication cost. But so amazing is this offer that you need only pay this levy once—and never again be bothered by it in your mortal life.

If for whatever reason you elect not to purchase the complimentary *Tokens of the World's Great Subway Systems,* you still profit:

The solid-gold *Venetian Gondolier's Boat Pole Toothpick* and velvet-lined presentation case are yours to treasure for as long as this incredible offer lasts.

Our *Distinctive Axe Marks of the Immortal Brazilian Rubber Planters* are in such short supply that an advance application in your name is already reserved for you. To protect your investment, *none* will be made.

REGISTERED WITH THE DEPARTMENT OF MOTOR VEHICLES

A dazzling proposition, you will agree. If you do not, your 560-piece set of *Belgium's Most Cherished Waffle Patterns,* together with your check or money order, will be buried at sea on or before midnight, April 15, 1982—the 70th anniversary, college-trained historians tell us, of the sinking of RMS *Titanic,* one of the 66 *Great Marine Disasters* commemorated in this never-yet-offered series, each individually bronzed, annealed, Martinized, and hickory-cured by skilled artisans working under the supervision of the Tulane University Board of Regents.

Please note that each comes wrapped in authentic North Atlantic seaweed, its salt content confirmed by affidavit.

Best of all, you need not order. Simply steal a new Rolls-Royce, fence it, and turn the bills into small denominations of used money (U.S. currency only, please). No salesman will call. The Polk McKinley Harding Coolidge Mint is not a U.S. Government body. This is not an offering.

The Polk McKinley Harding Coolidge Mint

P.S. If you have already begun your *Napkin Rings of the State Supreme Court Dining Rooms* collection, please disregard.

1981

FRANK CAMMUSO AND HART SEELY

OLDFINGER

YES, sir, what'll it be?
Diet Sprite with a slice of lemon.
Shaken, not stirred.
Coming up, Mr. . . .
Bond. James Bond.
And what brings you to Days Inn, Mr. Bond?
Wish I could say a holiday. Actually, I'm in town to see a lawyer. I'm being sued. Sexual harassment, of all things! Eight cases.
Good God, eight? Why, once is happenstance—
Yes, yes, I know, twice is coincidence, and eight is a bloody massacre. Say, do I know you? Never mind. Eight cases. How can you be charged for such a thing by someone named Pussy Galore? You should see the docket. Thumper v. Bond. Octopussy v. Bond. Once they

dreamed of becoming Mrs. James Bond. Now they hyphenate their names. It's *Ms.* Kissy Suzuki-Feldstein. Now they've got careers. It's *Professor* Holly Goodhead. Honey Ryder, *M.D.* God help the poor chap who unzips her gown during a physical. Back then we didn't call her Dr. No. I'm just tired of it all.

You do look fatigued.

Shouldn't I be? It doesn't matter that I saved England. Who cares that I stopped SPECTRE from developing its diamond-laser ray-gun death satellite? You'd think they'd thank me, but all they say is "He can't work with women. He has to control them." I can assure you those women never complained when we were alone. You should read their petty allegations: "During tour of stable, defendant abruptly threw plaintiff into hay, rolled onto plaintiff, and employed physical force to kiss plaintiff on mouth." Remember, now, these were exotic beauties; these were Bond girls! We're not talking about fondling Irma Bunt. You won't believe what else they're saying. That I'm a repressed homosexual! That I hate women! That I can't control my libido, that I'm a walking hormone, and that everything I say is a double-entendre about sex. Well, I find it all hard to swallow. They forced me to join AA. My travel budget is shot. They don't even let me smoke in the building. You try standing in the cold rain sixty times a day! I've been waiting two months for blood-test results. You'd think the mails were sabotaged by Russian agents—if there *were* Russian agents! But what riles me most is the secretaries. One has even become my boss. These days, on Her Majesty's Secret Service, *M* stands for Moneypenny!

You guard the Queen, Mr. Bond?

Queen? Hah. Try Fergie. God, just saying the name is like having a tarantula crawl across my chest. I was on the beach that day she dropped her top. In my Benzedrine nightmares, I used to see Pistols Scaramanga's third nipple. Now I see that odious Texan kissing her toes. I should have left with my old boss.

And where is he now?

Here in the States. He's a lobbyist for the Heritage Foundation—works with my old CIA counterpart Felix Leiter.

Not *the* Felix Leiter?

That's right. The next senator from Virginia. Actually, I haven't seen him in years. No time. I get weekends with the kids, you know. Traded the Aston Martin for a minivan. Q Branch added some extras. I haven't had to use the toddler-ejection seats, but the sleeping gas works wonders. Say, you do look familiar.

What if I remove this mustache, Mr. Bond?

Goldfinger! But I saw you squirt out that airplane window! How did you survive the fall?

Simple, 007. You should know I'd never fly without my golden parachute. I floated to the ground and adopted a new precious metal. Ever heard of Silverado Savings & Loan? Ha-ha-ha. I never needed to rob Fort Knox. The U.S. government gave it to me. But my best luck was being caught. I served a mere six months in federal prisons. Blofeld was there. Milken! Boesky! Pete Rose! We've rebuilt SPECTRE, Mr. Bond. And this time we want your help.

You're mad, Goldfinger, insane! You should know I'd never—Well, what, exactly, do you have in mind?

Talk shows. Sally. Oprah. Donahue. We're controlling the airwaves. Our topic is white-male persecution. Your assignment: To go public with your pain. To describe your suffering. To expose your oppression. It's perfect—the white male as victim. If we can turn back the clock there, we can restore everything—even the Cold War!

Damn it all, I'll do it. A toast to the old days, Goldfinger!

Sorry, but I have other customers. Another time, perhaps. Until then—good-bye, Mr. Bond.

1993

JOHN KENNEY

THE LAST CATALOGUE

Retailer J. Peterman Files for Bankruptcy
    —*The New York Times*, January 26, 1999

WHAT IS IT ABOUT A WASTEPAPER BASKET?

Hemingway used one. So did Scott Fitzgerald. The last tsar of Russia, Nicholas II, used one all the time before that nasty business at Yekaterinburg. "It" was a simple wastepaper basket, or "basque," as the French say. Perfect for throwing things away, as long as the "things" aren't too big. You can put it near a desk, or not. You can throw drafts of your novel or receipts from a store into it. The old, great ones were round, sturdy, made of strong woven wire. We found one just like it. Sort of. Ours is plastic and slightly scuffed.

Color: Prison gray.
Price: $125.

IS IT POSSIBLE TO LOVE A WATER COOLER?

Somewhere it is 1947. The country is back to work. The war is over. The "boys" are home. Everyone's wearing hats, even children. People eat lunch at Automats. Things are "Martinized." Cars are huge. Gravy is put on everything. And water coolers. Down at the end of the hall. In every office in America. Big, blue-green glass bottles holding clean, cold, crisp water. And by its side a long metal tube dispensing delicate conical paper cups so small that you have to fill one six or eight times for a satisfying drink. No matter. We've found one exactly like those old ones. Only in plastic. And empty. But you can fill it. How, we don't know. But good luck to you.

Price: $450.

A GENTLEMAN ALWAYS HAS REAMS OF PAPER HANDY.

I was talking once with the former Duchess of Windsor, Wallis Simpson, and I asked her what it was that made her fall in love with the King. She said—I'll never forget this—"Paper. He always has reams and reams of paper handy." No surprise there. Helen of Troy is said to have had the same weakness. Years ago, the really great paper was made from trees. We've found some just like that, reproduced perfectly. Packed neatly in stacks of five hundred sheets. Ten tidily wrapped packages to a box. Ideal for home or office.

Price: $85 per box.

HOW'S YOUR SHELVING?

Once, many years ago, a young man—say, a member of an Indian tribe somewhere out in the West where Indians lived—would leave his village on the eve of his sixteenth birthday and wander alone into the woods without food, water, or clothes. He was not allowed to return to the village until he had built himself some nice shelves. True story, I think. The Indian shelves were made of pine or oak or some other wood. We've searched the world for the same kind. Found a pressed polyvibrafoam reproduction that looks just like it right here in Kentucky.

Price: $230. (Brackets with metal screws: $65 each.)

DON'T JUDGE A MAN UNTIL YOU'VE WALKED A MILE ON HIS INDUSTRIAL CARPETING.

Garbo was obsessed with it. Jack Kennedy is said to have wooed Marilyn on it. Noël Coward wrote a play about it, though there's no "evidence" of that. The classic postwar industrial carpeting was thin, flimsy, and badly soiled. We've managed to locate a cache of just such a product. Yards of it, all brownish-gray, rolled up on huge spools near our loading dock.

Color: Army-mess-hall-beef brown.

Price: $18 sq. yd.

NEED ANY TONER?

I had just survived a nasty mishap when my single-engine Piper PA-28 Cherokee crashed in Egypt and I was laid up in a Cairo hospital. My nurse, a Bedouin, had wandered away into the night and was nowhere to be found. A fire broke out and I managed to drag myself to safety, only to be set upon by Israeli Mossad agents. I was interrogated for three days somewhere in the Negev, giving them only my name, my occupation, and my thoughts on the wholesale potential of a near-perfect replica of the Israeli Air Force beret. What this has to do with the fact that we have twelve gross of toner cartridges, I don't know. But we do. And they're for sale.

Color: Inky black.

Price: Make me an offer.

1999

STEVE MARTIN

THE ETHICIST

D EAR Ethicist:
Last week, while putting a man to death (I'm an executioner at a state prison), I noticed that several spectators were doing "the wave." I felt that this was wrong, so afterward I executed them, too. Then I asked their spouses to join me for dinner. Here's my question: When giving a dinner at home, is it the host's responsibility to serve healthful, low-calorie food?

When you are serving dinner to guests, remember that they are essentially a captive food audience. So, yes, it is wrong to offer only rich, fatty food. Generally, a host should ask his guests about their dietary preferences in advance—something you did not have time to do—or he should offer healthy alternatives.

My wife and I were at a restaurant on our anniversary and when I paid the bill I noticed that two numbers had been inverted, causing the total to be nine dollars more than what I owed. I went ahead and paid it. Was I wrong?

Sometimes this column gets letters so heinous that I question whether they should be published at all. The letter above was unsigned, naturally—a sure mark of a coward. I offer it here as a reminder that this must never happen again, anywhere, ever. Now let me answer the question: I have no idea.

I have recently written two biographies of the same famous politician. One is intentionally filled with disgusting lies; the other is based solely on truth. The problem is, they are identical. Which one should I publish?

The key word in your question is that the lies are "intentional." Your admitted intention makes the first biography wholly honest, whereas there might be errors in the one based on fact. Publish the one with the disgusting lies.

My wife is having an affair with a bartender, and I have been secretly filming her and her lover having intercourse. I then sell the tapes on the floor of the stock exchange. I would like her to be more wrong than I am. Who is more wrong?

She is more wrong. Her immoral actions have enabled your own immoral actions. Without her, you would not have committed your immoral act. Once I pushed a conflicted suicide off a bridge, and I felt fine afterward, because his action had engendered mine. I knew I was "less wrong" than he was, and I walked with a spring in my step for the rest of the day.

I am going to a country where it is legal and socially acceptable to eat people. I would like to eat my brother-in-law, who will be on the trip with me and is Canadian. I am from Iowa. Would this be ethical?

I am sure cannibalism is illegal in Iowa, but I'm not sure about Canada. I would suggest you stop in Canada first, take your brother-in-law to a police station and eat his foot, and see if anyone objects. If not, you can feel assured that the complete ingestion of your brother-in-law in a permissive country is perfectly ethical.

After I was banned from my nine-year-old son's Little League playing field, I began teaching him to scream at his coach. I would like to encourage him to include profanity in these adorable tirades, but, as it is banned from our household, would this make me a hypocrite?

You have created a philosophical conundrum. What happens when two contradictory moral laws seem to be in effect at the same time? Bertrand Russell said that it is possible for one law to indicate the truth or falsehood of another, even though the two contradict each other. However, it should be noted that in 1948 Russell entered into a lifelong feud over the issue with a Magic 8 Ball, which said, "Reply hazy, try again."

I am suing my neighbor's eleven-year-old daughter because she overheard my son Chester say, "I am going to blow up the school and everybody in it," and she then reported him to the principal. My son has become a pariah at school and has been kicked out of home-ec class. You should know that I have always been very strict with my son about not allowing him to take his homemade bombs outside his bedroom. Besides the lawsuit, I would like to retaliate in some other way, but my brother-in-law has told me that legal action is enough. What do you think?

You have strayed into the difficult philosophical area that Schopenhauer called "getting even." It is important that you utilize the court system to get even legally, and then, according to Schopenhauer's dictum, "give 'em a little kicker." Why not invite your neighbor over for dinner and serve him fatty, high-calorie food?

I am a sixth-grade teacher and would like to hang the Ten Commandments on the wall of my classroom. However, I am told that this is illegal. I'm not sure whether I should honor the Great God Jehovah, Lord of the Universe, or the Constitution of the United States. What should I do?

Easy. Change all the "Thou shalt not"s to "Don't"s. Cut the one about coveting your neighbor's wife (now regarded as "too little too late"). Change the word "Commandments" to "Suggestions." You now have "The Nine Suggestions." This should make everyone happy.

2001

BRUCE McCALL

UNDER THE PROVENÇAL DEADLINE

TRUDY and I had always dreamed of settling into some sunny southern European burg and turning our misadventures as hapless outsiders into publishing gold. But now, heading into this fourth sequel, even we wonder if maybe the vein hasn't been pretty much mined out. (*Editor's Note: A wonderfully felt paragraph, but the consensus here is that it's not an intro. Some of that old-time insouciance, please!*)

Pork and beans and Trudy's famous Jell-O salad again tonight. Yum! This snobby food-fetish thing—finding some exotic new recipe, hunting down the idiotically obscure ingredients, haggling with avaricious shopkeepers, fussing around in a steamy kitchen—to think how we used to dote on that whole precious foodie thing! Live and learn. That new supermarket, two towns over, is worth the drive for the frozen U.S. Parker House rolls alone. (*Editor's Note: Powerful stuff, but we worry that literal-minded readers just might think that you've become jaded, even a mite surly—"ugly American," so to speak. How about "We never stop marveling at the locals' passion for fine food" and leave it at that?*)

Talk about a backwater! The video store has three Stallones and *The Sound of Music,* dubbed. We caved last week and got satellite TV, first one in this broken-down community. Of course, the neighbors are all up in arms about the big dish. What a peevish bunch. And two-faced: Any day now they'll be coming over and begging to watch some Brazilian soccer game, right in the middle of *The Sopranos.* (*Editor's Note: Brilliantly, brutally honest. HOWEVER: I can understand how hard it must be by now to keep up the chipper, insouciant—that word again, but it fits!— tone of the first four books, yet I can't stress enough how inseparable that tone and your success have been. And, frankly, when you cashed the advance check we all thought you'd signaled your readiness to wear that lopsided, self-deprecatory grin for one more round. I don't want your millions of book-buying fans to sense that their American pal abroad isn't having a ball.*)

Trudy pointed out today that we haven't had a dinner invitation from a local in exactly one year. A-OK with us, if that's how they want to play it. We ran out of things to talk about with these yokels a lot longer than a year ago. "How soon are you returning to America?" That's the only damn question they could ever think of. (*Editor's Note: This is more of exactly what I mean. I have to delete the whole paragraph to save you from yourself. Where's the ingenuous guy with a dual-language dictionary who used to laugh off his gaffes and get all dewy-eyed just sitting in the town café?*)

The old bastard local winegrower had put a curse on our scraggly little vineyard, but until he tried running me down in the village today I hadn't quite realized the depth of his animosity. (*Editor's Note: Much better! I think if you make this funnier it can be a terrific little anecdote about your eccentric fellow-villagers. It was the way you came up smiling every time you were dumped on—the humility and the humanity—that made those first four books so great.*)

The phony little mayor and his delegation completely surrounded the house, their pitch torches blazing in the night. How ancient, Trudy and I wondered, was this local ceremony or vigil or whatever? Did they have a special name for it? Would they keep coming back, night after night? (*Editor's Note: Local color, outsider's awed perspective, Old World–New World interaction—splendid!*)

It was, the policeman assured me, just a few young bucks letting off steam. Tipping our car over the embankment—a prank, a "macho" thing, and absolutely nothing personal. He had a cousin who could come, perhaps tomorrow or the next day, and roll it back up the hill; please, some money for the long-distance call? I couldn't help thinking of the same situation back home: the endless waiting for the cops, the forms to fill out, lawyers and insurance agents and tow trucks, and certainly no mob of bystanders joking, calling out suggestions, making of it an occasion for fun. The gift for having fun—it was perhaps the best trait of this singular people, Trudy and I agreed on the long, long, long walk home. (*Editor's Note: You've regained the old stride—masterfully sketched!*)

I had finally broken the peasant's viselike grip on my wrist and handed over my gold Rolex; Trudy, meanwhile, was marveling at the sauce his wife labored over at her ancient stove, stirring with a crooked forefinger and spitting what appeared to be tobacco juice into the pan. "Could I have the recipe?" Trudy inquired. "No! Get out, American bitch!" It would clearly take time, and patience, to glean the secrets of this kitchen. "Out! Out! Out!" The salty spirit, the utter lack of ambiguity—by now we knew it was no mere empty social ritual but pure, personal hostility. We had connected, outsiders no more. (*Editor's Note: What an ending! They're gonna love this! Not to jump too far ahead, but have you given any thought to a sixth book?*)

2001

ANTHONY LANE

JEWELERS' CAESAR

One of the first scenes in the British writer Fay Weldon's new novel takes place amid "the peaches and cream décor" of the Bulgari jewelry store on Sloane Street in London. . . . Readers may not know that Bulgari, the Italian jewelry company, paid Ms. Weldon an undisclosed sum for a prominent place in the book, fittingly entitled The Bulgari Connection. —The *Times*, September 3, 2001

ANT.

Friends, Romans, Countrymen, lend me your earrings,
Within whose massy hoops, which feed the sense
That craves their argent light, there doth reside
A pearl beyond all price, except to those
Who have already oped their coffers vast
To that esteemed Bulgari, dearest merchant
I'th'affections of my noble friends,
To whom alone this unsurpassing pair
Is now available online, for nought
But fifteen hundred bucks and fifty cents.
Tush, enough of bargains; may mine eyes
Let fall their jewels on this unlucky stiff.
I come to bury Caesar, not to praise him.
The evil that men do lives after them,
The good is oft interred with their bones,
Unless these men of high estate have shown
The foresight to invest with prudence sound
Their assets, hedg'd more thickly than the glade
Wherein Dian, beloved of the moon,
Did trippingly ensnare the panting hart;
For if my Lords of Morgan and of Stanley,
And thou, fair Dean, whose arm doth yet
Embrace old Witter in its reach, do take
The proffered purse, in mutual assurance
Of thy unbounded funds, why then, we yield
The restless clay of this unhappy frame
Sans weeping, for we know our eldest sons
Will never have to do a stroke of work.
Brutus, whose liquidity I doubt,
Hath told you Caesar was ambitious;
If it were so, it was a grievous fault,
And grievously hath Caesar answer'd it,
Tho' not as grievously as those who mouth
Their wither'd answers to the empty air,
And find their cell phone orphan'd of all force,
When they forgot to charge it overnight;
Whereas the lusty Panasonick hath
A battery ingenious devised,
The Superflux T20, that endures

More deeply than the blasted oak, whose limbs,
Like to the babe's, will ne'er be sundered from
The bosom of the earth. And thus, hands-free,
Here, under leave of Brutus and the rest
(For Brutus is an honorable man,
So are they all, all honorable men),
Come I to speak in Caesar's funeral:
A heavy task, eas'd only by the ride,
More soft than any steed, that I enjoyed
Upon the sooty couch of my sedan.
Ah! Infiniti, whose very name
Doth footings to eternity vouchsafe,
With ABS as standard as the breath
Of mortals; ah, thy wheels, whose alloy trim
Outlives the jasper of the Afric soil,
Or marble of those columns orgulous
Which yet the uneyed Samson did, in love's
Despite, reduce to flinted waste! And all
For payments down of half a grand a month.

1. PLEB.
Methinks there is much reason in his sayings.

2. PLEB.
If thou consider rightly of the matter,
Caesar has had great wrong, and we are dopes.

1. PLEB.
Wherefore dopes? Fie! Rubies red as fire
Can you and I, who feast on orts and leavings,
Ill afford.

2. PLEB.
'Tis so; and yet I hear
Word that the King of Burger graciously
Doth even now his whoppers grill'd with flame
Unburthen, three for price of twain. Avaunt,
And dip our napkins in his sacred sauce.
Exeunt.

2005

IAN FRAZIER

CLASS NOTES

J ACK "Spicer" Conant tells us that when he was in Houston recently on a business trip he put in a call to Houstonite and class-
mate **Chuck Gales,** but Chuck didn't call back.

Jim Carmichael writes that he happened to see **Marc Weinstein** in
the Salt Lake City airport not long ago and pretended not to recognize
him.

Out of the blue the other day, **Bill Tolan** says, he realized he had
forgotten the names of **Marty Glimer, Todd Saalsten,** and **Andy
Camp.** A quick glance at our yearbook refreshed his memory.

Anne (Patterson) Simms asks, "What in the world was I thinking
of, going out with **Mike Stack**?" Don't know, Annie—but are you sure
his name wasn't **Russ**?

Arthur Stancik never liked **Jim McMickens,** and hasn't seen him in
years.

From rainy Seattle, **Alex Kostygian** sends a note inquiring about
"the name of the **skinny black guy** who was in our class for a few weeks
at the beginning of sophomore year and then dropped out." Sorry we
can't help you with that, Alex!

Fuadh Akmed Muhammad says he now can't believe he ever went
to school here.

Though **Geoff Emery** sat next to **Hotch Engleman** at every assembly for four years, today he can't bring his face to mind.

Mariah Miller told **Judith (Mandelbaum) Giles** and **Lacie (Stone)
McCarthy** she'd love to have lunch, but doesn't get into the city that
often. Judith, or maybe Lacie, had just returned from Italy.

Benjamin Kaplan, recently downsized, wonders why he should donate money to a school he can't afford to send his own children to. Ben,
you've got us there!

When **Marylin Cho** saw **Tony Lemire**'s name on her caller ID last
summer, she let the machine pick up. Her daughter, **Sophie** ('06), later
erased the message by mistake.

Gus Trebonyek and **Ted Antrim,** who lived just one floor apart in

Brainard junior and senior years, never met once during that entire time. Gus went on to a career in law, and Ted eventually became a consultant with a management firm. Ted moved to far-off Anchorage, Alaska. Gus, meanwhile, settled into a successful practice as a litigator in Detroit. Finally, as middle-aged men with wives and families, both Ted and Gus came back for the twenty-fifth reunion, where again their paths did not cross. They still don't know each other from Adam.

A luncheon buffet and cash bar at the Westin Hotel gave class members in the San Francisco area a chance for catching up and reminiscing last month. **Spencer Beale,** who attended, reports that nobody there looked at all familiar, and he thinks he might have been in the wrong room.

Wasn't **Kay Fortunaro** a number, with those tight sweaters she used to wear? Well, turns out that was someone else. A misidentification of a photo in our Class Register is to blame.

The secretary of **Fisk Pettibone** passes along the welcome news that "of course he remembers [us]" and will drop us a note when he has time.

MOVIN' ON: Often, mail sent to classmates returns unopened, but with a little sleuthing we discovered that **Melanie Ostroff** hasn't lived at the address we have for her since 1985! The house, a two-bedroom Colonial, belonged to her parents, who bought it in the sixties and have since died. The current residents went to public schools.

Mitchell DiMario, Sallie Stark, Chris Feinstock, Joel Bushwell, and **Will "Thirsty" Tabor** all rented cars for business travel on weekends within the past year, thus qualifying for certain perks and discounts. They may meet to talk about this next fall.

Bruce Dunlop couldn't pick **Tim Brandt, Roger Magnuson,** or **Larry Bollardi** out of a police lineup today. He hasn't a clue what became of them, or whether he might have confused them with some guys he used to hang out with at a summer camp in Maine.

Guy Forstman says he left **Rick Kelling**'s business card in the pocket of a suit that's at the cleaners, or possibly in a drawer at the office. Guy is sure it will turn up.

On the way to a sales appointment recently, **Bob Halmer** drove right by the campus. Though going fairly fast, he appeared to look much the same.

Cecily Spaeth-McCorkle makes more than any of her former teachers, according to a newsy e-mail she sent from the South of France.

Married the week after graduation, classmates **Alison Stammel** and **Randy Tinsley** divorced acrimoniously long ago. Both report that they are better off.

Wilson Yoshida very rarely thinks about anything having to do with his past, and throws away all letters or circulars bearing the school's return address. Wilson was the 2002 recipient of a "no-limits" checking account.

Lyle Kerner simply disappeared.

McMurdo Station, a lonely research outpost in Antarctica near the South Pole, has to be the last place on earth where you'd expect to run into your roommate from sophomore year. If anyone ever does, please write or call with details.

We have received the following from **Katie (Cole) Shearwood**, firing off a missive in the midst of her busy schedule:

Hello, all! As we formerly youthful (don't remind me!) friends and classmates wend our way closer to codger-hood, I can't help but sit back and wonder. What I'll be when I grow up is still up for grabs, though perhaps less so now than ever before. In '99 I left my longtime job as a group vice-president responsible for more than eight hundred people in a pre-public biotech company dealing with infrastructure issues—enjoyed the work, but felt a change was due—and founded KatieCorp, my own firm handling on-demand biosecurity auditing and database vulnerability analysis. Who would've guessed? I absolutely love it, and only regret that I didn't make the change weeks earlier. Plus, as an added bonus, I met my current spouse/partner/best friend/severest critic/terrific lover, Dennie Strube. (Dennie Shearwood, my ex, is history, though we remain good friends, and I kept his name.) I quickly had three children to add to my previous two and his four, and before we knew it all had left for colleges and graduate schools, where they are doing fine. I remain very concerned about the state of our nation and the world. As a new empty-nester, I find I have more time to think about what I, as a generation, have accomplished for right (and wrong). The success of KatieCorp, whose factories are now in Suriname and run themselves, causes me to look for new challenges. When I see my face in the mirror in the morning, peering between the lines for the hopeful young person I once was, I say, 'Katie—,' and then I tell myself various things. I've had to juggle so much (I'm with a small local circus here in Montreal) and yet I still get up every morning eager for what the day will bring, and no man I'd care to drink with would do otherwise.

Does anybody have any idea who Katie was?

2003

BRUCE McCALL

AIR POCKETS

DEAR Full-Fare Passenger Only,
This is the last edition of *Air Pockets* in its current form. With the next issue, our in-flight magazine will appear as a lively, fascinating, and informative paragraph on the back of your boarding pass. And it's yours to take with you.

As this airline's new chairman, I have the pleasure of announcing a host of other passenger-related initiatives inspired by our merger with the Fifteenth Circuit Bankruptcy Court:

- Baggage check-in and pickup at the luggage carousel are now two separate cash-pay opportunities.
- Lavatory Class, a low-cost alternative featuring aisle-free seating and almost unrestricted restroom privileges.
- SkyBump, our pioneering new in-flight fare-hike program.
- On landing, if you haven't finished sucking your complimentary throat lozenge, please stick it on the armrest for the next passenger.
- Try our groundbreaking new In-Flight Meal Insurance: pay a small fee and you won't be served an in-flight meal.
- Membership in our After-Dark Club entitles you to use of a flashlight, for reading and avoiding nasty tumbles in the aisle.

On top of all this, our fleet's recent switch to Liberian registry means no more cumbersome seat belts, life vests, or oxygen masks and an end to those boring preflight demonstrations. Jittery fliers needn't worry, though; they can join our exclusive Survivors' Club and rent a personal Air Troubleshooter Kit (fire-extinguisher deposit extra).

Spiraling senior-airline-executive compensation costs have challenged us to find ways of effectively boosting revenues while lowering service levels. By cinching the money belt even tighter, we have found that we can better serve the most important people of all: our shareholders. Accordingly, new profit requirements dictate that children under five be carried in the overhead compartments on all flights. Remember: Deposit ten dollars in nickels and set the time lock *before* bolting the compartment door shut. And, on the ground, we've simplified procedures dramatically, eliminating preflight passenger check-in service and seat selection. With our new AirSprint feature, all ticketed passengers in the departure lounge are invited to race for the jetway when the buzzer sounds. Passengers will be reassured to know that costly counter personnel have been transferred to such urgent duties as siphoning gas from cars in the parking lot to fuel our air fleet and filling in for those unionized flight mechanics who are always calling in sick.

I am also happy to report that our flight schedules are being continuously overhauled to minimize passenger convenience and to help our board members travel more easily to their favorite resorts and spas. For example, Santa Barbara has been added to our nonstop Nantucket–Hobe Sound–Nice–Columbus, Ohio route. Next spring will mark the inauguration of our nonstop annual Sioux Falls–Beijing Flight No. 0. (Return flights are in the advanced let's-consider-it stage.) And, as you know, we have just announced new partnerships with BulgAir, ParaguAir, and Air Eire, insuring that international travelers will have the opportunity to change planes three times on even the shortest routes. With the recent leasing of our hub to Wal-Mart, ours is now the world's first true "all-spoke" airline.

On a final note, immediately after your aircraft took off today the International Brotherhood of Airport Runway Pavers, Scrapers, and Stripers declared a wildcat strike against this airline, and therefore your plane cannot land at any airport in North America. Be assured that management will continue to bargain in good faith while seeking alternative landing sites in the nearest friendly country—but we cannot and will not be blackmailed by exorbitant landing fees that make a mockery of our policy of fiscal restraint. So please stow all loose articles and bring your seat to the full upright position.

2005

JONATHAN STERN

THE LONELY PLANET GUIDE TO MY APARTMENT

ORIENTATION

My Apartment's vast expanse of unfurnished space can be daunting at first, and its population of one difficult to communicate with. After going through customs, you'll see a large area with a couch to the left. Much of My Apartment's "television viewing" occurs here, as does the very occasional **making out with a girl** (see "Festivals"). To the north is the **food district,** with its colorful cereal boxes and **antojitos,** or "little whims."

WHAT TO BRING

A good rule of thumb is "If it's something you'll want, you have to bring it in yourself." This applies to water, as well as to toilet paper and English-language periodicals. Most important, come with plenty of cash, as there's sure to be someone with his hand out. In My Apartment, it's axiomatic that you have to grease the wheels to make the engine run.

WHEN TO GO

The best time to travel to My Apartment is typically after most people in their twenties are already showered and dressed and at a job. Visits on Saturdays and Sundays before 2 P.M. are highly discouraged, and can result in lengthy delays at the border (see "Getting There and Away").

LOCAL CUSTOMS

The population of My Apartment has a daily ritual of **bitching,** which occurs at the end of the workday and prior to ordering in food.

Usually, meals are taken during reruns of *Stargate Atlantis*. Don't be put off by impulsive sobbing or unprovoked rages. These traits have been passed down through generations and are part of the colorful heritage of My Apartment's people. The annual **Birthday Meltdown** (see "Festivals") is a tour de force of recrimination and self-loathing, highlighted by fanciful stilt-walkers and dancers wearing hand-sewn headdresses.

HEALTH

Rabies and hepatitis have almost completely been eradicated from My Apartment, owing to an intensive program of medication and education. However, travelers must still be wary of **sexually transmitted diseases.** While abstinence is the only certain preventative, it is strenuously not endorsed by the My Apartment government. Condoms and antibiotics are available on most evenings (see "Medical Services").

SOCIETY & CULTURE

The inhabitants of My Apartment tend to be insecure and combative. This is likely the result of living under the thumb of a series of **illegitimate dictators** (see "History") that have dominated the citizens in recent years. Since the Breakup of 2004 and the ensuing electoral reforms, the situation has become more democratic.

WOMEN TRAVELERS

Solo female travelers are often subjected to excessive unwanted male attention. Normally, these men only want to talk to you, but their entreaties can quickly become tiresome. Don't be afraid to be rude. Even a mild polite response can be perceived as an expression of interest. The best approach is to avoid eye contact, always wear a bra, and talk incessantly about your "fiancé, Neil."

DANGERS & ANNOYANCES

The ongoing economic recession has led to a large increase in **petty crime.** For the most part, this is limited to the "borrowing" of personal items and the occasional accidental disappearance of the neighbor's newspaper. However, the U.S. Department of State has issued a warning about several common cons—such as the "I'm out of small bills" scam, typically perpetrated when the delivery guy arrives.

VOLUNTEER ORGANIZATIONS

Various international agencies can place volunteers in projects working on areas such as job training, doing my laundry, election monitoring, developing opportunities for young women, running to the deli for me, and therapeutic massage.

THINGS TO SEE & DO

A ten-foot walk to the non-working fireplace brings musically inclined visitors to the popular **collection of novelty records,** which includes *Leonard Nimoy Sings.* The north-facing section of My Apartment is divided into two districts. In the lively Bedroom District, the excellent **drawer of snapshots of ex-girlfriends naked** is a good way to gain a deeper understanding of the history of the people, and is open for guided tours on most Saturdays between 2 A.M. and 3 A.M. The Western Quarter is home to the **bathtub with one working spa jet,** in which the recreation commissioner of My Apartment plans to hold an **international Jell-O wrestling tournament** in the spring of 2007.

PLACES TO EAT

Tourists often flock to the **salvaged wooden telephone-cable spool** in front of the TV as a convenient dining spot. More adventurous eaters might try **standing over the sink,** as the locals do. If you're willing to venture off the beaten track, there's **balancing your plate on the arm of the couch** or **using the toilet lid as a makeshift table.**

NIGHT LIFE

The music on offer tends toward late-seventies disco recordings, but they are sometimes embellished with impromptu live vocal performances. There was once a cockfight in My Apartment, though it was unplanned and will likely never happen again (see "Law Enforcement").

SPORTS & OUTDOOR ACTIVITIES

The **air-hockey table** probably still works.

EXCURSIONS

A short trip in almost any direction will bring travelers to one of many unique **Starbucks** outlets. Or try one of the nightly walking tours to the sidewalk in front of the brownstone across the street to watch **that red-head** getting out of the shower with her curtains open. And tourists are often sent around the corner to visit the **ATM machine** in order to stock up for the rigorous financial demands of a trip to My Apartment.

MULE RENTAL

Mules can be rented by the hour or the day and are situated near the **main closet.** Prices vary with the season and it's best to reserve in advance, since My Apartment's stable of twenty-six mules books up fast. They may not be the quickest form of transportation, but they provide a wonderful way to see My Apartment up close.

WILDLIFE

The dog's name is **Sadie.** Don't touch her.

2006

GEORGE SAUNDERS

ASK THE OPTIMIST!

DEAR Optimist:
     My husband, who knows very well that I love nothing more than wearing bonnets, recently bought a convertible. He's always doing "passive-aggressive" things like this. Like once, after I had all my teeth pulled, he bought a big box of Cracker Jacks. Another time, when I had

very serious burns over ninety percent of my body, he tricked me into getting a hot-oil massage, then tripped me so that I fell into a vat of hydrochloric acid. I've long since forgiven him for these "misunderstandings," but, tell me, is there a way I can be "optimistic" about this "bonnet" situation?

Mad Due to No More Bonnets
Cleveland, Ohio

Dear Mad:

You can still wear bonnets while riding in a convertible! You will just need to have more of them to start with! What I recommend? Buy a large number of bonnets, place them in the car, begin driving! When one blows off, put on another from your enormous stockpile! And just think of all the happiness you will create in your wake, as people who cannot afford bonnets scurry after your convertible, collecting your discards! Super!

Dear Optimist:

Upon returning from vacation, we found our home totally full of lemons. I mean totally. The cat even had one in its mouth. What do you recommend?

Sourpuss
Seattle, Wash.

Dear Sourpuss:

That is a tough one! What I recommend is, when life gives you lemons: (1) Buy a bunch of Hefty bags! (2) Fill the Hefty bags with lemons! (3) Lug the bags to the curb! And (4) Call a certified waste-disposal contractor to haul away the pile of lemons now rotting in the sun! Before long, like magic, your home will be lemon-free—and you can celebrate by going out and having something cold to drink! And don't forget to give Kitty a jaw massage!

Dear Optimist:

My wife is a terrific artist—except when it comes to me! Whenever she paints me, my legs are half the length of my torso, my face looks like the face of a frog, my feet are splayed outward unattractively like the feet of some hideous reptile, and I have a smug, pinched look on my face. Anyone else she paints, they look exactly like themselves. I pretend not to notice, but recently, at my wife's one-woman show, I could tell our friends were discussing this, and I felt embarrassed. How might I have taken this in a more optimistic way?

Hurt But Hopeful
Topeka, Kans.

Dear Hurt But:

After receiving your letter, I sent a private investigator to your home with a camera! And guess what! Have you looked in the mirror lately? Your legs are squat, you have the face of a frog, your feet are reptilian, and you do look smug and pinched! So not to worry! Your wife is a terrific artist!

Dear Optimist:

When I go to the zoo, I feel so sad. All those imprisoned animals sitting in their own feces. What do you suggest?

Animal Lover
Pasadena, Calif.

Dear Animal:

What I suggest is, stop going to the zoo! But, should you find yourself tricked into going to a zoo, think about it as follows: All those animals, coated with their own poop, pacing dry grassless trenches in their "enclosures," have natural predators, and might very well be dead if they were still in the wild! So ask yourself: Would I rather be dead, or coated in my own poop, repetitively pacing a dry grassless trench? I certainly know what *my* answer would be!

Dear Optimist:

A few years ago, I inadvertently declared war on the wrong country. Also, I perhaps responded a little slowly to a terrible natural disaster. Also, those of my friends who are not under indictment seem to be deserting me. Also, the organization of which I am in charge is all of a sudden facing a huge crushing debt. And I still have almost two years left in my job. Advice?

In Somewhat Over My Head
Washington, D.C.

Dear In Somewhat:

Stay the course! Admit to nothing! Disparage your enemies! Perhaps declare another war? Do you have any openings in your Cabinet?

Sounds like you could use a little Optimism! What would you pay? Have your people call my people!

Dear Optimist:

Recently, my wife left me for another man. Not only that, the other man was bigger, better-looking, and richer than me, and—at least according to my wife—better-endowed and with a nicer singing voice and less back hair. To tell the truth, I am feeling somewhat "pessimistic" about this situation. Advice?

> *Depressed Because My Penis Is Smaller,*
> *Relative to That of My Wife's New and*
> *More Handsome Lover*
> *Brighton, Mich.*

Dear Small-Penis:

Why not try to look on the bright side! At least he is not more articulate than you—

Dear Optimist:

Oh, yes, he is. I forgot that.

Dear Small-Penis:

No worries! I believe in you! She is clearly not the right woman for you, and by accepting this—

Dear Optimist:

Actually, Ralph speaks five languages and is just finishing up a translation from the Sanskrit of an ancient text on social deportment. And Judy is the right woman for me, I just know it. I could never love anyone else. I'd rather die.

Dear Small-Penis:

Wow, no wonder she left you! You are so negative! Also somewhat pigheaded!

Dear Optimist:

I know, right? That's exactly what Judy always said. Oh, what's the point of living anymore? I'm just going to take these fast-acting suicide pills and . . . and . . . and . . .

Dear Small-Penis:

You know, Small-Penis, you don't seem to understand Optimism at all! What is the essential quality of the Optimist? He is non-Pessimistic! What is the essential quality of the Pessimist? He thinks too much, then gets all depressed and paralyzed! Like you, Small-Penis! Me, I prefer to think as little as possible and stay peppy! Peppy and active! If something is bothering me, I think of something else! If someone tells me some bad news? I ignore it! Like, I knew this one guy, very Optimistic, who was being eaten by a shark and did not even scream but just kept shouting, "It's all for the best!" Now, that was an Optimist! In the end, he was just as dead, but he hadn't brought everybody else down! What a great guy! I really miss him! No, I don't! It's all good! I don't miss Todd at all, even though we were briefly lovers and I've never felt so completely inhabited, if you know what I mean! So *valued*! But no biggie! I'm certainly not going to start moping about it! Right? Right, Small-Penis? Hello! Oh, well, I guess he's off moping somewhere! Next letter!

Dear Optimist:

I am an emaciated single mother living in a vast famine-affected region with my four starving children. Rebels frequently sweep down from the hills with automatic weapons and kill many of us and violate and abuse the others. All our men are dead or have been driven away, and there is no food or fresh water to be had. I would be very appreciative of any advice you might be able to offer us.

Not Altogether Hopeful
Africa

Dear Hopeful:

Thanks so much for writing! Perhaps it would be of some consolation for me to tell you what a vast minority you are in! There are, relative to the world's population, very few people "in your boat"! Most of the rest of us are not starving or in danger, and, in fact, many of us do not even know that *you* are starving and in danger, and are just out here leading rich, rewarding lives, having all kinds of fun! Does that help? I hope so! And remember—trouble can't last forever! Soon, I expect, your difficulties will be over!

Dear Optimist:

Recently, my father-in-law backed over me with his car. When I complained, he backed over me again. When, from beneath the wheels of his car, I complained again, he got out of his vehicle, poured molten metal over me, hauled me to a public park, mounted me on a pedestal, and placed at my feet a plaque reading "SLOTH." What gives? I am trying to think about this incident in an optimistic way but am having some difficulties, as my chin itches and I am unable to reach it with my bronze-encrusted arms.

> *I Love Parks but, Hey, This Is Ridiculous*
> *Fort Myers, Fla.*

Dear Loves Parks:

Oh, really? Bronze-encrusted arms? Then how did you write that letter?

Dear Optimist:

Uh, one of my arms is not totally bronze-encrusted?

Dear Loves Parks:

Then why don't you scratch your chin with that arm?

Dear Optimist:

Uh, because I am holding my pen in that hand? And if I drop the pen I will not be able to bend to retrieve it, because my torso is totally encrusted in bronze? And the pigeons will, like, run away with the pen? Hey, I've got an idea. Why don't you suggest I *kill* myself? With fast-acting suicide pills, after first calling me "negative" and "pigheaded"?

Dear Loves Parks:

Is that you, Small-Penis? I thought the handwriting was similar! Were you faking it just now when you said you were taking those pills? And you're not really encrusted in bronze at all, are you?

Dear Optimist:

That's right, genius, I am *not* dead and *not* encrusted in bronze and am *not* giving up and in fact am going to go and try to get Judy on the phone right now. If she'll just *listen* to me, then I know she'll—

Dear Optimist:

I am a man trapped in a turkey's body. I have dim memories of my life as a human. But then I look down, and there are my wattles! Sometimes when it rains I find myself gazing up at the sky, mouth open, gullet slowly filling with rain. I'm really starting to feel bad about myself. Can you help?

Chagrined Gobbler
A Farm Near Albany

Dear Gobbler:

Of course I can help! Come to my house for some private counseling! Does Christmas work for you? Wait for me at the "waiting spot," a tree stump with an axe leaning against it! And do you happen to know a human trapped in a pig's body? I can also counsel him! Until then, I suggest eating as much as you can, preferably some high-quality corn! And keep your chin up, or your wattles up, or whatever!

Dear Optimist:

I was buried alive during the Eighteenth Century when I experienced a fit of narcolepsy and my family mistook my deep sleep for Death. In the two hundred and fifty-six years since, trapped in my moldering Body by the terrifying circumstances of my departure from this Life, my Soul has longed for freedom. And yet everyone who once would have prayed for me has long since gone on to Eternity, and I, desperately lonely, am haunted by the scuffing feet of dog-walkers and the skittering of leaves in Autumn, doomed to exist in this semi-death forever, in a perpetual state of mild Terror, until Time itself shall end and our Creator returns to redeem us all. Any thoughts about this?

Longing for the Sweet Peace of True
Death
Plymouth, Mass.

Dear Longing:

Do you mind some "tough love"? Did they even have that in your time? Have you honestly tried your best to get out of this situation? Have you, for example, clawed frantically at the lid of your coffin for sixty or seventy years, after which have you tried literally digging your way to the surface even though your mouth was filling with dirt and you were nearly overcome with a terrible feeling of claustrophobia? Or have you just been lying there feeling sorry for yourself all this—

Dear Optimist:

No, no, I think you misunderstand my situation. I can't move. My mind is active, I can fear and regret and dream, but I can't move at all.

I guess I thought when I said "dead" I assumed you'd understand that this meant—

Dear Longing:

No sense trying to blame me! I am not the bonehead who went through life with undiagnosed narcolepsy! I didn't mistake your sleep for death! I wasn't even alive in the eighteen-hundreds or whenever! You know what? Just lie there awhile and think about what you really want!

Dear Optimist:

I started out life as an angel, then, through a misunderstanding, became a "fallen angel," and am now Lucifer, Master of Evil. Although I know I should be grateful—I love working for myself, and I'm one of the two most powerful beings in the universe—I sometimes feel a certain absence, as if there's some essential quality I'm lacking. I've heard people, as I make my rounds, speak of something called "goodness." Usually when I hear someone use this word I get frustrated and immediately tempt them into doing something horrific—but lately, somehow, this isn't enough. Thoughts?

Satan
Hell

Dear Satan:

Clearly you are lonely! Here's what I recommend: Go visit Longing for the Sweet Peace of True Death, in his grave, in Plymouth, Massachusetts. He is lonely! You are lonely! A real win-win! Just reside with him there in his coffin awhile! I think he'll love it! Or maybe not! Maybe it will kind of scare him, to have Satan suddenly arrive in his cramped little coffin! Oh, I doubt it! Whatever! It's all good!

Dear Optimist:

I am feeling so great! I have totally internalized all the wonderful things you've taught over the years, via your column! I am just so excited!

Thrilled to Be Alive, Never Felt Better
Chicago, Ill.

Dear Thrilled:

Super! Did you have a question?

Dear Optimist:

No, not really!

Dear Thrilled:

Then what the heck! What is the name of this column? Is it "Make a Statement to the Optimist"? Is it "Come Up in Here and Act All Like Mr. Perfect"? Is it—

Dear Optimist:

No problem! I totally respect what you're saying! Many apologies and I hope you have a great day! You know, actually, I am going to go sit quietly somewhere and think about what I've done, so that if I did in fact do something wrong I won't, in the future, repeat my mistake!

Thrilled

Dear Thrilled:

Jeez, what an asshole! Well, that's about all the space we have, so—

Dear Optimist:

Damn it! Judy would not take my call. This is the worst day of my life.

Small-Penis

Dear Small-Penis:

We are done here! The column is finished for the day! Do I come to your work and mess with you?!

Dear Optimist:

I don't work! And thanks very much for rubbing *that* in. You know what? I've had it with you. I'm coming straight over to your house right now. Got it? How do you feel about that, smart guy?

Small-Penis

Dear Anyone:

Please call the police! I am sure it will be fine! Oh, God, he's here! He's breaking down the door! Please call the police! Help! Help!

Dear Optimist:

How do you like that? How does that feel, Mr. Superior?

Dear Everyone:
Ouch! Ouch! Oh, God!

Dear Everyone!
It is finished. The Optimist is no more. We are, at last, free of his arrogance. And, Judy, if you're out there: Size isn't everything. And articulate isn't everything, and tall isn't everything, and also, sweetie, I just had my back waxed. Give me some hope! I await your letter, darling!

Small-Penis, aka Steve

Dear Small-Penis, aka Steve:
Hi, Steve! How's it going? I'll be replacing the Optimist here at the column! Just call me the New Optimist! Super! Here's what I recommend: Turn yourself in! There will be good food in jail, and time for contemplation, and, who knows, you may even, eventually, have a great spiritual revelation and pull your head out of your ass! Isn't that better than living on the lam? Judy is not taking you back, no way, and I should know! Judy is staying with me forever!

Thrilled to Be Alive, Never Felt Better, aka the New Optimist

Dear Ralph, You Bastard!
Is that really you? You scum, you wife-stealer! Look what you've reduced me to! I am now a murderer! I murdered the Optimist! My God, the look on his face—even at the end, he was trying so hard to smile pleasantly!

Steve

Dear Steve-o:
Yup, you schmuck, it is me, Ralph! And guess what! I followed you over here! I am right outside! You'll never harass poor Judy again! I have with me a letter I've written, which I will plant on your corpse, so all the world will believe that, after killing the Optimist, you did away with yourself in a bizarre murder-suicide! You are a fool and the Optimist was a fool! If one really wants to be an Optimist, there is only one way: Win! Always win! Be superior and never lose! Slaughter your enemies and live on, so that you and only you are left to write the history books! Goodbye, Steve! Ralph rules! Here I come! Oh, you look so scared! There! I have done it! Steve is no more. I am going right home to make

Optimistic love to the beautiful Judy! And from now on this column is mine! No more working at the oil-change place while trying to write my Sanskrit book on weekends!

> *Thrilled, aka Ralph, aka the New Optimist*

Dear New Optimist:

I recently left my husband of ten years for a new man. Although I feel I basically did the right thing (my ex was small-penised and hairy-backed and not very articulate), I have to admit I feel a little guilty. What do you suggest?

> *Completely Happy, Almost*

Dear Almost Happy:

Don't worry about it! It's all good! What I'd recommend is, as soon as your new man gets home from wherever he is right now, make love to him more ferociously than you've ever made love to anyone in your life! Show your adoration by doing things to him you never even contemplated doing with that boring loser Steve!

Dear New Optimist:

Okay! Will do! As a matter of fact, he just rang the bell! Gotta go!

> *Completely Happy, All the Way*

P.S.: Say, how did you know my ex-husband's name was Steve?

Dear All the Way:

Don't be so negative! That's what got you in trouble in the first place, Judy! You think too much! Just be quiet and do what I say! Follow my lead! Hail Optimism! Long live the New Optimist! Open the door, Judy, open the door, so we can begin our beautiful new life together! And don't even think of back-talking me, Missy!

Dear New Optimist:

Okay! Super! Thanks for the advice! Come in, Ralph! God, you look flushed, and, honey, gosh, why are you holding that bludgeon?

> *Completely Happy, All the Way, Although*
> *Maybe Just a Little Bit Scared Now,*
> *aka Judy*

Dear Judy:

There will be no problems whatsoever, Judy, if you simply acknowl-edge my absolute supremacy in a way that continually pleases me! And this is not a bludgeon! It is a bouquet of flowers! Right? Right, Judy? Well, that's all the space we have! Not that I'm complaining! See you next time! Never doubt yourself, and, if you start feeling down, casti-gate yourself, and, if others try to put the slightest trace of doubt in your mind, rebuke them, and, should your rebuke not alter their speech, you may bring harm to them, even unto death, and, after they have died, feel free to arrange their rictus-stiffening mouths into happy hopeful smiles! And that's an order! Believe me, you'll be doing them a favor! Just kidding! You are special!

The New Optimist

2006

TESTAMENTS AND DECLARATIONS

THE DIARY OF A LADY

DURING DAYS OF PANIC, FRENZY, AND WORLD CHANGE

Monday. Breakfast tray about eleven; didn't want it. The champagne at the Amorys' last night was *too* revolting, but what *can* you do? You can't stay until five o'clock on just *nothing.* They had those *divine* Hungarian musicians in the green coats, and Stewie Hunter took off one of his shoes and led them with it, and it *couldn't* have been funnier. He is *the* wittiest number in the *entire* world; he *couldn't* be more perfect. Ollie Martin brought me home and we both fell asleep in the car—*too* screaming. Miss Rose came about noon to do my nails, simply *covered* with *the* most divine gossip. The Morrises are going to separate *any minute,* and Freddie Warren *definitely* has ulcers, and Gertie Leonard simply *won't* let Bill Crawford out of her sight even with Jack Leonard *right there in the room,* and it's all *true* about Sheila Phillips and Babs Deering. It *couldn't* have been more thrilling. Miss Rose is *too* marvelous; I really think that a lot of times people like that are a lot more intelligent than a lot of people. Didn't notice until after she had gone that the damn fool had put that *revolting* tangerine-colored polish on my nails; *couldn't* have been more furious. Started to read a book, but too nervous. Called up and found I could get two tickets for the opening of *Run like a Rabbit* to-night for forty-eight dollars. Told them they had *the* nerve of the world, but what *can* you do? Think Joe said he was dining out, so telephoned some *divine* numbers to get someone to go to the theatre with me, but they were all tied up. Finally got Ollie Martin. He *couldn't* have more poise, and what do *I* care if he *is* one? *Can't* decide whether to wear the green crêpe or the red wool. Every time I look at my fingernails, I could *spit. Damn* Miss Rose.

Tuesday. Joe came barging in my room this morning at *practically nine o'clock. Couldn't* have been more furious. Started to fight, but *too* dead.

Know he said he wouldn't be home to dinner. Absolutely *cold* all day; couldn't *move*. Last night *couldn't* have been more perfect. Ollie and I dined at Thirty-eight East, absolutely *poisonous* food, and not one *living* soul that you'd be seen *dead* with, and *Run like a Rabbit* was *the* world's worst. Took Ollie up to the Barlows' party and it *couldn't* have been more attractive—*couldn't* have been more people absolutely *stinking*. They had those Hungarians in the green coats, and Stewie Hunter was leading them with a fork—everybody simply *died*. He had *yards* of green toilet paper hung around his neck like a lei; he *couldn't* have been in better form. Met a *really new number,* very tall, *too* marvelous, and one of those people that you can *really* talk to them. I told him sometimes I get so *nauseated* I could *yip,* and I felt I absolutely *had* to do something like write or paint. He said why didn't I write or paint. Came home alone; Ollie passed out *stiff.* Called up the new number three times to-day to get him to come to dinner and go with me to the opening of *Never Say Good Morning,* but first he was out and then he was all tied up with his mother. Finally got Ollie Martin. Tried to read a book, but couldn't sit still. *Can't* decide whether to wear the red lace or the pink with the feathers. Feel *too* exhausted, but what *can* you do?

Wednesday. The most terrible thing happened *just this minute.* Broke one of my fingernails *right off short.* Absolutely *the* most horrible thing I ever had happen to me in my life. Called up Miss Rose to come over and shape it for me, but she was out for the day. I do have *the* worst luck in the *entire* world. Now I'll have to go around like this all day and all night, but what *can* you do? *Damn* Miss Rose. Last night *too* hectic. *Never Say Good Morning too* foul, *never* saw more poisonous clothes on the stage. Took Ollie up to the Ballards' party; *couldn't* have been better. They had those Hungarians in the green coats and Stewie Hunter was leading them with a freesia—*too* perfect. He had on Peggy Cooper's ermine coat and Phyllis Minton's silver turban; *simply* unbelievable. Asked simply *sheaves* of *divine* people to come here Friday night; got the address of those Hungarians in the green coats from Betty Ballard. She says just engage them until four, and then whoever gives them another three hundred dollars, they'll stay till five. *Couldn't* be cheaper. Started home with Ollie, but had to drop him at his house; he *couldn't* have been sicker. Called up the new number to-day to get him to come to dinner and go to the opening of *Everybody Up* with me to-night, but he was tied up. Joe's going to be out; he didn't *condescend* to say *where, of course.* Started to read the papers, but nothing in them except that

Mona Wheatley is in Reno charging *intolerable cruelty*. Called up Jim Wheatley to see if he had anything to do to-night, but he was tied up. Finally got Ollie Martin. *Can't* decide whether to wear the white satin or the black chiffon or the yellow pebble crêpe. Simply *wrecked* to the *core* about my fingernail. Can't *bear* it. *Never* knew *anybody* to have such *unbelievable* things happen to them.

Thursday. Simply *collapsing* on my *feet*. Last night *too* marvelous. *Everybody Up too* divine, *couldn't* be filthier, and the new number was there, *too* celestial, only he didn't see me. He was with Florence Keeler in that *loathsome* gold Schiaparelli model of hers that every *shopgirl* has had since *God* knows. He must be out of his *mind;* she wouldn't *look* at a man. Took Ollie to the Watsons' party; *couldn't* have been more thrilling. Everybody simply *blind*. They had those Hungarians in the green coats and Stewie Hunter was leading them with a lamp, and after the lamp got broken, he and Tommy Thomas did adagio dances—*too* wonderful. Somebody told me Tommy's doctor told him he had to ab-solutely get *right out of town,* he has *the* world's worst stomach, but you'd *never* know it. Came home alone, couldn't find Ollie *anywhere*. Miss Rose came at noon to shape my nail, *couldn't* have been more fascinating. Sylvia Eaton can't go *out the door* unless she's had a hypodermic, and Doris Mason *knows every single word* about Douggie Mason and that girl up in Harlem, and Evelyn North won't be *induced* to keep away from those three acrobats, and they don't *dare* tell Stuyvie Raymond *what* he's got the matter with him. *Never* knew anyone that had a more simply *fascinating* life than Miss Rose. Made her take that *vile* tangerine polish off my nails and put on dark red. Didn't notice until after she had gone that it's practically *black* in electric light; *couldn't* be in a worse state. *Damn* Miss Rose. Joe left a note saying he was going to dine out, so telephoned the new number to get him to come to dinner and go with me to that new movie to-night, but he didn't answer. Sent him three telegrams to *absolutely surely* come to-morrow night. Finally got Ollie Martin for to-night. Looked at the papers, but nothing in them except that the Harry Motts are throwing a tea with Hungarian music on Sunday. Think will ask the new number to go to it with me; they must have meant to invite me. Began to read a book, but too exhausted. *Can't* decide whether to wear the new blue with the white jacket or save it till to-morrow night and wear the ivory moire. Simply *heartsick* every time I think of my nails. *Couldn't* be wilder. Could *kill* Miss Rose, but what *can* you do?

Friday. Absolutely *sunk; couldn't* be worse. Last night *too* divine, movie *simply* deadly. Took Ollie to the Kingslands' party, *too* unbelievable, everybody absolutely *rolling*. They had those Hungarians in the green coats, but Stewie Hunter wasn't there. He's got a *complete* nervous breakdown. Worried *sick* for fear he won't be well by to-night; will absolutely *never* forgive him if he doesn't come. Started home with Ollie, but dropped him at his house because he *couldn't* stop crying. Joe left word with the butler he's going to the country this afternoon for the week-end; *of course* he wouldn't *stoop* to say *what* country. Called up *streams* of marvelous numbers to get someone to come dine and go with me to the opening of *White Man's Folly*, and then go somewhere after to dance for a while; can't *bear* to be the first one there at your own party. Everybody was tied up. Finally got Ollie Martin. *Couldn't* feel more depressed; never should have gone *anywhere near* champagne and Scotch together. Started to read a book, but too restless. Called up Anne Lyman to ask about the new baby and *couldn't* remember if it was a boy or girl—*must* get a secretary *next week*. Anne *couldn't* have been more of a help; she said she didn't know whether to name it Patricia or Gloria, so then of course I knew it was a girl *right away*. Suggested calling it Barbara; forgot she already had one. Absolutely *walking the floor* like a *panther* all day. Could *spit* about Stewie Hunter. Can't *face* deciding whether to wear the blue with the white jacket or the purple with the beige roses. Every time I look at those *revolting* black nails, I want to absolutely *yip*. I really have *the* most horrible things happen to me of anybody in the *entire* world. *Damn* Miss Rose.

1933

JAME*S* THURBER

THE *S*ECRET LIFE OF JAME*S* THURBER

I HAVE only dipped here and there into Salvador Dali's *The Secret Life of Salvador Dali* (with paintings by Salvador Dali and photographs of Salvador Dali), because anyone afflicted with what my grandmother's sister Abigail called "the permanent jumps" should do no more than skitter through such an autobiography, particularly in these melancholy times.

One does not have to skitter far before one comes upon some vignette which gives the full shape and flavor of the book: the youthful dreamer of dreams biting a sick bat or kissing a dead horse, the slender stripling going into man's estate with the high hope and fond desire of one day eating a live but roasted turkey, the sighing lover covering himself with goat dung and aspic that he might give off the true and noble odor of the ram. In my flying trip through Dali I caught other glimpses of the great man: Salvador adoring a seed ball fallen from a plane tree, Salvador kicking a tiny playmate off a bridge, Salvador caressing a crutch, Salvador breaking the old family doctor's glasses with a leather-thonged mattress-beater. There would appear to be only two things in the world that revolt him (and I don't mean a long-dead hedgehog). He is squeamish about skeletons and grasshoppers. Oh, well, we all have our idiosyncrasies.

Señor Dali's memoirs have set me to thinking. I find myself muttering as I shave, and on two occasions I have swung my crutch at a little neighbor girl on my way to the post office. Señor Dali's book sells for six dollars. My own published personal history (Harper & Bros., 1933) sold for $1.75. At the time I complained briefly about this unusual figure, principally on the ground that it represented only fifty cents more than the price asked for a book called *The Adventures of Horace the Hedgehog*, published the same month. The publishers explained that the price was a closely approximated vertical, prefigured on the basis of probable ceiling, which in turn was arrived at by taking into consideration the effect on diminishing returns of the horizontal factor.

In those days all heads of business firms adopted a guarded kind of double talk, commonly expressed in low, muffled tones, because nobody knew what was going to happen and nobody understood what had. Big business had been frightened by a sequence of economic phenomena which had clearly demonstrated that our civilization was in greater danger of being turned off than of gradually crumbling away. The upshot of it all was that I accepted the price of $1.75. In so doing, I accepted the state of the world as a proper standard by which the price of books should be fixed. And now, with the world in ten times as serious a condition as it was in 1933, Dali's publishers set a price of six dollars on his life story. This brings me to the inescapable conclusion that the price-fixing principle, in the field of literature, is not global but personal. The trouble, quite simply, is that I told too much about what went on in the house I lived in and not enough about what went on inside myself.

LET me be the first to admit that the naked truth about me is to the naked truth about Salvador Dali as an old ukulele in the attic is to a piano in a tree, and I mean a piano with breasts. Señor Dali has the jump on me from the beginning. He remembers and describes in detail what it was like in the womb. My own earliest memory is of accompanying my father to a polling booth in Columbus, Ohio, where he voted for William McKinley.

It was a drab and somewhat battered tin shed set on wheels, and it was filled with guffawing men and cigar smoke; all in all, as far removed from the paradisiacal placenta of Salvador Dali's first recollection as could well be imagined. A fat, jolly man dandled me on his knee and said that I would soon be old enough to vote against William Jennings Bryan. I thought he meant that I could push a folded piece of paper into the slot of the padlocked box as soon as my father was finished. When this turned out not to be true, I had to be carried out of the place kicking and screaming. In my struggles I knocked my father's derby off several times. The derby was not a monstrously exciting love object to me, as practically everything Salvador encountered was to him, and I doubt, if I had that day to live over again, that I could bring myself, even in the light of exotic dedication as I now know it, to conceive an intense and perverse affection for the derby. It remains obstinately in my memory as a rather funny hat, a little too large in the crown, which gave my father the appearance of a tired, sensitive gentleman who had been persuaded against his will to take part in a game of charades.

We lived on Champion Avenue at the time, and the voting booth was on Mound Street. As I set down these names, I begin to perceive an essential and important difference between the infant Salvador and the infant me. This difference can be stated in terms of environment. Salvador was brought up in Spain, a country colored by the legends of Hannibal, El Greco, and Cervantes. I was brought up in Ohio, a region steeped in the tradition of Coxey's Army, the Anti-Saloon League, and William Howard Taft. It is only natural that the weather in little Salvador's soul should have been stirred by stranger winds and enveloped in more fantastic mists than the weather in my own soul. But enough of mewling apology for my lackluster early years. Let us get back to my secret life, such as it was, stopping just long enough to have another brief look at Señor Dali on our way.

SALVADOR Dali's mind goes back to a childhood half imagined and half real, in which the edges of actuality were sometimes less sharp than the edges of dream. He seems somehow to have got the idea that this sets him off from Harry Spencer, Charlie Doakes, I. Feinberg, J. J. McNaboe, Willie Faulkner, Herbie Hoover, and me. What Salvie had that the rest of us kids didn't was the perfect scenery, characters, and costumes for his desperate little rebellion against the clean, the conventional, and the comfortable. He put perfume on his hair (which would have cost him his life in, say, Bayonne, N.J., or Youngstown, Ohio), he owned a lizard with two tails, he wore silver buttons on his shoes, and he knew, or imagined he knew, little girls named Galuchka and Dullita. Thus he was born halfway along the road to paranoia, the soft Poictesme of his prayers, the melting Oz of his oblations, the capital, to put it so that you can see what I am trying to say, of his heart's desire. Or so, anyway, it must seem to a native of Columbus, Ohio, who, as a youngster, bought his twelve-dollar suits at the F. & R. Lazarus Co., had his hair washed out with Ivory soap, owned a bull terrier with only one tail, and played (nicely and a bit diffidently) with little girls named Irma and Betty and Ruby.

Another advantage that the young Dali had over me, from the standpoint of impetus toward paranoia, lay in the nature of the adults who peopled his real world. There was, in Dali's home town of Figueras, a family of artists named Pitchot (musicians, painters, and poets), all of whom adored the ground that the *enfant terrible* walked on. If one of them came upon him throwing himself from a high rock—a favorite relaxation of our hero—or hanging by his feet with his head immersed in a pail of water, the wild news was spread about the town that greatness and genius had come to Figueras. There was a woman who put on a look of maternal interest when Salvador threw rocks at her. The mayor of the town fell dead one day at the boy's feet. A doctor in the community (not the one he had horsewhipped) was seized of a fit and attempted to beat him up. (The contention that the doctor was out of his senses at the time of the assault is Dali's, not mine.)

The adults around me when I was in short pants were neither so glamorous nor so attentive. They consisted mainly of eleven maternal great-aunts, all Methodists, who were staunch believers in physic, mustard plasters, and Scripture, and it was part of their dogma that artistic tendencies should be treated in the same way as hiccups or hysterics. None of them was an artist, unless you can count Aunt Lou, who wrote sixteen-stress verse, with hit-and-miss rhymes, in celebration of people's birthdays or on the occasion of great national disaster. It never occurred to me to bite a bat in my aunts' presence or to throw stones at them. There was one escape, though: my secret world of idiom.

Two years ago my wife and I, looking for a house to buy, called on a firm of real estate agents in New Milford. One of the members of the firm, scrabbling through a metal box containing many keys, looked up to say, "The key to the Roxbury house isn't here." His partner replied, "It's a common lock. A skeleton will let you in." I was suddenly once again five years old, with wide eyes and open mouth. I pictured the Roxbury house as I would have pictured it as a small boy, a house of such dark and nameless horrors as have never crossed the mind of our little bat-biter.

It was of sentences like that, nonchalantly tossed off by real estate dealers, great-aunts, clergymen, and other such prosaic persons, that the enchanted private world of my early boyhood was made. In this world, businessmen who phoned their wives to say that they were tied up at the office sat roped to their swivel chairs, and probably gagged, unable to move or speak, except somehow, miraculously, to telephone; hundreds of thousands of businessmen tied to their chairs in hundreds of thousands of offices in every city of my fantastic cosmos. An especially fine note about the binding of all the businessmen in all the cities was that whoever did it always did it around five o'clock in the afternoon.

Then there was the man who left town under a cloud. Sometimes I saw him all wrapped up in the cloud, and invisible, like a cat in a burlap sack. At other times it floated, about the size of a sofa, three or four feet above his head, following him wherever he went. One could think about the man under the cloud before going to sleep; the image of him wandering around from town to town was a sure soporific.

Not so the mental picture of a certain Mrs. Huston, who had been terribly cut up when her daughter died on the operating table. I could see the doctors too vividly, just before they set upon Mrs. Huston with their knives, and I could hear them. "Now, Mrs. Huston, will we get up on the table like a good girl, or will we have to be put there?" I could usually fight off Mrs. Huston before I went to sleep, but she frequently got into my dreams, and sometimes she still does.

I remember the grotesque creature that came to haunt my meditations when one evening my father said to my mother, "What did Mrs.
Johnson say when you told her about Betty?" and my mother replied,
"Oh, she was all ears." There were many other wonderful figures in the
secret, surrealist landscapes of my youth: the old lady who was always
up in the air, the husband who did not seem to be able to put his foot
down, the man who lost his head during a fire but was still able to run
out of the house yelling, the young lady who was, in reality, a soiled
dove. It was a world that, of necessity, one had to keep to oneself and
brood over in silence, because it would fall to pieces at the touch of
words. If you brought it out into the light of actual day and put it to the
test of questions, your parents would try to laugh the miracles away, or
they would take your temperature and put you to bed. (Since I always
ran a temperature, whenever it was taken, I was put to bed and left
there all alone with Mrs. Huston.)

Such a world as the world of my childhood is, alas, not yearproof. It
is a ghost that, to use Henley's words, gleams, flickers, vanishes away. I
think it must have been the time my little Cousin Frances came to visit
us that it began surely and forever to dissolve. I came into the house one
rainy dusk and asked where Frances was. "She is," said our cook, "up in
the front room crying her heart out." The fact that a person could cry
so hard that his heart would come out of his body, as perfectly shaped
and glossy as a red velvet pincushion, was news to me. For some reason
I had never heard the expression, so common in American families
whose hopes and dreams run so often counter to attainment. I went upstairs and opened the door of the front room. Frances, who was three
years older than I, jumped up off the bed and ran past me, sobbing, and
down the stairs.

My search for her heart took some fifteen minutes. I tore the bed
apart and kicked up the rugs and even looked in the bureau drawers. It
was no good. I looked out the window at the rain and the darkening
sky. My cherished mental image of the man under the cloud began to
grow dim and fade away. I discovered that, all alone in a room, I could
face the thought of Mrs. Huston with cold equanimity. Downstairs, in
the living room, Frances was still crying. I began to laugh.

Ah there, Salvador!

1943

GARRISON KEILLOR

END OF THE TRAIL

THE last cigarette smokers in America were located in a box canyon south of Donner Pass in the High Sierra by two federal tobacco agents in a helicopter who spotted the little smoke puffs just before noon. One of them, the district chief, called in the ground team by air-to-ground radio. Six men in camouflage outfits, members of a crack anti-smoking joggers unit, moved quickly across the rugged terrain, surrounded the bunch in their hideout, subdued them with tear gas, and made them lie face down on the gravel in the hot August sun. There were three females and two males, all in their mid-forties. They had been on the run since the adoption of the Twenty-eighth Amendment.

The chief, a trim, muscular man in neatly pressed khakis who carried a riding crop, paced back and forth along the line of motionless shoe soles. "What are you people using for brains? Can't you read?" he snapped, flicking the crop at their ankles. He bent down and snatched up an empty pack of Marlboros and thrust it in the face of a pale, sweaty man whose breath came in short, terrified gasps. "Look at this! This warning has been there for decades! Want me to read it to you? Want me to give you the statistics? What does it take to make you understand? Look at me! Speak up! I can't hear you!"

In fact, the smokers had been very subdued long before the acrid tear-gas fumes drifted into their hideout, a narrow cave near the canyon mouth. They knew the end was near. Days before, they had lost radio contact with the only other band of smokers they knew of: five writers holed up in an Oakland apartment. It had been three weeks since the Donner group's last supply drop from the air, forty pounds of barbecued ribs, ten Picnic Tubs of Jimbo deep-fried chicken, and six cartons of smokes, all mentholated. Agents who searched the cave found exactly two cigarettes. There was not a single shred of tobacco found in any of the thousands of discarded butts. The two cigarettes were hidden in the lining of a sleeping bag, and the general disorder in the cave—clothing and personal effects strewn from hell to breakfast—indicated that some smokers had searched frantically for a smoke that very morning. Blackened remnants of what appeared to be cabbage leaves lay in the smoldering campfire.

"Move 'em out of here!" the chief said. "They disgust me."

AMONG the personal effects were four empty packs, carefully slit open, the blank insides covered with handwriting. An agent picked them up and put them in a plastic bag, for evidence. They read:

Dear Lindsay & Matt—

This is to let y. know I'm OK & w. friends tho how this w. reach you I dont know. 5 of us are in the mts (dont know where). I never thot it wld come to this. All those yrs as ashtrays vanishd fr parties & old pals made sarc remarks & FAA crackd down & smoke sect. became closet, I thot if I just was discreet & smokd in prv & took mints I'd get by but then yr dad quit & I had to go undergrnd. Bsmnt, gar., wet twls, A/C, etc. Felt guilty but contd, couldnt stop. Or didnt. Too late for that now. Gotta go on midnt watch. More soon.

Love, Mother.

My Dear Children—

Down to 1 cart. PlMls. Not my fav. Down to 1 cg/day. After supper. Hate to say it but it tastes fant. So rich, so mild. I know you never approvd. Sorry. In 50s it was diffrnt, we all smokd. Felt like movies. So gracefl, tak'g cg from pk, the mtch, the lite, one smooth move. Food, sex, then smoke. Lng drags. Lrnd Fr. exh. Then sudd. it was 82 and signs apprd (Thanx for Not S). In my home! Kids naggng like fishwives & yr dad sudd. went out for track. I felt *ambushed*. Bob Dylan smokd, Carson, Beatles. I mean WE'RE NOT CRIMINALS. Sorry. Too late now. More soon.

Love, Mother.

Dear Kids—

This may be last letter, theyre closing in. Planes o'head every day now. Dogs in dist. Men w. ldspkrs. Flares. Oakland chapt got busted last pm. Was w. them on radio when feds came. Reminded me of when yr dad turnd me in. After supper. Knew he was nut but didnt know he was creep. Cops surr. our hse, I snk away thru bushes. No time to say g-b to y. Sorry. Wld you believe I quit twice yrs ago, once fr 8 mo. I'm not a terrible wom. y'know. Sorry. Know this is hard on y. Me too.

We're down to 2 pks & everybody's tense. Got to go chk perimtr. Goodbye.

Love, Mother.

Dear L & M—

This is it. They saw us. I have one left and am smokng it now. Gd it tastes gd. My last cg. Then its all over. I'm OK. I'm ready. Its a better thng I do now than I hv ever done. I love you both. . . .

THE five smokers were handcuffed and transported to a federal detention camp in Oregon, where they were held in pup tents for months. They were charged with conspiracy to obtain, and willful possession of, tobacco, and were convicted in minutes, and were sentenced to write twenty thousand words apiece on the topic "Personal Integrity" by a judge who had quit cigarettes when the price went to thirty-five cents and he could not justify the expense.

The author of the letters was soon reunited with her children, and one night, while crossing a busy intersection near their home in Chicago, she saved them from sure death by pulling them back from the path of a speeding car. Her husband, who had just been telling her she could stand to lose some weight, was killed instantly, however.

1984

VERONICA GENG

MY AND ED'S PEACE PROPOSALS

ED and I each have come up with a proposed plan for the cessation of hostilities between the Reagan administration and our household. Since our plans differ in certain minor respects (Ed taking a somewhat tougher line), we offer both versions, in the hope that they may at least stimulate the administration to consider negotiations toward ending the past six and a half years of drawn-out mutual aggression and mistrust. This is not a ploy or a farce on our part. We are even putting all our personal problems on the back burner while we press these initiatives. We now task the administration with showing how sincere *it* is by responding in a spirit of reconciliation and good faith.

MY PLAN	ED'S PLAN
1. Immediate suspension of Elliott Abrams, who will then be reflagged as a Kuwaiti vessel.	1. Ed given a line-item veto on presidential rhetoric.
2. Unconditional withdrawal of the Bork nomination; Bork allowed to head a presidential commission on the colorization of film classics.	2. Immediate amnesty for Ed's mother, a political prisoner of right-wing mailing lists.
3. Trade and assistance: As soon as the first two conditions are met, we will give support to the administration's economic goals by ceasing our costly flow of Mailgrams to the White House, thus freeing funds for disbursement to more productive sectors of the economy and enabling us to stop accepting aid from Ed's mother.	3. U.S. diplomatic relations with puppet regime of Pat Buchanan severed for an indefinite cooling-off period; in return, Ed will use all his influence to halt Latin-American incursions by Joan Didion.
4. National plebiscite on secular humanism, to be supervised by elected representatives from four regional productions of *La Cage aux Folles.*	4. Arms reduction: Ronald Reagan to enter into a one-on-one dialogue with Peter Ueberroth to achieve a 60-day suspension of Mike Scott of the Houston Astros for pitching defaced baseballs. This is just to give Ed an added incentive to abide by the remainder of the plan.
5. Timetable for routine Rorschach and Stanford-Binet testing of President Reagan.	5. Timetable for the election of someone else as president by the end of 1988.

1987

GEORGE W. S. TROW

YOU MISSED IT

YOU should have been there—it was great. How come you missed it? I'd get up earlier if I were you. I can't believe you missed it. Maybe you have a discipline problem.

You got here slightly too late. A moment ago we had crab cakes. Marie cooked them up. Did you see the sunset when you came in? No? I can't believe you didn't see it. The sky was huge and dark; curved; with wisps of light, just the way you like it. After the sun finally went down, Marie and I sat on the porch and watched an electric, vital blue just over the western horizon. You hardly ever get to see a blue like that. Marie, me, Billy—did I tell you he was there?—watched it together. Billy took me by the legs and tumbled me over and over until I burst out laughing; then he took Marie and placed her on top of me, and I laughed and laughed until I thought I would burst; and then—get this—Billy piled on top and rolled over the two of us like a steamroller. We couldn't stop laughing.

Are you comfortable? Can I get you something? Sure? Can I ask you a question? How come you weren't there? Were you taking some kind of examination or something? So anyway, we got up. I don't know if you've seen the way Marie looks in the new dress I bought her. It hangs on her so nicely. She stood up, and I watched the dress hang. I don't know if we missed you or not. Later on we thought, "He missed *us*," but that is different. Then the little boys and girls of the neighborhood came by. We wanted to remember to tell you about that. The oldest, the cute one who is called Shiloh, brought a lizard to Marie. That's what made her think to cook up the crab cakes. When she brought out the steaming mess of crab cakes, she put her hands on her hips and let the steam make her perspire—little drops running down her neck and even onto her breasts. "I wouldn't care to know anyone who isn't here with us," she said defiantly. You should have been there. But I've said that.

In my opinion, you're the kind of guy who missed Hell Week, railroads sending clouds of steam into the station, singing just to hear the sound of your own voice, and operetta. How could you have done it? With all your potential? How could you have been so stupid and lazy?

You weren't here when we had the intelligent debate about Vietnam. You skipped; you missed *the moment,* and don't pretend you didn't.

But I'm ahead of myself. Where was I? Well, after having such a wonderful time on the porch, we walked down Water Street. The lights were just beginning to come on. Suddenly we heard "The Gal from Joe's"—the Ellington tune. It *was* Joe's. An acre of pleasure spread out before our hungry eyes—room after room! Range-fed chicken, fish you can't get anymore, delicious beers, and turkeys from Tidewater farms like "Acrewood," "King's Forty," "Underlea," "Scrivesden," and "Rose Hall"—the last miraculously raised from its ashes. The best part was that jazz was being reborn in the back room. Maybe you heard about that—how suddenly a little white boy added a note to "A Night in Tunisia" at Joe's in such a way that the audience was reduced to utter respectful silence, at which point black and white men and women, each one an expert in the development of bebop and other modern jazz idioms, clasped hands while tears streamed down their faces. You had to see it. Why *didn't* you see it? Were you in *detention* or what?

Then Billy brought the novel out of its doldrums of postmodern irrelevancy. Somehow, with that wonderful natural spontaneity of his, he was able to capture what I was saying and cast it in novelistic terms. I was so enthralled with the rebirth of jazz that I must have communicated to him some quintessential American energy, which, together with his work in linguistics and his deep sympathy for Hispanics and women, came together to produce an American free-form prose that promises to enrich all our work. Whew. It took my breath away to hear it.

Then we walked out along the causeway. The little fisherfolk who go out in their boats just as they have for centuries raised a cheer: "Hurrah for the creators of a new American civilization!" they cried. The head man or person of the fisherfolk came out and explained that it is the custom—indeed, the stated purpose and goal—of the fisherfolk to be willing to die for the right to save the best fish for their sweethearts. Then in a very tender way they explained that *we* were their sweethearts, and they gave us all the fish. I erected an impromptu brazier, and Marie grilled them up. I gave Marie a little kiss, and Marie gave Billy a big hearty sloppy one, and we all three settled down to eat this corn tortilla of incomparable delicacy, which Marie had in her pocket.

Then we told stories about you. How you didn't get a National Merit Scholarship. (Remember how *easy* they were to get?) And how you missed seeing the Tall Ships. I mean, everybody saw the Tall Ships. I know people who were sick beyond endurance with seeing the Tall

Ships by *accident*—just running into the sight of them out a window or something—and apparently you never saw them once. And how about all those things you said you saw when we weren't with you, like the Liberation of Paris, and the '51 National League pennant race, and Elvis when he was under contract to Sam Phillips at Sun in Memphis?

Marie said she likes you anyway. She told a long story about taking a bicycle trip with you in France and stopping in an out-of-the-way restaurant that looked just perfect and all they had was toast. "How do you make it?" you asked. The man said nothing. "How much *is* it?" you asked. By the way, the man turned out to be a great artist, and the sketches Marie bought that day are worth a small fortune now. I wonder why you had to ask that. You made the man so sad. Marie liked him right away and made friends, or so she says.

Could I borrow about one hundred dollars? Your parts are on order. We had some corned beef, but that guy over there got the last serving.

1988

GEORGE W. S. TROW

A MAN WHO CAN'T LOVE

(DEDICATED TO WOMEN WHO LOVE TOO MUCH)

TODAY, instead of going through the usual routine, which, frankly, none of you seem to be getting that well, I thought I'd focus on these failed candidates, point out why they flunked, have a good time with their flaws. Let's look at what they did wrong.

I. CLAIRE

Claire is an attractive film reviewer in her early thirties. A stunning brunette, she's been in and out of a dozen "relationships" but is now "available" again. When I met her, she had just been through a painful and extremely self-destructive relationship with "Fred." "Fred," a ravishing film editor in his late thirties, was married and insisted on meeting her in obscure resorts on holidays *only*. (His wife belonged to a violent religious group, quite beyond animal sacrifice, self-flagellation, etc., which did not permit outsiders to participate in their festive seasons.) Claire, who was, as I say, a wildly attractive film reviewer, the graduate of a topnotch Eastern school, the daughter of attractive, highly educated people (her father was provost of a major interdenominational religious restaurant; her mother, an attractive, well-educated woman in her mid-fifties, doled out anabolic steroids and had corrupted many of the nation's finest athletes—in Canada, too), was beginning to wonder if she would ever have a happy, sustained relationship.

The answer is: *Not with me she can't*. Claire is making one simple, basic error, like many other attractive film reviewers; however often she changes the *externals* of her situation, basically the underlying problem remains untouched. The fact is, I don't date film reviewers. I date film *critics*. Claire came on with a clumsy "thumbs up, thumbs down" routine, which was, frankly, an embarrassment. One and a half stars for that one, Claire. I thought the plot was kind of contrived, and we've seen these characters before.

2. MARY

Mary is one of those women who can't seem to get a handle on life. She just drifts from day to day, unable to concentrate on her real ambition, which is to torment her daughter. We'll be hearing more about Mary later.

3. SUSAN

Susan cannot learn to classify men. In fact, she can't tell one from another. The subway, where there are hundreds of men, is a particular problem for her. So let's give it one more try for Susan. Sit down and listen. There are *three kinds of men:*

1. The Wheedler

At first he's all attention. She can't get enough of him, he can't get enough of her (so *she* thinks), but all the time she's putting garnishes on the dish of love, he's getting ready to move out.

2. The Tomcat

She's in heaven: she's finally met "The One." The trouble is just that—*trouble*. The reason he's so crazy about *her* is that he's crazy about every girl. He can't get enough! He's an absolute raving maniac! He's ready to go again! He's out the door! He's back!

Mary, above, was an amazing example of putting up with this. Mary's case was extreme. Frankly, I'd never heard of anything quite like it. This is what she told me:

> My husband admitted to me on our wedding night that he had "a secret ambition" and it was to populate an entire state. He said that he would be a "good husband" to me as long as I would "turn a blind eye" to the fact that he would be having thousands of children by other women. The code word for our deal was "Nebraska." It got so I couldn't bear to hear the name of any Midwestern state. Breakfast, lunchtime, dinner, it was always time to "go to Nebraska," or "see the Cornhuskers," or some similar term. Conventions and business trips were a strain for me—and apparently for him. And I'd be expected to nurse him back to health! But then he'd turn "sweet" and tell me I was the "only one," and I'd believe him! I can't believe what a fool I was! As soon as he had his strength again, he'd be back "in Omaha," or "going to Grand Island." It was a nightmare! It went on for over thirty years, and I believe that a high percentage of that state are his children. I have met some of his "other women"—how could I *not* meet them? There were hundreds, thousands of them—and they all swear by my husband, but to me it was a living daydream or unreality, and it's still going on! I'm out of my mind to put up with it!

3. The No-Goodnik

Frankly, this guy's just a heel. Don't expect him to change—*you* change. You take the crucial creative steps toward self-involvement with yourself and other women like yourself who have come to terms with coming to understand that he's not going to change, and realize that, unlike you, he's condemned to the nightmare of constantly looking at and desiring women. You have to face the fact that he's just no good. The fact is that if you deny it you just stay in the same patterns, which seem to change but don't. If you catch yourself talking to one of these men—at a bar or cocktail lounge is where they are—tell him, *I'm going to change,* and have the satisfaction of watching him walk right into that same old pattern of watching and desiring women who are unable or unwilling to see that *he won't change.* See that guy over there? Watch him. Think he's going to change? Uh-uh. I'm glad I'm with a person who is able to watch that striking upscale brunette begin to go through the *same patterns,* participating in the delusion that *he's* going to change. Can I buy you a drink while we wait?

1989

DAVID OWEN

HOW I'M DOING

IN the hope of establishing a more equitable framework by which the public can evaluate my effectiveness as a father, husband, friend, and worker, I am pleased to announce that the methodology heretofore used in measuring my performance is being revised. Beginning tomorrow, my reputation and compensation will no longer be based on year-long, cumulative assessments of my attainments but will instead be derived from periodic samplings of defined duration, or "sweeps."

From now on, ratings of my success as a parent will be based solely on perceptions of my conduct during the two weeks beginning March 7th (aka "spring vacation"), the two weeks beginning August 1st (aka "summer vacation"), the seven days ending December 25th, and my birthday. No longer will my ranking be affected by unsolicited anecdotal reports from minors concerning my alleged "cheapness," "strictness," and "loser" qualities, or by the contents of viewing diaries maintained by my dependents. Page views, click-throughs, and People Meter data concerning me will also be disregarded, except during the aforementioned periods. The opinions of my children will no longer be counted in evaluations of my sense of humor.

Public appraisals of my behavior at parties will henceforth not be drawn from overnight ratings provided by my wife; instead, my annual ranking will be based on a random sampling of my level of intoxication during the week following January 2nd. My official weight for the year will be my median weight during the four weeks beginning July 1st. All measures of my geniality, thoughtfulness, romantic disposition, and willingness to compromise will henceforth be calculated just three times per year: on September 15th (my wife's birthday), August 26th (our anniversary), and February 14th. My high-school grades, SAT scores, college grades, and income history will no longer be available for inclusion in any of my ratings, and in fact they will be expunged from my personal database. Evaluations of my success as a stock-market investor will no longer include the performance of my portfolio during the month of October.

Beginning in 2001, my annual compensation will cease to consist of my total income over the twelve months of the fiscal year; instead, my yearly pay will be adjusted to equal not less than thirteen times my nominal gross earnings during the four weeks beginning February 1st, when the holiday season is over, my children are back in school, and my local golf course has not yet reopened for the spring. My critics may object that my output during February is not representative of my output during the rest of the year, especially when I am at the beach. However, I believe (and my auditors concur) that the work I do during periods of cold, miserable weather provides the best available indication of my actual abilities as a worker and therefore constitutes the only fair and objective basis for calculating my true contribution to the economy. Conversely, my federal income-tax liability will henceforth be based on an annualized computation of my total earnings between Memorial Day and Labor Day.

These changes are being made as a part of my ongoing effort to insure that public data concerning me and my personality are the very best available. This new protocol may be further modified by me at any time without advance notice, and, in any case, is not legally binding. In addition, all assessments of my performance are subject to later revision, as improved information becomes available. Specifically, my lifetime ratings in all categories may be posthumously adjusted, within thirty days of my death, to reflect the content of newspaper obituaries regarding me, should any such be published, and the things that people say about me at my funeral.

2000

PAUL SIMMS

A PRAYER

L ORD?
Please don't let me die in a funny way.

Like being beaten to death with a shoe. Especially not my own shoe. And, if it absolutely has to be my own shoe, I'd rather not be wearing it at the time.

Or like choking on my own fist during a bar bet.

Perhaps I should clarify a little. I do know that I'm going to die someday. (Maybe soon! That's Your call.) And I know there's nothing funny about death—at least, that's the current thinking from this side. I'm just asking to not die in a way that leads people who don't know me to e-mail one another news items about my death. For instance:

Please don't let me get so fat that paramedics have to come to my house and cut out a wall to remove me but then bang my head against a load-bearing pillar in the process, thus killing me.

Please don't let me die on or near or—perhaps worst of all—because of a toilet. (This includes a urinal or a baseball-stadium-style urine trough, in addition to a standard commode.)

Please don't let my death in any way involve one of those giant in-flatable rats that union protesters put up outside nonunion job sites. Or a blimp of any kind. Until I see some evidence to the contrary, I'm going to have to say that my dying because of just about anything in-flatable would be something I'd rather avoid. A hot-air balloon, I guess, would be okay, but only if I'm actually in the balloon at the time. At least that would be kind of rugged and outdoorsy. What I'm trying to say is: If someone else's hot-air balloon falls out of the sky and smoth-ers me while I'm lying in a hammock reading *Hot Air Balloon Enthusi-ast* magazine, I'm going to be a little pissed.

I apologize for that language, Lord, but I'm just trying to be honest with You.

A vehicular accident? Fine. Bring it on. I understand that, statisti-cally, there's a pretty good chance of that happening anyway. Just please don't let it involve a moped. Or a go-kart.

Also, I'd prefer not to die in a head-on collision with someone who—against all odds—has the same name as me. Or anyone named, for instance, Roger Crash. Or Ed Oncollision. Or Jennifer Safedriver. I could go on, but I think You get the point.

I'm sure You get this one a lot, but: Please don't let me die during sex. Unless the technical cause of my death is a heart attack or a stroke. If I have to die during sex, please don't make the cause of death any of the following: extreme dehydration, a previously undiagnosed allergy to fruit-scented or "massage" oils, dermatological complications arising from severe rug burn, or anything involving the use or misuse of any object best described as "foreign."

Please don't let me die in a way that allows the *Post* to run a small item about my death on page 12 or 13 or so under the headline "DUDE, WHERE'S MY CORPSE?" Or "DUMB AND DEADER." Or "DEAD AND DEADER." Or "THE HOUSE OF SAND AND DEAD." Or "J. LO'S LATEST NUPTIALS POSTPONED DUE TO LETHAL TENT-RAISING MISHAP."

Please don't let me cut my own head off while trying to revive the lost Scouting pastime of mumblety-peg.

I would have to consider any fatality involving a prolapsed anus, of course, absolutely beyond the pale. I mean, come on, Lord.

Also—and I'm not trying to split hairs with You, Lord—when I ask You to not let me die in a funny way, I also mean please don't let me die in a noteworthily ironic way. Meaning: whether my death is "ha-ha" funny or the other kind of funny, neither of those is what I'm in the market for. For instance, please don't let me go on a Sleepwalkers Anonymous Outward Bound–type retreat and sleepwalk into a canyon or gorge in the middle of the night.

And, if You deem it necessary (or just amusing) to take my mind before You take my body, let's try to keep the progressive dementia noble and epically sad rather than comical. For example: Please let the last face I recognize be the photograph of a long-lost high-school girlfriend and not one of the plucky toddlers from the animated show *Rugrats*. In my final moments, let me awaken—apparently lucid—in the predawn hours calling out for a kiss on the forehead from a dead great-aunt rather than from the mustachioed black bartender on *The Love Boat*.

Or from the actor who played him, for that matter.

Even if I don't die in a funny way, I'd still rather not die on the same day as some other person who does die in a funny way. Because I don't want any version of the following conversation to occur between my friends:

FRIEND ONE: Did you read his obituary?

FRIEND TWO: Yeah. Nice piece.

FRIEND ONE: Very nice.

FRIEND TWO: He would have liked it.

FRIEND ONE: That he would have. That he would have.

(Awkward silence.)

FRIEND TWO: Did you see that other obituary about the banana wholesaler who actually slipped on the—

FRIEND ONE: Yeah. You couldn't make that up!

Well, that's about it, Lord.

Actually—as long as I've got You, let me just mention a few final ways for me to die that may or may not seem funny to You, depending on Your sense of humor.

I would rather be burned beyond all recognition than burned *almost* beyond all recognition, especially if the pictures are going to end up on the Internet.

If some kind of rare organism eats away at my body from the inside, please let it be microscopic. Or just slightly larger than microscopic. Let's put it this way: If it's big enough to have a face, that would be too big.

Thank You for Your time, Lord.

(Also: Ted Lange. That's the name of the actor who played the bartender on *The Love Boat* whose name I couldn't remember before. I Googled him for You, Lord. Which has got to count for something, right?)

2004

PAUL RUDNICK

MY LIVING WILL

1. If I should remain in a persistent vegetative state for more than fifteen years, I would like someone to turn off the TV.

2. If I remain motionless for an extended period and utter only guttural, meaningless sounds, I would like a Guggenheim.

3. If I am unable to recognize or interact with friends or family members, I still expect gifts.

4. If I am unable to feed, clean, or dress myself, I would like to be referred to as "Mr. Trump."

5. Do not resuscitate me before noon.

6. If I do not respond to pinches, pinpricks, rubber mallets, or other medical stimuli, please stop laughing.

7. If I no longer respond to loved ones' attempts at communication, ask them about our last car trip.

8. Once I am allowed to die a painless and peaceful death, I would like my organs donated to whoever can catch them.

9. If my death is particularly dramatic, I would like to be played by Hilary Swank, for a slam dunk.

10. If there is any family dispute over my medical condition, it must be settled with a dreidel.

11. Even if I remain in a persistent vegetative state for more than fifteen years, that still doesn't mean bangs.

12. If my doctor pronounces me brain-dead, I would like to see the new Ashton Kutcher movie.

13. If I remain unconscious during a painful, lingering illness, I would like the following life lessons to be published in a book entitled *Tuesdays with Paul:*
    i. Treasure every moment.
    ii. Love everyone.
    iii. If you bought this in hardcover, you're an idiot.

14. I do not wish to be kept alive by any machine that has a "Popcorn" setting.

15. I would like to die at home, surrounded by my attorneys.

16. If my loved ones insist that the cost of my medical care has become an impossible burden, show them a Polaroid of their "beach shack."

17. In lieu of flowers or donations, I would prefer rioting.

18. I would like my entire estate to become the property of my cat, Fluffy, who said, "He wouldn't want to live like this, with that zit."

19. Assume that, even in a coma, I can still hear discussions about my apartment.

20. If there is any talk of canonizing me, please remember that I have often held the elevator for people who were still getting their mail, that I have twice offered a cab to a woman in a fur coat even though I was totally there first, and that I always waited to make derogatory comments until after the couple with the double stroller was a block away.

21. In the event of an open coffin, I would like smoky evening eyes.

22. At my memorial service, I would like my clergyman to begin his eulogy with the words "I suppose, in a way, we all killed him."

2005

JACK HANDEY

WHAT I'D SAY TO THE MARTIANS

PEOPLE of Mars, you say we are brutes and savages. But let me tell you one thing: if I could get loose from this cage you have me in, I would tear you guys a new Martian asshole. You say we are violent and barbaric, but has any one of you come up to my cage and extended his hand? Because, if he did, I would jerk it off and eat it right in front of him. "Mmm, that's good Martian," I would say.

You say your civilization is more advanced than ours. But who is really the more "civilized" one? You, standing there watching this cage? Or me, with my pants down, trying to urinate on you? You criticize our Earth religions, saying they have no relevance to the way we actually live. But think about this: If I could get my hands on that god of yours, I would grab his skinny neck and choke him until his big green head exploded.

We are a warlike species, you claim, and you show me films of Earth battles to prove it. But I have seen all the films about twenty times. Get some new films, or, so help me, if I ever get out of here I will empty my laser pistol into everyone I see, even pets.

Speaking of films, I could show you some films, films that portray a different, gentler side of Earth. And while you're watching the films I'd sort of slip away, because guess what: The projector is actually a thing that shoots out spinning blades! And you fell for it! Well, maybe not now you wouldn't.

You point to your long tradition of living peacefully with Earth. But you know what I point to? Your stupid heads.

You say there is much your civilization could teach ours. But perhaps there is something that I could teach you—namely, how to scream like a parrot when I put your big Martian head in a vise.

You claim there are other intelligent beings in the galaxy besides earthlings and Martians. Good, then we can attack them together. And after we're through attacking them we'll attack you.

I came here in peace, seeking gold and slaves. But you have treated me like an intruder. Maybe it is not me who is the intruder but you.

No, not me. You, stupid.

You keep my body imprisoned in this cage. But I am able to transport my mind to a place far away, a happier place, where I use Martian heads for batting practice.

I admit that sometimes I think we are not so different after all. When you see one of your old ones trip and fall down, do you not point and laugh, just as we on Earth do? And I think we can agree that nothing is more admired by the people of Earth and Mars alike than a fine, high-quality cigarette. For fun, we humans like to ski down mountains covered with snow; you like to "milk" bacteria off of scum hills and pack them into your gill slits. Are we so different? Of course we are, and you will be even more different if I ever finish my homemade flamethrower.

You may kill me, either on purpose or by not making sure that all the surfaces in my cage are safe to lick. But you can't kill an idea. And that idea is: me chasing you with a big wooden mallet.

You say you will release me only if I sign a statement saying that I will not attack you. And I have agreed, the only condition being that I can sign with a long sharp pen. And still you keep me locked up.

True, you have allowed me reading material—not the "human reproduction" magazines I requested but the works of your greatest philosopher, Zandor or Zanax or whatever his name is. I would like to discuss his ideas with him—just me, him, and one of his big, heavy books.

If you will not free me, at least deliver a message to Earth. Send my love to my wife, and also to my girlfriend. And to my children, if I have any anyplace. Ask my wife to please send me a bazooka, which is a flower we have on Earth. If my so-called friend Don asks you where the money I owe him is, please anally probe him. Do that anyway.

If you keep me imprisoned long enough, eventually I will die. Because one thing you Martians do not understand is that we humans cannot live without our freedom. So, if you see me lying lifeless in my cage, come on in, because I'm dead. Really.

Maybe one day we will not be the enemies you make us out to be. Perhaps one day a little Earth child will sit down to play with a little Martian child, or larva, or whatever they are. But, after a while, guess what happens: the little Martian tries to eat the Earth child. But guess what the Earth child has? A gun. You weren't expecting that, were you? And now the Martian child is running away, as fast as he can. Run, little Martian baby, run!

I would like to thank everyone for coming to my cage tonight to hear my speech. Donations will be gratefully accepted. (No Mars money, please.)

2005

JACK HANDEY

THIS IS NO GAME

THIS is no game. You might think this is a game, but, trust me, this is no game.

This is not something where rock beats scissors or paper covers rock or rock wraps itself up in paper and gives itself as a present to scissors. This isn't anything like that. Or where paper types something on itself and sues scissors.

This isn't something where you yell "Bingo!" and then it turns out you don't have bingo after all, and what are the rules again? This isn't that, my friend.

This isn't something where you roll the dice and move your battle-ship around a board and land on a hotel and act like your battleship is having sex with the hotel.

This isn't tiddlywinks, where you flip your tiddly over another player's tiddly and an old man winks at you because he thought it was a good move. This isn't that at all.

This isn't something where you sink a birdie or hit a badminton birdie or do anything at all with birdies. Look, just forget birdies, okay?

Maybe you think this is all one big joke, like the farmer with the beautiful but promiscuous daughter. But what they don't tell you is the farmer became so depressed that he eventually took his own life.

This is not some brightly colored, sugarcoated piece of candy that you can brush the ants off of and pop in your mouth.

This is not playtime or make-believe. This is real. It's as real as a beggar squatting by the side of the road, begging, and then you realize, Uh-oh, he's not begging.

This is as real as a baby deer calling out for his mother. But his mother won't be coming home anytime soon, because she is drunk in a bar somewhere.

It's as real as a mummy who still thinks he's inside a pyramid, but he's actually in a museum in Ohio.

This is not something where you can dress your kid up like a hobo and send him out trick-or-treating, because, first of all, your kid's twenty-three, and, secondly, he really is a hobo.

All of this probably sounds old-fashioned and "square" to you. But if loving your wife, your country, your cats, your girlfriend, your girlfriend's sister, and your girlfriend's sister's cat is "square," then so be it.

You go skipping and prancing through life, skipping through a field of dandelions. But what you don't see is that on each dandelion is a bee, and on each bee is an ant, and the ant is biting the bee and the bee is biting the flower, and if that shocks you then I'm sorry.

You have never had to struggle to put food on the table, let alone put food on a plate and try to balance it on a spoon until it gets to your mouth.

You will never know what it's like to work on a farm until your hands are raw, just so people can have fresh marijuana. Or what it's like to go to a factory and put in eight long hours and then go home and realize that you went to the wrong factory.

I don't hate you; I pity you. You will never appreciate the magnificent beauty of a double rainbow, or the plainness of a regular rainbow.

You will never grasp the quiet joy of holding your own baby, or the quiet comedy of handing him back to his "father."

I used to be like you. I would put my napkin in my lap, instead of folding it into a little tent over my plate, like I do now, with a door for the fork to go in.

I would go to parties and laugh—and laugh and laugh—every time somebody said something, in case it was supposed to be funny. I would walk in someplace and slap down a five-dollar bill and say, "Give me all you got," and not even know what they had there. And whenever I found two of anything I would hold them up to my head like antlers, and then pretend that one "antler" fell off.

I went waltzing along, not caring where I stepped or if the other person even wanted to waltz.

Food seemed to taste better back then. Potatoes were more potatoey, and turnips less turnippy.

But then something happened, something that would make me understand that this is no game. I was walking past a building and I saw a man standing high up on a ledge. "Jump! Jump!" I started yelling. What happened next would haunt me for the rest of my days: The man came down from the building and beat the living daylights out of me. Ever since then, I've realized that this is no game.

Maybe one day it will be a game again. Maybe you'll be able to run up and kick a pumpkin without people asking why you did that and if you're going to pay for it.

Perhaps one day the Indian will put down his tomahawk and the white man will put down his gun, and the white man will pick up his gun again because, Ha-ha, sucker.

One day we'll just sit by the fire, chew some tobacky, toast some marshmackies, and maybe strum a tune on the ole guitacky.

And maybe one day we'll tip our hats to the mockingbird, not out of fear but out of friendliness.

If there's one single idea I'd like you to take away from this, it is: This is no game. The other thing I'd like you to think about is, could I borrow five hundred dollars?

(Author's Note: Since finishing this article, I have been informed that this is, in fact, a game. I would like to apologize for everything I said above. But please think about the five hundred dollars.)

2006

GEORGE SAUNDERS

PROCLAMATION

TEHRAN, Iran (July 29)—Iranian President Mahmoud Ahmadine-jad has ordered government and cultural bodies to use modified Persian words to replace foreign words that have crept into the language, such as "pizzas," which will now be known as "elastic loaves."

—Associated Press

OKAY, so this is it. I am telling you now. Our jihad declares this: no more English. Wait, I know. I am speaking English, but just this one last time. No more English, once I am done speaking. When done speaking, I will do that zipping thing one does with the lips, and after that: our glorious linguistic jihad begins! It is going to really kick ass. However, hang on. "Kick ass" does not please the Prophet. How do I know? I just do. From now on, we will say, like: Our new linguistic jihad is really going to "put the foot in the old rumpus." Got it? Or "rumpamundo" is okay. "Put the foot in the old rumpamundo." Yes, yes, I like that.

Some of you have asked, "Mahmoud, why are we doing this?" One even asked, "Mahmoud, why the heck are we doing this"—more about "heck" later, but for now . . . Remember, back in the seventies, when we took those American, uh, "visitors who did not intend to stay quite so long as they did, in fact, stay"? At the time everyone was going, "No, no, Mahmoud, bad idea"—but look how great it turned out! Now everyone is futzing over us, because why? Because we asserted our—Oh, right, no, you're right, absolutely, we must also purge our language of the expressions of the blood-drinkers. So "futz"? No. Thanks for pointing that out. How about "fuss"? "Fussing around"? What do you think? Show of hands? Too similar? Okay, instead of "futz," let it be, uh . . . let me get back to you on that one.

But you see my point. When we draw a line in the sand with the Western imperialists, they pay attention. When we try to be nice, they treat us badly. I write the guy a sixteen-page letter, and don't even get a note back! I put a lot of thought into that! I did, like, three drafts! I was trying to be an "egg that is good"! I was trying to offer "the branch of the olive"! But that "one who fucks" treated me like I was some "stupid rectum" from "HoboIntercourse"!

My friends, I am a simple man. That is why you elected me. I have never been anywhere other than our beloved country. I actually haven't even been to that many places here in our beloved country. I have pretty much been here in my beloved house, nonstop, since the seventies. In my beloved room. With the door locked. Having nightmares in which Hulk Hogan is waiting outside my room—look, as for Hulk Hogan, do not mention his name ever again! He will be referred to, if we even *need* to refer to him, which I doubt, as "Blond Blondie, Big Blondie!" In this way, we will disrespect him! In this way, he will be driven from my dreams! No more sneaking up behind me, "Blond Blondie, Big Blondie!," and putting me in a headlock, and I am naked, and have forgotten to study for all my exams!

No. For us, all Western decadence is finished. McDonald's, chief villain of the American imperialist program, will henceforth be known as "Burger King." That will really mess with everybody's head. Some enemy of the revolution here in Tehran goes into a McDon—Do we still even have McDonald's? I used to really like the cheeseburgers. The "snack that is surprisingly caloric because, you sense, there is even sugar in the bun." Anyway, some enemy of the revolution goes into a McDonald's, orders a Big Mac, and—ha-ha!—he is really in Burger King. I love it! He is undone.

Similarly, Burger King will be known as "Wendy's," KFC will be known as "Home Depot," Farouq's Funeral Home will be known as "Blockbuster Video," and Pamela Anderson will be known as "Mrs. President of Iran." Joking! I know she is already married! Didn't she just—Well, in any event, I am. At least, I think I am. Can you get my wife on my cell? Is this going out live? That Pam Anderson thing might have rubbed her the wrong—

Speaking of *women,* that is another thing: Don't you find that word provocative? Say it a few times, softly, kind of moaning it to yourself, while picturing some slut undulating. See what I mean? Provocative. So that is why we are outlawing that as well. No, just the word. At least for now.

Henceforth, let us call our sisters "that which is too hot to be seen." Or should it be "that whom are too hot to be seen"? To tell the truth, I am not nuts about the word "hot." It makes me . . . well, it makes me hot. Say it, kind of stretch it out: *hot.* No, that won't do. We shall call them "those who are dangerous to see, due to they are nasty, which is why we shall henceforth hide them under the new immense heavy tents of steel for which I own the patent."

Have I mentioned that? I am decided. Women are just too hot. Even in chadors, they are too damn hot. Try it, say it, really slowly, kind of prolonging the "ch" sound: *chador.* Right? See what I mean? So the chadors are off (stop it!) and the "comfort tents" are on. Here is one now. See how weighty, totally opaque (and therefore form-concealing) it is? This way, "those who are dangerous to see, due to they are nasty, which is why we, etc., etc." will no longer be able to make any sudden sexy moves, or be seen at all, even when a bright light is shining right on them (during, say, an interrogation), or have a free thought, since they are essentially being perpetually crushed by about a quarter ton of steel, like wearing a damn VW bug.

Oops. Sorry. My bad. Did not mean to say "VW." Meant to say "Volkswagen." And did not mean to say "damn." Meant to say "frigging." Ha-ha! Joking.

Let no one say our revolution is without humor. Anyone says that, I

will put my foot in his old rumpamundo in a way he will not soon forget. Trust me on this. I will "install, via rippage, an entirely new down-
low-nasty-nasty orifice-stinky," brother, and pronto, please believe me.

Because guess what? I have nukes coming. "Slender death-
containing tubes by which righteousness shall be enforced, as per me."

I shit you not.

2006

THE GREAT AND
THE GOOD

WHAT, ANOTHER LEGEND?

Trans-Ethnic Gesellschaft is pleased to announce the release of another album in its Geniture series of recordings devoted to giants in American jazz. These liner notes are by the noted jazz critic and historian Arthur Mice, whose efforts first brought Pootie LeFleur to public attention.

POOTIE LeFleur, a legendary figure in the development of American jazz, was discovered—or *re*discovered, rather—last summer placidly raking leaves on the courthouse lawn in Shibboleth, Louisiana. Although one hundred and twelve years old and in semiretirement (two days a week, he drops paper bags of water from his second-story window onto passersby below, for which he receives a small sum), Pootie has astonishing powers of recall, displaying the lucidity of a man easily fifteen years his junior. On a recent visit engendered by the production of this record, we got Pootie talking about the roots of the music he knows so well.

"Was there an ideal period when jazz was pure, untainted by any influence foreign to its African origins?" we asked.

"I spec' . . . um . . . *rebesac,* dey's a *flutterbug,* hee, hee, hee!" Pootie said, squinting very hard and making a popping sound with his teeth.

"And what of the blues? Don't the blues, with their so-called 'blue notes,' represent a significant deviation from standard European tonality?"

"T'se ketch a ravis, y'heah? A ravis, an' de *dawg,* he *all* onto a *runnin'* boa'd," replied the jazz great, leaning back in his chair expansively until his head touched the floor.

This album represents the distillation of over sixty hours of taped conversations with Pootie LeFleur (of which the above is but a fragment), plus all the significant available recorded performances by this authentic primitive genius, whose career spanned the entire jazz era, from Jelly Roll Morton to John Coltrane—including a three-month hiatus in 1903, when nobody in New Orleans could seem to get in tune.

Carlyle Adolph Bouguereau "Pootie" LeFleur was born into the fertile musical atmosphere of postbellum New Orleans. His mother had favorably impressed Scott Joplin by playing ragtime piano with her thighs, and his father was a sometime entrepreneur, who once owned the lucrative ad-lib franchise for all of Storyville and the north delta; for years, no New Orleans musician could shout "Yeh, daddy!" during or after a solo without paying Rebus LeFleur a royalty. The young boy taught himself to play the piano with some help from his uncle, the legendary "Blind" (Deaf) Wilbur MacVout, for two decades a trombonist with Elbert Hubbard, although Hubbard was an author and had no real need for a trombonist. When Pootie was five, he was given his own piano but misplaced it, requiring him to practice thereafter on the dining-room table.[1]

When Pootie was six, the LeFleur home was razed to make way for a bayou, and Pootie's father made the decision to relocate the family in St. Louis. Here Pootie tried his hand at composition. "The Most Exceedin' Interestin' Rag," the first effort which we have in manuscript, is clearly an immature conception; only two measures long, it contains a curious key signature indicated by a very large sharp accidental over the treble clef, and a flat and a half-moon drawn in the bass. The piece is melodically sparse (the entire tune consists of one whole note, with a smiling face drawn in it), but it does anticipate Pootie's characteristic economy by at least a decade. The material from this period (some of which is also available on *Pre-Teen Pootie*, 12″ Trans-Ethnic Gesellschaft TD 203) reveals a profusion of styles and influences. "Spinoza's Joy" has a definite Spanish, if not Sephardic, flavor, while "What Vous Say?" shows a hint of the Creole.

According to Dr. Ernst Freitag and Gustav Altschuler's encyclopedic *Dictionary of Jazz and Home Wiring Simplified* (Miffin Verlag, 1942), the next few years were ones of extreme financial deprivation for

---

1. Johnny St. Cyr recalled an anecdote about Pootie's habit of playing out scales and figures on the table. One night in 1938, Pootie, Kid Ory, Baby Dodds, and Tiny Grimes were at Small's Paradise having a late supper of miniature gherkins, and Pootie was occupied as usual tapping out a riff with his right hand. It finally became too much for Ory, and the famous tailgater put down his fork. "Stop that, Pootie," said the Kid. "It's annoying." Although attributed to many others, including Fletcher Henderson and Dorothy Parker, the remark was in fact made by Ory.

the LeFleurs. Pootie's father had squandered the family savings by investing in a feckless enterprise called Fin-Ray Cola, a tuna-flavored soft drink, and in an attempt to bring in some money Pootie invented a new note, located between F and F sharp, which he named "Reep," and tried peddling it door to door. Despite early bad luck, Pootie never lost faith in "my fine new note," as he called it, and some time later he hired a hall in Sedalia to test public reaction and attract financial backing. The playing of the note apparently made no impression on the casual Missourians, most of whom arrived too late to hear it.

IT was about this time that LeFleur played for James P. Johnson, who urged him to go to New York or any other city a thousand miles away. The story of that trip is probably the most fascinating in the entire history of jazz, but unfortunately Pootie claims to have forgotten it. By now a leader and innovator in his own right, Pootie organized himself and three other musicians into what Nat Hentoff has called a "quartet," and secured an engagement at Buxtehude's, a speakeasy in the heart of Manhattan's swinging Flemish district. His first wife, singer Rubella Cloudberry, evokes those exciting years in her autobiography, *A Side of Fries* (Snead House, Boston, 1951):

> Well, don't you know, Pootie come in one night and say, "Pack up, woman, we goin' to the Big Apple!" And I say, "Hunh?" And so he say, "Pack up, woman, we goin' to the Big Apple!" And I say, "The big what?" So we stayed in Chicago.[2]

The stimulating, rough-and-tumble atmosphere of Prohibition sparked LeFleur's group (the Mocha Jokers) and others to marvelous feats of improvisation, typified by the moment during one dinner show at Tony Pastor's when Bix Beiderbecke blew a brilliant version of "Dardanella" on a roast chicken.[3]

LeFleur's classical period begins with the reflective "Boogie for the Third Sunday After Epiphany" and ends with the tender and haunting "Toad" Nocturne. "Toad" opens with a simple piano motif in G, which

2. Of course, when LeFleur did make it to New York it was without his saxophonist, Crazy Earl Bibbler. Two days before the trip, Bibbler, an alcoholic, sold his lips to a pawnshop for twenty dollars.
3. As retold by Miff Mole.

is reworked into C, F, F minor, and B, finally retiring to E flat to freshen up. At the very end, following a tradition as old as the blues, everybody stops playing.

One of the hallmarks of LeFleur's career was his constant effort to adapt his style to contemporary trends—with the result that he was habitually accused of plagiarism. When the New Orleans style (or "Chicago style," as it was then called) waned, Pootie was eclipsed, but he reappears in 1939 as a member of the historic Savoy Sextet sessions, featuring Bird, Diz, Monk, Prez, and Mrs. Hannah Weintraub on vibes.[4] With a penchant for overstatement typical of the period, Pootie tried augmenting the sextet, changing it first into a septet, then an octet, then a nonet, a dectet, an undectet, and so on, ending up with the cumbersome "hundred-tet," which could only be booked into meadows. A major influence on him at this time was his attendance at a tradition-breaking rent-party jam session, during which nineteen consecutive choruses of "How High the Moon" were played in twelve seconds by "Notes" Gonzales—the brilliant and erratic disciple of Charlie Parker—who was later killed when his car crashed into the tower of the Empire State Building.

The next album in this series will cover Pootie's modern period, including the prophetic Stockholm concert, with Ornette Coleman on vinyl sax and Swedish reedman Bo Ek on Dacron flute, plus some very recent sides cut by Pootie at his own expense in the Record-Your-Voice booth at the West Side bus terminal in New York City.

1973

4. Hear especially the second take of "Schizoroonia on Hannah Banana—The Flip Side of Mrs. Weintraub" (Ulysses 906) for a remarkable polytonal chord cluster achieved when her necklace broke.

MARSHALL BRICKMAN

THE NEW YORK REVIEW OF GOSSIP

(JUICY TIDBITS FROM ALL AROUND THE LITERARY SCENE)

W HAT'S got **Noam Chomsky** smiling so mysteriously these days? Was it the party **Robert L. Heilbroner** (*Limits of American Capitalism, The Future as History*) threw for him at **Jilly's** to celebrate a smashing new paperback contract? **Noam** isn't talking. How about it, **Noam**? Your fans wouldn't mind a sample of those fabulous **Chomsky** "linguistics"! . . . **Bill Styron** edged out **Eliot Janeway** and **Nelson Algren** in the **Boris Pasternak** look-alike contest held at **Sam Wo's.** Proceeds of the evening will go to buy a new beard for **Alexander Solzhenitsyn.** . . . History freak **Will Durant** credits wife **Ariel** with a lot of the success he's enjoyed as a writer and as a human being, too. **Will's** really *nuts* about her, even after many decades of marriage. . . . No one can accuse craggy **Sam Beckett** (*Endgame, Malone Dies*) of not having a *great* sense of humor—or can they? Friends report the bleak playwright will often put an *haricot* or green bean into his ear during dinner "just for laughs." *Pretty funny,* **Sam**! . . . Crinkle-faced pepperpot **Henry Miller** is brooding because **Nathalie Sarraute** has never, ever phoned him in over thirty years. "So sue me. I say she's crispy and tart, like a September apple," he admitted at Big Sur's posh **Nepenthe** restaurant. No argument from this end, **Hank,** but why not come in out of the sun for a while? . . . **Jean-Paul Sartre** spends part of each day grappling with the mysteries of life, then jogs to keep the flab down. His stay-trim secret: an avocado stuffed with farmer cheese. "It's scrumptious, and packed with all the vitamins I need to ratiocinate," the sinewy existentialist revealed. . . . Close friends of **Rudyard Kipling** deny he's dead, and to prove it they're taking over the **Belmore Cafeteria** for a giant one-hundred-and-tenth-birthday blowout. . . . **Norm Mailer** (*Armies of the Night*), **Norm Podhoretz** (*Making It*), and **Norm Cousins** (*Talks with Nehru*) huddled at the **All-Norman Gala** thrown by **Paddy Chayefsky** at the **Parkway Restaurant** (Roumanien Broiling, unborn eggs). Also present: **Bernie Malamud** looking trendy in a blue suit, dancing to the exciting polyrhythms of *Petrouchka* (**Bob Craft** tickled the eighty-eight). . . . Is talented harmonist **Walter Piston** busily composing a brand-new cello concerto for **Mstislav Rostropovich** or not? **Walter,** no blabbermouth, won't say. But that twinkle in his eye must mean *something*! Better keep the rosin handy, **Mstislav**! . . . Was that **Dwight Macdonald** in a cream-and-tangerine Porsche trying to beat the lights down Park Avenue the other night at 2 A.M.? **Dwight,** sporting a new look in sideburns (both on the same side), explained how he makes the fifty-one blocks from **Hunter College** to **Union Square** without stopping. "I drop her into second, floor it, and scream my lungs out until I hit Twenty-third Street," the essayist confided. "After that, it's a piece of cake." Those in the know claim **Dwight'**s fuel-injection system and 11-inch disc brakes help him get manuscripts to the publisher more quickly, thereby preserving a certain freshness of insight and that fabulous **Macdonald** contemporaneousness. . . . **Jonas** and **Adolfas Mekas,** arriving at the **Bleecker St. Cinema** for a midnight showing of *Nosferatu,* encountered **Al** and **Dave Maysles** exiting. The four exchanged rueful smiles. . . .

EAVESDROPPINGS:

Henry Moore: "Some folks claim I'm a kook because I sculpt. But if you want to move concepts through a juxtaposition of plastic and tactile forms, what else can you be—a hockey player?"

    Lillian Hellman: "There's nothing wrong with a little housework."

    Leslie Fiedler: "Everybody's always asking me which comes first, my career or having fun. Honestly, I'm never sure what the right answer is!"

    André Malraux: "I'm a pretty lucky guy. I mean, when you've got your health (*santé*), that's pretty much the whole ball of wax, isn't it?"

    Henry Steele Commager: "Sometimes, in the middle of the night, I sneak down and make a bacon-and-onion sandwich. Just a lot of bacon, raw onion, mayonnaise, and white bread. Before morning I'm nauseous, but I can't help myself!"

QUICKIES:

. . . **Izzy Stone** and **Nancy** ("Zelda") **Milford** sweating it out on adjoining rowing machines at the **92nd St.** "**Y.**" . . .

... Gallic publishing dreamboat and pioneer pornster **Maurice Girodias** at the **Gotham Book Mart** for a **Joyce Society** meeting, thumbing a *Portable Emerson.* How's that, **Maury?** Going transcendental on us? ...

... **Tom** (*Gravity's Rainbow*) **Pynchon** lobbing hot chestnuts at the tourists on Fifth Avenue from the **Brentano's** penthouse, on a dare by **William** (*Fiction and the Figures of Life*) **Gass.** "What a gass, **Bill!**" chuckled **Tom.** ...

KEEP YOUR EYE ON:

Robert Penn Warren ("Incarnations"). **Bob** *hates* the idea of dating dull models or secretaries. **Warren,** who rarely dances, describes an ideal evening as a leisurely dinner, followed by lively discussion, coffee, then some late-night nit-picking. **Bob's** favorite bedside reading: **Paul Tillich's** *Grooming Tips.* ... **Alvin Toffler.** *Future Shock* **Al** eschews expensive hair-styling salons, does all his own tonsorial chores at home with a bowl and pinking shears. He calls his sexy new pompadour "the wave of the future."

DOWN MEMORY LANE WITH:

Rainer Maria Rilke. Lyric-poetry buffs will have no trouble remembering the main man of postsymbolist wordsmithery, "His Nibs," the fantastic **"Rags" Rilke.** Born in romantic Prague (near Czechoslovakia), the young, handsome **Rilke** went to Paris to become secretary to famous chipsmith **Auguste Rodin** (who put his *Kiss* on *everyone's* lips!). One day, **Rilke** noticed that certain words sounded alike. "Words such as 'mice' and 'advice,'" he was later to recall. "It was right then that I got into my poesy bag." A familiar figure in Saint-Germain, "Rags" cut a wide swath in the unofficial uniform of the vagabond versifier—suede knee-boots, a puff-sleeved raw-silk bolero shirt, green velvet breeches, and a large wooden hat. A favorite in rhyme circles for years, **Rilke** hit it *really* big in 1906 with his narrative poem *Die Weise von Liebe und Tod des Cornets Christoph Rilke.* Occasionally scored for being stodgy, **Rilke** loosened up toward the end of his life, and, with the encouragement of **Thomas Mann,** once mailed some sneeze powder to **Sylvia Beach.**

THE MAILBAG:

Dear Editor:

Where can I get the **Martin Buber** sweatshirt advertised in your last issue? Also, anyone having any pictures or interviews with **Pär Lagerkvist,** please contact me.

> Nan Sloat
> Maspeth, L.I.

Dear Nan:

The **Martin Buber** sweatshirts, pot holders, and ice-crushing bags, plus a glamorous 8×10 glossy photo of **Pär Lagerkvist** in a dwarf suit, are all available through the **Buber-Lagerkvist** Fan Exchange, Kungsgatan 72, Box 3, Stockholm, Sweden.

Dear Editor:

I have always been worried by the abruptness of Gerald's death in Chapter 5 of **E. M. Forster's** *The Longest Journey.* What happened? Why did **Forster** do that?

> Hadrian Kornbleet, Ph.D.
> Reed College
> Portland, Oregon

Dear Professor Kornbleet:

We'll bet you didn't like Leonard's seduction of Helen in *Howards End,* either. If surprises turn you off, better lay off the belles-lettres and get into something certain, like insurance.

Dear Editor:

What's **Gunnar Myrdal's** secret of always looking so fresh? Everybody I know thinks he's the absolute tops in sociohistorical analysis, too.

> Dmitri Reutershan
> Prairie du Chien, Wis.

Dear Dmitri:

Before lecturing or undertaking any serious talking, **Gunnar** always pops a clove into his mouth and puts one under each arm. As a result, he's the only Swedish economist around who emits an aroma of mince pie.

Dear Editor:

One day recently, I saw **Letty Cottin Pogrebin** wearing a pair of black slacks. Less than a week later, I saw **Susan Sontag** wearing what appeared to be *identical slacks*! Realizing the importance of individuality in attire as well as prose style, I must ask, Do you feel **Susan** was trying to "make it hot" for **Letty**?

Sri Murtiswammy
Trenton, N.J.

Dear Sri:

No, it was probably just a coincidence, as **Letty** and **Sue** are "best of friends." Looks like you're guilty of what **Lionel Trilling** would call "the Intentional Fallacy"! (Incidentally, criticism fans who have not already done so may still order the **NYRG** durable vinyl tablecloth, clearly imprinted with a refutation of the Intentional Fallacy, in Professor **Trilling**'s own words. The text is cogent and aesthetically pleasing, and, like the professor himself, can be wiped clean with a damp cloth.)

1975

IAN FRAZIER

THE BLOOMSBURY GROUP LIVE
AT THE APOLLO

(LINER NOTES FROM THEIR NEW BEST-SELLING ALBUM)

I.

Live albums aren't supposed to be as exciting, as *immediate* as the actual stage performances they record, but (saints be praised!) the Bloomsbury Group's newest, *Live at the Apollo,* is a shouting, foot-stomping, rafter-shaking exception to this rule. Anyone who has not seen John Maynard Keynes doing his famous strut, or Duncan Grant playing his bass while flat on his back, can now get an idea of what he's been missing! The Bloomsbury Group has always stood for seriousness about art and skepticism about the affectations of the self-important, and it has been opposed to the avowed philistinism of the English upper classes. *Live at the Apollo* is so brilliantly engineered that this daring Neo-Platonism comes through as unmistakably as the super-bad Bloomsbury beat. A few critics have complained that the Bloomsbury Group relies too heavily on studio effects; this album will instantly put such objections to rest. The lead vocals (some by "Mister White Satin" Lytton Strachey, the others by Clive Bell) are solid and pure, even over the enthusiastic shouts of the notoriously tough-to-please Apollo crowd, and the Stephen Sisters' chorus is reminiscent of the Three Brontës at their best. There is very little "dead air" on this album, even between cuts. On Band 3 on the flip side, there is a pause while the sidemen are setting up, and if you listen carefully you can hear Leonard Woolf and Virginia Stephen coining withering epigrams and exchanging banter with the audience about Macaulay's essay on Warren Hastings. Very mellow, very close textual criticism.

Lytton Strachey, who has been more or less out of the funk-literary picture since his girlfriend threw boiling grits on him in his Memphis hotel room in March of 1924, proves here that his voice is still as sugar-cured as ever. In his long solo number, "Why I Sing the Blues," he really soars through some heartfelt lyrics about his "frail and sickly childhood" and "those painfully introverted public-school years." The song is a triumph of melody and phrasing, and it provides some fascinating insights into the personality of this complex vocalist and biographer.

Much of the credit for the album's brilliance must go to G. E. Moore, who wrote *Principia Ethica*, the group's biggest hit, as well as to Lady Ottoline Morrell, the sound technician and backstage mama. The efforts of professionals like these, combined with Bloomsbury's natural dynamism, have produced that rarest of rarities—a live album that is every bit as good as being there.

II. SAILCAT TURNER REMINISCES ABOUT THE FOUNDING OF THE BLOOMSBURY GROUP

People will tell you nowadays, "Well, the Bloomsbury Group this or the Bloomsbury Group that," or "Bertrand Russell and Sir Kenneth Clark were members of the original Bloomsbury Group," or some such jive misinformation. I don't pay 'em no mind. Because, dig, I knew the Bloomsbury Group before there ever *was* a Bloomsbury Group, before anybody knew there was going to *be* any Bloomsbury Group, and I was in on the very beginning.

One night in '39, I was playing alto with McShann's band uptown at the old Savoy Ballroom—mostly blues, 'cause we had one of the better blues shouters of the day, Walter Brown—and Dizzy Gillespie was sittin' out front. So after the set Diz comes up to me and he says, "Sailcat, I got this chick that you just *got* to hear. Man, this chick can *whale*." So he takes me over to Dan Wall's Chili Joint on Seventh Avenue, and in the back there they got a small combo—two horns, some skins, and a buddy of mine named Biddy Fleet on guitar. They're just runnin' some new chords when from this table near the stage this chick steps up. She's got what you might call a distracted air. She looks around the room nervous-like, and then she throws back her head and sound comes out like no sound I ever heard before. Man, I sat there till eight o'clock in the morning, listening to her. I asked Diz who this chick was, and he says, "Don't you know? That's little Ginny Stephen." Now, of course, everybody talks about Virginia Woolf, author of *To the Lighthouse*, and so on. When I first knew her, she was just little Ginny Stephen. But man, that chick could *whale.*

I liked her music so much that me and Diz and Billie Holiday and Ginny and Ginny's sister Vanessa started hanging out together. So one day Ginny says to me, "Sailcat, I got this economist friend of mine, he's really outta sight. Would you like to meet him?" So I said sure, and she took me downtown to the Village Vanguard, and that was the first time I ever heard John Maynard Keynes. Of course, his playing wasn't much back then. Truth is, he shouldn't have been on the stage at all. Back then he was doin' "What Becomes of the Broken Hearted," but it sure didn't sound like the hit he later made it into. Back then he was still doin' "What Becomes of the Broken Hearted" as a *demonstration,* with charts and bar graphs. Later, of course, he really started cookin' and smokin'. That cat took classical economic theory and bent it in directions nobody ever thought it could go.

Now, Ginny and John, they were pretty tight, and they had this other friend they used to run with. This was a dude named Lytton Strachey, that later became their lead singer. He also won a wide reputation as an author and a critic. After hours, they used to sit around and jam and trade aphorisms. Me and Cootie Williams and Duncan Grant and Billie Holiday and Leonard Woolf, who later married Ginny, and Ella Fitzgerald, who had just taken over Chick Webb's band, and James (Lytton's brother) and Dizzy and the Duke and Maynard Keynes and Satchmo and Charles Mingus and Theodore Llewelyn Davies and Thelonious

Monk and Charles Tennyson and Miles Davis and Ray Charles and Hilton Young (later Lord Kennet) all used to sit in sometimes too. We smoked some reefer. Man, we used to *cook*.

Well, that was the beginning. Later, a lot of people dropped out, and Lytton and Ginny and Vanessa and Maynard and Leonard and Duncan and some of the others started to call themselves the Bloomsbury Group, after their old high school over in England. They asked me and Diz to join, but Diz was supposed to go on tour with Billy Eckstine's band, and as for me, well, I wasn't too crazy about the group's strong Hellenic leanings. Now, of course, I wish I'd said yes.

III. VIRGINIA WOOLF TALKS FRANKLY ABOUT THE BLOOMSBURY GROUP

Being a member of the Bloomsbury Group has brought me out of myself and taught me how to open up to other people. At the beginning, all of us—Leonard, Clive, Vanessa, Lytton, Duncan, Maynard, and me— we were like different states of mind in one consciousness. It was like we each had one tarot card but it didn't make sense until we put all the cards together, and then when we did—it was beautiful. Like in *2001*, when that monkey figures out how to use that bone. Everything was merged.

Of course, we still have our problems. The interpersonal vibes can get pretty intense when we're touring, going from one Quality Court to another and then to another and then another. Sometimes I wonder if I have room to grow as an artist. But usually it works out okay. Like the time I told Lytton that our new reggae number "Mrs. Dalloway" might work better as a short story or even a novel. We talked it out, and Lytton told me I was thinking too linear. Later, I had to admit he was right.

The hardest thing about being a member of the Bloomsbury Group is learning how to be a person at the same time you're being a star. You've got to rise above your myth. We've reached the point where we're completely supportive of each other, and that's good. But at the same time we all have our own separate lives. I've been getting into video, Maynard recorded that album with Barry White, Duncan's been doing some painting—we have to work hard to keep in touch with each other and ourselves, but it's worth it. The way I figure it, there's really nothing else I'd rather do.

1975

IAN FRAZIER

KIMBERLEY SOLZHENITSYN'S CALENDAR

*Two years have passed since the Russian novelist and Nobel Prize win-
ner Alexander Solzhenitsyn left the Soviet Union to take up residence in
the West.* —News item

May 1—Derby Day buffet at Andrei and Bev Sakharov's. Bring cranberry ketchup for the ham.

May 2—Twins to band camp. Drinks with André and Nan Malraux.

May 8—Welcome Wagon visit in A.M. Remind Al to drain dehumidi-
fier pan again.

May 9—Sunday dinner at the Lévi-Strausses'. (Claude and JoAnn.
Children: Sean, 7, and I think Jason, about 4.) 1003 Red Fox Trail,
Walden Estates.

May 10—Pick up twins at band camp. Take Al's old Siberia clothes to
Fire Dept. Rummage Sale.

May 11—Crêpes Club here: Mimi Sartre, Megs Ionesco, Barb Dubuf-
fet, Wendy Szent-Györgyi, Tracy Robbe-Grillet, Gail Miró.

May 12—Remind Al—bring patio trays up from basement. Nobel
Prize winners' Spaghetti Dinner. Get Al's marimba fixed.

May 15—Al's Rotary Meeting: Brown Derby. 8:00 P.M.: To P.-T.A.
Mummers' *Barefoot in the Park* with Mikhail & Candy Baryshnikov.

May 17—Ecology Day. Al's old *Cancer Ward* notes to recycling center.
Twins' swimming lesson—2:30: Leisure Time Pool.

May 20—Leave Subaru at the shop: oil & lube. Twins to the Sakharovs'. Sam & Patsy Beckett for lunch and paddle tennis.

May 21—Hog roast at the Lévi-Strausses'.

May 24—Get twins' band uniforms cleaned for Memorial Day Parade. Al's slide show at Church Guild—"Russia: Land of Contrasts."

May 26—Blocked Writers' Benefit Car-Wash & White Sale: Church parking lot, 9:00 A.M. Evening: Gals' poker night at Cindy Böll's.

May 31—Memorial Day Horse Show: 2:00 P.M. Bring covered dish.

1976

VERONICA GENG

RECORD ROUNDUP

The Supreme Court refused to hear an appeal by former President Richard M. Nixon from a ruling by the United States Court of Appeals under which large portions of some 6,000 hours of White House tape recordings will eventually be released to the public.

—The *Times*, November 30, 1982

PICK HIT:
The Benefit Concert

MUST TO AVOID:
Bad Rap

Nixon, Haldeman & Dean: Blunder Down the Road *(District of Colum-bia)*   Not up to their *Smoking Gun* debut, though audio-wiz producer Alex Butterfield's notorious "walls of sound" remain serviceable. The B side is dismissable on the merits, but with Dick's country-bluesy growl on "Can of Worms" and Brushcut Bob's proto-new-wave incantation of "$900,000," side one will pass as professional heat-taking at its baddest. But bad is as good as they get on this outing. Which is as it should be, and the profundo-paranoiac high of Nixon/Dean's smoochfest-as-dialectic "They Are Asking for It / What an Exciting Prospect" didn't change my mind. Bet they didn't change theirs either. **B MINUS**

Nixon & Dean: Bad Rap *(Panmunjom import)*   The biggest ripoff of this or any century, with no less than eleven of twelve cuts mere soup's-on rephrasings of Nixon's own '50s and '60s anthems (all six extended-play "Crises" plus "Pumpkin Papers," "Communist Issue," "Anna Chennault," "Hoover Told Me," and the man's all-purpose signature tune, the self-fulfilling "This Thing Burns My Tail"). Besides which, when Tricky isn't covering himself he's covering Janis Joplin's "Bobby Was a Ruthless (Characterization Bleeped)," a charisma-grab not half as perverse as smoothie Dean's foray into faux-gospel backup antiphonies ("Absolutely!" "Totally true!" "That's correct!"), musically okay—Tormé meets Torquemada—but commercially misguided. **D MINUS**

Nixon, Dean & Haldeman: The Benefit Concert *(Creep)*   You can't play jailhouse mariachi with church-charity-bazaar chops, but these guys can—and did, in the definitive March 21, 1973, concert to aid prisoners of conscience victimized by Sirica-style justice. Unified by the rhythmically haunting Latinfluence of former house band Liddy & His Cubans while aspiring to the bigger, cleaner sound of Vesco & the Mexican Laundry, the gang finds its groove in a three-route statement melding socio-folkie concern ("How Much Money Do You Need?"), absurdist riffs ("Who Is Porter?"), and spiritual smarts ("As God Is My Maker / We Need More Money")—for sheer ride-this-thing-out stay-ing power, the greatest album of all time. Dean, in superb voice (shoo-in airplay hit: "Cancer"), comes into his own as a soloist forever peerless even by the standard later set in the legendary Capitol Hill sessions. El Tricko, feeling his Quaker oats, pours on that baritone cream and serves up instant classic ("It Is Wrong That's for Sure"), while Halde-man brings home the metaphysical bacon with late-breaking robotica-sardonica, *viz.* "fatal flaw / verbal evil / stupid human errors / dopes," and none dare call it doowop. Not that all this means I have to like it, but I love it. And they almost get away with it. **A**

Nixon, Dean, Haldeman & Ehrlichman: Wild Scenario *(Enemies List Productions)*   Search-and-seize tempos, thesaurus lyrics about "furtherance" and "concomitance"—as long as they kept breaking a few simple rules, there was no reason why this ensemble couldn't parlay its deeply involved harmonies into a pure celebration of criminal liability or even better. Ehrlichman's showboat presence here is an acoustic plus, and though his surprisingly apt cover of Liza's "That Problem Goes On and On" hardly bespeaks the "deep six" poet whose witty improvs would quasi-compensate for the group's ultimately fatal loss of the Dean pipes, it wears far better than Nixon's descent into bubblegum-maudlin, "We Can't Harm These Young People"—so indictably undanceable that you ignore it at your own peril. **B**

Big Enchilada *(N.Y. Bar Association)*   How you respond to this morose tribute compilation, which offers touching originals by Kleindienst ("Mitchell and I"), Haldeman ("Cover Up for John"), and Ehrlichman (the catchy title tune, natch) as well as ye-olde-memory-lane perfunctoriana (the Chief's "Good Man"), depends on your tolerance for sodden wee-hours-in-the-studio sentimentality about an aging master-performer never adequately recorded in his own right. I'd feel better about Henry Petersen wailing "LaRue broke down and cried like a baby / Not fully he broke down / But when it came to testifying about John Mitchell / He just broke down and started to cry" if Petersen knew as much about blues changes as he does about LaRue's tear ducts, or if I knew as much about Mitchell as I would if somebody had bothered to mike him where it would do the most good. Still, on this one they make you care, or at least they would if they knew how.

B MINUS

Nixon, Haldeman, Ehrlichman, Dean & Mitchell: Inaudible *(Sony)* Dumb title, and every word of it is true. Either Butterfield was asleep at the switch or this is a concept move for the Japanese abstraction market—a waste of plastic and, with Mitchell sitting in, an even worse waste of Enchilada exotica. Giveaway: "Yeah, yeah—the way, yeah, yeah, I understand. Postponed—right, right, yeah / Yeah, yeah / Right / Yeah / (Inaudible)." But they've never sounded looser.

C PLUS

Nixon & Kleindienst: Let's Stand Up for People *(Grand Jury)* This tortured after-you-Alphonse act recycles the basics of limited-hang-out obscurity into strategically meaningless polyrhythms aching to transcend their own pungency. That a lot of it is artfully incoherent must mean Dick & Dick thought the long-overdue synthesis might just come naturally, but the album divides too neatly into standard-issue I-know-you-know hooks, standard-issue you-know-I-know hooks, and standard-issue I-thought-you-ought-to-know-I-know-you-know hooks, plus a defiantly throwaway A-side opener, "Would You Like Coffee? Coca-Cola?"—one of those ersatz-icky coat-the-palate numbers played with such jumpy, nerve-jangled insincerity that it leaves you nursing few illusions about this pair's ability to cross over to simple pop truths. **C MINUS**

Nixon & Dean: The Dean Farewell Tour *(Washington Post)* You want soulful resignation, they've got soulful resignation, and they've got it with spark (fave: "Feet to the Fire"). You want the rush of live jamming, they've got that too, with sound effects ("I Am Sorry, Steve, I Hit the Wrong Bell"). Nifty strokes that put this partnership's final stamp on an electronic heritage. **A MINUS**

Nixon, Rogers, Haldeman & Ehrlichman: Really Ticklish *(Dash)* Even more painful than was intended. Sideman Rogers (who?) may be the turnoff element here, but by this time the group was so beset by personnel instability that distinctions are moot. Synth-zomboid Haldeman's "Façade of Normal Operations" tells more than it knows, and only Ehrlichman has the spirit to lighten the prevailing funk, mustering a Segrettiesque sense of theater and playfulness for two Randy Newman–type persona pieces, "Suspend These Birds" and "Dean Is Some Little Clerk." Maybe I'm taking it personally, but it seems to the Dean of American Rock Criticism, aka Some Other Little Clerk, that the dream was over, and not a point in time too soon. **F PLUS**

1983

ROGER ANGELL

BABE RUTH: MY TEAMMATE, MY LOVER

BABE Ruth and I were teammates on the Yankees—and lovers, too. It was no big deal back then. After Sunday games were over, lots of players and writers would come by our little flat in the Morrisania section of the Bronx for one of Babe's famous bean dinners. I also remember the evening when Babe, wearing his familiar pink housecoat, turned out a nice catfish stew for Commissioner Kenesaw Mountain Landis. Everyone in baseball knew how it was with me and Babe. After the company had gone home and we'd done the dishes, he would lie in my arms and I'd whisper, "You are my bambino."

Babe was a fine singer as well as a great cook. He was a natural mezzo-soprano. As we know, Harry Frazee, the owner of the Boston Red Sox, sold Babe to the Yankees in 1919 because he needed cash to back a Broadway musical. What hasn't been told is that he hoped to land Babe for the ingénue role in *No, No, Nanette*. It was all-day games back then, and once the Sultan of Swat had become a fixture at Yankee Stadium he'd have plenty of time to wrap up his work in the Bronx, hop on the subway, and sing and dance on Broadway that evening. An understudy would fill in for him at the Saturday matinées and when the Yanks were away on road trips. That was Frazee's plan, at least. As it transpired, however, there was a two-year production delay and by the time *Nanette* went into rehearsal Babe had grown too fat for the role. Louise Groody got the part instead. He was heartbroken.

The reason was steroids. These were readily available in the early nineteen-twenties, in the form of breakfast food. All you had to do was read the label. Babe went into a bit of a slump in the spring of '22 and, looking for a lift, downed a hundred and twenty-seven bowls of Wheatnutz in one sitting. Typical Ruthean excess. By nightfall, his weight was up by fourteen pounds and he'd turned contralto. The svelte Babe had gone forever, except at the ankles.

The Babe and I were also involved with the Yankees' famous decision to wear pin-striped uniforms. He wasn't a cross-dresser, but one night I was playing pinochle with him in a little Worth frock that had been given to me by Lady Cunard—tight in the bodice but flaring to that cute kneetop hem—and Babe said, "Say, wouldn't that organza stripe look great on our plain white unies!" Excited, we called Colonel Jacob Ruppert, the Yankees' owner, who came right up for a look. He agreed—he was that kind of executive—and once again baseball history was made.

Not everyone was as broadminded about our relationship. Lou Gehrig seemed a mite stuffy about Babe's ways, but he cheered up when he understood that what Ruth wanted from him was something quite special. Babe had been raised in an orphanage, and one day at Comiskey Park he popped the question—asked Lou if he'd legally adopt him. "Kid," he said (he called everybody "kid"), "you play like an old man, so why not be mine?" Lou was tickled—he was that kind of baseball immortal—but in the end his mother, Mom Gehrig, said no.

I'd only played on the Yanks with Babe for a couple of seasons when it became clear that I should give my full attention to our arrangement, undistracted by cheering and umps and train trips. So I quit. Babe never turned up at our place until late—he had a marriage and fatherhood to take care of, downtown—but I needed a whole day to get ready. Shopping, making dinner, and laying out his evening togs made the hours fly by. He'd come in smoking a cigar and full of that day's doings—"I bopped one good offa Walberg!" I can hear him exclaiming—and before you knew it the doorbell would ring and another of our soirées would be under way. Jimmy Walker, Neysa McMein, George Bernard Shaw, Jack Dempsey, Harpo Marx, J. Edgar Hoover, Theda Bara, Jimmie Foxx, Bernarr Macfadden, Edna St. Vincent Millay—ask rather who *didn't* make it uptown to our tasteful nest. Night ran into dawn, and lucky late-stayers might get to hear the Babe (insouciant on the lap of John McCormack, the great Irish tenor) reprise his tender "Caro nome," from *Rigoletto*, or—standing tall with a bat held high—give us one more spirited "Apparvi alla luce" as La Fille du Régiment.

Us old baseball bores are all the same, and it's time for me to get off the field here. If you're wondering which Yankee was the Babe's sweetie for so long, I'll give you a little tip. Look carefully at the mid-twenties team photos and maybe you'll notice that on Babe's cap the famous "NY" logo is interlocked in a slightly different way than on the other guys'. The "Y" is sort of on top, instead of underneath. Then look for another smiling old Yankee with the same variation. That's me! That was our symbol, and Babe and I got our couturier to appliqué it onto our uniforms and, later, our hankies and hand towels. Everyone knew but nobody cared. Those were the days.

2002

FRANK GANNON

DONALD RUMSFELD ORDERS
BREAKFAST AT DENNY'S

THAT'S a good question. Am I ready to order? Let me answer it a little off to the side.

First of all, there *are* things that we know. I can look at this menu and see that. But there's a danger there. Do I "know" that hash browns are not included in the Original Grand Slam Breakfast? It says that on the menu, which, by the way, is nicely laminated and we're grateful to the laminator. But getting back to the hash-brown potatoes. I should "know" that they're not included.

The real truth is, there are no "knowns." This is a whole new menu. Are we in the past? No. Are we using the past's menu? No. Are there things that we know we know? Not exactly.

There are known unknowns. That is to say that there are things that we now know we don't know. But there are also unknown unknowns. These are things that we don't know we don't know. Got that? I want you to note that on the check.

By the way, the Meat Lover's Skillet is a fine piece of work. Thank you for putting that together.

Now, as far as ordering. First, juice. And a small glass of skim milk. Then, to answer the question that I know you were going to ask, yes, this maybe isn't the healthiest place to eat, but we're here. That much is not debatable. We're here. Here. Not someplace else. Not *there*. Back in philosophy class, that's what we used to call a "given." Now, who said we should be here? We don't know. Who picked this place? I can't say.

Who drove the car? I wasn't paying attention. Who's paying for this? That will become clear. Where do we sit? Anywhere you like. Do you like a booth or a movable seat? Makes no difference. Do you want to sit facing the door? Not at this time.

All these questions are not "givens." We can talk about them and we will talk about them when the time is right. Now is not the time or the place to talk. It's the time to order, and that's exactly what we're doing.

Now, another thing. Does this place have a hell of a lot of cholesterol on the menu? Sure. Does cholesterol result in clogged arteries? Probably. Do clogged arteries cause cardiac events? Sometimes. Is it a good idea to clog up all your arteries so your blood stops moving completely? I doubt it. Has the blood completely stopped moving in several parts of my body? Sure. Am I going to grab my chest, fall on the ground, and twist my face into a grotesque mask of pain? Absolutely. Am I gonna go ahead and order the Original Grand Slam Breakfast? You betcha.

Look. I want bacon *and* sausage. Now, let me stop right here. Bacon is, we all know, and nobody seriously doubts it anymore, very similar to sausage. They both come from pigs, they're both cooked, and they're both eaten. They're similar. S-I-M-I-L-A-R. They're not the same. S-A-M-E. If they were the same, I wouldn't be ordering both of them. I don't think the most liberal person in the world can deny *that*, unless he wants to maintain the existence of a parallel universe, with spacemen and ray guns.

Now, is there going to be a cost for this? Sure. Will it be a high cost? I don't know. Am I going to pay for it? Don't know. Am I going to pretend I'm going to the bathroom and then just bolt on the check? Maybe. Are they going to catch me getting into my car? Not if I send somebody out to start the car and pull it up right outside the door so I can just run out and dive into the back seat. Do I have a good chance of getting away with it? Absolutely. Is this a crime? I personally think of it as defending myself from breakfast items of exorbitant price. Period.

It's just a rational way of dealing with expense, a very forward-looking, sensible way of dealing with breakfast in a very cost-conscious manner. That's all.

Thank you very much.

2003

JESSE LICHTENSTEIN

WHAT WOULD JESUS TEST-DRIVE?

Thirty-three percent of the public thought Jesus would not drive a sport utility vehicle, while 29 percent thought he would, 31 percent offered no opinion and 7 percent volunteered the reply that he would not drive, but walk.

—The *Times*, referring to a poll by the Pew Research Center and the Pew Forum

EDGEWATER CADILLAC

SALES ASSOCIATE: And here's our deluxe SUV, the Escalade. Comes in sable black, protective cladding, onboard DVD Navigation System, seventeen-inch seven-spoke cast-aluminum wheels.

JESUS: It catches the eye.

SALES ASSOCIATE: All the luxury and craftsmanship you've come to expect from a Cadillac, but with the physical road presence to exceed all SUV vehicles in its class. Go ahead, hop in.

JESUS: Nice.

SALES ASSOCIATE: Ten-way power adjusting seats with power lumbar support and side bolsters. Let's drive.

JESUS: All right. I notice the windows are really dark.

SALES ASSOCIATE: Full tint job. Most of our high-profile clients demand it, so we keep it on the floor model.

JESUS: Gotcha. It handles really well.

SALES ASSOCIATE: Deceptively smooth.

JESUS: Okay, let's say I'm just curious: could I switch the wheels for twenty-two-inch chrome Momos and add a brushed billet grille, Corsa exhaust tips, Kicker Solo-Baric L7 subs, and a Magna Charger with a 4.5-p.s.i. boost?

SALES ASSOCIATE: Piece of cake.

JESUS: What's the gas mileage?

SALES ASSOCIATE: [*snickers*] Sorry? Didn't catch that.

JESUS: I'm just messing with you.

BIEGLER HONDA AND MITSUBISHI

SALES ASSOCIATE: Listen to that—almost silent.

JESUS: Amazing! It sounds more like a refrigerator than a car. It's eerie.

SALES ASSOCIATE: On these hybrids, the gasoline engine doesn't kick in until you top twenty-two m.p.h.

JESUS: There it goes, I hear it. That's fascinating.

SALES ASSOCIATE: Take a left here.

JESUS: So, honestly, how many miles per gallon are we talking about?

SALES ASSOCIATE: In town, you'll get about sixty m.p.g.s. On the freeway, I can get you sixty-six.

JESUS: Sixty-six?! Really?

SALES ASSOCIATE: I know, it's a marvel. They should have had these years ago. Goodbye, staggering gas prices. So long, dependence on foreign oil cartels. And there's the environmental aspect—you feel a little better about yourself at the end of the day.

JESUS: So how fast can it go?

SALES ASSOCIATE: It's perfectly adequate for freeway speeds. You aren't going to be able to push eighty-five up a mountain pass with a U-Haul in the back, but for most people that's not a problem.

JESUS: Oh. So it's a little weak, then.

SALES ASSOCIATE: You really won't notice it much in your everyday life.

JESUS: What if I want to peel out at a stoplight?

SALES ASSOCIATE: Well, it starts out with the electric motor, so . . .

JESUS: I see. Suppose some kid in a Corvette cuts me off, then floors it and starts to pull away?

SALES ASSOCIATE: Well, I mean . . .

JESUS: Because it sounds like you're trying to sell me a shiny new golf cart.

RIVERSIDE HUMMER

SALES ASSOCIATE: How's it feel?

JESUS: Powerful.

SALES ASSOCIATE: What did I tell you—it's a rush. It's like crack cocaine.

JESUS: It really is a remarkable feeling, being this high up.

SALES ASSOCIATE: Like riding a bull. That's a seriously mean *toro* beneath you, amigo. Who says size doesn't matter, eh?

JESUS: It's really big.

SALES ASSOCIATE: You know, I envy you. I remember my first drive—I knew I could never go back. I've got two of these mothers at home now, Xena the Warrior and Sharon. As in Stone. Gotta take turns with them or they get jealous.

JESUS: I don't know. I don't think it would fit in my garage.

SALES ASSOCIATE: Well, mortgage rates these days are rock bottom. A lot of my customers are refinancing and using the money to fix up the garage, add a deck, a Jacuzzi, a shooting range, what have you. So you could remodel the whole garage, have more space for your tools—you said you were a carpenter?

JESUS: Mostly finish work. Cabinets.

SALES ASSOCIATE: Well, you can haul a pretty pile of cabinets in the back of this baby. And cabinets ain't everything. Let me ask you this: Are you married?

JESUS: No.

SALES ASSOCIATE: Correct answer. Now, take a look at me. Am I a handsome man?

JESUS: Um . . .

SALES ASSOCIATE: Hey, tell it like it is—I'm no movie star, I know that. But let me ask you this: How many women did I pick up in Xena last week alone?

JESUS: Come again?

SALES ASSOCIATE: I'm not talking about a friendly ride around the block. I'm not talking about "let me drop you off at your pedicure appointment." The question is: How many women did I spread like Philadelphia cream cheese in the back of my H2 last week?

JESUS: Um, look . . .

SALES ASSOCIATE: Go on, how many?

JESUS: I really couldn't . . .

SALES ASSOCIATE: How many?

JESUS: I have no idea. Two? Three?

SALES ASSOCIATE: Unh-unh.

JESUS: Ten?

SALES ASSOCIATE: Please. Now you're pissing on my parade. Five. Five! In one week! And that's me. Now, take you. You've got the whole retro-fashion thing going for you—the sandal thing, the beard. Unusual for a man commanding six tons of steel, you follow? Keeps 'em guessing. And let me ask you this: Ever wondered what a

Volkswagen Beetle sounds like as it's crushed to scrap metal beneath your front axle?

JESUS: Not really . . .

SALES ASSOCIATE: Like angels on high, amigo. Angels rejoicing on high.

2003

PAUL RUDNICK

INTELLIGENT DESIGN

DAY NO. 1:

And the Lord God said, "Let there be light," and lo, there was light. But then the Lord God said, "Wait, what if I make it a sort of rosy, sunset-at-the-beach, filtered half-light, so that everything else I design will look younger?"

"I'm loving that," said Buddha. "It's new."

"You should design a restaurant," added Allah.

DAY NO. 2:

"Today," the Lord God said, "let's do land." And lo, there was land.

"Well, it's really not just land," noted Vishnu. "You've got mountains and valleys and—is that lava?"

"It's not a single statement," said the Lord God. "I want it to say, 'Yes, this is land, but it's not afraid to ooze.' "

"It's really a backdrop, a sort of blank canvas," put in Apollo. "It's, like, minimalism, only with scale."

"But—brown?" Buddha asked.

"Brown with infinite variations," said the Lord God. "Taupe, ochre, burnt umber—they're called earth tones."

"I wasn't criticizing," said Buddha. "I was just noticing."

DAY NO. 3:

"Just to make everyone happy," said the Lord God, "today I'm thinking oceans, for contrast."

"It's wet, it's deep, yet it's frothy; it's design without dogma," said Buddha, approvingly.

"Now, *there's* movement," agreed Allah. "It's not just 'Hi, I'm a planet—no splashing.' "

"But are those ice caps?" inquired Thor. "Is this a coherent vision, or a highball?"

"I can do ice caps if I want to," sniffed the Lord God.

"It's about a mood," said the Angel Moroni, supportively.

"Thank you," said the Lord God.

DAY NO. 4:

"One word," said the Lord God. "Landscaping. But I want it to look natural, as if it all somehow just happened."

"Do rain forests," suggested a primitive tribal god, who was known only as a clicking noise.

"Rain forests here," decreed the Lord God. "And deserts there. For a spa feeling."

"Which is fresh, but let's give it glow," said Buddha. "Polished stones and bamboo, with a soothing trickle of something."

"I know where you're going," said the Lord God. "But why am I seeing scented candles and a signature body wash?"

"Shut up," said Buddha.

"You shut up," said the Lord God.

"It's all about the mix," Allah declared in a calming voice. "Now let's look at some swatches."

DAY NO. 5:

"I'd like to design some creatures of the sea," the Lord God said. "Sleek but not slick."

"Yes, yes, and more yes—it's a total gills moment," said Apollo. "But what if you added wings?"

"Fussy," whispered Buddha to Zeus. "Why not epaulets and a sash?"

"Legs," said Allah. "Now let's do legs."

"Are we already doing dining-room tables?" asked the Lord God, confused.

"No, design some *creatures* with legs," said Allah. So the Lord God, nodding, designed an ostrich.

"First draft," everyone agreed, and so the Lord God designed an alligator.

"There's gonna be a waiting list," Zeus murmured appreciatively.

"Now do puppies!" pleaded Vishnu. "And kitties!"

"*Ooooo!*" all the gods cooed. Then, feeling a bit embarrassed, Zeus ventured, "Design something more practical, like a horse or a mule."

"What about a koala?" asked the Lord God.

"Much better," Zeus declared, cuddling the furry little animal. "I'm going to call him Buttons."

DAY NO. 6:

"Today I'm really going out there," said the Lord God. "And I know it won't be popular at first, and you're all gonna be saying, 'Earth to Lord God,' but in a few million years it's going to be timeless. I'm going to design a man."

And everyone looked upon the man that the Lord God designed.

"It has your eyes," Zeus told the Lord God.

"Does it stack?" inquired Allah.

"It has a naïve, folk-artsy, I-made-it-myself vibe," said Buddha. The Inca sun god, however, only scoffed. "Been there. Evolution," he said. "It's called a shaved monkey."

"I like it," protested Buddha. "But it can't work a strapless dress." Everyone agreed on this point, so the Lord God announced, "Well, what if I give it nice round breasts and lose the penis?"

"Yes," the gods said immediately.

"Now it's intelligent," said Aphrodite.

"But what if I made it blond?" giggled the Lord God.

"And what if I made you a booming offscreen voice in a lot of bad movies?" asked Aphrodite.

DAY NO. 7:

"You know, I'm really feeling good about this whole intelligent-design deal," said the Lord God. "But do you think that I could redo it, keeping the quality but making it at a price point we could all live with?"

"I'm not sure," said Buddha. "You mean, what if you designed a really basic, no-frills planet? Like, do the man and the woman really need all those toes?"

"Hello!" said the Lord God. "Clean lines, no moving parts, functional but fun. Three bright, happy, wash 'n' go colors."

"Swedish meets Japanese, with maybe a Platinum Collector's Edition for the geeks," Buddha decided.

"Done," said the Lord God. "Now let's start thinking about Pluto. What if everything on Pluto was brushed aluminum?"

"You mean, let's do Neptune again?" said Buddha.

2005

CHRISTOPHER BUCKLEY

JEEVES AND W.

I WAS lying in bed after a rather depressing night, listening to the birds twitter in the trees, when Jeeves shimmered into the room.

"What ho, Jeeves."

"Good morning, sir."

"What's all this I hear about your heading up some Iraq Study Group? Have you been talking to my father again?"

"Might I suggest the blue suit today? Something about this November suggests blue."

Sometimes Jeeves can be evasive, which is when I apply the old iron hand that we W.s are known for.

"Now, see here, Jeeves, I can handle this Iraq business myself."

"Yes, sir. But, if I may, there does seem to be something of a clamor for an exit strategy."

"Dash it, Jeeves, the only exit strategy is victory."

"Yes, sir. So Dr. Kissinger keeps insisting. And yet, as the Bard would suggest, ripeness is all."

"What are you talking about?"

"*King Lear,* sir. A play by the late Mr. Shakespeare."

"Just spit it out."

"As you may recall, sir, I had suggested replacing Mr. Rumsfeld before the election, rather than after."

"Deuced good idea, Jeeves. See to it immediately. Walk him up the scaffold, and no blindfold. That'll get us a few votes."

We W.s are slow to anger, but, when the feeling comes, the ground around us trembles.

"If I may, sir?"

"What is it, Jeeves?"

"The election is over."

"Oh. Dash it all, Jeeves, you might have told me."

"I believe there was some mention of it in the newspapers."

"Well, don't be so mysterious. How'd we do? Another unqualified triumph?"

"Not as satisfactorily as one might have hoped, sir. One might even be tempted to say that we took rather a thumping."

"Hmm. Wondered why there've been so many Democrats lurking about. Every time I look up from my desk, they're tiptoeing about with tape measures. It's deuced annoying, Jeeves. How's a president supposed to concentrate?"

"I have spoken with the Secret Service about it, sir. I have asked them to limit Democratic visitors to no more than two per day."

"That Pelosi woman. Sat there like a cobra. Froze my blood, Jeeves. Could hardly get up out of my chair."

"I keenly regret it, sir. I shall ask the Secret Service to be on the lookout especially for her. Meanwhile, perhaps if you appealed to her maternal side? I believe the lady is a mother of five and a grandmother. Perhaps a tasteful arrangement of seasonal flowers, accompanied by an appropriate sentiment? 'Every hyacinth the garden wears / dropped in her lap from some once lovely head.' "

"What are you going on about now?"

"A poem, sir, by a Mr. Khayyam. A Persian person."

"Well, stop it. You're making my head spin. And that Reid fellow who was with her—good Lord, he could give the Grim Reaper a run for his money. Where do the Democrats find these people, Jeeves? In a funeral parlor?"

"I believe the gentleman is from the state of Nevada, sir. The 'Battle Born' state, as the state flag has it. Admitted to the Union during the Civil War."

"I tried to jolly him up by giving him one of my nicknames. You know how I like to crack the old ice by giving people nicknames."

"I am acquainted with your tendency toward the spontaneous assignment of the fraternal sobriquet. Might I inquire just what you called him?"

"Cactus Butt."

"Doubtless a reference to the flora of his natal environs. And was the future Senate Majority Leader amused, sir, by your jeu d'esprit?"

"He just stared at me. Deuced uncomfortable, let me tell you."

"Perhaps the gentleman is not inclined to persiflage. But, if I may, sir, with respect to Iraq?"

"All right, then. Give it to me straight up."

"Might I suggest, sir, a regional conference?"

"Dash it, Jeeves, we're at war. You can't go conferencing with bullets flying all over the place."

"Indeed, sir. And yet if we were to invite, say, Iran and Syria and some of the other affected countries to sit down for what is, I believe, referred to as 'networking,' it might take some of the pressure off yourself?"

"You mean the sort of how-d'ye-do where everyone sits at one of those huge U-shaped tables and makes endless orations all day?"

"That would be the general notion, yes, sir."

"Now, steady on, Jeeves. You know I hate those things. You sit there with an earphone, listening to interpreters jibber-jabber about how it's all your fault. I'd rather take my chances playing Blinky with Cobra Woman and Cactus Butt."

"You wouldn't actually have to attend personally, sir. Indeed, I could represent you, if that would be agreeable."

"I say, would you, Jeeves?"

"Certainly, sir. Indeed, sir, it is my impression that you have been working much too hard as it is. Might I suggest that you winter at the ranch in Crawford? I believe the climate there this time of year is thought to be salubrious."

"But what if the vice-president wants to come down and go quail-hunting?"

"I have taken the liberty of speaking with the Secret Service, sir, and have asked that they replace Mr. Cheney's shotgun cartridges with blanks."

"Jeeves, you're a genius. Pack my things. We leave immediately."

"Thank you, sir. I endeavor to give satisfaction."

2006

EXPLANATIONS
AND
ADVISORIES

ROBERT BENCHLEY

SO YOU'RE GOING TO NEW YORK

TO the traveler who is returning to New York after a summer in Europe, full of continental ways and accustomed to taking in with an appraising eye such points of interest as have been called to his attention by the little books he bought at Brentano's, perhaps a few words will not be amiss to refresh his memory about his homeland. One forgets so easily.

We approach New York by the beautiful North River, so-called because it is on the west of the island, the scene of many naval battles during the Civil War and referred to by Napoleon as "*le robinet qui ne marche pas*" ("the faucet which does not work"). All true Americans, on sailing up the harbor, will naturally feel a thrill of pride as the tall towers (incorrectly called "the tall towers of Ilium") raise their shaggy heads through the mists, and will naturally remark to one another: "Well, after all, there isn't anything like Little Old New York." These will be the last kind words they speak of New York until they are abroad again next year.

(We are purposely omitting any satirical reference to the Statue of Liberty and Prohibition, but there will be any number of amateur satirists on board who will make them for you in case you feel the need of them. The editors of this work believe, with Beaumarchais, that "obedience to law is liberty" and, so long as Prohibition is a law of this country, will do or say nothing to discredit it. It is, however, fairly safe to slip a couple of small bottles of Napoleon brandy into the pockets of your overcoat if you carry it over your arm.)

The word for douanier is *customs-house officer*, and you will find that the American customs are much less exacting than those of foreign countries, owing to the supremacy of American industries and their manufacturing efficiency which makes it possible for them to make better goods at lower prices than those of Europe. The only articles which one is not allowed to bring into America in any quantity are:

Wearing apparel, jewelry, silks, laces, cottons (woven or in the bale), living equipment, books, gifts, raw hides, marble slabs, toothpaste, sugar cane, music (sheet or hummed), garters (except black with a narrow white band), sun-burn acquired abroad, moustaches grown abroad (unless for personal use), cellulose, iron pyrites, medicine (unless poison), threshing-machines, saliva, over four lungfuls of salt air, and any other items that you might possibly want to bring in.

The customs thus disposed of, we take a cab and tell the driver to drive slowly to our hotel. This will be difficult at first, owing to the hold which the French or German language has got on us. We may not have noticed while we were abroad (and certainly the foreigners never noticed it) how like second-nature it comes to speak French or German, but, on landing in America, we shall constantly be finding ourselves (especially in the presence of friends who have been at home all summer) calling waiters "*Garçon*" or saying to drivers: "*Nicht so schnell, bitte!*" This will naturally cause us a little embarrassment which we will explain away by saying that we really have got so used to it that it is going to take us a couple of days to get the hang of English. Some way should be found to make Americans as glib in foreign languages while they are abroad as they are when they get back to New York. Then there will be no more wars.

AMERICAN money will cause us quite a lot of trouble, too, especially those new bank-notes. Compiling statistics ahead of time, we may say that roughly one million returning Americans will remark to friends, during the month of September: "Say, I thought I had a ten-shilling note here," or "I'll be giving one of these dollars for ten francs the first thing I know." The fact that they are not the same size at all will not enter into it. Sharp-tempered people who have been in New York throughout the torrid season may have to take the matter into their own hands and shoot a great many returned travelers.

The new money will, however, present quite a problem, owing to the tendency of those who have been accustomed to wadding five- and ten-franc notes (to keep them from falling apart) leaving dollar bills similarly wadded around in peignoir pockets or tossing them off as tips. New York waiters, during the month of September, will probably reap a harvest of wadded dollar bills. Or maybe, when it is a matter of a loss of seventy-five cents, the travelers will catch themselves just in time and remember that they are back in America.

Now that we are safe and sound at our hotel, or home, or favorite speakeasy, we have the whole of marvelous New York before us. New York was founded by the Dutch in the seventeenth century (the editors will not give you the exact date because by looking it up for yourself you will remember it better) and is a veritable gold-mine of historic associations. We must divide our days up wisely, in order to get the most out of our stay here, and to renew old friendships and revisit familiar scenes. We shall also spend a few days looking over old bills which we neglected to pay before sailing.

The old friendships will not be so difficult to renew. The first old friend we meet will say: "Hi!" cheerily and pass on. The second will say: "Not so hot as it was last week, is it?" and the third will say: "When are you going to take your vacation?" This will get us back into the swing again, and we can devote the rest of our time to studying points of interest. Most of these will either have been torn down or closed.

There is an alternate, or Trip B, from Europe to New York. If we follow this, we stay right on the boat and go back to Cherbourg.

1929

PETER DE VRIES

A HARD DAY AT THE OFFICE

I RECENTLY worked in an office where they had a number of those signs reading "Think," the motto of the International Business Machines Corporation, which so many other business firms seem to be adopting. The signs became almost at once a bone of contention between my employer and me, though not because I was not responsive to them; I have always reacted unqualifiedly to wall injunctions, especially the monosyllabic kind. Confronted, for example, with the exhortation "Smile," my face becomes wreathed in an expression of felicity that some people find unendurable. The "Think" signs, one of which was visible from my desk, so I saw it every time I raised my head, were equally effective. As a consequence, by midmorning of my first day on the job I was so immersed in rumination that the boss, a ruddy, heavy-set fellow named Harry Bagley, paused on his way past my desk, evidently struck by a remote and glazed look in my eye.

"What's the matter with you?" he asked.

"I was just thinking," I said, stirring from my concentration.

"What about?"

"Zeno's paradoxes," I answered. "The eight paradoxes by which he tries to discredit the belief in plurality and motion, and which have come down to us in the writings of Aristotle and Simplicius. I was recalling particularly the one about Achilles and the tortoise. You remember it. Achilles can never catch up with the tortoise for, while he traverses the distance between his starting point and that of the tortoise, the tortoise advances a certain distance, and while Achilles traverses this distance, the tortoise makes a further advance, and so on ad infinitum. Consequently, Achilles may run ad infinitum without overtaking the tortoise. *Ergo* there is no motion."

"A fat hell of a lot of good this is doing us," Bagley said.

"Oh, I know Zeno's old hat and, as you say, fruitless from a practical point of view," I said. "But here's the thought I want to leave with you. It's amazing how many of our values are still based on this classic logic, and so maybe the semanticists, under Korzybski and later Hayakawa, have been right in hammering home to us a less absolutistic approach to things."

"Yes, well, get some of this work off your desk," Bagley said, gesturing at a cluster of documents that had been thickening there since nine o'clock.

"Right," I said, and he bustled off.

I FELL to with a will, and by noon was pretty well caught up. But as I sat down at my desk after lunch, my eye fell on the admonitory legend dominating the opposite wall, and I was soon again deep in a train of reflections, which, while lacking the abstruseness of my morning cogitations, were nevertheless not wholly without scope and erudition. My face must have betrayed the strain of application once more, for Bagley stopped as he had earlier.

"Now what?" he said.

I put down a paper knife I had been abstractedly bending.

"I've been thinking," I said, "that the element of the fantastic in the graphic arts is, historically speaking, so voluminous that it's presumptuous of the Surrealists to pretend that they have any more than given a contemporary label to an established vein. Take the chimerical detail in much Flemish and Renaissance painting, the dry, horrifying apparitions of Hieronymus Bosch—"

"Get your money," Bagley said.

"But why? What am I doing but what that sign says?" I protested, pointing to it.

"That sign doesn't mean this kind of thinking," Bagley said.

"What kind, then? What do you want me to think about?" I asked.

"Think about your work. Think about the product. Anything."

"All right, I'll try that," I said. "I'll try thinking about the product. But which one?" I added, for the firm was a wholesale-food company that handled many kinds of foods. I was at pains to remind Bagley of this. "So shall I think of food in general, or some particular item?" I asked. "Or some phase of distribution?"

"Oh, good God, I don't know," Bagley said impatiently. "Think of the special we're pushing," he said, and made off.

The special we were pushing just then was packaged mixed nuts, unshelled. The firm had been trying to ascertain what proportions people liked in mixed nuts—what ratio of walnuts, hazelnuts, almonds, and so on—as reflected in relative sales of varying assortments that the company had been simultaneously putting out in different areas. I didn't see how any thinking on my part could help reach any conclusion about that, the more so because my work, which was checking and collating credit memoranda, offered no data along those lines. So I figured the best thing would be for me to dwell on nuts in a general way, which I did.

SHORTLY after four o'clock, I was aware of Bagley's bulk over me, and of Bagley looking down at me. "Well?" he said.

I turned to him in my swivel chair, crossing my legs.

"Nuts, it seems to me, have a quality that makes them unique among foods," I said. "I'm not thinking of their more obvious aspect as an autumnal symbol, their poetic association with festive periods. They have something else, a *je ne sais quoi* that has often haunted me while eating them but that I have never quite been able to pin down, despite that effort of imaginative physical identification that is the legitimate province of the senses."

"You're wearing me thin," Bagley said.

"But now I think I've put my finger on the curious quality they have," I said. *"Nuts are in effect edible wood."*

"Get your money," Bagley said.

I rose. "I don't understand what you want," I exclaimed. "Granted the observation is a trifle on the precious side, is that any reason for firing a man? Give me a little time."

"You've got an hour till quitting time. Your money'll be ready then," Bagley said.

MY money was ready by quitting time. As I took it, I reflected that my wages from this firm consisted almost exclusively of severance pay. Bagley had beefed about having to fork over two weeks' compensation, but he forked it over.

I got another job soon afterward. I still have it. It's with an outfit that doesn't expect you to smile or think or anything like that. Anyhow, I've learned my lesson as far as the second is concerned. If I'm ever again confronted with a sign telling me to think, I'll damn well think twice before I do.

1953

WOODY ALLEN

A LOOK AT ORGANIZED CRIME

IT is no secret that organized crime in America takes in over forty billion dollars a year. This is quite a profitable sum, especially when one considers that the Mafia spends very little for office supplies. Reliable sources indicate that the Cosa Nostra laid out no more than six thousand dollars last year for personalized stationery, and even less for staples. Furthermore, they have one secretary who does all the typing, and only three small rooms for headquarters, which they share with the Fred Persky Dance Studio.

Last year, organized crime was directly responsible for more than one hundred murders, and *mafiosi* participated indirectly in several hundred more, either by lending the killers carfare or by holding their coats.

Other illicit activities engaged in by Cosa Nostra members included gambling, narcotics, prostitution, hijacking, loansharking, and the transportation of a large whitefish across a state line for immoral purposes. The tentacles of this corrupt empire even reach into the government itself. Only a few months ago, two gang lords under federal indictment spent the night at the White House, and the President slept on the sofa.

HISTORY OF ORGANIZED CRIME IN THE UNITED STATES

In 1921, Thomas (The Butcher) Covello and Ciro (The Tailor) Santucci attempted to organize disparate ethnic groups of the underworld and thus take over Chicago. This was foiled when Albert (The Logical Positivist) Corillo assassinated Kid Lipsky by locking him in a closet and sucking all the air out through a straw. Lipsky's brother Mendy (alias Mendy Lewis, alias Mendy Larsen, alias Mendy Alias) avenged Lipsky's murder by abducting Santucci's brother Gaetano (also known as Little Tony, or Rabbi Henry Sharpstein) and returning him several weeks later in twenty-seven separate mason jars. This signaled the beginning of a bloodbath.

Dominick (The Herpetologist) Mione shot Lucky Lorenzo (so nicknamed when a bomb that went off in his hat failed to kill him) outside a bar in Chicago. In return, Corillo and his men traced Mione to Newark and made his head into a wind instrument. At this point, the Vitale gang, run by Giuseppe Vitale (real name Quincy Baedeker), made their move to take over all bootlegging in Harlem from Irish Larry Doyle—a racketeer so suspicious that he refused to let anybody in New York ever get behind him, and walked down the street constantly pirouetting and spinning around. Doyle was killed when the Squillante Construction Company decided to erect their new offices on the bridge of his nose. Doyle's lieutenant, Little Petey (Big Petey) Ross, now took command; he resisted the Vitale takeover and lured Vitale to an empty midtown garage on the pretext that a costume party was being held there. Unsuspecting, Vitale walked into the garage dressed as a giant mouse, and was instantly riddled with machine-gun bullets. Out of loyalty to their slain chief, Vitale's men immediately defected to Ross. So did Vitale's fiancée, Bea Moretti, a showgirl and star of the hit Broadway musical *Say Kaddish,* who wound up marrying Ross, although she later sued him for divorce, charging that he once spread an unpleasant ointment on her.

Fearing federal intervention, Vincent Columbraro, the Buttered Toast King, called for a truce. (Columbraro had such tight control over all buttered toast moving in and out of New Jersey that one word from him could ruin breakfast for two-thirds of the nation.) All members of the underworld were summoned to a diner in Perth Amboy, where Columbraro told them that internal warfare must stop and that from then on they had to dress decently and stop slinking around. Letters formerly signed with a black hand would in the future be signed "Best Wishes," and all territory would be divided equally, with New Jersey going to Columbraro's mother. Thus the Mafia, or Cosa Nostra (literally, "my underwear" or "our underwear"), was born. Two days later, Columbraro got into a nice hot tub to take a bath and has been missing for the past forty-six years.

MOB STRUCTURE

The Cosa Nostra is structured like any government or large corporation—or group of gangsters, for that matter. At the top is the *capo di tutti capi*, or boss of all bosses. Meetings are held at his house, and he is responsible for supplying cold cuts and ice cubes. Failure to do so means instant death. (Death, incidentally, is one of the worst things that can happen to a Cosa Nostra member, and many prefer simply to pay a fine.) Under the boss of bosses are his lieutenants, each of whom runs one section of town with his "family." Mafia families do not consist of a wife and children who always go places like the circus or on picnics. They are actually groups of rather serious men, whose main joy in life comes from seeing how long certain people can stay under the East River before they start gurgling.

Initiation into the Mafia is quite complicated. A proposed member is blindfolded and led into a dark room. Pieces of Crenshaw melon are placed in his pockets, and he is required to hop around on one foot and cry out, "Toodles! Toodles!" Next, his lower lip is pulled out and snapped back by all the members of the board, or *commissione;* some may even wish to do it twice. Following this, some oats are put on his head. If he complains, he is disqualified. If, however, he says, "Good, I like oats on my head," he is welcomed into the brotherhood. This is done by kissing him on the cheek and shaking his hand. From that moment on, he is not permitted to eat chutney, to amuse his friends by imitating a hen, or to kill anybody named Vito.

CONCLUSIONS

Organized crime is a blight on our nation. While many young Americans are lured into a career of crime by its promise of an easy life, most criminals actually must work long hours, frequently in buildings without air-conditioning. Identifying criminals is up to each of us. Usually they can be recognized by their large cufflinks and their failure to stop eating when the man sitting next to them is hit by a falling anvil. The best methods of combating organized crime are:

1. Telling the criminals you are not at home.
2. Calling the police whenever an unusual number of men from the Sicilian Laundry Company begin singing in your foyer.
3. Wiretapping.

Wiretapping cannot be employed indiscriminately, but its effectiveness is illustrated by this transcript of a conversation between two gang bosses in the New York area whose phones had been tapped by the FBI:

ANTHONY: Hello? Rico?
RICO: Hello?
ANTHONY: Rico?
RICO: Hello.
ANTHONY: Rico?
RICO: I can't hear you.
ANTHONY: Is that you, Rico? I can't hear you.
RICO: What?
ANTHONY: Can you hear me?
RICO: Hello?
ANTHONY: Rico?
RICO: We have a bad connection.
ANTHONY: Can you hear me?
RICO: Hello?
ANTHONY: Rico?
RICO: Hello?
ANTHONY: Operator, we have a bad connection.
OPERATOR: Hang up and dial again, sir.
RICO: Hello?

Because of this evidence, Anthony (The Fish) Rotunno and Rico Panzini were convicted and are currently serving fifteen years in Sing Sing for illegal possession of Bensonhurst.

1970

GARRISON KEILLOR

THE PEOPLE'S SHOPPER

SHOP THE CO-OP WAY AND SAVE!

THESE FINE PEOPLES ARE HAPPY TO SERVE YOU

THE WHOLE WHEAT FOOD CO-OP

The WWFC Coordinating Council has approved the following statement for publication. The Council voted on the statement line-by-line, and where the vote was not unanimous the minority opinion appears in brackets.

WHOLE WHEAT FLOUR
Ground on Our Own Millstone 12¢ lb.
[*8¢*]

ORANGES
6¢ ea.

MILK
39¢ ½ gal. 82¢ gal.
[*What's the markup for—the pleasure of your company? 78¢*]

CARROTS
15¢ lb.
[*The carrots are not too crisp because the big honchos in this so-called organization don't know how to call an electrician to fix the cooler,*]

which has not worked for six weeks now. In fact, it's like a steam pit in there. If the "coordinators" would come around once in a while they might find out about these things. The oranges are shriveled up, also the lettuce, and the carrots are like rubber. Organic or not, I wouldn't feed it to apes. Diane.]

HOME MADE YOGHURT
Delicious 75¢ qt.
[*Anyone who can in good conscience sell this stuff for 75¢ should be forced to eat it.*]

ACORN SQUASH
30¢ ea.
[*I will not accept more than 21¢ per squash and I am giving away the bread and milk free until this group shows a little more sensitivity to the women, who do about 2/3rds of the work. That's no lie either.*

I am at the store 1–4 p.m. Mondays and 5–8 Thursdays—the tall woman with reddish hair and glasses. See me for bargains. Marcia.]

SHARP CHEDDAR
80¢ lb.
[*Stuff it in your ear, hippie ripoff artist! We're busting out of this pukehole!*]

SUPPORT [*THE BOYCOTT OF*]
YOUR NEIGHBORHOOD CO-OP

PEOPLE'S CANDY COLLECTIVE

Last August, five of us pulled out of the Whole Wheat Co-op to form the Collective. Hopefully this article will try to explain what we're doing and where we go from here.

At Whole Wheat we were making sesame-seed cakes and oat balls. We enjoyed our work, but we wanted to branch out into wholesome chocolates and nut bars. This proved to be traumatic for the Co-op hierarchy, which was into macrobiotic and organic gardening, the whole elitist grocery bag. They took the position that candy is bad for the people, it ruins their teeth, spoils their appetite, etc. Finally, we split. Our purpose was to set up a candy store where the decision-making would be shared by the whole community and everyone could contribute his ideas.

First, we visited the existing candy store in the neighborhood, Yaklich's. We assured Mr. Yaklich and his son Baron that our intention was to cooperate, not compete, and we agreed not to sell cigarettes, cigars, newspapers, magazines, or adult books, which they are very much into. They are also into point spreads, and we agreed not to do that, either.

Second, we tried to get some Indian, black, and Chicano representation (of which there was none) in the Collective, but that was a problem, since there was none in the neighborhood, either, and attendance at our meetings would've meant a long ride on the bus for them.

Finally, we began soliciting community input. We began at the nearby grade school, where we met a lot of people who, though unfamiliar with the theory of running a collective, were very helpful and gave us a lot of new ideas. They suggested such things as licorice whips, nougat bars, sourballs, jawbreakers, bubble gum, soda pop, frozen delights, cupcakes, and Twinkies.

These are yet to be discussed, but it appears we have several alternatives: to go back to Whole Wheat, to help the grade-school community set up its own candy collective, or to serve them and their needs in order to create a broader base of support within which we can seek to familiarize them with where we are at. We invite anyone concerned to stop by the store (upstairs from the Universal Joint).

ST. PAUL'S EPISCOPAL DROP-IN HAIR CENTER

If you've decided to get a haircut, that's your decision, but why go to a straight barber and pay $3.50 for a lot of bad jokes? Come to St. Paul's Hair Center (in the rectory basement) where Rev. Ray and Rev. Don are waiting to see you. The price is right on and the rap is easy. Ray and Don are trained barbers, but more than that they know how hard this move can be and offer warm supportive pre- and post-trim counseling. They're people-oriented, not hair-oriented, and if you just want to come in and *talk* about haircuts, well, that's cool, too.

PEOPLE'S MEATS

Most of us accept strict vegetarianism as the best way, but many find it difficult to change their eating habits. People's Meats is an interim solution. All of our meat comes from animals who were unable to care for themselves any longer. Hoping to phase out the operation, we do not advertise hours, prices, or location. We do not deliver.

PEOPLE'S USED FURNITURE

One sign of what's going on in our society is the trend toward larger and harder beds. Queen-size, king-size, wider, firmer—beds that resemble a flat plain and the sleepers ships passing in the night, not knowing one another at all. We reject that kind of sleep with our Warm Valley Bed. It is built narrow and soft and shaped like a trough, gently urging its occupants toward the middle, to spend the night in each other's arms. No matter how hard you fight it (and we all do), the Warm Valley Bed brings the two of you together into warm mutually reinforcing physical contact. The bed of commitment. Specify depth.

THE UNIVERSAL JOINT GARAGE & BODY SHOP

The way it is at the U.J. is like the five of us, Sully, Bill, Butch, Duke, and Bud, we're totally together because we stay high together and when you come in with your car, say the car is really bummed out and won't even start, before we even *touch* that car we're going to sit down with you and get you up there together with us.

Now, a lot of folks can't dig that. They say, "Here's my car. When can you fix it?" or some other kind of linear crap. Well, we just got to talk that person loose. Because we are not in that *fix* matrix at all. We say, "We're not there yet. We're *here*." Or we say, "You on a wrench trip? Okay, here's a wrench!" But that's not where he's at or the car either, and on a simple planetary level they both know it. The car and him are one circuit, one continuum, and the ignition switch is right there in his head. Like we say, "The key is *not* the key! Tools are *not* the tools!"

So what we do is get very loose and very easy and very high. The afternoon goes by and the whole shop is like suspended up there in its own holding pattern, we're all sitting around listening to the leak in the air hose and *digging* it, and slowly that person gets to copping to that car through us. It's tremendous, a stone—you feel the energy really flowing. So we're all sitting there revving on *that* and then the car starts to get off on it and pretty soon that *car* gets going. Sometimes it starts by itself, other times we got to do some laying on of hands, but it's *going*. Wide open, you can feel it vibrating. So all that comes right back to *us*. Like the car is going *rmmm-rmmm-rmmm* and *we're* going *rmmm-rmmm-rmmm,* and the next thing you know that person gets in the car and he just like takes *off*! Which was his Karma all this time— to *go*. Like he was in this place, now he's in another place, pretty soon he'll be somewhere else, and so on, but you know, it's all one road.

THE PHANTOM STOMACH ALTERNATIVE CAFÉ

The Stomach originated as a study group within the Whole Wheat Co-op, for people interested in vegetables as a tool in therapy. We were somewhat divided between eggplant and kohlrabi, but we got along pretty well. All of us felt that eating vegetables helped us free ourselves from authoritarian life-systems and become more self-sufficient and honest with ourselves and more whole. Wholeness was the key. But as we pushed it farther we came to feel that vegetables were merely rais- ing us to a higher ego-level that was rather empty and intellectual. We felt whole but we didn't feel full. It was then that we discovered "the other stomach."

The group was on a five-day fast in order to get beyond food and onto a different thought plane where we could meditate with our stom- achs and find out what they wanted. One night we went up to the roof of an apartment building to cool off, and as we lay there we saw a great membrane descending from the sky. The membrane shone with a pale moist light. As it came near, we saw hamburgers in it, a thousand of them, and pizzas—pepperoni, sausage, anchovy-and-sausage, mush- room—along with French fries, Cokes, onion rings, Big Macs, Pronto Pups, chow mein, Reubens, malts, frosted doughnuts, buttered pop- corn—everything right there within reach. We heard tremendous bursts of thunder from the membrane, and then a voice said, "Eat!"

We said, "But we can't. We're fasting, and besides it's not our kind of food."

And it said again, louder, "Eat!"

So we did—the stuff looked good—and to our surprise, it *was* good. It was hot and tasty and crisp, and the more we ate the more there was of it. We kept saying, "It is our thing, it is our thing!" Because we'd never felt that way before. A spreading circle of warmth from the stom- ach to all parts of the body. A great calorie rush.

The next night, the membrane came again. This time, we'd invited all of our friends. Hundreds of people joined in the feast. There was enough for everyone, and we became aware of a very profound physical sensation that we never got from veggies. Now we know: Around the little vegetable stomach there is a second and much greater stomach, which eggplant cannot satisfy. This second stomach is the whole body. As the voice said to us the second night, "You are not *what* you eat. You *are* eating." You only realize that if you eat the right food.

We're trying to carry out this philosophy in our café. We sell burgers that make people listen to themselves and understand themselves and we got a machine that turns out a single continuous French fry. The endless potato. When there are no customers in the place, we like to open the front door and let the French fry go out into the community to make contact with people. Some of them, like us, have eaten their way back to the beginning.

1973

CATHLEEN SCHINE

SEEK DWELLINGS FOR MX

IN an appeal to "neighborly spirit," President Reagan is asking homeowners to help ease the plight of the country's growing number of homeless MX missiles. Speaking at the annual convention of the North American Bungalow League (NABUNGLE), Mr. Reagan cited a new Pentagon study predicting approximately five hundred thousand undomiciled missiles in the United States by 1984. He urged each American family to open its door to a needy missile, "like we used to do." Calling his plan "MX Housekeeper," the President noted that "there are a far greater number of lovely guest rooms in this great country than homeless ICBMs."

Mr. Reagan went on to describe the nationwide crisis. "Rusting and dented, their spare parts stuffed haphazardly into shopping bags, the vagrant missile is getting to be a common sight in most of America's major cities," he said. "In the Southwest, you can see whole families of uprooted MXs squeezed into '74 Buicks, Ford Rancheros, and two-door Toyota Coronas. And every spring in Fort Lauderdale, Florida, thousands of young, barefoot MX missiles crowd the beaches, where they sing 'Michael, Row the Boat Ashore' and spend their nights in sleeping bags."

The President warned that the Soviet Union continues to have a "substantial monopoly" on missile shelters. He proposed four additional programs to close the shelter gap:

Amtrak Pack: In a plan that has already divided the nation's redcaps, roomettes on Amtrak's New York–to–Miami line would be reserved for qualifying missiles. Connecting return-trip tickets on the Silver Meteor would be provided upon arrival at destination. Complimentary wine-and-cheese basket.

Woodstock Pack: Research funds have been appropriated to study the feasibility of erecting tents on the famed six-hundred-acre site in upstate New York to house up to three hundred thousand MX missiles for a three-day music festival featuring Country Joe & the Fish and Suzanne Somers. Car pools from Colorado and Vermont.

Bundling Pack: A salute to America's pioneers and the spirit of self-reliance, this nationwide bundling board would permit missiles to huddle side by side for warmth. Defending the plan, Mr. Reagan commented, "Even if all the homeless MX missiles were placed end to end in a line, that line would stretch from San Diego to Boston without compromising more than three or maybe four so-called wilderness areas."

Au-Pair Pack: As an adjunct to the Pershing-missile scholarship program, the au-pair pack would arrange for the placement of thousands of au-pair missiles with French, English, and German families willing to share their homes in exchange for occasional babysitting.

The President also called on municipal governments to pitch in. He singled out New York City, which has one of the largest populations of homeless MXs in the country, as the ideal location for a pilot program. Fleets of vans would cruise midtown Manhattan in the evenings, making special stops at the Port Authority Bus Terminal and Pennsylvania Station, two places at which transient missiles tend to congregate. Teams of highly trained social workers would seek out the missiles and offer them doughnuts. The vans would then shuttle the missiles to city shelters for social services and showers.

Mr. Reagan thanked the churches and synagogues that have been providing cots and coffee for missiles in their areas. But he cautioned, "You have to do more than throw hot coffee at problems if we really believe in our hearts that every American missile has the right to a roof over its warheads."

1983

STEVE MARTIN

SIDE EFFECTS

Dosage: Take two tablets every six hours for joint pain.

Side Effects: This drug may cause joint pain, nausea, headache, or shortness of breath. You may also experience muscle aches, rapid heartbeat, and ringing in the ears. If you feel faint, call your doctor. Do not consume alcohol while taking this pill; likewise, avoid red meat, shellfish, and vegetables. Okay foods: flounder. Under no circumstances eat yak. Men can expect painful urination while sitting, especially if the penis is caught between the toilet seat and the bowl. Projectile vomiting is common in 30 percent of users—sorry, 50 percent. If you undergo disorienting nausea accompanied by migraine and raspy breathing, double the dosage. Leg cramps are to be expected; one knee-buckler per day is normal. Bowel movements may become frequent—in fact, every ten minutes. If bowel movements become greater than twelve per hour, consult your doctor, or any doctor, or just anyone who will speak to you. You may find yourself becoming lost or vague; this would be a good time to write a screenplay. Do not pilot a plane, unless you are among the 10 percent of users who experience "spontaneous test-pilot knowledge." If your hair begins to smell like burning tires, move away from any buildings or populated areas, and apply tincture of iodine to the head until you no longer hear what could be taken for a "countdown." May cause stigmata in Mexicans. If a fungus starts to grow between your eyebrows, call the Guinness Book of World Records. May induce a tendency to compulsively repeat the phrase "no can do." This drug may cause visions of the Virgin Mary to appear in treetops. If this happens, open a souvenir shop. There may be an overwhelming impulse to shout out during a Catholic Mass, "I'm gonna wop you wid da ugly stick!" You may feel a powerful sense of impending doom; this is because you are about to die. Men may experience impotence, but only during intercourse. Otherwise, a powerful erection will accompany your daily "walking-around time." Do not take this product if you are uneasy with lockjaw. Do not be near a ringing telephone that works at 900 MHz or you will be very dead, very fast. We are assuming you have had chicken pox. You also may experience a growing dissatisfaction with life along with a deep sense of melancholy—join the club! Do not be concerned if you arouse a few ticks from a Geiger counter. You might want to get a one-month trial subscription to *Extreme Fidgeting*. The hook shape of the pill will often cause it to become caught in the larynx. To remove, jam a finger down your throat while a friend holds your nose to prevent the pill from lodging in a nasal passage. Then throw yourself stomach first on the back portion of a chair. The expulsion of air should eject the pill out of the mouth, unless it goes into a sinus cavity, or the brain. WARNING: This drug may shorten your intestines by twenty-one feet. Has been known to cause birth defects in the user retroactively. Passing in front of TV may cause the screen to moiré. Women often feel a loss of libido, including a two-octave lowering of the voice, an increase in ankle hair, and perhaps the lowering of a testicle. If this happens, women should write a detailed description of their last three sexual encounters and mail it to me, Bob, Trailer Six, Fancyland Trailer Park, Encino, CA. Or e-mail me at hot-guy.com. Discontinue use immediately if you feel that your teeth are receiving radio broadcasts. You may experience "lumpy back" syndrome, but we are actively seeking a cure. Bloated fingertips on the heart-side hand are common. When finished with the dosage, be sure to allow plenty of "quiet time" in order to retrain the eye to move off stationary objects. Flotation devices at sea will become pointless, as the user of this drug will develop a stone-like body density; therefore, if thrown overboard, contact your doctor. (This product may contain one or more of the following: bungee cord, plankton, rubber, crack cocaine, pork bladders, aromatic oils, gunpowder, corn husk, glue, bee pollen, dung, English muffin, poached eggs, ham, Hollandaise sauce, crushed saxophone reeds.) Sensations of levitation are illusory, as is the sensation of having a "phantom" third arm. User may experience certain inversions of language. Acceptable: "Hi, are how you?" Unacceptable: "The rain in Sprain slays blainly on the phsssst." Twenty minutes after taking the pills, you will feel an insatiable craving to take another dose. AVOID THIS WITH ALL YOUR POWER. It is advisable to have a friend handcuff you to a large kitchen appliance, ESPECIALLY ONE THAT WILL NOT FIT THROUGH THE DOORWAY TO WHERE THE PILLS ARE. You should also be out of reach of any weaponlike utensil with which you could threaten friends or family, who should also be briefed to not give you the pills, no matter how much you sweet-talk them.

1998

ZEV BOROW

SUPERSTRING THEORY FOR DUMMIES

Though human brains are not wired to picture a world beyond the familiar three dimensions of space, one can begin to overcome this myopia by pretending to be antlike creatures in a two-dimensional fantasy world like the one in Edwin A. Abbott's story Flatland. *Confined to the surface of a plane, the Flatlanders can move left and right or forward or backward, but the idea of up and down is inconceivable to them.*
—From an explanation of superstring theory in the *Times*

PRETEND that you are a barnacle attached to the bottom of a big whaling ship like the one in *Moby-Dick*. It is very cold and wet and dark where you are, on the underside of the boat. Now imagine that the boat is a speedboat instead, and that you're its tanned Filipino captain with great abs. You are moving very fast. Still, your drink could use refreshing, and you can't for the life of you figure out why. This is just like superstring theory, except with boats, and your having great abs.

WALK over to a mirror and stare at your reflection. Now pretend that that reflection no longer resembles you at all. Pretend that your reflection actually more closely resembles the smiling face of Ned Beatty.

Now slam your forehead into the mirror three times, hard. You are bleeding. Of course. Superstring theory.

PRETEND that you are Russell Crowe in *Gladiator*. Find a gladiator costume. Put it on. Engage in swordplay. Slay a tiger with your bare hands and offer it to the Emperor as a sign of respect. Very, *very* superstring theory.

IMAGINE that you did better on your SATs than you did. A lot better. Now imagine that you smoked, say, a quarter of the pot that you smoked during your sophomore year in college. Now imagine that you never decided to leave school the following summer in order to try your luck with Cirque du Soleil. Finally, imagine that instead you became a Harvard-educated physicist who now often attends conferences in Oslo during the summer months. Imagine that you know Oslo is a city, probably somewhere in Europe, and that you understand all about superstring theory.

CLOSE your eyes and scream as loud as you can. Next, open your eyes and shut your mouth very tight. Think about how one might be able to open one's eyes and close one's eyes and shut one's mouth very tight and scream all at the same time. Now relax and check out a rerun of *The Sopranos*. Superstring theory is not so tough.

IMAGINE that you have some money in the stock market. What if one day you woke up to find that your stocks had lost 20 percent of their value? And what if the very next day you woke up to find that those same stocks had bounced back? Imagine if you paid attention to all this, but not so much, and still decided to go ahead and buy one of those cool flat-screen TVs. Imagine if that TV showed nothing but new episodes of *The Sopranos*, and that in one episode one of the show's delightfully piquant secondary characters explained superstring theory, to you and only you.

FIND a pencil and a five-year-old. Now tell the five-year-old that you'd like to bet him or her five dollars that you can make a pencil bend just by waving it in the air. Place the bet. Then hold the pencil horizontally at one end and move it up and down rapidly, in a sort of wavelike motion. Take your money. Before walking away, explain to the five-year-old that the reason you can make a pencil bend in the air, and are now five dollars richer, is because of a little something called superstring theory, something that he or she might not understand but you do.

2000

IAN FRAZIER

RESEARCHERS SAY

ACCORDING to a study just released by scientists at Duke University, life is too hard. Although their findings mainly concern life as experienced by human beings, the study also applies to other animate forms, the scientists claim. Years of tests, experiments, and complex computer simulations now provide solid statistical evidence in support of old folk sayings that described life as "a vale of sorrows," "a woeful trial," "a kick in the teeth," "not worth living," and so on. Like much common wisdom, these sayings turn out to contain more than a little truth.

Authors of the twelve-hundred-page study were hesitant to single out any particular factors responsible for making life tough. A surprise, they say, is that they found so many. Before the study was undertaken, researchers had assumed, by positive logic, that life could not be *that* bad. As the data accumulated, however, they provided incontrovertible proof that life is actually worse than most living things can stand. Human endurance equals just a tiny fraction of what it should be, given everything it must put up with. In a personal note in the afterword, researchers stated that, statistically speaking, life is "just too much," and as yet they have no plausible theory how anyone gets through it at all.

A major disadvantage to living which the study called attention to is, of course, death. In fact, so obvious are its drawbacks that no one before had thought to examine or measure them empirically. Death's effects on life, the scientists pointed out, are two: First, death intrudes constantly and unpleasantly by putting life at risk at every stage, from infancy through advanced adulthood, degrading its quality and compromising happiness. For individuals of every species, death represents a chronic, worrisome threat that they can never completely ignore.

Secondly, and far worse, death also constitutes an overwhelmingly no-win experience in itself. Many of life's well-known stress producers—divorce, loss of employment, moving, even fighting traffic—still hold out hope of a better outcome in the future. After all, one may end up with a better spouse, exciting new job, beautiful home, or fresh bottle from the drive-through liquor store. Death, by contrast, involves as much trouble as any conventional stress, if not more. Yet, at the end of the medical humiliations, physical suffering, money concerns, fear, and tedium of dying, one has no outcome to look forward to except being dead. This alone, the study found, is enough to give the entire life process a negative tinge.

Besides dying, life is burdened with countless occurrences that are almost equally unacceptable to active and vital individuals. In many cases which the scientists observed, humans no longer functioned properly after the age of seventy or seventy-five. A large majority of subjects in that age range exhibited significant loss of foot speed, upper-body strength, reflexes, hair, and altitude of vertical leap. Accompanying these impairments were other health glitches, sometimes in baffling number and variety. Such acquired traits carried the additional downside of making their possessors either "undesirable" or "very undesirable" to members of the opposite sex in the key eighteen-to-thirty-five demographic. Researchers were able to offer no credible hope for the development of treatments to deal with these creeping inadequacies.

Somewhat simplifying the study's collection of data was the natural law first discovered by Newton that things are rough all over. Thus, what happens to you will always be just as bad (relatively speaking) as what happens to anybody else. Or, to frame it another way, no problem is effectively "minor" if you yourself have it. One example is the mattress cover, or quilted pad, that goes over the mattress before you put on the fitted sheet, and that pops loose from one corner of the mattress in the middle of the night nearly 60 percent of the time, experts say. After it does, it will often work its way diagonally down the bed, taking the fitted sheet with it, until it becomes a bunched-together ridge of cloth poking up at about kidney level. The problem it represents to the individual experiencing it at that moment is absolute, in the sense that it cannot usefully be compared with difficulties in the lives of people in China or anywhere. The poke in the kidneys and the press of bare mattress against the face are simply the accumulating misery of life making itself known.

Nine out of ten of the respondents, identified by just their first initials for the purpose of the survey, stated that they would give up completely if they knew how. The remainder also didn't see the point of going on any longer but still clung to a slight hope for something in the mail. Quitting the struggle and lying face down on the floor was a coping strategy favored by most or all. Situations like having to wait an entire day for a deliveryman to deliver a breakfront and the guy didn't say exactly when he would be there and in the end didn't come and didn't even bother to call were so pointless and awful that the hell with the whole deal, many respondents said.

Interestingly, the numbers bear them out. The point, or points, of going on with existence, when charted and quantified, paint a very grim picture indeed. Merely trying to get a shoe off a child has been shown to release a certain chemical into the system which causes a reaction exactly opposite to what the task requires. Despite vigorous effort and shouting, the thing won't come off, for Christ's sake, as can be seen in the formula written out in full in Figure 7. Furthermore, that level of suffering doesn't include the additional fact that a person's spouse may not consider what the person does every day to be "work," because he or she happens occasionally to enjoy it; so what is he or she supposed to do, get a job he or she hates, instead? From a mathematical standpoint, this particular problem is an infinite regression.

Flammia Brothers Pharmaceuticals, which paid somebody to say it paid for the study, frankly admits that it does not as yet have the answers. In the interim, it offers a wide array of experience-blocking drugs, which consist of copyrighted names without pills to go with them, and which certainly might work, depending on one's susceptibility, financial history, and similar factors. Hundreds of thousands of notepads with the Flammia Brothers' logo and colorful drug names at the top of every page are already in circulation in doctors' offices and examining rooms, and a soothing poultice may be made of these pages soaked in water and driveway salt from Ace Hardware. (Most health-insurance plans may or may not cover the cost of the salt, excluding delivery.)

Other large drug manufacturers, while not willing to go quite as far, still substantially follow the Flammia Brothers' program. The fact that life is beyond us has been firmly established by now. All the information is in, and no real dispute remains. But with the temporary absence of lasting remedies, and looking to a future when they won't be necessary, the manufacturers' consortium suggests that consumers send them money in cash or check, no questions asked. Major health organizations have unanimously endorsed this goal. Originally, the consortium explained that the companies might need the money to develop a new generation of drugs narrowly focused on curing many previously uncured problems. More recently, however, they have backed off of that.

Why we were brought into the world in the first place only to suffer and die is an area of research in which much remains to be done. Like other problems thought impossible in the past, this one, too, will someday be solved. Then anybody afflicted with questions like "Why me?" "What did I do to deserve this?" "How did I get in this lousy mess?" and so on could be given a prescription, maybe even through diagnostic services provided online. The possibilities are exciting. At the same time, we must not underestimate our adversary, life itself. Uncomfortable even at good moments, difficult and unfair usually, and a complete nightmare much too often, life will stubbornly resist betterment, always finding new ways of being more than we can stand.

2002

DON STEINBERG

BRAINTEASERS: THE AFTERMATH

Problem: In a terrible car accident, a man is killed and his son is rushed to the hospital for surgery. As the boy is wheeled into the operating room, the surgeon looks at the patient and says, "I cannot operate on this child. He is my son." How is this possible?

Answer: The surgeon is the boy's mother.

Subsequently: Interns plead with the female surgeon, saying that her stubbornness about operating on the boy is jeopardizing his health, yet she steadfastly refuses. It is decided that the boy's broken foot must wait until another surgeon is summoned. Suddenly, the door bursts open—it is the boy's father, alive. "Just do the surgery, Elaine!" he shouts.

"Hey," she replies, "do I come to your job and tell you how to drive?"

. . .

Problem: A king wants to hire a royal adviser, so he invites his kingdom's three wisest men to engage in a contest of wits. He sits them down facing one another and walks behind them, putting a cap on each man's head. He tells them that he has given each of them a red cap or a white cap; in fact, he has placed red caps on all three heads. No one can see what he himself is wearing; there are no mirrors or other ways to cheat. The king says, "Raise your hand if you see someone wearing a red hat." All three men raise their hands. Then the king says, "All right, now, if you know what color your cap is, stand up."

For several minutes, no one moves. Then wise man No. 3 stands up. "I am wearing a red cap!" he proclaims. How did he know?

Answer: Wise man No. 3 first imagined himself wearing a white cap. "If I have a white cap," he reasoned, "then when wise man No. 2 raised his hand he must have been looking at wise man No. 1's red cap. Wise man No. 1, being smart, would have realized immediately that the red cap seen by No. 2 had to be his, and he would have stood up. Wise man No. 2 would have reached the same conclusion and he would have stood up quickly as well. Since neither of the others stood up, I must not be wearing a white cap. I must be wearing a red one."

Subsequently: Wise man No. 3 is made the king's royal adviser. Two days later, the king consults with him. "The people of my kingdom are unhappy," he says. "There is much misery and disease, farmland lies fallow, and war may be imminent. What shall I do?"

The wise man thinks for a moment. Then he says, "Sire, do any of those people happen to be wearing a red hat?"

. . .

Problem: I was born in Boston, and my parents were born in Boston. Yet I was not born a United States citizen. How is this possible?

Answer: I was born before 1776, before the United States was created.

Subsequently: Like many others, I became a proud U.S. citizen in 1776. The ensuing years have been arduous for me, and I bear no small shame for the unholy means by which I have sustained myself for more than two centuries. You see, I am not only a U.S. citizen . . . I am also a vampire.

.   .   .

Problem: A traveler visits an island inhabited by two types of people, knights and knaves. Knights always tell the truth; knaves always lie. The visitor falls in love with a local girl and wants to marry her. But before marrying he wants to be sure she is not a knave. An island tradition prohibits men from speaking to women until they are married. So the traveler must ask the girl's brother, who may be a knight or a knave and is not necessarily the same type as his sister. The traveler is allowed to ask the brother one question to find out if his potential bride-to-be is a knave. What is the question?

Answer: Are you and your sister of the same type? If the brother answers yes, then, no matter whether he is a knight or a knave, his sister must be a knight. If the brother answers no, the sister must be a knave.

Subsequently: The bride's brutal honesty soon sours the marriage, and the visitor leaves the strange island heartbroken, vowing never again to book travel through the Internet. Knights and knaves gradually intermarry, and within three generations everybody on the island lies occasionally, at unpredictable times.

2003

GEORGE SAUNDERS

A SURVEY OF THE LITERATURE

THE Patriotic Studies discipline may properly be said to have begun with the work of Jennison et al., which first established the existence of the so-called "fluid-nations," entities functionally identical to the more traditional geographically based nations ("geo-nations"), save for their lack of what the authors termed "spatial/geographic contiguity." Citizenship in a fluid-nation was seen to be contingent not upon residence in some shared physical space (i.e., within "borders") but, rather, upon commonly held "values, loyalties, and/or habitual patterns of behavior" seen to exist across geo-national borders.

For approximately the first five years of its existence, the Patriotic Studies discipline proceeded under the assumption that these fluid-nations were benign entities, whose existence threatened neither the stability nor the integrity of the traditional geo-nation. A classic study of this period was conducted by Emmons, Denny, and Smith, concerning the fluid-nation Men Who Fish. Using statistical methods of retro-attribution, the authors were able to show that, in a time of national crisis (the Battle of the Bulge, Europe, 1944), American citizens who were also citizens of Men Who Fish performed their duties every bit as efficiently (+/- 5 Assessment Units) as did members of the control group, even when that duty involved inflicting "harm" to "serious harm" on fellow-citizens of Men Who Fish who were allied at that time with the opposing geo-nation (i.e., Germany). During this battle, as many as seventy-five hundred (and no fewer than five thousand) German soldiers who were also citizens of Men Who Fish were killed or wounded by American soldiers who were citizens of Men Who Fish, leading the authors to conclude that citizens of Men Who Fish were not "expected, in a time of national crisis, to respond significantly less patriotically than a control group of men of similar age, class, etc., who are not citizens of Men Who Fish."

Significant and populous fluid-nations examined during this so-called "Exoneration Studies" period included Men with Especially Large Penises; People Who Say They Hate Television but Admit to Watching It Now and Then, Just to Relax; Women Who When Drunk Berate the Sport of Boxing; and Elderly Persons Whose First Thought Upon Hearing of a Death Is Relief That They Are Still Alive, Followed by Guilt for Having Had That First Feeling.

A watershed moment in the history of the discipline occurred with the groundbreaking work of Randall, Clearly, et al., which demonstrated for the first time that individuals were capable of holding multiple fluid-nation citizenships. Using the newly developed Anders-Reese Distance-Observation Method, the authors were able to provide specific examples of this phenomenon. A Nebraska man was seen to hold citizenship in Men Who Sit Up Late at Night Staring with Love at Their Sleeping Children and also in Farmers Who Mumble Soundless

Prayers While Working in Their Fields. In Cincinnati, Ohio, twin sisters were found to belong to Five-Times-a-Week Churchgoers as well as to Clandestine Examiners of One's Own Hardened Nasal Secretions. An entire family in Abilene, Texas, was seen to belong to Secretly Always Believe They Are the Ugliest in the Room, with individual members of this family also holding secondary citizenships in fluid-nations as diverse as Listens to Headphones in Bed; Stands Examining Her Breasts in Her Closet; Brags Endlessly While Actually Full of Doubt; Makes Excellent Strudel; and Believes Fervently in the Risen Christ.

At the time, awareness of this work among the general public was still low. This would change dramatically, however, with the publication, by Beatts, Daniels, and Ahkerbaj, of their comprehensive study of the fluid-nation Individuals Reluctant to Kill for an Abstraction.

In this study, 155 citizens of the target fluid-nation were assessed per the Hanley-Briscombe National-Allegiance Criterion, a statistical model developed to embody the Dooley-Sminks-Ang Patriot Descriptor Statement, which defined a patriot as "an individual who, once the leadership of his country has declared that action is necessary, responds quickly, efficiently, and without wasteful unnecessary questioning of the declared national goal."

Results indicated that citizens of Individuals Reluctant to Kill for an Abstraction scored, on average, thirty-nine points lower on the National-Allegiance Criterion than did members of the control group and exhibited nonpatriotic attitudes or tendencies 29 percent more often. Shown photographs of citizens of an opposing geo-nation and asked, "What sort of person do you believe this person to be?," citizens of Individuals Reluctant to Kill for an Abstraction were 64 percent more likely to choose the response "Don't know, would have to meet them first." Given the opportunity to poke with a rubber baton a citizen of a geo-nation traditionally opposed to their geo-nation (an individual who was at that time taunting them with a slogan from a list of Provocative Slogans), citizens of Individuals Reluctant to Kill for an Abstraction were found to be 71 percent less likely to poke than members of the control group.

The authors' conclusion ("Within this particular fluid-nation, loyalty to the fluid-nation may at times surpass loyalty to the parent geo-nation"), along with the respondents' professed willingness to subjugate important geo-national priorities, and even accept increased national-security risks, in order to avoid violating the Cohering Principle of their fluid-nation (i.e., not killing for an abstraction), led to the creation of a new category of fluid-nation, the "Malignant" fluid-nation.

At this time—coincidentally but fortuitously—there appeared the work of Elliott, Danker, et al., who made the important (and at the time startling) discovery that multiple fluid-nation citizenship *did not occur in random distributions.* That is, given a known fluid-nation citizenship, it was theoretically possible to predict an individual's future citizenship in other fluid-nations, using complex computer-modeling schemes. The authors found, for example, that citizens of Overinvolved Mothers tended to become, later in life, citizens of either Overinvolved Grandmothers or (perhaps paradoxically) Completely Uninterested Grandmothers, with high rates of occurrence observed also in Women Who Collect Bird Statuary and Elderly Women Who Purposely Affect a "Quaint Old Lady" Voice.

The implications of these data vis-à-vis the so-called Malignant fluid-nations were clear. Work immediately began within the discipline to identify and develop new technologies for the purpose of identifying those fluid-nations most likely to produce future citizens of Malignant fluid-nations. The most sophisticated and user-friendly of these tools proved to be the Rowley Query Grid, which successfully predicted the probability that citizens of Tends to Hold Him/Herself Aloof from the Group (previously thought to be innocuous) would, in time, evolve into citizens of Individuals Reluctant to Kill for an Abstraction. Subsequently, dozens of these "Nascent-Malignant" fluid-nations were identified, including Bilingual Environmentalists, Crusty Ranchers, Angry Widowers, and Recent Immigrants with an Excessive Interest in the Arts.

Needless to say, these findings resulted in dramatic improvements in both the National Security Index and the Unforeseen-Violence Probability Statistic.

Entire research departments have now embarked on the herculean task of identifying all extant fluid-nations, with particular emphasis, of course, on links to known Malignant fluid-nations. The innovative work of Ralph Frank, in which fifty individuals waiting for a bus in Portland, Oregon, were, briefly and with their full consent, taken into custody and administered the standard Fluid-Nation Identifier Questionnaire, indicated the worrisome ubiquity of these fluid-nations. At least ninety-seven separate fluid-nations were detected within this random gathering of Americans, including, but not limited to: Now Heavy

Former Ballerinas; Gum-Chompers; People Who Daydream Obsessively of Rescuing Someone Famous; Children of Mothers Who Were Constantly Bursting into Tears; Men Who Can Name Entire Lineups of Ball Teams from Thirty Years Ago; Individuals in Doubt That Someone Will Ever Love Him/Her; and Individuals Who Once Worked, or Considered Working, as Clowns. A closer analysis of the fluid-nations identified indicated that *nearly 50 percent of these* had been, would soon be, or very possibly could eventually be linked to Individuals Reluctant to Kill for an Abstraction, or to another Malignant fluid-nation.

It is thus no longer a question of whether a large number of Americans belong to fluid-nations; it is, rather, a question of how willing Americans are to freely confess these citizenships, and to then undergo the necessary mitigative measures so that the nation need have no doubt about their readiness to respond in an emergency.

This is not, of course, just an American issue; leaders of other geo-nations have now begun to recognize the potential gravity of this threat. Throughout the world, at any given moment, the justifiable aims of legitimate geo-nations are being threatened by reckless individuals who insist upon indulging their private, inscrutable agendas. The prospect of a world plagued by these fluid-nations—a world in which one's identification with one's parent geo-nation is constantly being undermined—is sobering indeed. This state of affairs would not only allow for but require a constant, round-the-clock reassessment of one's values and beliefs prior to action, a continual adjustment of one's loyalties and priorities based on an evaluation and reevaluation of reality—a process that promises to be as inefficient as it is wearying.

The above summary has, of necessity, been brief. It will be left to future scholars, working in a time of relative calm, once the present national crisis has receded, to tell the full story, in all the rich detail it deserves.

2003

JOHN KENNEY

YOUR TABLE IS READY

You do not seize control at Masa. You surrender it. You pay to be putty.
And you pay dearly. . . . Lunch or dinner for two can easily exceed
$1,000.

> —From the *Times*'s review of Masa, a sushi restaurant that
> was given four stars

AM I very rich? Since you ask, I will tell you. Yes, I am. I happen to be one of the more successful freelance poets in New York. The point being, I eat where I like. And I like sushi. As does my wife, Babette.

Unfortunately, we were running late. This worried me. I had been trying to get a reservation at Masa since 1987, seventeen years before it opened, as I knew that one of the prerequisites of dining there was a knowledge of the future. I also knew of the restaurant's strict "on-time" policy. Babette and I arrived exactly one minute and twenty-four seconds late. We know this because of the Swiss Atomic clock that diners see upon arrival at Masa.

The maître d' did not look happy. And so we were asked, in Japanese, to remove our clothes, in separate dressing cabins, and don simple white robes with Japanese writing on the back that, we soon found out, translated as "We were late. We didn't respect the time of others." Babette's feet were bound. I was forced to wear shoes that were two sizes too small. The point being, tardiness is not accepted at Masa. (Nor, frankly, should it be.)

The headwaiter then greeted us by slapping me in the face and telling Babette that she looked heavy, also in Japanese. (No English is spoken in the restaurant. Translators are available for hire for three hundred and twenty-five dollars per hour. We opted for one.)

And so it was that Babette, Aki, and I were led to our table, one of only seven in the restaurant, two of which are always reserved—one for former Canadian prime minister Pierre Trudeau, who died five years ago, and the other for the actress and singer Claudine Longet, who ac-

cidentally shot and killed her boyfriend, the skier Spider Sabich, in
1976.

There are no windows in Masa. The light is soft, and, except for the
tinkling of a miniature waterfall and the piped-in sound of an airplane
losing altitude at a rapid rate, the place is silent. We sat on hemp pillows, as chairs cost extra and we were not offered any, owing to our tardiness.

Thirty-five minutes later, we met our wait staff: nine people, including two Buddhist monks, whose job it is to supervise your meal, re-
align your chakras, and, if you wish, teach you to play the oboe.
Introductions and small talk—as translated by Aki (which, we later
learned, means "Autumn")—lasted twenty minutes. I was then slapped
again, though I'm not sure why.

Before any food can be ordered at Masa, one is required to choose
from an extensive water menu (there is no tap water at the restaurant).
With Aki's help, we selected an exceptional bottle of high-sodium Polish sparkling water known for its subtle magnesium aftertaste (a taste I
admit to missing completely). Henna tattoos were then applied to the
bases of our spines. Mine depicted a donkey, Babette's a dwarf with unusually large genitals.

Then it was time to order—or to be told what we were having, as
there is no menu. Babette and I had been looking forward to trying an
inside-out California roll and perhaps some yellowtail. Not so this
night. I was brought the white-rice appetizer and Babette was brought
nothing. Aki said this was not uncommon, and then told us a story
about his brother, Akihiko ("Bright Boy"), who has, from the sound of
it, a rather successful motor-home business outside Kyoto.

I noticed another guest a few tables away being forced to do
pushups while the wait staff critiqued his wife's outfit. Aki saw me
looking at them and translated the words on the back of their robes:
"We were twenty minutes late. We are bad."

It was then that our entrées arrived and we realized why this restaurant is so special. Before us were bay scallops, yellow clams, red clams,
and exotic needlefish, all lightly dusted with crushed purple shiso
leaves. Unfortunately, none of these dishes was for us. They were for
the wait staff, who enjoyed them with great gusto while standing beside
our table. They nodded and smiled, telling us, through Aki, how good
it all tasted. Aki told us that this was very common at fine Japanese
restaurants and urged us to be on time in the future, even though he
said we would never be allowed on the premises again. He then gave us

a brochure for a motor home. Babette and I were strongly advised to order more water.

For dessert, I ordered nothing, as I was offered nothing. Babette was given a whole fatty red tuna wrapped in seaweed, served atop a bowl of crushed ice and garnished with a sign reading, "Happy Anniversary, Barbara" (*sic*).

Our bill came to eight hundred and thirty-nine dollars. Aki said we were lucky to get out for so little and then begged us to take him with us when we left. We caught a cab and got three seats at the bar at Union Square Café.

2005

FRANK GANNON

PRE-APPROVED FOR PLATINUM

DEAR Occupant:
You've been pre-approved! What does that mean? Let us tell you.

Just the other day, we were sitting around asking ourselves, "Where are we going to find exactly the kind of person we need?" This was a hard question, because our standards and specifications are stringent. We spent weeks asking ourselves this question. We got sick of looking at one another because we were meeting so often with the same people and asking the same question over and over. One of us started to ridicule another one of us for his slight Midwestern "twang." Another one of us broke down sobbing. It was a trying period. There were some pretty heated confrontations in there, let me tell you! Some of us didn't make it.

But, finally, after countless cups of coffee and cigarettes and frantic phone calls and consultations and trips to the bathroom and looking things up in the dictionary and the thesaurus and just throwing our hands up in despair, we came up with somebody. And that somebody just happened to be someone you know—you!

We know you. You are a person who appreciates life. You know how to savor the little things. You know how a good bowl of chicken soup is supposed to taste, and you're not settling for crap. *What is this? Take it away and bring me some real soup. I don't drink dishwater. Now go!* You've said that more than once.

You appreciate the opposite sex. You like them as people, and you hate it when they are treated as one-dimensional objects. They're not playthings. You hate the way they can bump into a "glass ceiling" sometimes. You hate unfairness. You've hated it since you were a child. Life is too short for a playing field that is not precisely level. It makes you upset if anyone even alludes to it. Because you know that a member of the opposite sex is a three-dimensional being whose features are composed in a pleasant way. A way that you find exciting. And you're not ashamed of that.

We know what kinds of actions you like to take. We don't have to spell things out for you. We don't think that you are the sort of person who wants everything explained. Because you already know a whole lot. You couldn't even get everything you know into a book. Forget about books—you couldn't get everything you know into a room. Unless the room is really pretty big, like a garage.

We're not limiting you. Limits aren't for you. Even the sky isn't your limit. That's why we know you're going to take advantage of our one-time offer to consolidate all of your credit-card debt into one account with one easy-to-remember card. And your wallet is going to have that "sleek" look that the wallets owned by so many of the truly knowledgeable people have.

That look isn't for everyone. Most people have huge bulgy wallets with stuff sticking out. They can't even take their wallets out of their pockets without a bunch of lint and gum wrappers coming out with them. They look like such idiots when they do that. They look, truth be told, like they have brain damage. Like they need someone to go with them and open the door for them and remind them to pay for things before they walk out with a bunch of stuff and get arrested. Frankly, that's what they deserve. Some hard prison time. Maybe that will straighten them out. It can't hurt.

They just can't own up to it, though. They say their mother never taught them the right way to act. Then they go and blame it on her. That is pathetic.

You're not like that, and I and the other people here would just like to say that we appreciate people like you. You're a breed apart. You're going to be enjoying zero-percent interest for the first six months.

Then you will have a truly great variable rate of 9.4 percent. But those bulgy-wallet people won't. May they rot in Hell. We hate to use language like that, but sometimes it just fits. This really couldn't happen to a better person. God didn't make many of you. We mean that.

2005

LARRY DOYLE

MAY WE TELL YOU OUR SPECIALS THIS EVENING?

WE have several.

For an appetizer, the chef has prepared a slaughter of baby salmon on toast points of nine grains—blue corn, barley, rye, chaff, stover, found rice, horse-rolled oats, balsa, and fermented teff flown in daily from Ethiopia—and fancy assorted nuts, which may contain up to 10 percent peanuts. The salmon is very fresh; it was hatched just this morning.

The chef is also offering a personal favorite, his hot spiced rocks. These are igneous and sedimentary varietals, half-washed and heated to nine hundred degrees Fahrenheit, then gleefully sprinkled with international peppers.

For the more adventurous, we have a selection of freshly purchased water crackers spread with unmarked pastes, jellies, and unguents found in the kitchen.

We are also featuring a tasting gavage, in which every appetizer on the menu is wheeled to your table and forced down the gullets of two to four people. The price is twenty-eight dollars per person, plus a nominal service charge. To accompany this course, the chef recommends a bottle of the Pete, which is quite sneaky tonight. It comes in cherry or mixed berry, and is served in brown paper.

Our special soup tonight is Georgian alligator turtle, prepared and presented in its own shell. This soup is served cold and slimy, and, in the traditional manner, with the head and legs attached. We recommend that you not touch the head, as it can snap your finger clean off before you can say, "Hey, this turtle is still alive."

In addition to our usual salad, our chef offers a faux tuna niçoise, which he is recommending not be eaten by anyone trying to limit his mercury consumption.

We also have an iceberg-lettuce leaf, wetted and centered on the plate.

With your soup and salad, the chef suggests two or three cocktails, and not Cosmopolitans or candy-assed Martinis but real men's drinks. He is recommending an interesting Thai vodka that he managed to get into this country; the "liquor" is chilled into an aspic, spooned into a shot glass, then served between the breasts of Alicia over there.

Before I tell you the entrées, there is one change to the menu: We are out of the pan-fried squirrel brains tonight, as our supplier fell out of a tree this morning.

Our fish tonight is a Blue Happy, which is a euphemism. It is mostly filleted and sunbaked, then disinfected and served with what may or may not be capers. Blowholes can be requested for an additional charge.

The pasta is a single, comically long strand of spaghetti with a surprise at the end. The sauce is of no consequence.

And, finally, tonight we are offering a very special entrée that has been the subject of much debate in the kitchen. It is roast loin of Oliver, a pig that our chef has raised since infancy. Oliver was the runt in a litter of nine, and was, as you can see in this picture, bottle-fed by the chef as a young boy. Oliver grew strong and proud and was soon beating his siblings in their rutting games. Extremely smart, Oliver has thrice saved our chef from fires caused by careless smoking. However, in his latter years Oliver has grown bitter and incontinent, and just yesterday he ate the chef's brand-new cell phone.

Once we receive our first order this evening, Oliver will be smothered by a pillow filled with virgin goose down. This may take the chef some time. Oliver will then be hacked to pieces and charbroiled on a specially blessed grill. His loin will be laid to rest on a bed of tears, with asparagus and a confit of something. The chef would like to serve Oliver to you personally, and give a short eulogy. He will remain tableside, drinking steadily as you eat in silence. Because of the singular nature of this dish and its extreme emotional cost, it is priced at eighteen thousand dollars.

Would you like to order now, or do you need a few moments?

2005

BRUCE McCALL

GETTING STARTED

CONGRATULATIONS on choosing your new Type A-30/Type A-31/Type Q-2/Type Q-3/Type AQ-1/Type AQ-2/Type AQ-2.5/Type AQ-2000 (Type AQ-2000 is discontinued) hand-held portable unit.

To operate in Cell Phone mode, see pp. 10–14. An unfamiliar voice will answer when you place your first call. A nonrefundable fifty-dollar surcharge will appear on your monthly bill if you press END before hearing the complete message.

To operate in Camera mode, see pp. 15–19 or press any green key.

To operate in 3-D Cam, Spy-Cam, or Sky-Cam mode, turn the Microsoft Snoop-Cam function (on thumbwheel below viewfinder) to ON/OFF. If your unit is not a Type AQ-1, you will need a fifty-foot Kord-Pak (see Accessories, pp. 520–608) to prevent reverse power surgeback.

Never leave your unit in a freezer, convection oven, or cyclotron unless the Cell Phone function is set to END CHARGING (U symbol; Ü symbol on German-language units).

The default setting for the Entertainment function is Adults Only. To switch to Mature, XXX, or Taboo, gently slap unit until the function you have chosen appears. Your credit card is not required at this time.

To operate in Cheese Grater mode, see pp. 20–26.

Important: If your unit has three red keys on the back (see diagram, p. 7), carefully lay it down and evacuate the premises.

To operate in Magic Fingers mode, see pp. 27–36. (If you are not a licensed masseur/masseuse, see p. 37.)

Always grip unit lightly while cradling it in the palm of your hand, with the logo facing *up*. The unit's "creeping" tendency is normal. If unit becomes hot to the touch, use the Cell Phone function to call your local firehouse or volunteer fire department.

Do not attempt to manually fold the attached satellite dish.

To operate in Spot Welding mode, see pp. 38–42. Welding mask included with Type AQ-2.5 units only.

To operate in Pants Pressing mode, see pp. 43–47.

Note: Your unit is equipped to predict the winner of the next Irish parliamentary election (Leprechaun key), but you *must* enter candidate names on the Gaming keypad at least twenty-four hours before voting begins.

To operate in Radio Habana Shortwave mode, see pp. 48–52.

To operate in Men's Beard Shave mode, see pp. 53–55.

To operate in Ladies' Leg Shave mode, see pp. 56–57.

Microphone-feedback-adjustment dial on Type AQ-3 units is found on the faceplate (see Unit Overview, p. 2). In Types A-1 through A-18, the microphone-feedback-adjustment dial is the # key. Press until you hear a squealing noise.

To operate in Pencil Sharpener mode, see pp. 58–62.

To operate in Two Carolinas Redneck Culture Museum Audio Tour mode, press TOK2ME button on the thumbwheel after seeing pp. 63–64.

This unit has been approved by the Association of American Underwriters as resistant to vibration from Antarctic drilling.

To operate in Marine Haircut mode, see pp. 65–95.

To operate in Kaleidoscope mode, see pp. 96–327.

To operate in Pedometer mode, see pp. 328–329. *Do not* move your feet while switching to Pedometer setting.

Do not attempt to read the Controls/Functions section (pp. 1–4) without the help of a licensed engineer. A list of recommended engineers can be found on p. 400.

Recording the purchase date of your unit with your lawyer or guardian could void your warranty.

If you are using your unit in the horse latitudes (see map, pp. 202–223), it cannot be switched from Marine Haircut mode to Calculator mode without a Supplementary BatteryPak or plug-in access to a power grid.

Calculator-mode note: Never attempt to compute the distance to Betelgeuse from earth while watching C-SPAN. (See p. 401.)

To operate in Sonar mode, see pp. 402–408. Sonar mode operation may interfere with Cell Phone reception.

To operate GPS function (Types A-3, A-2, A-1.5 only), register your whereabouts before startup by aligning Venus, the nearest Wal-Mart, and the heel of your left shoe. A Kangaroo iconograph should begin flashing on the screen.

If you plan to use your unit as a Cell Phone only, disregard this paragraph. It is unnecessary to preset any logarithms.

Your unit (see Type list above) has become obsolete since purchase date. Do *not* attempt to discard it in a slag pile, bog, recycling receptacle, or mine pit. Switch off unit before destroying. Any person throwing away a unit without switching it off will be reported to the Department of Homeland Security.

2005

LARRY DOYLE

I'M AFRAID I HAVE SOME BAD NEWS

YOU might want to sit down. I wouldn't sit like that. You're going to develop a real nice case of lumbosacral strain, and it's going to hurt for the rest of your life. You'll end up going to a chiropractor twice a week for the next sixteen years, and every time you go he's going to ask you if you've been doing your exercises and you're going to admit that you lost the sheet, and he's going to give you another sheet and charge you a hundred bucks. Meanwhile, the pain will be getting worse and you won't feel like having sex anymore and your husband is going to start looking around, and who could blame him—you've gone from being a reasonably attractive wife to a whiny sack of no sex.

Your husband? I'll get to him.

So he's out there, banging some hooker (not wanting to start a relationship, out of respect for you), completely unaware that he's being filmed for an HBO documentary. Of course, he catches this new hepatitis G, which makes hepatitis C look like hepatitis A, and which also makes your kidneys explode, possibly harming innocent bystanders. You, in turn, are going to take up with your chiropractor, the only man still willing to touch you, and that's going to get expensive.

So, if I were you, I'd sit up straight.

Anyway, your husband has what we call a "medical condition." Without getting too technical, I should warn you that this next part is going to make me look smart and you feel stupid, and it's also pretty gory.

Your husband was admitted with extreme pain in the abdomen, which is obviously not our fault. Now, pain in the abdomen can be caused by any number of things, from comical food poisoning, which strikes in the middle of a fancy dinner party, to fatal—or *noncomical*—food poisoning, to a three-hundred-pound tumor composed of hair and teeth, possibly the overgrown unborn twin that his mother mourned instead of ever loving him.

We didn't want to rule anything out, so we opened him up.

There were no multi-hundred-pound tumors; that's the good news.

However, it's a real mess in there. There's a lot of intestinal tubing squishing around—what you call "guts"—as well as an assortment of small, esoteric organs they don't spend a lot of time on in medical school. And bear in mind that everything's pretty much the same color, not like in the textbooks.

After securing the kidneys as a precaution, I took a step back and opened the floor to suggestions. This is a teaching hospital, so there's always a bunch of smart-ass interns wandering around thinking they know everything. The "diagnoses" put forth—crazy, scary stuff—were summarily dismissed, because God forbid one of these snot-nosed wanna-docs is right.

I did a little preliminary exploratory surgery, employing what is known as the "scream test," which involves poking various organs and seeing if the patient responds. This usually indicates a problem. The procedure is trickier when the patient is sedated, of course, but I've been known to get a decent scream out of patients who were technically dead. So I did some poking and prodding, but then I remembered that I had this eye appointment, so I decided to close him up. And that's when . . . well, you might want to stand up and sit back down again. I don't know why; I find it helps, and I'm the doctor.

First, the good news. Your husband's portfolio looks great; I can't believe he got into Apple at 12—pre-split 12. I'd say the prognosis for your long-term financial health is excellent. However, last month your husband dumped seventy-eight thousand dollars' worth of Clo-Pet, the pet-cloning outfit, two days before it was revealed that Dr. Kalabi was not in fact cloning clients' beloved companions but instead was creating look-alikes using plastic surgery and transplanting pieces from other pets. Yesterday, the SEC and the IRS swooped in and froze all your husband's accounts—which may explain his abdominal pain—and then, talk about bad luck, this morning the CEO of your health-insurance carrier fled to Argentina with a transgender dominatrix, owing me literally millions of dollars.

So, unless you've got fourteen thousand dollars in cash or a certified check, I'm going to have to leave Douglas wide open on the table.

Excuse me? He's not your husband? Then whose—

God damn it. I'm going to have to go through that whole thing again. Great. Okay, well, then, who is your husband?

Oh.

I'm afraid I have some very bad news.

2006

IAN FRAZIER

HOW TO OPERATE THE
SHOWER CURTAIN

DEAR Guest:
   The shower curtain in this bathroom has been purchased with care at a reputable "big box" store in order to provide maximum convenience in showering. After you have read these instructions, you will find with a little practice that our shower curtain is as easy to use as the one you have at home.

You'll note that the shower curtain consists of several parts. The top hem, closest to the ceiling, contains a series of regularly spaced holes designed for the insertion of shower-curtain rings. As this part receives much of the everyday strain of usage, it must be handled correctly. Grasp the shower curtain by its leading edge and gently pull until it is flush with the wall. Step into the tub, if you have not already done so. Then take the other edge of shower curtain and cautiously pull it in opposite direction until it, too, adjoins the wall. A little moisture between shower curtain and wall tiles will help curtain to stick.

Keep in mind that normal bathing will cause you unavoidably to bump against shower curtain, which may cling to you for a moment owing to the natural adhesiveness of water. Some guests find the sensation of wet plastic on their naked flesh upsetting, and overreact to it.

Instead, pinch the shower curtain between your thumb and forefinger near where it is adhering to you and simply move away from it until it is disengaged. Then, with the ends of your fingers, push it back to where it is supposed to be.

If shower curtain reattaches itself to you, repeat process above. Under certain atmospheric conditions, a convection effect creates air currents outside shower curtain which will press it against you on all sides no matter what you do. If this happens, stand directly under showerhead until bathroom microclimate stabilizes.

Many guests are surprised to learn that all water pipes in our system run off a single riser. This means that the opening of any hot or cold tap, or the flushing of a toilet, interrupts flow to shower. If you find water becoming extremely hot (or cold), exit tub promptly while using a sweeping motion with one arm to push shower curtain aside.

REMEMBER TO KEEP SHOWER CURTAIN *INSIDE* TUB AT ALL TIMES! Failure to do this may result in baseboard rot, wallpaper mildew, destruction of living-room ceiling below, and possible dripping onto catered refreshments at social event in your honor that you are about to attend. So be careful!

This shower curtain comes equipped with small magnets in the shape of disks which have been sewn into the bottom hem at intervals. These serve no purpose whatsoever and may be ignored. Please do not tamper with them. The vertical lines, or pleats, which you may have wondered about, are there for a simple reason: user safety. If you have to move from the tub fast, as outlined above, the easy accordion-type folding motion of the pleats makes that possible. The gray substance in some of the inner pleat folds is a kind of insignificant mildew, less toxic than what is found on some foreign cheeses.

When detaching shower curtain from clinging to you or when exiting tub during a change in water temperature, bear in mind that there are seventeen mostly empty plastic bottles of shampoo on tub edge next to wall. These bottles have accumulated in this area over time. Many have been set upside down in order to concentrate the last amounts of fluid in their cap mechanisms, and are balanced lightly. Inadvertent contact with a thigh or knee can cause all the bottles to be knocked over and to tumble into the tub or behind it. If this should somehow happen, we ask that you kindly pick the bottles up and put them back in the same order in which you found them. Thank you.

While picking up the bottles, a guest occasionally will lose his or her balance temporarily, and, in even rarer cases, fall. If you find this occurring, remember that panic is the enemy here. Let your body go limp, while reminding yourself that the shower curtain is not designed to bear your weight. Grabbing onto it will only complicate the situation.

If, in a "worst case" scenario, you do take hold of the shower curtain, and the curtain rings tear through the holes in the upper hem as you were warned they might, remain motionless and relaxed in the position in which you come to rest. If subsequently you hear a knock on the bathroom door, respond to any questions by saying either "Fine" or "No, I'm fine." When the questioner goes away, stand up, turn off shower, and lay shower curtain flat on floor and up against tub so you can see the extent of the damage. With a sharp object—a nail file, a pen, or your teeth—make new holes in top hem next to the ones that tore through.

Now lift shower curtain with both hands and reattach it to shower-curtain rings by unclipping, inserting, and reclipping them. If during this process the shower curtain slides down and again goes onto you, reach behind you to shelf under medicine cabinet, take nail file or curved fingernail scissors, and perform short, brisk slashing jabs on shower curtain to cut it back. It can always be repaired later with safety pins or adhesive tape from your toiletries kit.

At this point, you may prefer to get the shower curtain out of your way entirely by gathering it up with both arms and ripping it down with a sharp yank. Now place it in the waste receptacle next to the john. In order that anyone who might be overhearing you will know that you are still all right, sing "Fat Bottomed Girls," by Queen, as loudly as necessary. While waiting for tub to fill, wedge shower curtain into waste receptacle more firmly by treading it underfoot with a regular high-knee action as if marching in place.

We are happy to have you as our guest. There are many choices you could have made, but you are here, and we appreciate that. Operating the shower curtain is kind of tricky. Nobody is denying that. If you do not wish to deal with it, or if you would rather skip the whole subject for reasons you do not care to reveal, we accept your decision. You did not ask to be born. There is no need ever to touch the shower curtain again. If you would like to receive assistance, pound on the door, weep inconsolably, and someone will be along.

2007

PAST
IMPERFECT

S. J. PERELMAN

NO STARCH IN THE DHOTI, S'IL VOUS PLAÎT

U P until recently, I had always believed that nobody on earth could deliver a throwaway line with quite the sang-froid of a certain comedian I worked for in Hollywood during the thirties. You probably don't recall the chap, but his hallmark was a big black mustache, a cigar, and a loping gait, and his three brothers, also in the act, impersonated with varying degrees of success a mute, an Italian, and a clean-cut boy. My respect for Julio (to cloak his identity partially) stemmed from a number of pearls that fell from his lips during our association, notably one inspired by an argument over dietary customs. We were having dinner at an off-Broadway hotel, in the noisiest locale imaginable outside the annual fair at Nizhnii-Novgorod. There were at least a dozen people in the party—lawyers, producers, agents, brokers, astrologers, tipsters, and various assorted sycophants—for, like all celebrated theatrical personages, my man liked to travel with a retinue. The dining room was jammed, some paid-up ghoul from Local 802 was interpreting the "Habanera" on an electric organ over the uproar, and, just to insure dyspepsia, a pair of adagio dancers were flinging themselves with abandon in and out of our food. I was seated next to Julio, who was discoursing learnedly to me on his favorite subject, anatomical deviations among showgirls. Halfway through the meal, we abruptly became aware of a dispute across the table between several of our companions.

"It is *not* just religious!" one was declaring hotly. "They knew a damn sight more about hygiene than you think in those Biblical days!"

"That still don't answer my question!" shouted the man he had addressed. "If they allow veal and mutton and beef, why do they forbid pork?"

"Because it's unclean, you dummy," the other rasped. "I'm trying to tell you—the pig is an unclean animal!"

"What's that?" demanded Julio, his voice slicing through the alter-cation. "The pig an unclean animal?" He rose from his chair and re-peated the charge to be certain everyone within fifty feet was listening. "The pig an unclean animal? Why, the pig is the cleanest animal there is—except my father, of course." And dropped like a falcon back into his chow mein.

As I say, I'd gone along for years considering Julio preeminent in tossing off this kind of grenade, and then one Sunday, a few weeks ago, in the *Times* magazine, I stumbled across an item that leaves no doubt he has been deposed. The new champ is Robert Trumbull, the former Indian correspondent of the paper and a most affable bird with whom I once spent an afternoon crawling around the Qutb Minar, outside New Delhi. In the course of an article called "Portrait of a Symbol Named Nehru," Mr. Trumbull had the following to say: "Nehru is ac-cused of having a congenital distaste for Americans because of their all too frequent habit of bragging and of being patronizing when in unfa-miliar surroundings. It is said that in the luxurious and gracious house of his father, the late Pandit Motilal Nehru—who sent his laundry to Paris—the young Jawaharlal's British nurse used to make caustic re-marks to the impressionable boy about the table manners of his father's American guests."

IT was, of course, the utter nonchalance of the phrase "who sent his laundry to Paris" that knocked me galley-west. Obviously, Trumbull wasn't referring to one isolated occasion; he meant that the Pandit made a practice of consigning his laundry to the post, the way one used to under the academic elms. But this was no callow sophomore ship-ping his wash home to save money. A man willful and wealthy enough to have it shuttled from one hemisphere to another could hardly have been prompted by considerations of thrift. He must have been a con-summate perfectionist, a fussbudget who wanted every last pleat in order, and, remembering my own Homeric wrangles with laundrymen just around the corner, I blenched at the complications his overseas dis-patch must have entailed. Conducted long before there was any air ser-vice between India and Europe, it would have involved posting the stuff by sea—a minimum of three weeks in each direction, in addition to the time it took for processing. Each trip would have created prob-lems of customs examination, valuation, duty (unless Nehru senior got friends to take it through for him, which was improbable; most people detest transporting laundry across the world, even their own). The old gentleman had evidently had a limitless wardrobe, to be able to dispense with portions of it for three months at a time.

The major headache, as I saw it, though, would have been coping with the *blanchisseur* himself. How did Pandit Motilal get any service or redress out of him at such long range? There were the countless vexations that always arise: the missing sock, the half-pulverized button, the insistence on petrifying everything with starch despite the most detailed instructions. The more I thought about it, the clearer it became that he must have been embroiled in an unending correspondence with the laundry owner. I suggest, accordingly, that while the exact nature of his letters can only be guessed at, it might be useful—or, by the same token, useless—to reconstruct a few, together with the replies they evoked. Even if they accomplish nothing else, they should help widen the breach between East and West.

Allahabad,
United Provinces,
June 7, 1903

Pleurniche et Cie.,
124, Avenue de la Grande Armée, Paris

My dear M. Pleurniche:
You may be interested to learn—though I doubt that anything would stir you out of your vegetable torpor—that your pompous, florid, and illiterate scrawl of the 27th arrived here with insufficient postage, forcing me to disgorge one rupee three annas to the mailman. How symbolic of your character, how magnificently consistent! Not content with impugning the quality of the cambric in my drawers, you contrive to make me *pay* for the insult. That transcends mere nastiness, you know. If an international award for odium is ever projected, have no fear of the outcome as far as India is concerned. You can rely on my support.

And à propos of symbols, there is something approaching genius in the one that graces your letterhead, the golden fleece. Could any trademark be more apt for a type who charges six francs to wash a cummerbund? I realize that appealing to your sense of logic is like whistling an aria to the deaf, but I paid half that for it originally, and the Muslim who sold it to me was the worst thief in the bazaar. Enlighten me, my dear fellow, since I have never been a tradesman myself—what passes through your head when you mulct a customer in this outrageous fashion? Is it glee? Triumph? Self-approbation at the cunning with which you have swindled your betters? I ask altogether without malice, solely from a desire to fathom the dark intricacies of the human mind.

To revert now to the subject of the drawers. It will do you no good to bombinate endlessly about sleazy material, deterioration from pounding on stones, etc. That they were immersed in an acid bath powerful enough to corrode a zinc plate, that they were wrenched through a mangle with utmost ferocity, that they were deliberately spattered with grease and kicked about the floor of your establishment, and, finally, that a white-hot iron was appliquéd on their seat—the whole sordid tale of maltreatment is writ there for anybody to see. The motive, however, is far less apparent, and I have speculated for hours on why I should be the target of vandalism. Only one explanation fits the facts. Quite clearly, for all your extortionate rates, you underpay your workmen, and one of them, seeking to revenge himself, wreaked his spite on my undergarment. While I sympathize with the poor rascal's plight, I wish it understood that I hold you responsible to the very last sou. I therefore deduct from the enclosed draft nine francs fifty, which will hardly compensate me for the damage to my raiment and my nerves, and remain, with the most transitory assurances of my regard,

Sincerely yours,

PANDIT MOTILAL NEHRU

Paris,
July 18, 1903

Pandit Motilal Nehru,
Allahabad, U.P., India

Dear Pandit Motilal:

I am desolated beyond words at the pique I sense between the lines in your recent letter, and I affirm to you on my wife's honor that in the six generations the family has conducted this business, yours is the first complaint we have ever received. Were I to list the illustrious clients we have satisfied—Robespierre, the Duc d'Enghien, Saint-Saëns, Coquelin, Mérimée, Bouguereau, and Dr. Pasteur, to name but a handful—it would read like a roll call of the immortals. Only yesterday, Marcel Proust, an author you will hear more of one of these days, called at our *établissement* (establishment) to felicitate us in person. The work we do for him is peculiarly exacting; due to his penchant for making notes on his cuffs, we must observe the greatest discretion in selecting which to launder. In fine, our function is as much editorial as sanitary, and he stated unreservedly that he holds our literary judgment in the highest esteem. I ask you, could a firm with traditions like these stoop to the pettifoggery you imply?

You can be sure, however, that if our staff has been guilty of any oversight, it will not be repeated. Between ourselves, we have been zealously weeding out a Socialist element among the employees, malcontents who seek to inflame them with vicious nonsense about an eleven-hour day and compulsory ventilation. Our firm refusal to compromise one iota has borne fruit; we now have a hard core of loyal and spiritless drudges, many of them so lacklustre that they do not even pause for lunch, which means a substantial time saving and consequently much speedier service for the customer. As you see, my dear Pandit Motilal, efficiency and devotion to our clientele dominate every waking thought at Pleurniche.

As regards your last consignment, all seems to be in order; I ask leave, though, to beg one trifling favor that will help us execute your work more rapidly in future. Would you request whoever mails the laundry to make certain it contains no living organisms? When the current order was unpacked, a small yellow-black serpent, scarcely larger than a pencil but quite dynamic, wriggled out of one of your *dhotis* and spread terror in the workroom. We succeeded in decapitating it after a modicum of trouble and bore it to the Jardin d'Acclimatation, where the curator identified it as a krait, the most lethal of your indigenous snakes. Mind you, I personally thought M. Ratisbon an alarmist—the little émigré impressed me as a rather cunning fellow, vivacious, intelligent, and capable of transformation into a household pet if one had leisure. Unfortunately, we have none, so fervent is our desire to accelerate your shipments, and you will aid us materially by a hint in the right quarter, if you will. Accept, I implore of you, my salutations the most distinguished.

> Yours cordially,
> OCTAVE-HIPPOLYTE PLEURNICHE

Allahabad, U.P.,
September 11, 1903

Dear M. Pleurniche:

If I were a hothead, I might be tempted to horsewhip a Yahoo who has the effrontery to set himself up as a patron of letters; if a humanitarian, to garrote him and earn the gratitude of the miserable wretches under his heel. As I am neither, but simply an idealist fatuous enough to believe he is entitled to what he pays for, I have a favor to ask of you, in turn. Spare me, I pray, your turgid rhetoric and bootlicking protestations, and be equally sparing of the bleach you use on my shirts. After a single baptism in your vats, my sky-blue *jibbahs* faded to a ghastly greenish-white and the fabric evaporates under one's touch. Merciful God, whence springs this compulsion to eliminate every trace of color from my dress? Have you now become arbiters of fashion as well as littérateurs?

In your anxiety to ingratiate yourselves, incidentally, you have exposed me to as repugnant an experience as I can remember. Five or six days ago, a verminous individual named Champignon arrived here from Pondichéry, asserting that he was your nephew, delegated by you to expedite my household laundry problems. The blend of unction and cheek he displayed, reminiscent of a process server, should have warned me to beware, but, tenderhearted ninny that I am, I obeyed our Brahmin laws of hospitality and permitted him to remain the night. Needless to say, he distinguished himself. After a show of gluttony to dismay Falstaff, he proceeded to regale the dinner table with a disquisition on the art of love, bolstering it with quotations from the Kamasutra so coarse that one of the ladies present fainted dead away. Somewhat later, I surprised him in the kitchen tickling a female servant, and when I demurred, he rudely advised me to stick to my rope trick and stay out of matters that did not concern me. He was gone before daylight, accompanied by a Jaipur enamel necklace of incalculable value and all our spoons. I felt it was a trivial price to be rid of him. Nevertheless, I question your wisdom, from a commercial standpoint, in employing such emissaries. Is it not safer to rob the customer in the old humdrum fashion, a franc here and a franc there, than to stake everything on a youth's judgment and risk possible disaster? I subscribe myself, as always,

Your well-wisher,
PANDIT MOTILAL NEHRU

Paris,
October 25, 1903

Dear Pandit Motilal:

We trust that you have received the bundle shipped five weeks since and that our work continues to gratify. It is also pleasing to learn that our relative M. Champignon called on you and managed to be of assistance. If there is any further way he can serve you, do not hesitate to notify him.

I enclose herewith a cutting which possibly needs a brief explanation. As you see, it is a newspaper advertisement embodying your photograph and a text woven out of laudatory remarks culled from your letters to us. Knowing you would gladly concur, I took the liberty of altering a word or two in places to clarify the meaning and underline the regard you hold us in. This dramatic license, so to speak, in no way vitiates the sense of what you wrote; it is quite usual in theatrical advertising to touch up critical opinion, and to judge from comment I have already heard, you will enjoy publicity throughout the continent of Europe for years to come. Believe us, dear Pandit, your eternal debtor, and allow me to remain

Yours fraternally,
OCTAVE-HIPPOLYTE PLEURNICHE

Allahabad,
November 14, 1903

Dear M. Pleurniche:

The barristers I retained immediately on perusing your letter—Messrs. Nankivel & Fotheringay, of Covent Garden, a firm you will hear more of one of these days—have cautioned me not to communicate with you henceforth, but the urge to speak one final word is irresistible. After all, when their suit for a million francs breaks over you like a thunderclap, when the bailiffs seize your business and you are reduced to sleeping along the *quais* and subsisting on the carrot greens you pick up around Les Halles, you may mistakenly attribute your predicament to my malignity, to voodoo, djinns, etc. Nothing of the sort, my dear chap. Using me to publicize your filthy little concern is only a secondary factor in your downfall. What doomed you from the start was the humbling incompetence, the ingrained slovenliness, that characterizes everyone in your calling. A man too indolent to replace the snaps he tears from a waistcoat or expunge the rust he sprinkles on a brand-new Kashmiri shawl is obviously capable of any infamy, and it ill becomes him to snivel when retribution overtakes him in the end.

Adieu then, *mon brave*, and try to exhibit in the dock at least the dignity you have failed to heretofore. With every good wish and the certainty that nothing I have said has made the slightest possible impression on a brain addled by steam, I am,

Compassionately,

PANDIT MOTILAL NEHRU

1955

MICHAEL J. ARLEN

MORE, AND *STILL* MORE, MEMORIES
OF THE NINETEEN-TWENTIES

WHAT a summer! Everyone was in the South of France. Willie Maugham was at Antibes. Margot Asquith was at Jimmy Sheean's. Jimmy Sheean was at Margot Asquith's. In June, we all went up to Paris to watch the Prince of Wales, then the most popular man of his time, fall off his horse at Auteuil. When he did, the crowd rushed across the track, picked up the young heir apparent, and carried him on their shoulders all the way to his room at the Ritz. Despite the twenty-two-mile walk through heavy traffic, with the Prince in obvious pain from a broken collarbone, it was a stirring occasion. Later, in the lobby of the hotel, I noticed a slight, dark-haired American lady making her way discreetly toward the service elevator. "We shall be hearing more about that girl," I remember remarking to Sherwood Anderson, who was covering the spectacle for the Seattle *Post-Intelligencer.* I was right. That girl was Helen Wills Moody.

This was in 1928. Back in New York, Jimmy Walker was mayor and the whole city had embarked on a frenzy of high spirits and wild living. On Broadway, Fred and Adele Astaire, fresh from a season's triumphs in *Kumquats of 1928*, were polishing new routines for the opening of *Kumquats of 1929*. Out in Hollywood, a young Spanish actor, Rodolpho d'Antonguolla, was already making a name for himself (Rudolph Valentino), subject to approval by the Los Angeles District Court. It was the era of prohibition, bootleg gin, and the infield single. Charles D. Flent was the best-loved man in America, and Calvin Coolidge was in the White House.

We were living at the time in a fashionable apartment on upper Fifth Avenue. On the advice of Bascomb W. Bascomb, my father had invested heavily in the rising bail-bond market, and our house was then a gathering place for many of the famous luminaries of the day. On the same evening, one might see such glittering personages as William S. (Big Bill) Thompson, William T. (Big Bill) Tilden, or William S. (Big Bill) Hart. Often, Otto Kahn, the banker, would come bustling in late in the evening with a bagful of money or Radio stock, which he would distribute to the guests. Noël Coward frequently made an appearance, as well as many other literary figures of the time: Bunny Wilson, Victor Hugo, Joseph Moncure March, Bruno Brockton. Sad, clever Bruno Brockton. If only he had published!

One of the best-known gatherings in New York in this period was the famous Oxford Group, a collection of writers, playwrights, and wits who met every Wednesday evening for lunch in the old Oxford Hotel, on Thirty-seventh Street. The members of the Oxford Group had a reputation for dazzling humor and repartee, to say nothing of sheer animal hunger, and to be invited to their table was one of the most sought-after honors that could befall a visitor to the city. It was at one of these lunches, I recall, that the famous exchange between S. S. Van-Flogel, the columnist, and Leo Tolstoy, the Russian novelist and count, took place. Tolstoy, whose novel *War and Peace* had earlier attracted much critical attention, had been traveling incognito in New York on the IRT, and was brought to the lunch late one evening by John Cameron Gilpin, the artist. Swiftly, the conversation turned to a discussion of the celebrated novel. It was widely known in New York that VanFlogel had had it "in" for Tolstoy for some time, and, suddenly, in a caustic tone, he asked the Russian if he wouldn't have written the book differently if he "had been a woman." There was a stunned silence. VanFlogel's biting wit was feared as far north as Sixty-third Street, and it was doubtful whether the elderly Russian could hold his own against the columnist. Tolstoy looked around him at the company. His eyes met Gilpin's. "Which woman?" he replied quickly. The rest is history.

This was the year when the stock market began its unparalleled rise. Men were making fortunes overnight. A few even made money during the day. A veritable fever, or fervor, of speculation swept Wall Street, which now, thanks to the Securities and Exchange Commission, higher margin rates, sound money, cold feet, and the Kellogg-Briand Pact, is no longer possible. It was the Golden Age of Sport. Dempsey knocked out Carpentier. Tunney knocked out Dempsey. Babe Ruth hit five hundred and three home runs. Charles D. Flent was the most popular man in America, and Francis X. Bushman was in the White House, visiting Calvin Coolidge.

SCOTT Fitzgerald was much in the news at this time, and his exploits were helping to set the pace for his generation. Fitzgerald, who had attended Princeton some years earlier, had been dropped from the football squad for being "too thin," and had always regretted not having had a chance to play John O'Hara's Yale team in the Bowl. One evening, toward the end of the football season, we were all sitting around in the Plaza fountain—Maxwell Perkins, Burton Rascoe, K. K. Huneker, Ellsworth Vines, Fitzgerald, and myself—when Fitzgerald leaped to his feet and cried, "Let's go up to New Haven and beard the bulldog!" Rascoe quickly commandeered a carriage from the hack stand on Fifty-ninth Street, and we all piled in for the trip to Connecticut. By the time we reached New Haven, the Yale team had already left the practice field, but Fitzgerald jumped out of the carriage and ran through the college quadrangles yelling, "Fire in the engine room, men! Everybody out to the Bowl!" What a night that was! The undergraduates poured out of the dormitories and we all swept out to the great stadium. By this time, Fitzgerald and the rest of us had dressed in football gear, but Yale unfortunately fielded its first lacrosse team. I remember Fitzgerald turning to me as we all trooped back to the dressing room and saying, "Twenty years from now, we shall all have a good laugh over this." Sad, brilliant Scott Fitzgerald. Was he more than just a regional writer? I have always maintained that he was.

MY most lasting memory of the times, however, is of the day I went, with John Middleton Mommsen, to meet the Lone Eagle, the young aviator whose daring exploits and pioneering spirit had made him the most famous figure in the land. We found the youthful pilot working in overalls beside a frail little craft, apparently made out of buckboard and canvas, with the legend "Spirit of St. Louis" hand-stenciled on its side. He spun the propeller. The engine gave a few fitful coughs and lay still. He spun it again. There was no response. The third time, he put his whole lanky body into the effort. The engine roared into action. Lindbergh—for it was he—stepped back and turned toward us. "It's a serviceable machine," he said shyly, "but it will never replace the Zeppelin."

How little the three of us knew then. War clouds were already gathering over Europe. The Zeppelin was doomed.

1960

BRUCE McCALL

THE PICKWICK CAPERS

Stand-up comedy is so brutal in terms of what works or what doesn't. . . .
You can get away with murder when you're writing. —Jerry Seinfeld, in
USA Today

MY Dear Thackeray,
        Hastily, a scribble, from my dressing chamber—foetid mop-closet that it be!—at the Hog & Varlet. But what of bodily discomfitures, when the Soul flies so! For I now have at hand as *pretty* a little fourteen minutes of vocalized risibility as this old Town has yet heard, or any old Town in the good old Realm. The "Corn Riots" jape makes a smart opening volley, followed by the "Lord Palmerston's Pantaloons," for a nice change in the pace; whilst at the finale, what better than that I do the "Poor Laws" set-piece?

Concerning your query: Worry not, Thackeray, I have over breakfast dashed off another two chapters of *Expectations*.

But, alas! The fateful Knock, and I am "on"! Wish me well.

—Boz

Thackeray—

Come up instanter to Manchester, for I fear that, short of a *complete* reworking, all is *lost*. Such barracking from the front tables, and *ale-bottles* hurled from the back. The "Corn Riot" sailed through the Ether, over their heads, and into that Oblivion where dead jokes dwell.

I console myself betimes by lining out more yardage on *Gt. Expects;* no tipplers obtrude whilst one sits composing one's prose, free from the hubbub of poltroons more beguiled by far by their *own* wit, than that of the *Performer*. Come quickly!

—Desperately, Boz

P.S. Should Wilkie C. choose to join, so much the better for doctoring back to health my maimed fourteen minutes!

My Estimable Collins,

I am deep in your debt for "physicking" my comedic Muse. You are, veritably, the "Surgeon of Smilery." I inclose a fair copy of the revised fourteen mins., which my new Agent, Mr. Blitz, believes fully strong enough to render t'morrow eve at the Ironmongers' Smoker. It has taxed my energies & invention more than ten *Nicklebys*—I do three fresh chapters of *Expects.* nowadays, for one good stand-up minute. Do you like the East India Co. joke? I practise my Hindoo expression in the looking-glass, the better to put it over.

—Faithfully, Boz

Dear Thackeray,

Collins returns my fourteen mins., *unread*, mewling that it is "ill fortune" to see another's Work, when one is *oneself* performing! For it transpires that Wilkie C. is to première his own mirthful (!) rodomontade this very evening in the back room at White's Club. Pray attend, and tell me what he has thieved of my own life's blood, my Act!

—Boz

Mr. Collins, Sir,

Thackeray tells of your stupendous success with a "Corn Riot" joke last evening, at White's. I find this fascinating, though not, I grant, as much so as do my Solicitors.

Tit for tat, I am performing a new "Victoria Regina & the Gillie" notion in my monologue to-night at the Lyceum, which would not, I think, sound entirely unfamiliar to you!

—C. D.

Dear Thackeray,

Regarding your inquiry, I have misplaced the *Grt. Expectations* ms., but it is of no moment, I shall recapitulate the 14 chapters to-day on the train to Newcastle.

Prosody! Had ever tho't my Novelizing a true Sisyphusean Labour; yet only now can know the far greater agony & pain of that Institution of Intellectual Industry nonpareil, Stand-Up.

It is all in the timing of things, Thackeray; what *swarms* with Life on the flat, written page becomes but a dead grey *mackerel* in its utterance upon the stage, without the properly measured *timing* of its delivery. Nor can it, cf. Collins, be taught.

I close with the promise to read your new Book soonest. Now, off to audit Trollope, who begs my attendance at his new Routine at a local caravansary. . . .

—Boz

Mr. Collins, Sir,

That I choose to publickly indorse Musgrave's Ague Elixir should be of no account to you, whose success has not made necessary the support of seven in service, three houses, and a villa, plus several barouches.

—D.

Bulwer-Lytton,

I surmise that the Thack tattles, and puts you up to what he, himself, would fain do, namely, to pester and afflict a busy Entertainer with verbal Boils. *Gt. Expect'ns* (I lack time to write it out entire) goes forward. It picks up speed. It careers. I have the idea of a cataclysmic Stage Coach Crash, which would dispatch Pip, Magwitch, Jaggers, Miss Havisham, and Bentley Drummle, and leave Herbert Pocket to wrap it up in an Epilogue, shortening the epic by two doz. chapters. Stand-up teaches nightly, that Brevity is the Thing.

—The Boz

Thack!

If I may so address you, for we stage-folk ever prefer the *informal* against the *formal* amongst ourselves . . .

Enclosed cutting from this morning's *Optic* shows who bested whom at last evening's Crimean War Relief Benefit Recital. 'Tis true, Thack—Collins was *heckled* by the Duke of Clarence himself when he quite forgot the punch-line to the "Irish Question" soliloquy! (Do you know a "ghost" who could pick up *Gt. Expect.* where I left off months ago? No time!)

—The Boz

Trollope,

The Lady whom you so flippantly described as my "niece" last Evening at the Garrick is, in fact, Miss Joywell, my protégée, and a distinguished Graduate of my Comedic Work Shop.

Yrs., The Boz

B.-L.,

Have reserved two tickets for you & a friend at Blackpool Tuesday eve next, late show. Come thither. Silly goose, 'twas but a jest, anent the Stage Coach Crash! I now think I can quickly be done with *Gt. Ex.* by this expedient, that Pip suddenly wakes, to find all was a dream.

—Believe me, the Boz

Thack!

Finished *Expectations* after oysters & champagne in the early hours of this morning, only to get the d—— thing away, so I can work on perfecting a wonderful new Disraeli jest. Alas, I cannot attend your Début as Napoleon III as some friends ask me down for the weekend. (I am told that that vixen Actress Miss L—— is invited also!) Must rush!

Love you, The Boz

Dear Mister Collins,

I have at hand your most interesting Proposal, received today. "Dickens & Collins," I believe, and so, too, my client, would sound more comely; he suggests that you trust his ear for names, which is not unremarked. We must also insist that his name always take the topmost place, type twice the size of yours, owing to his greater fame, and, likewise, that his share of all proceeds be 75 percent, as his Reward for "pulling you along" with him in regards ticket sales and public Curiosity. Perhaps we can thus conjoin with you, to the end of concluding a fair Contract.

Very sincerely yours,
Blitz (for the Boz)

1993

PAUL RUDNICK

THE GOSPEL OF DEBBIE

RECENT works like *The Passion of the Christ* and *The Da Vinci Code* seek to illuminate the life of Jesus. Not long ago, an additional text was discovered in an ancient linen backpack found in a cave outside Jerusalem, surrounded by what appeared to be early-Roman candy wrappers and covered with stickers reading "I ♥ All Faiths" and "Ask Me About Hell." A parchment diary found inside the backpack appears to contain the musings of one Debbie of Galilee. Many of the pages are still being translated from high-school Aramaic; here are some persuasive excerpts:

OCTOBER 5

I saw him in the marketplace! Everyone says that he's the son of God, but I don't care one way or the other because he's just so CUTE!!! Okay, he's not hot like a gladiator or a centurion, but he's really sensitive and you can tell that he thinks about things and then goes, "Be nice to people," and I'm like, that is SO TRUE, and I wonder if he's seeing anyone!

OCTOBER 21

Everyone says that he's just totally good and devoted to all humanity and that he was sent to save us and that's why he doesn't have time for a girlfriend, although I swear I saw Mary Magdalene doodling in the sand with a stick, writing "Mrs. Jesus Christ" and "Merry Xmas from Mary and Jesus Christ and All the Apostles," with little holly leaves all around it. And I'm like, Mary, are you dating Jesus? and she says, no, he's just helping me, and I'm like, you mean with math? and she's like, no, to not be such a whore. And I said, but that is so incredibly *sweet,* and we both screamed and talked about whether we like him better when he's healing the lame or with a ponytail.

DECEMBER 25

I wanted to get him the perfect thing for his birthday, so I asked Matthew and he said, well, myrrh is good, but then Luke said, oh please, everyone always gives him myrrh, I bet he wishes those wise men had brought scented candles, some imported marmalade, and a nice box of notecards. So I go, okay, what about accessories, like a new rope belt or clogs or like I could make him a necklace with his name spelled out in little clay letters? and Mark said, I love that, but Luke rolled his eyes and said, Mark, you are just such an Assyrian. So I go to see Mary, Jesus' mom, and she said that Jesus doesn't need gifts, that he just wants all of us to love God and be better people, but I asked, what about a sweater? and she said medium.

JANUARY 2

Oh my God, oh my God, I couldn't believe it, but I was right there, and Jesus used only five loaves of bread and two fish to feed thousands of people, and it was so beautiful and miraculous, and my brother Ezekiel said, whoa, Jesus has invented canapés and I said shut up! And then my best friend Rachel asked, I wonder if he could make my hair really shiny, and I said, you are so disgusting, Jesus shouldn't waste his time on your vanity, and then Jesus smiled at me and I'm telling you, those last seven pounds, the stubborn ones, they were totally gone! And I spoke unto the angry Roman mob and I said, behold these thighs! Jesus has made me feel better about me!

MARCH 12

Everyone is just getting so mean. They're all going, Debbie, he is so not divine, Debbie, you'll believe anything, Debbie, what about last year when you were worshipping ponchos? And I so don't trust that Judas Iscariot, who's always staring at me when I walk to the well and he's saying, hey, Deb, nice jugs, and I'm like, oh ha ha ha, get some oxen.

APRIL 5

So Mary Magdalene tells me that Jesus and all the apostles had this big party and that it got really intense and Jesus drank from this golden goblet and now it's missing and the restaurant is like, this is why there's a surcharge.

APRIL 23

It's all over. And it's been terrible and amazing and I don't know what any of it means or who's right and who's wrong but maybe I'll figure it out later. Anyway, I'll always remember what Jesus said to me. He said, Debbie, I can foresee that someday you'll meet someone, someone wonderful, but for right now let's at least think about college.

2004

BILLY FROLICK

1992 HOUSE

INTRODUCTION:

The assignment for Mrs. Stanfill's eighth-grade social-studies class was to pick a year in U.S. history and live for a week as if it were that year, without any of the conveniences available in today's modern society. I chose 1992, and for extra credit I persuaded my family to participate in the experiment along with me. Bill Clinton was elected President in 1992. A postage stamp cost twenty-nine cents, and Whitey (sp?) Houston had a No. 1 song with "I Will Always Love You," from a movie starring someone named Kevin Costner, on whom my mother apparently had a major crush.

SCIENTIFIC CONTROLS:

My brother Chris was the most reluctant to participate in the project, as he is way obsessed with the new Maroon 5 CD that he downloaded and didn't like having to listen to crud like Billy Ray Cyrus and Boyz II Men for the duration of the control period. He has a massive DVD collection, which was out of bounds, too, given that DVDs had not been invented in the olden days of 1992. Though Chris has an abiding attachment to one of the girls on *The Real World: Philadelphia,* I told him that, for the sake of historical verisimilitude, he had to learn to live without her—and TiVo or his iPod—for a week.

My stepdad Larry's reaction to the assignment was interesting. He said that maybe he'd go out of town to play golf for the week of the experiment because he wasn't actually "in the picture" in 1992. My mom nixed that suggestion.

Since the Internet was not in common use back then, Larry needed to check his stocks in the newspaper, which he had to start buying at Starbucks because he usually reads the news online. Thank God Starbucks was around in 1992. (I think. Not sure, and, under the terms of the experiment, I couldn't Google it.) But I do know that he couldn't order his usual caramel macchiato, because evidently in 1992 Starbucks barely even served coffee, let alone specialty drinks!!!!

My mom had a "procedure" scheduled for the week of the project and asked if I would make an exception for her, because my cousin Sharon's bat mitzvah was less than a month away and my mom wanted to make sure she looked okay in the pictures. It's too bad, because they definitely had bat mitzvahs and photography in 1992. But Botox was not readily available.

So, to keep the integrity of the research project intact, I denied her request and called Dr. Mussman (on a land-line—duh!) to cancel her appointment. By the time she found out and called Dr. Mussman back, the slot was filled, and my mom and I became engaged in a significant altercation. As domestic conflict no doubt existed in 1992, this worked well within the parameters of the experiment. My mother wanted to punish me by depriving me of something that I care about, but just about everything that's important to me was basically already off limits for the week anyway.

I learned that one of the biggest hardships endured by people back in 1992 was not being able to use cell phones. At first, I had thought that maybe I could just cut back on the number of calls I made, thinking that usage plans were more limited. However, my research (at the library!) unearthed the fact that cell phones really were not in widespread use back then; there were only humongous car-phone versions, prevalent among early executives in the hip-hop industry.

Attending school for a week without my cell phone aroused feelings of depression. It seemed like everyone around me was text-messaging each other, and after a while I became convinced that they were text-messaging about me. I felt really humiliated, and it made me appreciate the world I live in today.

RESEARCH SEGMENT:

Not having the use of a cell phone piqued my curiosity regarding how schoolchildren communicated all those years ago. Since my mother was not speaking to me and Larry wasn't around (he did end up going to Myrtle Beach), I turned to primary sources (in the form of classic cinema) for answers. I found *The Breakfast Club* and *Pretty in Pink* in the library—on *videotape*. Through studying these movies, I learned that back in the eighties and nineties students would hand-write things on little pieces of paper called "notes" and try to pass them to each other in class without getting caught.

Upon my return to school, no one wanted to engage in this practice with me because they were all text-messaging each other (probably about me).

BASIC SURVIVAL OBSERVATIONS:

During the period of the experiment, my family subsisted on bread, pasta, rice, and potatoes, just as people did before the turn of the century. My mother said that if you had mentioned food combining or wheat intolerance back in 1992 they might have thrown you into a pond to see if you floated. I have no idea what that means, or who "they" are, but it was the first thing she had said to me in three days and I wanted to avoid another altercation, so I wrote it down.

I discovered that eating so much starch was giving me severe headaches. This, I felt, might explain some of the heinous stuff that was happening in the world back in 1992—weirdos like Ross Perot and Jeffrey Dahmer, or all the rioting that went down in Los Angeles that year. Maybe the grunge look, too.

CONCLUSION:

In conclusion, 1992 was clearly a very confusing, difficult time in which to live in the United States of America. Having to use landlines and eat carbohydrates were hardships for the people to endure, but Americans are nothing if not resilient. If I had been a teenager in 1992, I would have been really challenged to find alternative ways to keep my life interesting, stay thin, and communicate with my peers.

Speaking of which, someone is text-messaging me. I'm *so* grateful to live in 2005!:)

2005

PAUL RUDNICK

FURTHER PROOF THAT
LINCOLN WAS GAY

The first draft of the Gettysburg Address began, "Four score and seven years ago-ish . . ."

When Lincoln was a boy, he would walk twenty miles through the snow every morning to buy magazines.

Lincoln was raised in a log cabin with a dirt floor, which he vacuumed.

Lincoln liked to say, "All men are created equal, except at the beach."

Lincoln's greatest regret was the movie version of *Phantom.*

Lincoln named his horse Mister Horse.

Lincoln wanted to call it "The Emancipation Proclamation—The New Sensation!"

Lincoln urged Congress to bind the nation's wounds "with malice toward none, with charity for all," although under his breath he murmured, "except for a certain red-headed lieutenant, and he knows why."

As a young country lawyer, Lincoln often bartered his services for house seats.

For more than four years during his twenties, Lincoln shared a bed with his friend Joshua Fry Speed. It is now believed that he loved Joshua Fry Speed for his winning personality, and not because his name sounds like a George Foreman product.

The friendship finally ended when Speed told Lincoln, "You're not the President of me!"

Another friend, Billy Greene, said that Lincoln's thighs were "as perfect as a human being's could be." Lincoln was said to have responded, "It's called Pilates."

Lincoln was known as the Rail-Splitter. Few people realize that this was a cocktail.

When Lincoln was told that Lee had surrendered, he gasped and exclaimed, "Oh no she didn't!"

Just before his first inauguration, he told Mary Todd Lincoln to go home and take one thing off.

Lincoln grew his beard because he thought it looked hot on Ethan Hawke.

Upon entering Ford's Theatre on that fateful night, Lincoln whispered to his wife, "I hear it's slow."

2005

FIELD NOTES
FROM ALL OVER

SUSAN ORLEAN

SHOW DOG

F I were a bitch, I'd be in love with Biff Truesdale. Biff is perfect. He's friendly, good-looking, rich, famous, and in excellent physical condition. He almost never drools. He's not afraid of commitment. He wants children—actually, he already has children and wants a lot more. He works hard and is a consummate professional, but he also knows how to have fun.

What Biff likes most is food and sex. This makes him sound boorish, which he is not—he's just elemental. Food he likes even better than sex. His favorite things to eat are cookies, mints, and hotel soap, but he will eat just about anything. Richard Krieger, a friend of Biff's who occasionally drives him to appointments, said not long ago, "When we're driving on I-95, we'll usually pull over at McDonald's. Even if Biff is napping, he always wakes up when we're getting close. I get him a few plain hamburgers with buns—no ketchup, no mustard, and no pickles. He loves hamburgers. I don't get him his own French fries, but if I get myself fries I always flip a few for him into the back."

If you're ever around Biff while you're eating something he wants to taste—cold roast beef, a Wheatables cracker, chocolate, pasta, aspirin, whatever—he will stare at you across the pleated bridge of his nose and let his eyes sag and his lips tremble and allow a little bead of drool to percolate at the edge of his mouth until you feel so crummy that you give him some. This routine puts the people who know him in a quandary, because Biff has to watch his weight. Usually, he is as skinny as Kate Moss, but he can put on three pounds in an instant. The holidays can be tough. He takes time off at Christmas and spends it at home, in Attleboro, Massachusetts, where there's a lot of food around and no pressure and no schedule and it's easy to eat all day. The extra weight goes to his neck. Luckily, Biff likes working out. He runs for fifteen or twenty minutes twice a day, either outside or on his Jog-Master.

When he's feeling heavy, he runs longer, and skips snacks, until he's back down to his ideal weight of seventy-five pounds.

Biff is a boxer. He is a show dog—he performs under the name Champion Hi-Tech's Arbitrage—and so looking good is not mere vanity; it's business. A show dog's career is short, and judges are unforgiving. Each breed is judged by an explicit standard for appearance and temperament, and then there's the incalculable element of charisma in the ring. When a show dog is fat or lazy or sullen, he doesn't win; when he doesn't win, he doesn't enjoy the ancillary benefits of being a winner, like appearing as the celebrity spokesmodel on packages of Pedigree Mealtime with Lamb and Rice, which Biff will be doing soon, or picking the best-looking bitches and charging them six hundred dollars or so for his sexual favors, which Biff does three or four times a month. Another ancillary benefit of being a winner is that almost every single weekend of the year, as he travels to shows around the country, he gets to hear people applaud for him and yell his name and tell him what a good boy he is, which is something he seems to enjoy at least as much as eating a bar of soap.

PRETTY soon, Biff won't have to be so vigilant about his diet. After he appears at the Westminster Kennel Club's show, this week, he will retire from active show life and work full time as a stud. It's a good moment for him to retire. Last year, he won more shows than any other boxer, and also more than any other dog in the purebred category known as Working Dogs, which also includes Akitas, Alaskan malamutes, Bernese mountain dogs, bullmastiffs, Doberman pinschers, giant schnauzers, Great Danes, Great Pyrenees, komondors, kuvaszok, mastiffs, Newfoundlands, Portuguese water dogs, Rottweilers, St. Bernards, Samoyeds, Siberian huskies, and standard schnauzers. Boxers were named for their habit of standing on their hind legs and punching with their front paws when they fight. They were originally bred to be chaperons—to look forbidding while being pleasant to spend time with. Except for show dogs like Biff, most boxers lead a life of relative leisure. Last year at Westminster, Biff was named Best Boxer and Best Working Dog, and he was a serious contender for Best in Show, the highest honor any show dog can hope for. He is a contender to win his breed and group again this year, and is a serious contender once again for Best in Show, although the odds are against him, because this year's judge is known as a poodle person.

Biff is four years old. He's in his prime. He could stay on the circuit for a few more years, but by stepping aside now he is making room for his sons Trent and Rex, who are just getting into the business, and he's leaving while he's still on top. He'll also spend less time in airplanes, which is the one part of show life he doesn't like, and more time with his owners, William and Tina Truesdale, who might be persuaded to waive his snacking rules.

Biff has a short, tight coat of fox-colored fur, white feet and ankles, and a patch of white on his chest roughly the shape of Maine. His muscles are plainly sketched under his skin, but he isn't bulgy. His face is turned up and pushed in, and has a dark mask, spongy lips, a wishbone-shaped white blaze, and the earnest and slightly careworn expression of a small-town mayor. Someone once told me that he thought Biff looked a little bit like President Clinton. Biff's face is his fortune. There are plenty of people who like boxers with bigger bones and a stockier body and taller shoulders—boxers who look less like marathon runners and more like weight-lifters—but almost everyone agrees that Biff has a nearly perfect head.

"Biff's head is his father's," William Truesdale, a veterinarian, explained to me one day. We were in the Truesdales' living room in Attleboro, which overlooks acres of hilly fenced-in fields. Their house is a big, sunny ranch with a stylish pastel kitchen and boxerabilia on every wall. The Truesdales don't have children, but at any given moment they share their quarters with at least a half-dozen dogs. If you watch a lot of dog-food commercials, you may have seen William—he's the young, handsome, dark-haired veterinarian declaring his enthusiasm for Pedigree Mealtime while his boxers gallop around.

"Biff has a masculine but elegant head," William went on. "It's not too wet around the muzzle. It's just about ideal. Of course, his forte is right here." He pointed to Biff's withers, and explained that Biff's shoulder-humerus articulation was optimally angled, and bracketed his superb brisket and forelegs, or something like that. While William was talking, Biff climbed onto the couch and sat on top of Brian, his companion, who was hiding under a pillow. Brian is an English toy Prince Charles spaniel who is about the size of a teakettle and has the composure of a hummingbird. As a young competitor, he once bit a judge—a mistake Tina Truesdale says he made because at the time he had been going through a little mind problem about being touched. Brian, whose show name is Champion Cragmor's Hi-Tech Man, will soon go back on the circuit, but now he mostly serves as Biff's regular escort. When

Biff sat on him, he started to quiver. Biff batted at him with his front leg. Brian gave him an adoring look.

"Biff's body is from his mother," Tina was saying. "She had a lot of substance."

"She was even a little extreme for a bitch," William said. "She was rather buxom. I would call her zaftig."

"Biff's father needed that, though," Tina said. "His name was Tailo, and he was fabulous. Tailo had a very beautiful head, but he was a bit fine, I think. A bit slender."

"Even a little feminine," William said, with feeling. "Actually, he would have been a really awesome bitch."

THE first time I met Biff, he sniffed my pants, stood up on his hind legs and stared into my face, and then trotted off to the kitchen, where someone was cooking macaroni. We were in Westbury, Long Island, where Biff lives with Kimberly Pastella, a twenty-nine-year-old professional handler, when he's working. Last year, Kim and Biff went to at least one show every weekend. If they drove, they took Kim's van. If they flew, she went coach and he went cargo. They always shared a hotel room.

While Kim was telling me all this, I could hear Biff rummaging around in the kitchen. "Biffers!" Kim called out. Biff jogged back into the room with a phony look of surprise on his face. His tail was ticking back and forth. It is cropped so that it is about the size and shape of a half-smoked stogie. Kim said that there was a bitch downstairs who had been sent from Pennsylvania to be bred to one of Kim's other clients, and that Biff could smell her and was a little out of sorts. "Let's go," she said to him. "Biff, let's go jog." We went into the garage, where a treadmill was set up with Biff's collar suspended from a metal arm. Biff hopped on and held his head out so that Kim could buckle his collar. As soon as she leaned toward the power switch, he started to jog. His nails clicked a light tattoo on the rubber belt.

Except for a son of his named Biffle, Biff gets along with everybody. Matt Stander, one of the founders of *Dog News,* said recently, "Biff is just very, very personable. He has a je ne sais quoi that's really special. He gives of himself all the time." One afternoon, the Truesdales were telling me about the psychology that went into making Biff who he is. "Boxers are real communicators," William was saying. "We had to really take that into consideration in his upbringing. He seems tough, but there's a fragile ego inside there. The profound reaction and hurt when you would raise your voice at him was really something."

"I *made* him," Tina said. "I made Biff who he is. He had an over-bearing personality when he was small, but I consider that a prerequi-site for a great performer. He had such an *attitude*! He was like this miniature *man*!" She shimmied her shoulders back and forth and thrust out her chin. She is a dainty, chic woman with wide-set eyes and the neck of a ballerina. She grew up on a farm in Costa Rica, where dogs were considered just another form of livestock. In 1987, William got her a Rottweiler for a watchdog, and a boxer, because he had always loved boxers, and Tina decided to dabble with them in shows. Now she makes a monogrammed Christmas stocking for each animal in their house, and she watches the tape of Biff winning at Westminster ap-proximately once a week. "Right from the beginning, I made Biff think he was the most fabulous dog in the world," Tina said.

"He doesn't take after me very much," William said. "I'm more of a golden retriever."

"Oh, he has my nature," Tina said. "I'm very strong-willed. I'm brassy. And Biff is an egotistical, self-centered, selfish person. He thinks he's very important and special, and he doesn't like to share."

BIFF is priceless. If you beg the Truesdales to name a figure, they might say that Biff is worth around a hundred thousand dollars, but they will also point out that a Japanese dog fancier recently handed Tina a blank check for Biff. (She immediately threw it away.) That check notwith-standing, campaigning a show dog is a money-losing proposition for the owner. A good handler gets three or four hundred dollars a day, plus travel expenses, to show a dog, and any dog aiming for the top will have to be on the road at least a hundred days a year. A dog photographer charges hundreds of dollars for a portrait, and a portrait is something that every serious owner commissions, and then runs as a full-page ad in several dog-show magazines. Advertising a show dog is standard procedure if you want your dog or your presence on the show circuit to get well known. There are also such ongoing show-dog expenses as entry fees, hair-care products, food, health care, and toys. Biff's stud fee is six hundred dollars. Now that he will not be at shows, he can be bred several times a month. Breeding him would have been a good way for him to make money in the past, except that whenever the Truesdales were enthusiastic about a mating they bartered Biff's service for the pick of the litter. As a result, they now have more Biff puppies than Biff earnings. "We're doing this for posterity," Tina says. "We're doing it for the good of all boxers. You simply can't think about the cost."

On a recent Sunday, I went to watch Biff work at one of the last shows he would attend before his retirement. The show was sponsored by the Lehigh Valley Kennel Club and was held in a big, windy field house on the campus of Lehigh University, in Bethlehem, Pennsylvania. The parking lot was filled with motor homes pasted with life-size decals of dogs. On my way to the field house, I passed someone walking an Afghan hound wearing a snood, and someone else wiping down a Saluki with a Flintstones beach towel. Biff was napping in his crate— a fancy-looking brass box with bright silver hardware and with luggage tags from Delta, USAir, and Continental hanging on the door. Dogs in crates can look woeful, but Biff actually likes spending time in his. When he was growing up, the Truesdales decided they would never reprimand him, because of his delicate ego. Whenever he got rambunctious, Tina wouldn't scold him—she would just invite him to sit in his crate and have a time-out.

On this particular day, Biff was in the crate with a bowl of water and a gourmet Oinkeroll. The boxer judging was already over. There had been thirty-three in competition, and Biff had won Best in Breed. Now he had to wait for several hours while the rest of the working breeds had their competitions. Later, the breed winners would square off for Best in Working Group. Then, around dinnertime, the winner of the Working Group and the winners of the other groups—sporting dogs, hounds, terriers, toys, non-sporting dogs, and herding dogs—would compete for Best in Show. Biff was stretched out in the crate with his head resting on his forelegs, so that his lips draped over his ankle like a café curtain. He looked bored. Next to his crate, several wire-haired fox terriers were standing on tables getting their faces shampooed, and beyond them a Chihuahua in a pink crate was gnawing on its door latch. Two men in white shirts and dark pants walked by eating hot dogs. One of them was gesturing and exclaiming, "I thought I had good dachshunds! I thought I had *great* dachshunds!"

Biff sighed and closed his eyes.

While he was napping, I pawed through his suitcase. In it was some dog food; towels; an electric nail grinder; a whisker trimmer; a wool jacket in a lively pattern that looked sort of Southwestern; an apron; some antibiotics; baby oil; coconut-oil coat polish; boxer chalk powder, a copy of *Dog News;* an issue of *ShowSight* magazine, featuring an article subtitled "Frozen Semen—Boon or Bane?" and a two-page ad for Biff, with a full-page, full-color photograph of him and Kim posed in front of a human-size toy soldier; a spray bottle of fur cleanser; another Oinkeroll; a rope ball; and something called a Booda Bone. The apron was for Kim. The baby oil was to make Biff's nose and feet glossy when he went into the ring. Boxer chalk powder—as distinct from, say, West Highland-white-terrier chalk powder—is formulated to cling to short, sleek boxer hair and whiten boxers' white markings. Unlike some of the other dogs, Biff did not need to travel with a blow dryer, curlers, nail polish, or detangling combs, but, unlike some less sought-after dogs, he did need a schedule. He was registered for a show in Chicago the next day, and had an appointment at a clinic in Connecticut the next week to make a semen deposit, which had been ordered by a breeder in Australia. Also, he had a date that same week with a bitch named Diana who was about to go into heat. Biff has to book his stud work after shows, so that it doesn't interfere with his performance. Tina Truesdale told me that this was typical of all athletes, but everyone who knows Biff is quick to comment on how professional he is as a stud. Richard Krieger, who was going to be driving Biff to his appointment at the clinic in Connecticut, once told me that some studs want to goof around and take forever but Biff is very businesslike. "Bing, bang, boom," Krieger said. "He's in, he's out."

"No wasting of time," said Nancy Krieger, Richard's wife. "Bing, bang, boom. He gets the job done."

After a while, Kim showed up and asked Biff if he needed to go outside. Then a handler who is a friend of Kim's came by. He was wearing a black-and-white houndstooth suit and was brandishing a comb and a can of hair spray. While they were talking, I leafed through the show catalogue and read some of the dogs' names to Biff, just for fun—names like Aleph Godol's Umbra Von Carousel and Champion Spanktown Little Lu Lu and Ranchlake's Energizer O'Motown and Champion Beaverbrook Buster V Broadhead. Biff decided that he did want to go out, so Kim opened the crate. He stepped out and stretched and yawned like a cat, and then he suddenly stood up and punched me in the chest. An announcement calling for all toys to report to their ring came over the loudspeaker. Kim's friend waved the can of hair spray in the direction of a little white poodle shivering on a table a few yards away and exclaimed, "Oh, no! I lost track of time! I have to go! I have to spray up my miniature!"

TYPICALLY, dog contestants first circle the ring together; then each contestant poses individually for the judge, trying to look perfect as the judge lifts its lips for a dental exam, rocks its hindquarters, and strokes its back and thighs. The judge at Lehigh was a chesty, mustached man with watery eyes and a grave expression. He directed the group with hand signals that made him appear to be roping cattle. The Rottweiler looked good, and so did the giant schnauzer. I started to worry. Biff had a distracted look on his face, as if he'd forgotten something back at the house. Finally, it was his turn. He pranced to the center of the ring. The judge stroked him and then waved his hand in a circle and stepped out of the way. Several people near me began clapping. A flashbulb flared. Biff held his position for a moment, and then he and Kim bounded across the ring, his feet moving so fast that they blurred into an oily sparkle, even though he really didn't have very far to go. He got a cookie when he finished the performance, and another a few minutes later, when the judge wagged his finger at him, indicating that Biff had won again.

You can't help wondering whether Biff will experience the depressing letdown that retired competitors face. At least, he has a lot of stud work to look forward to, although William Truesdale complained to me once that the Truesdales' standards for a mate are so high—they require a clean bill of health and a substantial pedigree—that "there just aren't that many right bitches out there." Nonetheless, he and Tina are optimistic that Biff will find enough suitable mates to become one of the most influential boxer sires of all time. "We'd like to be remembered as the boxer people of the nineties," Tina said. "Anyway, we can't wait to have him home."

"We're starting to campaign Biff's son Rex," William said. "He's been living in Mexico, and he's a Mexican champion, and now he's ready to take on the American shows. He's very promising. He has a fabulous rear."

Just then, Biff, who had been on the couch, jumped down and began pacing. "Going somewhere, honey?" Tina asked.

He wanted to go out, so Tina opened the back door, and Biff ran into the back yard. After a few minutes, he noticed a ball on the lawn. The ball was slippery and a little too big to fit in his mouth, but he kept scrambling and trying to grab it. In the meantime, the Truesdales and I sat, stayed for a moment, fetched ourselves turkey sandwiches, and then curled up on the couch. Half an hour passed, and Biff was still happily pursuing the ball. He probably has a very short memory, but he acted as if it were the most fun he'd ever had.

1995

BETSY BERNE

THE TIRED CHRONICLES

I'VE noticed recently that the main topic of conversation among my friends is tiredness. Actually, there is an underlying contest over who is more tired and who has truly earned his or her tiredness. I am not speaking of the downtrodden poor, who don't have the time to discuss the intricacies of fatigue. I am talking about upper-middle-class martyrs in their thirties and forties, for whom all tiredness is not equal. There are several categories among us. There are the tired married people with kids. There are the tired single people who work at home. There are the tired single people who are somewhat employed outside the home. And, of course, there are the tired people who have real jobs (a minority in this group).

According to the tired married people with kids, there is no contest. They are the royalty of the tired kingdom. They are smug with exhaustion. I belong to the tired-single-people-who-work-at-home group, and in the tired race I don't have a prayer. I have more than enough friends in the married-with-kids group, and I've gone many rounds of tiredness discussions. Generally, I try to head them off at the pass with a gentle "You must be so exhausted," hoping the acknowledgment will suffice. Unfortunately, this only sends them into their litany. When I talk to a member of this group, I try not to let it slip out that I may be a tiny bit tired, too. Sometimes it does slip out, and it can nip a tiredness conversation in the bud.

Conversations with my neighbor usually begin with a few basic pleasantries. He says, "Hi." I reply, "Hi, how are you?" He answers, "Exhausted." And we are off and running. I chime in, "I'm tired, too." We proceed to try and outdo each other. My neighbor beats me every time, because he is a single busy tired person who works somewhat outside the home. Sure I'm tired, but I'm not particularly busy. By his estimation, he averages three or four hours of sleep a night. He also naps at random, which is the true mark of a tired person who works at home (or somewhat at home). Whether naps count as sleep is unclear. (The tired married people with kids do not nap, or, if they do, they don't come clean.)

My neighbor and I are very specific in our chronicling of tiredness. We include time of actual tuck-in and amount of actual shut-eye, number of times awakened (including cause and effect), amount of human interaction in the day (a major factor in tiredness calculation), number of trips out of the house, and number of naps. Our conversation usually sends my neighbor back to bed.

By now it might be time to mention my brother, the jazz musician. He is bone tired. This is because he is a member of yet another group, the international-jet-set tired people. My brother is always on the road playing gigs—from Istanbul to Helsinki to Houston Street. When he is on tour in Italy, for example, not only must he deal with the adulation of fans but he must consume sumptuous free meals and stay in Tuscan castles. And he must always hang after a gig. "Hang" is jazz lingo for drinking all night with fans, who are often female. You can imagine the tiredness this can lead to.

Just last year, my big-wheel writer friend joined the ranks of the international-jet-set tired group. Now she, too, is always flying off to exotic locales—in her case, to work on a movie she has written. She, too, is forced to consume sumptuous free meals and stay in Tuscan castles. And, as if that weren't tiring enough, she is also searching for a mate. Finding a mate requires an inordinate amount of human interaction, naturally leading to you know what. Every day, on the phone, my friend rattles off her packed schedule, including both lunch and dinner dates, with an occasional party thrown in. My schedule is not packed, and the conversation is rather one-sided. Yet after I hang up I am overcome with exhaustion. In fact, I don't think I want to talk to any more members of the international-jet-set tired group. In fact, I might not want to talk to any members of any tired group. Instead, I will silently examine my own life, which will inevitably land me in the position I am most accustomed to: prone.

1995

JOHN UPDIKE

PARANOID PACKAGING

MAYBE the madness began with strapping tape. Its invention seemed to excite people, so that packages arrived more and more impenetrably wrapped, in layer upon layer of the tough, string-reinforced stuff. Where tearing fingers used to do the job, an X-Acto knife and a surgical precision had to be mustered. Domestic injuries mounted, but the tape kept coming, along with flesh-colored plastic tape that wouldn't tear—just stretched, like tortured flesh—no matter how hard you pulled.

Then one day, in the long twilight of the Reagan presidency, the cereal and sugar boxes that had always said "Press Here" ceased to yield, when pressed, the little pouring holes we remembered from childhood. Rather, our thumbnails broke, and turned purple overnight. Padded book envelopes, which used to open with an easy tug on the stapled turned-over flap, were now taped *over* the staples. The taping was tenacious, multilayered. Postal regulations, some said: too many clerks were calling in sick after cutaneous contact with half-bent staple ends. Sometime under Bush, with everybody distracted by televised bulletins from the Gulf War, the self-sealing book envelope was promulgated. Now there was no hope of a tidy opening and a thrifty reuse; nothing less than a hatchet or a machete would free the contents, in a cloud of fast-spreading gray fluff.

All this time, childproof pill bottles had been imperceptibly toughening and complicating, to the point where only children had the patience and eyesight to open them. Though the two arrows were lined up under a magnifying glass and superhuman manual force was exerted, the top declined to pop off. Similarly, the screw-tops on the can of creosote and the bottle of Liquid-Plumr refused to slip into the grooves that in theory would lift them up—up and free. Instead, they rotated aimlessly no matter how much simultaneously downward and sideways, or semicircular, pressure was applied. Occasionally, an isolated householder did enjoy a moment of success with these recalcitrant containers; manufacturers, swiftly striking back, printed the instructions in even smaller type or, less readably yet, in raised plastic letters.

The corporations, it seemed, did not want their products released into use—any upsurge in demand might interfere with their lucrative downsizing programs.

The little bags of peanuts with which the downsizing airlines had replaced in-flight meals became, as the Clinton administration warily settled into the seats of power, impossible to open. The minuscule notch lettered "Tear Here" was a ruse; in truth, the plastic-backed tinfoil, or tinfoil-backed plastic, had been reinforced in that very place. Mounting frustration, intensified by the normal claustrophobia, cramping, and fright of air travel, produced dozens of cases of apoplexy and literally thousands of convulsively spilled peanuts. Even the little transparent sacs of plastic cutlery for airplane meals (when these were actually served) proved seamlessly resistant, and yielded up their treasure only when pierced from within by a painstakingly manipulated fork.

Such consumer-resistant packaging devices were all as bows and arrows before the invention of gunpowder, however, once the maker of Vanish, a brand of mysterious crystals alleged to be able to clean toilet bowls, came up with a red child-resistant cap, shaped like a barred "O," a three-dimensional "Ө," whose accompanying arc-shaped directions read, "To open: Squeeze center while pulling up." Well, good luck, Mr. and Mrs. America: squeeze until your face turns red, white, and blue. No amount of aerobic finger exercise will ever pack in the squeeze power needed to release those crystals into that murky toilet bowl.

Either as a nation we have grown feeble or the policy of containment, once preached as the only safe tactic for dealing with the Communist menace, has now refocused upon the output of capitalism, in all its sparkling, poisonous, hazardous variety. They—the corporate powers that control our lives—have apparently decided, in regard to one product after another, to make it, advertise it, ship it, *but not let us into it*. Be it aspirin, creosote, salted peanuts, or Vanish, it is too wonderful for us—too potent, too fine. We rub the lamp, but no genie is released. We live surrounded by magic caskets that keep their tangy goodness sealed forever in.

1996

DAVID BROOKS

CONSCIENTIOUS CONSUMPTION

YOU'RE a highly cultured person who has never cared all that much about money, but suddenly, thanks to the information-age economy, you find yourself making more dough than you ever expected. The problem is: How to spend all that income without looking like one of the vulgar yuppies you despise? Fortunately, a Code of Financial Correctness is emerging. It's a set of rules to guide your consumption patterns, to help you spend money in ways that are spiritually and culturally uplifting. If you follow these precepts, you'll be able to dispose of up to four or five million dollars annually in a manner that shows how little you care about material things.

Rule No. 1: Only vulgarians spend a lot of money on luxuries; restrict your lavish spending to necessities. When it comes to members of the cultivated class, the richer they get the more they emulate the Shakers. It's crass to spend sixty thousand dollars on a Porsche, but it's a sign of elevated consciousness to spend sixty-five thousand dollars on a boxy and practical Range Rover. It's decadent to spend ten thousand dollars on an outdoor Jacuzzi, but if you're not spending twenty-five thousand dollars turning a spare bedroom into a new master bath, with a freestanding copper tub in the middle of the floor and an oversized slate shower stall, it's a sign that you probably haven't learned to appreciate the simple rhythms of life.

An important corollary to Rule No. 1 is that you can never spend too much money on a room or a piece of equipment that in an earlier age would have been used primarily by the servants. It's vulgar to spend fifteen thousand dollars on a sound system and a wide-screen TV, but it's virtuous to spend fifty thousand dollars on a utilitarian room, like the kitchen. Only a bounder would buy a Louis Vuitton briefcase, but the owner of a German-made Miele White Pearl vacuum cleaner, which retails for $749, clearly has his priorities straight.

Rule No. 2: It is perfectly acceptable to spend lots of money on anything that is "professional quality," even if it has nothing to do with your profession. For example, although you are not likely ever to climb Mt. Everest, an expedition-weight three-layer Gore-Tex Alpenglow-reinforced Marmot Thunderlight jacket is a completely reasonable purchase. You may not be planning to convert your home into a restaurant, but a triple-doored Sub Zero refrigerator and a ten-thousand-dollar AGA cooker with a warming plate, a simmering plate, a baking oven, a roasting oven, and an infinite supply of burners is still a sensible acquisition.

Rule No. 3: You can never have too much texture. The high-achieving but grasping consumers of the nineteen-eighties surrounded themselves with smooth surfaces—matte black furniture, polished lacquer floors, and sleek faux-marbleized walls. To demonstrate your spiritual superiority to such people, you'll want to build an environment full of natural irregularities. Everything they made smooth you'll want to make rough. You'll hire squads of workmen with ball-peen hammers to pound some rustic authenticity into your broad floor planks. You'll import craftsmen from Umbria to create the look of crumbling frescoed plaster in your foyer. You'll want a fireplace built from craggy stones that look as if they could withstand a catapult assault. You'll want sideboards with peeling layers of paint, rough-hewn exposed beams, lichenous stone walls, weathered tiles, nubby upholstery fabrics. Remember, if your furniture is distressed your conscience needn't be.

The texture principle applies to comestibles, too. Everything you drink will leave sediment in the bottom of the glass: yeasty microbrews, unfiltered fruit juices, organic coffees. Your bread will be thick and grainy, the way wholesome peasants like it, not thin and airy, as shallow suburbanites prefer. Even your condiments will be admirably coarse; you'll know you're refined when you start using unrefined sugar.

Rule No. 4: You must practice one-downmanship. Cultivated people are repelled by the idea of keeping up with the Joneses. Thus, in order to raise your own status you must conspicuously reject status symbols. You will never display gilt French antiques or precious jewelry, but you will proudly dine on a two-hundred-year-old pine table that was once used for slaughtering chickens. Your closet doors will have been salvaged from an old sausage factory. Your living-room rugs will resemble the ponchos worn by Mexican paupers. The baby gates on the stairs will have been converted from nineteenth-century rabbit hutches. Eventually, every object in your house will look as if it had once been owned by someone much poorer than you.

You will never spend large sums on things associated with the rich, like yachts, caviar, or truffles. Instead, you will buy unpretentious items associated with the proletariat—except that you'll buy pretentious versions of these items, which actual members of the proletariat would find preposterous. For example, you'll go shopping for a basic food like potatoes, but you won't buy an Idaho spud. You'll select one of those miniature potatoes of distinction that grow only in certain soils of northern France. When you need lettuce, you will choose only from among those flimsy cognoscenti lettuces that taste so bad on sandwiches. (You will buy these items in boutique grocery stores whose inventory says "A Year in Provence" even as their prices say "Ten Years Out of Medical School.")

Accordingly, you will pay hugely inflated prices for all sorts of things that uncultivated people buy cheap: coffee at three seventy-five a cup, water at five dollars a bottle, a bar of soap for twelve dollars. Even your plain white T-shirt will run fifty dollars or more. The average person might be satisfied with a twenty-dollar shovel from Sears, but the sophisticated person will appreciate the heft and grip of the fifty-nine-dollar English-made Bull Dog brand garden spade that can be found at Smith & Hawken. When buying your necessities, you have to prove that you are serious enough to appreciate the best.

Rule No. 5: If you want to practice conscientious consumption, you'll want to be able to discourse knowledgeably about everything you buy. You'll favor catalogues that provide some helpful background reading on each item. You'll want your coffee shop and your bookstore to have maxims from Emerson and Arendt on the walls, because there is nothing more demeaning than shopping in a store that offers no teleological context for your purchases. You'll only patronize a butcher who hosts poetry readings. Remember, you are not merely a pawn in a mass consumer society; you are the curator of your purchases. You are able to elevate consumption above the material plane. You are able to turn your acquisitions into a set of morally informed signifiers that will win the approbation of your peers. You are able to create a life style that compensates for the fact that you abandoned your early interest in poetry and grew up to be a corporate lawyer. You care enough to spend the very most.

1998

LOUIS MENAND

THE END MATTER

IT is 2:30 A.M. of a Monday, spring semester, 1983. Things are looking extremely good. Forty-eight hours of high-intensity stack work and some inspired typing have produced the thirty-page final paper for Modern European History (Mr. Blague, MW 9–10) that you were supposed to be working on all semester but that an unfortunate dispute involving a car, which, as you have repeatedly pointed out, really wasn't in such good shape when you borrowed it, has prevented you from giving the time and attention you sincerely intended. Now, as you contemplate the pile of neatly typed 20-lb. Eaton noncorrasable bond on your desk, you are satisfied that you have turned out, in two days, the intellectual and moral equivalent of three months' steady application, a paper that Professor Blague will recognize as the work of a powerful and unexpectedly mature historical mind. Only the notes and the bibliography remain. You have scored an emergency supply of No-Doz, the collegian's friend. Your Smith-Corona portable electric typewriter, the high-school graduation gift of proud grandparents and a machine expressly designed to meet the exigencies of the all-nighter, shows every sign of being equal to its historic task. Two-thirty is by no means an unreasonable hour of the night. You anticipate a decent five or six hours of sleep before class time. And you are, of course, so wrong. You are not nearing the finish line at all. There is a signpost up ahead: you are about to enter The End Matter.

Annotation may seem a mindless and mechanical task. In fact, it calls both for superb fine-motor skills and for adherence to the most exiguous formal demands. Throw in sleep deprivation and a mild case of caffeine jitters, and the combination is guaranteed to produce flawed page after flawed page. In the world of End Matter, there is no such thing as a flyspeck. Every error is an error of substance, a betrayal of ignorance and inexperience, the academic equivalent of the double dribble. That the decorums of citation are the arbitrary residue of ancient pedantries whose raisons d'être are long past reconstructing does not reduce the penalties for nonconformity. You are on page 3 of your endnotes before you remember that *ibid* is supposed to end with a period, since it is an abbreviation for *ibidem* ("in the same place"). What genius decided that it was worth saving a character by this practice no longer matters. What matters is that it is now three-thirty in the morning and you have to retype three pages of notes. Or perhaps it suddenly strikes you, with the force of panic, that maybe, as a foreign term, *ibid.* should be underlined. You quickly discover that, by continually hand-adjusting the typewriter's platen (the "roller," in layman's language), in order to superscript your endnote numbers, you have thrown the alignment out of whack, and when you roll the page back up to underline the *ibid.*s you type the line right through the word. You have to pull the paper out and start over.

You also need to remember that, even in the United States, the city in which Harvard University Press is situated is cited as Cambridge, Mass., while the city where Cambridge University Press is found is simply Cambridge. (Not that the British care; they happen to be complete slobs about citation.) And which is it: the Belknap Press of Harvard University Press, the Belknap Press, or Harvard University Press? What is the Belknap Press, exactly? The whole subfield of publishers' names is a thornbush of institutional idiosyncrasy. There is no such thing as the University of Mississippi Press. It is the University Press of Mississippi (just as Indiana University must never be called the University of Indiana, even though that, in fact, is what it is). Once, there was Charles Scribner's Sons; now it is Scribner. Make sure you have the right one. Knopf is both cooler and more kosher than Alfred A. Knopf, but W. W. Norton is a publishing house and Norton is a character in *The Honeymooners*. The student who types Macmillan & Co., Inc., instead of Macmillan & Co. is inviting a big red circle from the Blague marking pen, even though Macmillan & Co., Inc., is what it says on the title page. Little, Brown insists on its baffling comma (what's wrong with Little and Brown?); the comma-free Harcourt Brace Jovanovich is not a law firm but possibly hopes to be mistaken for one. Then there is the special hell of reprints—the Penguins and Plumes and Harper-Torchbooks, the Bantams, the Dovers, and the Signets. It seems undignified to cite the publisher of a book that cost $2.95 and was originally printed somewhere else. And if the pagination is different is it a new ed., or still a repr.? Is an "expanded edition" a rev. ed. or a 2nd ed.? You suspect that there are rules covering these things, but it is now 4 A.M. and you have no idea how to find out.

As you reach the far shores of the bibliography, and Phoebus rims the quad with reddening fire, questions such as where to put the name of the editor (after the title or before?); how to list an article in a col-lection (under the author of the article or under the editor of the col-lection, or both?); when you are supposed to include the issue number, as well as the volume number, of a journal; and when to precede page numbers by a colon and when by pp. assume an unbearable, almost an existential weight. The mistakes metastasize. As you are typing note 65, you realize, many pages too late, that you have two note 11s. You discover that you have been op-citing a work that you never cited. You curse yourself for not buying the corrasable bond. Flakes of whiteout litter the surface of the now unpleasantly hot Smith-Corona. You have started to make corrections with a pencil. You look at the page you just pulled out of the typewriter. It looks like a ransom note.

The worst part of the miserable ordeal is that, no matter how dili-gently you adhere to the conventions of one style of citation, Professor Blague will prefer a different one. If you use the *MLA Style Manual,* he will use Turabian; if it is Turabian you have relied on, he will turn out to be a lifelong Chicagoan. (Whatever you do, incidentally, do not look for guidance in the pages of *The New Yorker,* where house style requires quotation marks for book titles and the insertion of commas in places where other periodicals don't even have places.)

Correct citation, like virtually every other aspect of academic writ-ing, is a moving target. There is no uniform system. The natural sci-ences, and fields, like sociology, that pose as such, cite by last name and date of publication (Merton 1957a) and regard first names as a literary indulgence (R. K. Merton, *Social Theory and Social Structure* [hereafter *STSS* in text]). Law journals weirdly print article titles in itals (*Notes on Promissory Estoppel in Collective Bargaining Disputes*) and book titles all caps (SECOND RESTATEMENT OF CONTRACTS). They also precede page numbers, after the initial reference, with "at" (*Bush v. Gore,* at 7), an af-fectation that you would be shot for if you adopted it in an English paper. Recently, though, the humanities have been drifting in this hardhat, Men at Work direction by reducing titles to tech-speak ("*Cider House* subverts the conventions of monologism Irving elabo-rates in the texts after *Garp*") and by inserting page references in the text ("what Judith Butler has referred to as 'sex' [*GT* 87]"). Students using an older sister's edition of the *MLA Style Manual,* published be-fore these new forms became standard, had better hope that their liter-ature professors are too old to know the difference.

. . .

THE notion that the personal computer has eliminated the bone-crushing inefficiency of the typewriter, and turned composing The End Matter into a drive in the word-processing park, belongs to the myth that all work on a computer is "fun"—one of the Digital Age's cruellest jokes. It's true that typing a term paper no longer feels like working in a zinc quarry. You don't rely on No-Doz these days (*please*); you use, thanks to a roommate's very obliging psychopharmacologist, Provigil, a med being considered for military pilots who want to stay alert for twenty-four hours at a stretch. Though your laptop may not have all the gigabytes that you deserve but that your chintzy grandparents, who lease a brand-new Lexus *every year*, declined to spring for, it does have a hard drive capable of storing the equivalent of eighty billion three-by-five file cards, probably enough to get you through college (after which you will need to upgrade). And, yes, your term paper for Sexing the Victorians: Gender and Transgression in European Modernity (Ms. Slick, M 2–5) is now sixty-five elegantly formatted laser-printed pages, including a four-color cover page and scanned-in illustrations of nineteenth-century dildos and the like. But The End Matter remains an interminable twilight struggle. The potential for rage and heartbreak is even greater, in fact, for the very technology that is supposed to speed the task of information processing is now your most insidious foe.

First of all, it is time to speak some truth to power in this country: *Microsoft Word is a terrible program.* Its terribleness is of a piece with the terribleness of Windows generally, a system so overloaded with icons, menus, buttons, and incomprehensible Help windows that performing almost any function means entering a treacherous wilderness of pop-ups posing alternatives of terrifying starkness: Accept/Decline/Cancel; Logoff/Shut Down/Restart; and the mysterious Do Not Show This Warning Again. You often feel that you're not ready to make a decision so unalterable; but when you try to make the window go away your machine emits an angry beep. You double-click. You triple-click. *Beep beep beep beep beep.* You are being held for a fool by a chip.

When, in the old days, you hit the wrong key on your typewriter, you got one wrong character. Strike the wrong keys in Word and you are suddenly writing in Norwegian Bokmal (*Bokmal?*). And you have no idea how you got there; you can spend the rest of the night trying to get out. In the end, you stop the random clicking and dragging and pulling-down and have recourse to the solution of every computer moron: with a sob of relief, you press Ctrl/Alt/Del. (What do Control and Alt *mean*, by the way? Does anyone still know?) A message appears: "You will lose any unsaved information in all programs that are running." O.K.? Cancel? End task? End life? The whole reason for rebooting was that you didn't *have* access to your information, so how can you save it? You can always pull the plug out of the wall. That usually ends your "session" (a term borrowed—no accident—from psychoanalysis).

Few features of Word can be responsible for more user meltdowns than Footnote and Endnote (which is saying a lot in the case of a program whose Thesaurus treats "information" as "in formation," offering "in order" and "in sequence" as possible synonyms, and whose spellcheck suggests that when you typed the unrecognized "decorums" you might have meant "deco rums"). To begin with, the designers of Word apparently believe that the conventional method of endnote numbering is with lowercase Roman numerals—i, ii, iii, etc. When was the last time you read anything that adhered to this style? It would lead to sentences like:

In the Gramscian paradigm, the "intellectual"[lxxxvii] is, by definition, always already a liminal status.[lxxxviii]

(Hmm. Not bad.) To make this into something recognizably human, you need to click your way into the relevant menu (View? Insert? Format?) and change the i, ii, iii, etc., to 1, 2, 3, etc. Even if you *wanted* to use lowercase Roman numerals somewhere, whenever you typed "i" Word would helpfully turn it into "I" as soon as you pressed the space bar. Similarly, if, God forbid, you ever begin a note or a bibliography entry with the letter "A.," when you hit Enter, Word automatically types "B." on the next line. Never, btw (which, unlike "poststructuralism," is a word in Word spellcheck), ask that androgynous paper clip anything. S/he is just a stooge for management, leading you down more rabbit holes of options for things called Wizards, Macros, Templates, and Cascading Style Sheets. Finally, there is the moment when you realize that your notes are starting to appear in 12-pt. Courier New. Word, it seems, has, at some arbitrary point in the proceedings, decided that although you have been typing happily away in Times New Roman, you really want to be in the default font of the original document. You are confident that you can lick this thing: you painstakingly position your cursor in the Endnotes window (not the text!, where irreparable damage may occur) and click Edit, then the powerful Select All; you drag the arrow to Normal (praying that your finger doesn't lose contact with the mouse, in which case the window will disappear, and trying not to wonder what the difference between Normal and Clear Formatting might be) and then, in the little window to the right, to Times New Roman. You triumphantly click, and find that you are indeed back in Times New Roman but that all your italics have been removed. What about any of this can be considered "high-speed"?

THE special difficulty that digitization presents to scholarship has to do with the Internet—specifically, how to cite sources from the Web. The editors of one of the long-standing authorities in the style game, *The Chicago Manual of Style,* have arrived with some advice. This new *Chicago Manual* is the fifteenth edition of a work that made its publishing début in 1906. (Before that, it served an incarnation as the in-house style sheet at the University of Chicago Press.) It is important to note at the outset that the new edition has 956 pages and retails for $55. The only reasons to buy it are (1) that you want to start up a press and (2) that you want it to be exactly like the University of Chicago Press. *The Chicago Manual of Style* is, fundamentally, the in-house authority for bookmaking at the Press. It explains things like half titles; CIP (Cataloguing-in-Publication) data; bound-in errata pages; and the distinctions between perfect, notch, and burst bindings—matters of no relevance to the average term-paper writer. The text is organized in the manner of the *Tractatus Logico-Philosophicus,* with numbered points (**1.1, 1.2** . . . **1.11, 1.12,** and so on). Data are dispensed accordingly, in the ground-upward manner of logical positivism, and at ground level the points can be very elementary—e.g., "**1.112** *Content of the jacket.* Hardcover books are often protected by a coated paper jacket (or dust jacket)." Useful information for the man from Mars.

Every style book has its idiosyncrasies (part of the moving-target syndrome). Chicago used to insist on rendering dates in the form 15 August 2003, and ordinals as 2d and 3d, in the legal style, rather than 2nd and 3rd (which Word is programmed to superscript for you without asking). The *Manual* has now abandoned the former style and made the latter optional. Its authors also join the rest of the civilized world in consigning the dreadful op. cit. (along with its cousin, that desiccated old roué loc. cit.) to the lexical dustbin. One major addition (besides what the preface tantalizingly describes as "more attention to Canadian terms and usage") is a ninety-page section on Grammar and

Usage. For some reason—possibly for the convenience of our Martian friend—the authors felt it necessary to cover the field from scratch. Thus: "**5.1** *Definition.* Grammar consists of the rules governing how words are put together." On the other hand, common sources of solecism receive less attention than they might. The College Board would still not have avoided the mistake it made on a recent PSAT exam, where it replaced the phrase "Toni Morrison's genius" with "her," if it had consulted the Chicago discussion of pronouns and antecedents.

The chapter on Punctuation (separate from Grammar and Usage) notes that Chicago has finally dispensed with the practice of italicizing punctuation following a title (e.g., "*The Chicago Manual of Style,* a leading authority"), which is a welcome change, since Word's click-and-drag highlighting feature has problems performing this function. (If you wiggle the mouse a millimeter too far, trying to get that comma in, you highlight the entire line.) The authors are straightforward on two matters that many students are apparently hardwired at birth to find boggling: whether periods and commas belong inside or outside quotation marks, and whether inverted commas (sometimes called "single quotation marks") are an appropriate way to indicate an "ironic" usage. (Inside and no.) Some of the advice is frankly a matter of taste. "An exclamation point added in brackets to quoted material to indicate editorial protest or amusement is strongly discouraged, since it appears contemptuous," the authors counsel. "The Latin expression *sic* (thus) is preferred." First of all, the reason the bracketed exclamation point appears contemptuous is that you use it when you wish to express contempt. There is nothing wrong with contempt. Second (which Chicago insists on, although generations of pedants have believed "secondly" to be the proper usage), *sic* is a far more damning interpolation, combining ordinary, garden-variety contempt with pedantic condescension. Elsewhere in Punctuation, the instructions are sometimes the reverse of enlightened. What could the authors possibly have been thinking when they committed the following sentence to print: "The semicolon, stronger than a comma but weaker than a period, can assume either role [!]"?

On the aggravating business of citing a Web page, Chicago recommends giving the entire URL, usually in addition to any print data (journal volume number, year, page range, and so on), plus a "descriptive locator" (where to find the quotation on the screen, since electronic editions sometimes do not paginate), plus the date accessed. This can make for a very long note. Here is one of the samples the *Manual* offers, as it would appear if you reproduced it in Word:

Hlatky, M. A., D. Boothroyd, E. Vittinghoff, P. Sharp, and M. A. Whooley. 2002. Quality-of-life and depressive symptoms in post-menopausal women after receiving hormone therapy: Results from the Heart and Estrogen/Progestin Replacement Study (HERS) trial. *Journal of the American Medical Association* 287, no. 5 (February 6), http://jama.ama-assn.org/issues/v287n5/rfull/joc10108.html#aainfo (accessed January 7, 2002).

Try to prevent Word from doing that blue thing to whatever it recognizes as a hyperlink. There is undoubtedly a way to reset this, but it is deep within the bowels of the machine, guarded by dozens of angry pop-ups. Microsoft *wants* you to go on the Internet.

Attention to the new demands of electronic media informs almost every chapter of the new *Manual*. There are discussions about (besides citation) preparing electronic publications, editing and proofreading onscreen, and electronic-publishing rights and permissions. The authors are sensible about these matters; they're aware that this is an area very much "under construction." In all departments, in fact, the authors allow themselves plenty of wiggle room, quoting a passage from the 1906 edition: "Rules and regulations such as these, in the nature of the case, cannot be endowed with the fixity of rock-ribbed law. They are meant for the average case, and must be applied with a certain degree of elasticity." This is modest and becoming, but it is beside the point. The problem isn't that there are cases that fall outside the rules. The problem is that *there is a rule for every case,* and no style manual can hope to list them all. But we want the rules anyway. What we don't want to be told is "Be flexible," or "You have choices." "Choice" is another of modern life's false friends. Too many choices is precisely what makes Word such a nightmare to use, and what makes a hell of, for example, shopping for orange juice: Original, Grovestand, Home Style, Low Acid, Orange Banana, Extra Calcium, PulpFree, Lotsa Pulp, and so on.

The *Manual* does have lotsa lists, it's true. Still, it can be oddly silent about common usage mistakes. Sixty-seven pages are devoted to Names and Terms. Writers are instructed, in the subsection on Titles and Offices, to lowercase offices (pope, rabbi, ayatollah) and uppercase titles (Pope John Paul II, Rabbi Avraham Yitzhak ha-Kohen Kuk, Ayatollah Khomeini). The authors do not, however, warn against the frequent and well-meaning substitution of "Dr." for "Professor." Contrary to the assumption informing this practice, "doctor" is not the higher-status term; virtually all professors are doctors, but by no means are all doctors professors.

Chicago prefers a "down" style for the names of political and cultural movements (anarchist, mugwump, abstract expressionism), but this is possibly due to the desire to have a sleeker and more modern-looking page, for the rule runs into hard cases rather quickly. The authors concede right at the outset of the subsection on Names of Organizations that efforts to distinguish, by upper- and lowercase, between communism as an ideology and Communism as a political party are usually hopeless (was John F. Kennedy an anticommunist or an anti-Communist, or both?), and that Communist and Communism might as well be uppercased everywhere they appear. On the other hand, they countenance "nazi" as an adjective ("nazi tactics," as opposed to "the Nazis' tactics")—but what about "marxist"? The *Manual* does not propose this as an option.

The authors declare for pop art but do not mention popism (or Popism) and for conceptualism without mentioning conceptual art (or Conceptual Art). They have heard of structuralism and postmodernism (both lowercase) but (like Microsoft) do not recognize poststructuralism (this from one of Derrida's American publishers). Pragmatism (the philosophy) is unlisted, but it can create problems; George W. Bush is (arguably) a pragmatist, but he is no Pragmatist. "Classicism" is lowercased, but "romanticism" is "sometimes capitalized to avoid ambiguity"—though if you were capitalizing "Romanticism" it would look silly to lowercase "classicism" in the same paragraph. The authors scoff, delightfully, at brand-name and trademark shibboleths. Despite corporate bluster, they point out, there is no legal requirement to use ® or ™, as the Motion Picture Academy wants you to do with Oscar, or to write "Kleenex facial tissue" instead of "Kleenex," as the makers of Kleenex would like you to do when referring to their fine product. Less helpfully, the authors offer "photocopier" as a generic alternative to "Xerox machine," but do not explain whether you Xerox or xerox a piece of paper.

The section on Ellipses is seven pages. The authors distinguish between a three-dot method, a three-or-four-dot method, and what they designate "the rigorous method" (with the unfortunate implication that the other methods are for scholarly lightweights). For some reason, they do not address, even in the "rigorous" section, the problem of quoting a passage that includes ellipses in the original. Does placing brackets around the ellipsis imply that the ellipsis was interpolated or that it was not? The *Manual* authors now recommend disposing of the periods in the abbreviation of academic degrees (PhD instead of Ph.D.). On the important matter of the correct abbreviation of United States, though, the authors strike a note that recurs, all too disturbingly, in other places in the *Manual.* It is the note of permissiveness. "*U.S.* traditionally appears with periods," they advise. And then—it's almost a non sequitur—"Periods may nonetheless be omitted in most contexts. Writers and editors need to weigh tradition against consistency." The mental fuse is shorted. You had always thought that tradition *was* consistency. Also, as long as the authors are into lists, would it not have been helpful to list that small number of proper names which must, in all circumstances, be preceded by Mr.?

Mr. Rogers
Mr. Shawn
Mr. T
Mr. Tambourine Man
Mr. Tibbs

The sections that people who are not operating a printing press will consult most often are the two devoted to Documentation. But Documentation is where the *Manual*'s ecumenism starts to shade into anarchism (the condition, not the party). Consider the subsection on Series (that is, books published in a series with, usually, a general editor). The editor of the series, the *Manual* says, is "usually omitted, but see 17.92–93." Abbreviations for volume and number "may be omitted." The series title "may be omitted to save space." Some works "may be treated bibliographically either as multivolume works or as a series of volumes," depending on "the emphasis." And when a series has gone on so long that the editors re-start the numbering as "new series" or "second series," we learn that "books in the old series are identified by *o.s.,* *1st ser.,* or whatever fits." At which point the sleep-deprived might decide that, on due and balanced consideration, *nothing* is what fits, and move on.

Some people will complain that the new *Chicago Manual* is too long. These people do not understand the nature of style. There is, if not a right way, a best way to do every single thing, down to the proverbial dotting of the *i.* Relativism is fine for the big moral questions, where we can never know for sure; but in arbitrary realms like form and usage even small doses of relativism are lethal. The *Manual* is not too long. It is not long enough. It will never be long enough. The perfect manual of style would be like the perfect map of the world: exactly coterminous with its subject, containing a rule for every word of every sentence. We would need an extra universe to accommodate it. It would be worth it.

2003

MIKE ALBO AND VIRGINIA HEFFERNAN

THE UNDERMINER

MY FRIEND
My friend must be a bird
Because it flies.
Mortal, my friend must be
Because it dies!
Barbs has it, like a bee.
Ah, curious friend.
Thou puzzlest me.
                                —Emily Dickinson

GRADUATION DAY

Hey, there. Whew, what a day. First I did the Ellipticycle for an hour and then I had to run to the dean's small cocktail party for honors students and then I had to hurry up and turn in that Green Form so I could graduate.

You know, the Green Form.

The Green Form? You didn't turn it in?! No, it's that green form that we got at orientation when we first came here, four years ago. Yeah, sorry, but it kind of *is* important. It's the Green Form. They told us never to lose it, remember? No, not the blue registration card, the *green* form! Maybe you just put it in your wallet and you didn't even know or something. Check it.

Wow . . . your wallet. You actually keep everything all crammed in together like that? No, it's just kind of amazing. I would freak out if I couldn't streamline my wallet. Oh—I think you dropped this twenty-dollar bill. Oh, no, wait, it's actually mine. Sorry.

You are so funny, you. Man, am I going to miss college and all your crazy flakiness. Ha-ha! You've always been the funny, crazy one in our gang. With all your plans and your spilling wallet and your poetry writing and music and acting and whatever you have going on at the time! You're like the outsider of the gang. Not *outsider* outsider. But I mean, like, like outsider art. You know, like cute, sweet, drunk, weird. Like those artists who build towers in their back yards out of, like, TV-dinner trays, or who scratch the entire Bible into a bar of soap with their fingernails and end up in mental institutions. I mean, like not obviously insane but more like all your efforts may not be fully embraced by the public, but you're gonna just do it anyway, no matter what. And that's just great.

Well, anyway. You majored in Kurdish folklore, right? Wow. I was so surprised you didn't get honors, since you tried so hard to be schmoozy with your adviser—I mean, I'm sure that's probably a good strategy. That's the way you get ahead in this dog-eat-dog world.

So what are you doing this summer? You got a job as an intern? Cool beans! Where? An art gallery in New York! Bonwyck Gallery? Weird! Did they expand their program? I thought it was just for teens. No, I'm sure I'm wrong.

And after that—any life plan? Nothing yet? Yeah, I know. It's so hard to choose the right path. It's, like, one false move and you may end up leading an entirely different life, full of flaws and mishaps. Huh.

OPEN-MIKE NIGHT, KAFKA-FÉ COFFEE HOUSE

Oh, my God, I am so glad I got a chance to see your band perform. Wow, that was fun! That was just fun! Really fun! I got here right at the end, but I pretty much caught enough to understand your whole deal. Sorry the crowd was so small. . . . But they were all clapping. You really got a lot of applause. Did you have a lot of family and friends in the audience? It just seemed like everyone knew you or something. Oh, you wait tables here, too? I guess that internship ended, huh? Well, cool for you. At least the staff here is supportive. The way they clapped for you. Wow, that was fun!

Look at you and your outfit! That is a super pair of retro moon boots. They're the trend right now, I know. Trends are so interesting to follow, especially for someone cutting-edge like you who's so hyper-attuned to the whole "appearance industry." The way you keep up with things, and spend your money on magazines. Like, I know that, for you, you need to be really good about skin care.

Unbelievable. Your singing voice is so different from your appearance. It's, like, when I close my eyes I would imagine the person singing was a sultry, sexy vocalist from prewar Berlin, and then I open my eyes and there you are! You and your big shiny American face!

So are you still with Carl from college? That is so sweet that you guys are trying to work things out. Long-distance, right? Yeah. Sometimes those actually work. No, really! Sometimes they really do! Sometimes! How fun! Really fun!

Well, anyway, what are you doing later? Oh, yeah, I guess you have to clean up here. Send steamed water through the cappuccino machines and wipe out the coffee thermoses and stuff. Wow, I totally remember having to do that in my job after high school! It was better since I did it in Rome, but still.

Me? I'm going to Crish Crash, probably. Crish Crash? You know, the huge, huge warehouse party that's happening tonight. It's probably why there wasn't much of a crowd here—like, everyone in the city under twenty-five is going. This artist friend is meeting me. He's scouting for models for his photo series. I know you sort of have contempt for institutions, but RISD was good to him.

No, I mean, you said that once. Like, when you didn't get in. Whatever.

Crish Crash. You haven't heard about it? Weird. Yeah, you kind of have to know how to find it. And sort of know the right way to ask. Wait. Here's the address. If someone stops you at the door, just act like you know someone—that's what a lot of people who show up uninvited do.

AT A FRENCH BISTRO

You're here early! Wait. Are you sick? You look sort of tired. Oh, you went out drinking last night? It's so great how you can still do those college things. You're so crazy!

Did you throw up? No, no, I just smelled throw-up for a second.

You're having a Bloody Mary? No. I'm not drinking anymore. I'll just have a peppermint tea. No, go ahead and go for it. Don't let me stop you. I've just realized there's a little more to life. But go ahead, have fun. You're so crazy!

So I have some huge news. I didn't want you to hear it from someone else, but guess what? I just made two million dollars from my book deal. Yeah, yeah. I'm pretty happy about it, and my agent's pretty happy about it, and I can't talk about the details of the deal, but if you could just do me a huge, huge favor and just don't mention it to anyone? I know how you kind of have a problem keeping secrets! No, just joking. I'm joking, I'm joking. You do, though!

OUTSIDE A NIGHT CLUB CALLED HUSH

Excuse me? I'm sorry, but this is a private party and—

Oh, my God. Hi! I didn't recognize you. Jeez, you look so different! Jesus Christ! This is insane! I can't believe how different you look! Did you get a haircut? No? It just seems fluffier or something. Hmm? No, I don't wash my hair anymore. I just rinse it. At first it was dirty, but then it became cleaner than if you use shampoo, because, if you think that shampoo cleans your hair, it doesn't. It's full of chemicals and detergents that permanently strip your hair of important oils and then in a few years you experience aggressive balding.

So you came all dressed up for the movie-première party! That's so cute, because if you knew this scene you'd always really dress down. But we're probably just jaded.

Are you here alone? Trawling around the film scene, huh? Right, right. Trolling around the film scene. Yeah, everyone is still clamoring for a part of the indie-film pie. This is sort of a weird party for that, but . . . you know, maybe you'll get a chance to show off a script to some hungry producer, or at least sleep with one! Ha! You crazy, funny weirdo!

. . . So you're still here. I would have thought you'd left by now. I mean the party, not the city. Were you invited to the screening, or just the after-party? Oh. Well. By the way, how is Carl?

You did?

Oh, wow. I'm sorry you're dealing with that. I sort of saw that coming. Anyway, sweetie, really? That must be such a world of hurt for you. Who are you hanging out with now? Do you still see that girl who is my friend Amy's assistant?

You're taking a trip? Trajanja? Yes, of course I've heard of it! The small communal hard-to-get-to island off the coast of Belize? I went there last spring. It'll be good for you. I'm sure you got your shots. Oh. You didn't? Wow, I wish we'd talked before. I'm sorry, but, yes, those shots are kind of important. Without them you have a really high risk of developing a lot of long-term stomach problems and you don't really get to leave your room. Yeah, you could try to get them today, I guess. I mean, apparently they don't really "kick in" for, like, a week, but . . . yeah, you could try. Maybe they've made some medical advances since last spring.

Hey, it looks like they're opening the party to the general public. You could check it out! It'll be crowded, but, you know, you may as well just check out the whole deal.

Listen, I'm doing a ten-mile bike ride in the morning and I have to get to bed, but you take care of yourself, okay? Maybe you shouldn't go in. Save your energy for your trip. Don't go slutting around all night. Go home and take care of yourself. I worry about you, you crazy thing.

2004

NANCY FRANKLIN

MODEL CITIZENS

IF you watched the first episode of the fourth installment of UPN's *America's Next Top Model* last week, you may have noticed that I was not one of the contestants competing for the hundred-thousand-dollar contract with Cover Girl cosmetics, the model-management contract with Ford Models, and the spread in *Elle*, even though I fulfilled many of the show's stated eligibility requirements: I am not currently a candidate for public office; I am not shorter than five feet seven; my age is between eighteen and twenty-seven if you divide it by any number between 1.778 and 2.667; and, to the best of my recollection, I have not had previous experience as a model in a national campaign within the past five years. As for the stipulation that applicants must "exhibit . . . a willingness to share their most private thoughts in an open forum of strangers," is there anyone left on the planet who doesn't fit into this category? Also, I can totally work it, bring it, feel it, slam it, serve it, and own it—to use the terms that the fashion photographers, advisers, and judges fall back on when coaching the contestants or explaining their decision to keep them on the show or boot them.

The reason I'm not on the show is that I didn't want a tarantula crawling on my face; I'm funny that way. In a photo shoot for a jewelry ad in the third installment of *ANTM*, last fall, the models had to pose with a tarantula, either on or near their face. In one shot, the huge beast adjusts itself so that one leg is on the girl's eyelid and another is in the corner of her mouth. Another girl—the one with the most assertive personality—freaks out and cries, because she's terrified of spiders and so much rides on her being able to act like a pro. The contestants all regularly comment on one another to the camera, and one of them says during this scene, "Eva's really stressing. She's worried that her inability to perform with the spider on her face is going to send her home, so I don't think that she really is cut out to be America's Next Top Model." Since I, too, have an inability to perform with spiders on my face, I thought I wasn't cut out for it, either. But Eva was able to pull herself together, and she looked gorgeous in her picture with Spidey—*and* she went on to win the entire competition. So I guess I should have gone ahead and sent in an application, arachnophobia be damned.

The supermodel Tyra Banks created *America's Next Top Model,* and she is also the host and one of the show's executive producers. The aspiring models view her both as the bearer of a magic ticket out of poverty, obscurity, stripping, or waitressing and as a comforting, maternal, Oprah-like figure. Even while she is pondering which chick will be thrown out of the nest each week, Banks dispenses plentiful hugs to her charges, at one point getting down on a bathroom floor to console a distressed girl. During each episode, she makes sure the contestants understand the hardships of the modeling life—facing rejection, working in countries where they don't speak the language, putting makeup on in a moving limousine—and gives them the kind of challenges they would face as pros, such as wearing stiletto heels while posing in a bikini on volcanic rock along the coast of Jamaica. Oh, my God—now *I'm* crying.

One refreshing aspect of *ANTM* is that there is more diversity among the contestants than one usually sees in reality shows. In the last series, or "cycle," there was an Indian woman, and all the cycles have featured several black semifinalists, as well as a couple of plus-size hopefuls. (The show has not, however, stepped up—to use another of its recurring exhortatory phrases—when it comes to Asian and Latino women. Not that United Nations–style casting guarantees loftiness or anything. The Indian woman believed that she was "setting a goal for Indians: They're either engineers or doctors. But we can go outside of that. We can use our intelligence in this industry.") Banks, who has healthy, womanly curves, has included cautionary tales relating to the body-image problems that occur in the modeling business; the last cycle had a finalist who was a half inch under six feet tall and weighed a hundred and fifteen pounds, and another confessed to having problems with food, though she balked at the label "bulimic," because she didn't throw up after every single meal. Comments about the tall drink of water were left to the girls, who all live together for eight weeks and have the usual fights and dish the usual dirt on one another; for the model who was avowedly obsessed with thinness, Banks brought in a nutritionist, but the young woman resisted help—an accurate illustration of the difficulty that even experts often have in treating such disorders. It's hard not to think, though, that it was a little unfair to the extreme cases to let them get so far along in the competition, since they didn't have the remotest chance of winning; they're there, it seems, mainly to short-circuit potential complaints from viewers who may consider the modeling profession itself partly responsible for the fact that so many young women hate their bodies.

Much as Banks wants to come across as a hey-girlfriend confidante to the contestants, she in fact heightens the atmosphere of anxiety, by drawing out the elimination at the end of each episode for as long as possible, and by emphasizing that the loser will have to leave "immediately." For some contestants, immediately may not be soon enough. One girl from Oklahoma, after living in a gigantic suite at the Waldorf-Astoria for a while, had simply had it. "In Oklahoma, people look at me," she said. "I don't feel like people are looking at me here. I'm not having that much fun." While the opportunity these women are angling for is real, and even has benefits for the losers—two of whom appeared on UPN sitcoms last week—you can't help wondering why they want it so much, when success in the world they're trying to enter seems to hinge on how much of themselves they can make disappear. In this week's episode, Banks says to the girls, "Part of being a top model is about being a blank palette." And the stylist for the photo shoots, Jay Manuel, says after a session, "My concern with Toccara is that she allows too much of her personality to get in the way." At one point during a shoot, when a model strikes a less than erect pose, she is rewarded with this evaluation: "I love the broken-down-doll look." In the third cycle, the girls have to walk into a room wearing high heels that are two sizes too small and a dress that is too tight—the point being that a model has to smile through all kinds of discomfort. Nolé Marin, the fashion director of a magazine for gay men, and one of the arbiters of style who sit in judgment at the end of each episode—the others are Banks, a photographer named Nigel Barker, and the former super-model Janice Dickinson—says to one of the less graceful girls, "You look like the broken Tin Man. You needed a major oil job." Sometimes looking broken is good; sometimes it's not. It's all so confusing! This is actually among the most humane comments heard during the series from Marin, who is—and let's ourselves be fashion judges for a moment here—a chubby little bespectacled bald man with an unattractive soul patch. None of the judges offer much in the way of constructive criticism; it's always either "I'm loving the look, honey. I'm *loving* the look" or "Lose the pearls! Ugh! This is a model contest, not a secretary contest." (And yet—one more schmatte in the bundle of contradictions that is the fashion world—Mikimoto pearls are given out as a reward to a couple of the models.) Dickinson is a stun gun in human form, zealously zapping the girls as they parade before her. Referring to a picture of the bulimic woman, who is five feet ten, weighs a hundred and thirty pounds, and has a flat stomach, she says, "You look about two months pregnant there."

America's Next Top Model is fascinating, if you like trying to figure out life's little mysteries, such as how it could possibly be that someone has "wanted to model since I was three years old," and why models are trained to walk like people who have hip dysplasia. If you already think that models are vacuous, apparently you are not alone: even models themselves make that assumption. As one of the contestants, who is surprised (and shouldn't be) by how much Banks has on the ball, says, "I mean, you see Tyra, and you think boobs and lingerie. And she's got a brain—I mean, who woulda thought?"

2005

ANTHONY LANE

SPACE CASE

STAR WARS: EPISODE III

*S*ITH. What kind of a word is that? Sith. It sounds to me like the
noise that emerges when you block one nostril and blow through
the other, but to George Lucas it is a name that trumpets evil. What is
proved beyond question by *Star Wars: Episode III—Revenge of the Sith*,
the latest—and, you will be shattered to hear, the last—installment of
his sci-fi bonanza, is that Lucas, though his eye may be greedy for sensation, has an ear of purest cloth. All those who concoct imagined
worlds must populate and name them, and the resonance of those
names is a fairly accurate guide to the mettle of the imagination in
question. Tolkien, earthed in Old English, had a head start that led him
straight to the flinty perfection of Mordor and Orc. Here, by contrast,
are some Lucas inventions: Palpatine. Sidious. Mace Windu. (Isn't that
something you spray on colicky babies?) Bail Organa. And Sith.

Lucas was not always a rootless soul. He made *American Graffiti*,
which yielded with affection to the gravitational pull of the small town.
Since then, he has swung out of orbit, into deep nonsense, and the new
film is the apotheosis of that drift. One stab of humor and the whole
conceit would pop, but I have a grim feeling that Lucas wishes us to
honor the remorseless non-comedy of his galactic conflict, so here goes.
Obi-Wan Kenobi (Ewan McGregor) and his star pupil, Anakin Sky-
walker (Hayden Christensen), are, with the other Jedi knights, defending the Republic against the encroachments of the Sith and their
allies—millions of dumb droids, led by Count Dooku (Christopher
Lee) and his henchman, General Grievous, who is best described as a
slaying mantis. Meanwhile, the Chancellor of the Republic, Palpatine
(Ian McDiarmid), is engaged in a sly bout of Realpolitik, suspected by
nobody except Anakin, Obi-Wan, and every single person watching
the movie. Anakin, too, is a divided figure, wrenched between his Jedi
devotion to selfless duty and a lurking hunch that, if he bides his time

and trashes his best friends, he may eventually get to wear a funky black mask and start breathing like a horse.

This film is the tale of his temptation. We already know the outcome—Anakin will indeed drop the killer-monk Jedi look and become Darth Vader, the hockey goalkeeper from hell—because it forms the substance of the original *Star Wars*. One of the things that make Episode III so dismal is the time and effort expended on Anakin's conversion. Early in the story, he enjoys a sprightly light-sabre duel with Count Dooku, which ends with the removal of the Count's hands. (The stumps glow, like logs on a fire; there is nothing here that reeks of human blood.) Anakin prepares to scissor off the head, while the mutilated Dooku kneels for mercy. A nice setup, with Palpatine egging our hero on from the background. The trouble is that Anakin's choice of action now will be decisive, and the remaining two hours of the film—scene after scene in which Hayden Christensen has to glower and glare, blazing his conundrum to the skies—will add nothing to the result. "Something's happening. I'm not the Jedi I should be," he says. This is especially worrying for his wife, Padmé (Natalie Portman), who is great with child. Correction: with children.

What can you say about a civilization where people zip from one solar system to the next as if they were changing their socks but where a woman fails to register for an ultrasound, and thus to realize that she is carrying twins until she is about to give birth? Mind you, how Padmé got pregnant is anybody's guess, although I'm prepared to wager that it involved Anakin nipping into a broom closet with a warm glass jar and a copy of *Ewok Babes*. After all, the Lucasian universe is drained of all reference to bodily functions. Nobody ingests or excretes. Language remains unblue. Smoking and cursing are out of bounds, as is drunkenness, although personally I wouldn't go near the place without a hip flask. Did Lucas learn nothing from *Alien* and *Blade Runner*—from the suggestion that other times and places might be no less rusted and septic than ours, and that the creation of a disinfected galaxy, where even the storm troopers wear bright-white outfits, looks not so much fantastical as dated? What Lucas has devised, over six movies, is a terrible puritan dream: a morality tale in which both sides are bent on moral cleansing, and where their differences can be assuaged only by a triumphant circus of violence. Judging from the whoops and crowings that greeted the opening credits, this is the only dream we are good for. We get the films we deserve.

· · ·

THE general opinion of *Revenge of the Sith* seems to be that it marks a distinct improvement on the last two episodes, *The Phantom Menace* and *Attack of the Clones*. True, but only in the same way that dying from natural causes is preferable to crucifixion. So much here is guaranteed to cause either offense or pain, starting with the nineteen-twenties leather football helmets that Natalie Portman suddenly dons for no reason, and rising to the continual horror of Ewan McGregor's accent. "Another happy landing"—or, to be precise, "anothah heppy lending"—he remarks, as Anakin parks the front half of a burning star-cruiser on a convenient airstrip. The young Obi-Wan Kenobi is not, I hasten to add, the most nauseating figure onscreen; nor is R2-D2 or even C-3PO, although I still fail to understand why I should have been expected to waste twenty-five years of my life following the progress of a beeping trash can and a gay, gold-plated Jeeves.

No, the one who gets me is Yoda. May I take the opportunity to enter a brief plea in favor of his extermination? Any educated movie-goer would know what to do, having watched that helpful sequence in *Gremlins* when a small, sage-colored beastie is fed into an electric blender. A fittingly frantic end, I feel, for the faux-pensive stillness on which the Yoda legend has hung. At one point in the new film, he assumes the role of cosmic shrink—squatting opposite Anakin in a noirish room, where the light bleeds sideways through slatted blinds. Anakin keeps having problems with his dark side, in the way that you or I might suffer from tennis elbow, but Yoda, whose reptilian smugness we have been encouraged to mistake for wisdom, has the answer. "Train yourself to let go of everything you fear to lose," he says. Hold on, Kermit, run that past me one more time. If you ever got laid (admittedly a long shot, unless we can dig you up some undiscerning alien hottie with a name like Jar Jar Gabor), and spawned a brood of Yo-dettes, are you saying that you'd leave them behind at the first sniff of danger? Also, while we're here, what's with the screwy syntax? Deepest mind in the galaxy, apparently, and you still express yourself like a day-tripper with a dog-eared phrase book. "I hope right you are." Break me a fucking give.

The prize for the least speakable burst of dialogue has, over half a dozen helpings of *Star Wars*, grown into a fiercely contested tradition, but for once the winning entry is clear, shared between Anakin and Padmé for their exchange of endearments at home:

"You're so beautiful."
"That's only because I'm so in love."
"No, it's because I'm so in love with you."

For a moment, it looks as if they might bat this one back and forth forever, like a baseline rally on a clay court. And if you think the script is on the tacky side, get an eyeful of the décor. All of the interiors in Lucasworld are anthems to clean living, with molded furniture, the tranquillity of a morgue, and none of the clutter and quirkiness that signify the process known as existence. Illumination is provided not by daylight but by a dispiriting plastic sheen, as if Lucas were coating all private affairs—those tricky little threats to his near-fascistic rage for order—in a protective glaze. Only outside does he relax, and what he relaxes into is apocalypse. *Revenge of the Sith* is a zoo of rampant storyboards. Why show a pond when CGI can deliver a lake that gleams to the far horizon? Why set a paltry house on fire when you can stage your final showdown on an entire planet that streams with ruddy, gulping lava? Whether the director is aware of John Martin, the Victorian painter who specialized in the cataclysmic, I cannot say, but he has certainly inherited that grand perversity, mobilized it in every frame of the film, and thus produced what I take to be unique: an art of flawless and irredeemable vulgarity. All movies bear a tint of it, in varying degrees, but it takes a vulgarian genius such as Lucas to create a landscape in which actions can carry vast importance but no discernible meaning, in which style is strangled at birth by design, and in which the intimate and the ironic, not the Sith, are the principal foes to be suppressed. It is a vision at once gargantuan and murderously limited, and the profits that await it are unfit for contemplation. I keep thinking of the rueful Obi-Wan Kenobi, as he surveys the holographic evidence of Anakin's betrayal. "I can't watch anymore," he says. Wise words, Obi-Wan, and I shall carry them in my heart.

2005

PERSONAL
HISTORY

THE NIGHT THE BED FELL

I SUPPOSE that the high-water mark of my youth in Columbus, Ohio, was the night the bed fell on my father. It makes a better recitation (unless, as some friends of mine have said, one has heard it five or six times) than it does a piece of writing, for it is almost necessary to throw furniture around, shake doors, and bark like a dog, to lend the proper atmosphere and verisimilitude to what is admittedly a somewhat incredible tale. Still, it did take place.

It happened, then, that my father had decided to sleep in the attic one night, to be away where he could think. My mother opposed the notion strongly because, she said, the old wooden bed up there was unsafe: it was wobbly and the heavy headboard would crash down on father's head in case the bed fell, and kill him. There was no dissuading him, however, and at a quarter past ten he closed the attic door behind him and went up the narrow twisting stairs. We later heard ominous creakings as he crawled into bed. Grandfather, who usually slept in the attic bed when he was with us, had disappeared some days before. (On these occasions he was usually gone six or eight days and returned growling and out of temper, with the news that the Federal Union was run by a passel of blockheads and that the Army of the Potomac didn't have any more chance than a fiddler's bitch.)

We had visiting us at this time a nervous first cousin of mine named Briggs Beall, who believed that he was likely to cease breathing when he was asleep. It was his feeling that if he were not awakened every hour during the night, he might die of suffocation. He had been accustomed to setting an alarm clock to ring at intervals until morning, but I persuaded him to abandon this. He slept in my room and I told him that I was such a light sleeper that if anybody quit breathing in the same room with me, I would wake instantly. He tested me the first night—which I had suspected he would—by holding his breath after my regular breathing had convinced him I was asleep. I was not asleep, however, and called to him. This seemed to allay his fears a little, but he took the precaution of putting a glass of spirits of camphor on a little table at the head of his bed. In case I didn't arouse him until he was almost gone, he said, he would sniff the camphor, a powerful reviver. Briggs was not the only member of his family who had his crotchets. Old Aunt Clarissa Beall (who could whistle like a man, with two fingers in her mouth) suffered under the premonition that she was destined to die on South High Street, because she had been born on South High Street and married on South High Street. Then there was Aunt Sarah Shoaf, who never went to bed at night without the fear that a burglar was going to get in and blow chloroform under her door through a tube. To avert this calamity—for she was in greater dread of anesthetics than of losing her household goods—she always piled her money, silverware, and other valuables in a neat stack just outside her bedroom, with a note reading: "This is all I have. Please take it and do not use your chloroform, as this is all I have." Aunt Gracie Shoaf also had a burglar phobia, but she met it with more fortitude. She was confident that burglars had been getting into her house every night for forty years. The fact that she never missed anything was to her no proof to the contrary. She always claimed that she scared them off before they could take anything, by throwing shoes down the hallway. When she went to bed she piled, where she could get at them handily, all the shoes there were about her house. Five minutes after she had turned off the light, she would sit up in bed and say "Hark!" Her husband, who had learned to ignore the whole situation as long ago as 1903, would either be sound asleep or pretend to be sound asleep. In either case he would not respond to her tugging and pulling, so that presently she would arise, tiptoe to the door, open it slightly and heave a shoe down the hall in one direction and its mate down the hall in the other direction. Some nights she threw them all, some nights only a couple of pairs.

BUT I am straying from the remarkable incidents that took place during the night that the bed fell on father. By midnight we were all in bed. The layout of the rooms and the disposition of their occupants is important to an understanding of what later occurred. In the front room upstairs (just under father's attic bedroom) were my mother and my brother Herman, who sometimes sang in his sleep, usually "Marching Through Georgia" or "Onward, Christian Soldiers." Briggs Beall and myself were in a room adjoining this one. My brother Roy was in a room across the hall from ours. Our bull terrier, Rex, slept in the hall.

My bed was an iron cot, one of those affairs which are made wide enough to sleep on comfortably only by putting up, flat with the middle section, the two sides which ordinarily hang down like the sideboards of a drop-leaf table. When these sides are up, it is perilous to roll too far toward the edge, for then the cot is likely to tip completely over, bringing the whole bed down on top of one with a tremendous banging crash. This, in fact, is precisely what happened, about two o'clock in the morning. (It was my mother who, in recalling the scene later, first referred to it as "the night the bed fell on your father.")

Always a deep sleeper, slow to arouse (I had lied to Briggs), I was at first unconscious of what had happened when the iron cot rolled me onto the floor and toppled over on me. It left me still warmly bundled up and unhurt, for the bed rested above me like a canopy. Hence I did not wake up, only reached the edge of consciousness and went back. The racket, however, instantly awakened my mother, in the next room, who came to the immediate conclusion that her worst dread was realized: the big wooden bed upstairs had fallen on father. She therefore screamed, "Let's go to your poor father!" It was this shout, rather than the noise of my cot falling, that awakened my brother Herman, in the same room with her. He thought that mother had become, for no apparent reason, hysterical. "You're all right, mamma!" he shouted, trying to calm her. They exchanged shout for shout for perhaps ten seconds: "Let's go to your poor father!" and "You're all right!" That woke up Briggs. By this time I was conscious of what was going on, in a vague way, but did not yet realize that I was under my bed instead of on it. Briggs, awakening in the midst of loud shouts of fear and apprehension, came to the quick conclusion that he was suffocating and that we were all trying to "bring him out." With a low moan, he grasped the glass of camphor at the head of his bed and instead of sniffing it poured it over himself. The room reeked of camphor. "Ugf, ahfg!" choked Briggs, like a drowning man, for he had almost succeeded in stopping his breath under the deluge of pungent spirits. He leaped out of bed and groped toward the open window, but he came up against one that was closed. With his hand, he beat out the glass, and I could hear it crash and tinkle in the alleyway below. It was at this juncture that I, in trying to get up, had the uncanny sensation of feeling my bed above me! Foggy with sleep, I now suspected, in my turn, that the whole uproar was being made in a frantic endeavor to extricate me from what must be an unheard-of and perilous situation. "Get me out of this!" I bawled. "Get me out!" I think I had the nightmarish belief that I was entombed in a mine. "Gugh!" gasped Briggs, floundering in his camphor.

BY this time my mother, still shouting, pursued by Herman, still shouting, was trying to open the door to the attic, in order to go up and get my father's body out of the wreckage. The door was stuck, however, and wouldn't yield. Her frantic pulls on it only added to the general banging and confusion. Roy and the dog were now up, the one shouting questions, the other barking.

Father, farthest away and soundest sleeper of all, had by this time been awakened by the battering on the attic door. He decided that the house was on fire. "I'm coming, I'm coming!" he wailed in a slow, sleepy voice—it took him many minutes to regain full consciousness. My mother, still believing he was caught under the bed, detected in his "I'm coming!" the mournful, resigned note of one who is preparing to meet his Maker. "He's dying!" she shouted.

"I'm all right!" Briggs yelled, to reassure her. "I'm all right!" He still believed that it was his own closeness to death that was worrying mother. I found at last the light switch in my room, unlocked the door, and Briggs and I joined the others at the attic door. The dog, who never did like Briggs, jumped for him—assuming that he was the culprit in whatever was going on—and Roy had to throw Rex and hold him. We could hear father crawling out of bed upstairs. Roy pulled the attic door open, with a mighty jerk, and father came down the stairs, sleepy and irritable but safe and sound. My mother began to weep when she saw him. Rex began to howl. "What in the name of God is going on here?" asked father.

The situation was finally put together like a gigantic jigsaw puzzle. Father caught a cold from prowling around in his bare feet but there were no other bad results. "I'm glad," said mother, who always looked on the bright side of things, "that your grandfather wasn't here."

1933

WOLCOTT GIBBS

THE HUNTRESS

EVEN now, in the comparative security of a city of seven million people, I sit dreaming of Miss Sellers, the most dangerous woman in the world. For three years Miss Sellers was, in a sense, my employee, although she kept me in a steady panic, and I had neither dignity nor grace in her presence.

At that time, I was the editor of a New England weekly newspaper, dedicated to the social activities of the community, which were repetitious, and the interests of the Republican party, which were corrupt beyond belief. Miss Sellers was my reporter, a heritage from my predecessor, and certainly the most successful practical joke of his negligible career. She was a native New Englander, which, next to being a Jukes, is of course this world's surest guarantee of great peculiarity. She weighed about two hundred and fifty pounds, and as a rule she wore a rusty red garment, shapeless and without sleeves, like an old-fashioned nightgown. Her face was large and gray and sparsely bearded, and it glistened continually with perspiration. Her eyes protruded and never winked. Her hair was arranged, Japanese fashion, in a tower of diminishing black buns, which sometimes contained an exhausted flower. On the whole, it is impossible to describe her more graphically than to say that she resembled the late William Jennings Bryan, unkindly made up to play Madame Butterfly.

It was Miss Sellers' simple duty to report to me, in pencil on ruled sheets of yellow paper, the weddings, births, deaths, and other minutiæ of a community of three thousand people. She did this, I am obliged to admit, acceptably enough, being particularly eloquent in her obituaries, which were written more or less from the triumphant point of view of the earthworm. Unsolicited, Miss Sellers also contributed other articles, largely of an editorial nature and directed principally against the Catholic Church, of which she disapproved. These, however, were somewhat controversial in tone, having to do with vast papal conspiracies to take over the county government, and they were not printed. She also contributed poetry, and, country newspapers being what they are, some of this *was* printed. It, too, was dark and menacing, and, being largely incomprehensible, gained the paper a considerable reputation for profundity among the simple lobstermen. I have lost what copies I ever had of these compositions, but one at least persists in my memory. It was called "Sardak Y Noval," which Miss Sellers, being pinned down, condescended to explain was the name of a "mythical pool." It began:

> *Down through the depths of the depthless,*
> *Narrow and sombre and cool,*
> *Down in the heart of the heartless,*
> *Oh, where is the soul of the pool?*
> *Oh, silence is golden, while silver is sound*
> *As the motto proverbial saith,*
> *But the silence of Sardak, that stillness profound,*
> *The silence of Noval is . . . DEATH!*

I can still remember it all, but this, I think, is enough to convey the essence of Miss Sellers' gloomy gift.

NONE of these extra activities, of course, had the slightest bearing on Miss Sellers' value to me as a journalist. It also happened, however, that she was the victim of a series of delusions which made my contacts with her matters of the greatest anxiety and embarrassment. Her paramount idea was that almost all men, not too near the cradle or the grave, had carnal designs upon her person. This is certainly not a novel fixation, and I suppose it has its pathos, but Miss Sellers' precautions against unavenged rape were so bizarre and elaborate that they deserve to be noted. In the first place, she had procured (in an interview which must have mystified the village doctor) a "certificate of chastity," stating that Edith Sellers had been examined and found to be a virgin; in the second, she had picked up, God knows where, an enormous old revolver, minus both hammer and ammunition, with which to threaten any wretch too passionate or abandoned to be disarmed by the certificate. Both these articles were kept in the side pocket of her Ford runabout, and both figured freely and forbiddingly in her conversation.

This, too, would have been harmless enough from my point of view, except that, of all men, Miss Sellers was most inclined to suspect the editors who employed her, apparently expecting them to demand a sort of journalistic *droit du seigneur* in exchange for her salary. The certificate and the revolver, indeed, became commonplaces in our interviews, and I was threatened with them daily, though never directly.

"Just let any of them try their dirty monkey tricks on me," Miss Sellers would say, staring at me with unmistakable menace.

I learned from the villagers, who were largely exempt from Miss Sellers' suspicions and therefore inclined to find her diverting, that one previous editor had become so unnerved by these persistent innuendoes that he had resigned and, in his anxiety to get as far as possible from Miss Sellers, had bought a candy store in Austin, Texas.

Eventually it became clear, even to Miss Sellers, that I was unlikely to attack her, and our relationship entered an even more embarrassing phase. She decided that a great, but purely platonic, love had sprung up between us. This spiritual kinship involved the writing (on her part) of a sequence of poems, not primarily designed for publication, and many references, ingeniously but much too thinly disguised, to the dear new bond between us. It was Miss Sellers' hideous fancy to pretend that she was writing a book, in which the principal characters were designated simply as "the boy" and "the girl." To make it even easier, "the boy" was the editor of a newspaper, while "the girl," a poetess of considerable power, worked for him as a reporter. On the slightest provocation, or none, and certainly in any company, Miss Sellers would outline the latest chapter in this work. Once, I remember, "the boy" was dying of pneumonia (almost all the chapters contained a satisfactory amount of sickness and catastrophe) and "the girl" brought him around with a sonnet. As a *roman à clef*, it had an enormous vogue among the happy villagers.

Our love also involved telepathy. Occasionally, in the newspaper office, I would answer the phone, to hear that unmistakable voice—Miss Sellers always spoke in the tone generally reserved by elderly ladies for children or small animals.

"Hello," it would say.

"Hello, Miss Sellers."

"You *knew!*" There would be a sound which I could picture only as Miss Sellers blowing hard into the mouthpiece. "Isn't it marvellous!"

"Oh, I ought to know your voice by this time, Miss Sellers."

"Oh, *no!*" More blowing. "Oh, it's *much* more than that!"

The final confirmation of our psychic tie-up, however, came one evening when I was working late at the office. There was a frosted-glass panel in the door, and a strong light in the hall, so that anybody standing outside cast a sharp shadow on the pane. Looking up suddenly, I saw an outline that, from the triple bun on top to the gigantic waist, could have belonged to only one person in the world.

"Come in, Miss Sellers," I said hopelessly.

Miss Sellers came in, pale with some delicious blending of fright and rapture.

"It's uncanny! It frightens me," she cried. "Why, you *felt* me out there!"

I looked at the lighted panel, and at Miss Sellers, but I knew it was no use.

"Yes," I said, "it frightens me too."

A little after that, I resigned from the paper myself, partly because of Miss Sellers, and partly because I had no real interest in misleading the taxpayers. I left quietly, almost furtively, and I didn't see Miss Sellers. A few months ago, however, I got a letter from her. Our romance, it appears, has left no scars. Indeed, she didn't even mention it, being too preoccupied with news. There was a new editor after I left, an extremely disagreeable man, who had tried to take away her pistol and cause her "other troubles." Miss Sellers didn't specify just what these "other troubles" were, but I gathered that he'd tried to have her committed. He hadn't succeeded. In fact, the victory was magnificently with Miss Sellers. The editor had been driving along in a storm when a branch was blown down on his skull, fracturing it. He wasn't dead, but he was in the hospital, and nobody believed he'd ever be the same. Miss Sellers said that this was obviously the hand of God, and seemed to be somewhat alarmed at her own powers. In the meantime, there is a new editor—"a rather delicate boy." She hopes that he's stronger than he looks. So do I.

1935

PETER DE VRIES

ONE

MY first impression of Trenkle was the same as my last, and both were identical with all those that lay changelessly between: that of a man bent on talking in epigrams. He had a nickname he was completely oblivious of. Among ourselves, we who knew him never called him Trenkle, or Philip, either, which was his first name; we called him One, after the indefinite pronoun he constantly used—"One should always look at El Grecos on an empty stomach," and "Life is a carnival at which one should throw the balls at the prizes," and "There are types of innocence of which one should not be guilty," and so on. This "one" device seems more naturally suited to Englishmen than to Americans. The homes where he and I met, some years ago, were largely in and around Westport, immediately beyond which, one (to borrow the locution) is, after all, on one's way to Bridgeport. Conversation may be, as One believed, a lost art, but it probably never did prosper on the aphoristic plane on which he strove to twinkle.

I remember the first time I saw One, at a cocktail party for a couple who had just announced their engagement. In the course of some standard persiflage about matrimony, somebody asked One, then thirty-four and espaliered against the mantel, when *he* was going to take the step. One reached for his Manhattan, which was on a nearby table. "Getting married is like sitting down on garden furniture," he said. "One does it cautiously."

A young advertising man I was sitting next to—a chap in his late twenties named Dick Fillmore—looked at me and murmured, "Judas Priest!" But within the month he was to find One at his own dinner table.

Dick and his wife, Madge, had just settled in a house in Darien, and in the process of striking social roots Madge was inviting people wholesale. This time she had practically everybody in the group I went around with. An excellent cook had prepared a capital dinner topped off with Nesselrode pudding. Having finished his, One set his napkin down and turned to Madge with a gleam in his eye.

"Stendhal," said One, who frequently built his effects on those of the masters, "Stendhal is reported to have said, on first eating ice cream, 'What a pity it isn't a sin!' " He gestured toward his dessert dish. "This *is* a sin."

"Tell Dodie," Madge said, with a wave toward the cook, who was just then emerging from the kitchen. Dick scraped his chair back with a jittery motion and said, "Let's have our coffee in the living room."

In there, One got off an epigram somewhat better than his usual. The subject was, fittingly enough, epigrams themselves, and after the coffee, when we were sitting around drinking highballs, One quoted liberally from Wilde, Shaw, and Voltaire. "Epigrams," he said, at length, "what are they?"

There was a silence. One picked up his drink, sipped slowly, and set it down again. "Epigrams," he said, "are canes with which we swagger in our youth but on which in old age we must lean."

Virginia Woolf, in her *Orlando,* describes the effect of actual wit on an eighteenth-century reception room where wit is delusively held by the frequenters of the salon to be a nightly staple. The poet Pope is announced. He steps inside and delivers three mots in rapid succession. People sit in dead silence for twenty minutes. Then they turn in consternation and slink, one by one, from the room.

This at the Fillmores' was by no means a salon; this was just a bunch of us. But we were similarly immobilized; if not for twenty minutes, perhaps because we had so much less to lose—about as much less, I suppose, as One had to offer than Pope. People on the fringe turned away, muttering resentfully; somebody snickered and looked at his feet; arms reaching for highball glasses converged like the spokes of a wheel on the large central coffee table. "Ju—das—" Dick began, but before he could get to "Priest" Madge's bright voice cried restoratively, "Who's for Ping-Pong?"

THE person who remains in my memory as most able to take One in his stride was a man of markedly earthier grain even than Dick. Into a small cluster of listeners to whom, at the opening of an exhibition at a country art gallery, One was expounding Surrealism as inverted Romanticism hove a short, portly figure in a double-breasted suit. He was the owner of a rope-and-twine business. His name was Wentworth, and his wife was on the arrangements committee and had a watercolor in the show.

"The symbol of Romanticism was a swan," One said. "That of Surrealism, half a swan."

"I'll buy that," Wentworth said from the periphery, looking around and nodding.

Wentworth haunted the brisker conversation all evening, buying heavily. Among his purchases were these generalizations of One's:

"Polo is merely the cavalry of croquet."

"Nothing resembles reverence so much as intense profanity. It is the soul on one knee."

"Strict chastity is itself a kind of promiscuity. It lacks the principle of selection."

"You can say that again!" Wentworth responded to the last, as he had to the first and second, respectively, with "And how!" and "Check!"

One moved off in search of less robust approval.

I HAVE an almost total recall of One's aphorisms, partly because he used them again and again but also, it must be confessed, because they exerted a fascination over me, especially when the gulf between the frequently debatable content and the always impeccably classic form was arresting enough to make me think of a hot dog under a glass bell.

Here are a few more of One's apothegms and paradoxes, as they occur to me:

"No sculpture is successful that does not inspire in us the desire to feel it—and leave us sheepish when we have done so."

"There is such a thing as smiling uproariously. I have done so once or twice in my life."

"The American principle: God helps those that help themselves. The Russian: God help those that help themselves. Only, the Russians do not believe in Him!"

"Eggnog is absurd."

"One reason I cannot order hash in a restaurant is the necessity of telling the waiter to omit the poached egg. One should not have to edit what one eats."

"Attacking the foibles of the human race is a good deal like swatting mosquitoes—one cannot do it without slapping oneself."

"I do not know whether the retaliation is intentional or not, but the food in museums is about on a par with the murals in restaurants."

"Time goes in one year and out the other."

"There is truly no such thing as a little garlic. Ideally, it should be rubbed on the cook."

"Conscience is like the emergency brake on an automobile. It is never used in an emergency, only when one is morally parked."

"Nature abhors a vacuum cleaner."

IT'S possible that One fancied himself another La Rochefoucauld, who would be quoted by the grandchildren of those out of whom, in life, he got no rise. The only response I ever heard that "worked" with him was the familiar "I know exactly what you mean!" One evening, he said to a group of us, "The music of Delius resembles nothing so much as pink stucco—if you know what I mean."

"Well—" I began, but was overridden by a woman wearing leather jewelry, who bobbed her head brightly and said, "I know exactly what you mean"—a signal of kinship that sent One happily into amplification.

"Not, you understand, that weathered pink of old missions fifty miles south of Los Angeles," he continued, "and not, you understand, the pink of the houses in Los Angeles, either, but, you see, the pink of the ice-cream stands on the outskirts of it."

Gassed into near-insensibility by this flow of subtlety, I laughed along with the woman, but whereas hers was a laugh of head-nodding appreciation, mine was a laugh of gentle, addled despair, the helpless laugh of someone trying to pick up quicksilver with his fingers.

But splitting the atom of meaning with One wasn't always a harmless pastime, and there was one occasion in particular when I got embroiled in the exegesis myself.

I was having dinner with One and another companion in the garden of a restaurant on the banks of the Saugatuck, near Westport. Travel on the Continent was discussed, and at last One, turning on the lathe of inference the sum of notes compared and anecdotes exchanged, said, "There are, usually, people and people. There are Frenchmen and Frenchmen. There are Englishmen and Englishmen. There are Irishmen and Irishmen, and there are, of course, Germans and Germans. But there are," he concluded, reaching for his coffee cup, "only Swedes."

I saw a hand whip away a vacant chair next to mine and a splendidly formed chap with ginger hair take a position over One.

"I heard that, Mac," he said, "and I'll thank you to take it back."

I got to my feet. "You don't understand," I said.

"There's nothing to understand," he said. "He'll take it back or I'll help him."

I could not imagine anything more certain to dissolve at the touch of analysis than what One had said (any more than I could remember ever having heard anyone being asked to take back anything that tenuous), but, eager to avoid a scene, I struck out hurriedly, "He means Swedes keep a steady level—none of the stock crotchets that make caricatures out of other nationalities." I laughed. "But maybe there are Swedes as *well* as Swedes, eh? In which case," I said, reaching the nadir of inanity, "I'm sure you'd be one of the Swedes."

"I'm Scotch-American," he said, compounding the confusion.

"Then what—" I began, and he waved to the table behind me.

At it was a dainty girl with cornflower eyes and hair like plaited gold. Her head down and her hands folded in her lap, she smiled deferentially at us. One rose with airy good nature and went over to her. The Scotch-American stood watchfully by, looking as though he might bring One's career to the anachronistic close that would have seemed so apt—ceremonial notice of offense, in the form of a card, and a rendezvous in the woods at dawn. But, with a bow that put us back still another hundred years, One said to the girl, "I have seen bottled honey, but I have never held it up to the sun. Now I know what it must look like, and it is with pride—not humility, by any means—that I embrace the opportunity of apologizing to such a vision."

"We'll let it go at that," the Scotch-American said.

"Honey—" One resumed.

"Never mind the 'honey' stuff. I'll call her that," the Scotch-American said as I caught hold of One's coattail to pull him back to our table before he would have to apologize for the way he was apologizing.

"This . . ." I said, helpless against the current bearing me on into an idiom where I had no business. "This," I said, with a wave at the poor Saugatuck, "is not nearly the Danube."

I NEVER saw One again after that. He took an apartment in New York that autumn, and finally disappeared from the orbit of my friends. I heard of him only once more. About a year ago, I ran across somebody who said he'd had word that One was living in London, managing a private art gallery. I hope his quest fares better there than here—for it's as an endless quest that I see his life. I see him venturing, groomed and gloved, each evening through the British fog, looking for the one door, the bright door beyond which blooms at last that indoor paradise of bandied conceits and oral arabesques he never found in Fairfield County.

If there's anything to the maxim that once hotboxed our conversation, then the reverse of it must also be true, namely that canes are like epigrams, swaggered with in youth, leaned on in old age. What, then, about middle life? Because it occurs to me now that One is in his forties and that he always carried a stick. I've racked my brain trying to complete the apothegm he left unfinished, but the number of things that you can do with a stick in your prime that have symbolic value are few. There's hailing cabs, swiping at bothersome dogs, and clacking it along picket fences, but none of these have symbolic value. Hailing cabs comes closest, but it's too thin. There's only one other thing I can think of that you might do with a cane. Push doorbells.

One wouldn't buy it, I don't suppose, but then I'm not trying to sell it, either.

1951

S. J. PERELMAN

DISQUIET, PLEASE, WE'RE TURNING!

OF all the fantasies cherished by the public about the craft of fiction, perhaps the most venerated concerns the moment of creativity—the instant at which, presumably, the divine spark infuses a writer and sets him frenziedly wooing his muse. The popular conception of an author, in fact, is almost total fantasy. The average reader imagines him as a rather Byronic, darkly brooding individual, an amalgam of Baudelaire, Robinson Jeffers, and MacKinlay Kantor, who sits in his study garbed in a smoking jacket and velvet tam-o'-shanter, his brow furrowed in thought as he puffs on a meerschaum, awaiting the flash of inspiration essential to the work of genius. Suddenly a lightning zigzag cleaves the gloom, narrowly missing the bust of Homer on the bookshelf: the Idea has been born. With a stifled cry—sometimes there is not even time for a stifled cry—the author seizes his quill and begins covering page after page of foolscap. Useless for wife and family to plead with him to take rest or nourishment; the all-consuming urge to create, the *furor scribendi,* is upon him and will not be stilled. E'en if it destroys him, he must press forward till he writes "Finis" to his masterpiece.

The series of events that climaxed in the present narrative had a somewhat different origin. They began on the sweltering summer morning in 1955 when Avrom Goldbogen—better known to the world of entertainment and various referees in bankruptcy as Michael Todd— first swam into my ken. I was seated in the dingy office on lower Sixth Avenue where I daily immured myself with an intractable typewriter, staring despondently at the rear wall of the adjacent apartment house. Three weeks before, the venetian blind veiling one of the windows had magically risen and I beheld, standing there in pearly nakedness, a lady of such flawless proportions that I was transfixed. She had obviously just emerged from the bath, to judge from the droplets of moisture that clung to her marble limbs, and the innocence of her pose, her sheer Eve-like rosy perfection as she stretched forth her arms and luxuriated in the morning sunshine, wrung my withers. Unhappily, as I was craning forward for a better view my head struck the windowpane. The impact startled her out of her reverie, and a second later the blind crashed downward, abruptly terminating my idyll. For weeks afterward, I kept expecting the vision to recur, but all I ever saw was an unshaven citizen in his undershirt, clearly an enforcer for the Mafia, glaring at me suspiciously through the blind, and I desisted.

I was sitting there, as I say, stirring the dead ashes of desire when the phone rang and a crisp female voice came over the wire. "This is Candide Yam, Michael Todd's beautiful Chinese secretary," it declared. "Mr. Todd just called me from the Coast. He wants to know if you ever read a work authored by Jules Verne entitled *Around the World in Eighty Days*."

"When I was eleven years old, lambie," I said patiently. "I also read *Toby Tyler, or Ten Weeks with a Circus, Phil the Fiddler,* by Horatio Alger, *Sink or Swim,* by Oliver Optic—"

"My, you really *are* a well-read person," she said. "I don't get much chance to talk to people like you in this job."

"Then why don't we have lunch?" I proposed. "I know a quiet little drop here in the Village—a droplet, so to speak—where we can relax over a vodka Martini and chat about books and stuff."

"Slow down, brother," she said. "There'll be plenty of time for that when we're filmy."

"Filmy?" I repeated. My mood, instinct with romance, conjured up a vision of this exciting person, clad in filmy black negligee, forcing kumquats into my mouth and pleading for love, and I was suddenly on the *qui vive.* "Look, where are you? I can be there in ten minutes. The Plaza bar, the Drake—"

"No, no—*filming,* dear," she corrected, in a voice that rivaled little silver bells. "Like in a movie."

"What movie?" I asked, bewildered. "I'm not involved in any flick I know of."

"Oh, yes, you are," she said. "The Michael Todd production of

Around the World in Eighty Days—that's why he wants you to reread the book. I'm sending down a copy by messenger in twenty minutes. Be there."

I hung up and, after a quick peek at the apartment window opposite to make sure my Lorelei had not reappeared, tried to recall what I could about Mike Todd. Having written for the theater sporadically in the past, I knew he had produced several shows of passing consequence, like *Star and Garter, The Hot Mikado,* and *Up in Central Park,* but his reputation, even by Broadway standards, was not fragrant with frankincense and myrrh. Playwrights who had dealt with the man showed a tendency to empurple; they castigated him as a cheap chiseler reluctant to disgorge royalties, a carnival grifter with the ethics of a stoat. My association with showmen of the type, notably Billy Rose, had taught me that, in Joyce's felicitous phrase—James Joyce, that is, not Joyce Matthews—they were as full of wind and water as a barber's cat. Still, I remembered the enjoyment Verne's novel had given me in youth, and if, in my present becalmed state, the project looked as though it might yield up enough to keep the pot boiling there was no harm in discussing it with Todd.

The book, when it arrived, proved to be a children's version bound in gleaming yellow calf, with my name—misspelled, naturally—so freshly emblazoned in gold on it that a few grains sifted into my palm. In due course, Todd rang up my agent and offered even fewer for my services on the screenplay. There then ensued the usual choleric exchange of insults and recriminations that attends all negotiations in the film industry, and ultimately a figure was arrived at which, in the hallowed phrase, we could both live with. Todd was living with his, I found when I reached Hollywood a week later, in opulence; he occupied a luxurious villa at the Beverly Hills Hotel, subsisting chiefly on champagne and caviar and smoking Flor de Magnificos, which cost a dollar apiece—frequently two at the same time. As he wove a verbal tapestry about the production he envisioned, the wonders of the Todd-AO process, the stars he planned to inveigle into cameo roles, and the *réclame* that would accrue to everyone concerned, I took stock of this *luftmensch* to whom I had indentured myself. Squat, muscular, intensely dynamic, he was the very pattern of the modern major moviemaker—voluble, cunning, full of huckster shrewdness, slippery as a silverfish, and yet undeniably magnetic. In short, a con man, a *tummler* with a bursting Napoleonic complex. Forever in movement, he walked in a fighter's crouch, as if both to ward off a blow and dodge a summons.

The key to his nature, as I was to learn in our association, was his mouth, which bore a marked resemblance to a rattrap. Those thin lips, I sensed, could be merciless, but at the moment they were busy weaving blandishments.

"We'll kill 'em, Jack," he predicted ebulliently. "It's going to be the picture of the century—we'll blow those civilians out the back of the theater. Rolls-Royces . . . town houses . . . emeralds and rubies the size of your nose. They'll be naming ships after us!" I was reminded of Walter Burns wooing Hildy Johnson in *The Front Page*. "Okay, now, get lost, and remember this, you bum—no hanging around the water cooler. We start shooting with a finished script six weeks from today in Spain."

TO chronicle with any accuracy the arguments, intrigues, stratagems, and frustrations I was embroiled in over the next several months would be virtually impossible. One factor, however, was constant: Todd's utter, neurotic refusal to part with money. A compulsive gambler, he would toss away thousands on the turn of a card or the convulsions of dice, but when my stipend or those of my co-workers fell due Todd automatically vanished. Week after week, it took cajolery, pleas, and threats of legal action to collect one's salary. All the while, of course, our impresario lived like the Medici, running up awesome bills that he waved away airily on presentation. Whether they were ever settled, even after he hit the mother lode, was doubtful. His *chutzpah*, however, was indisputable, for, as became more and more obvious daily, his million-dollar epic was a classic shoestring operation. In Hollywood, he held endless whispered consultations in corners with squat Neanderthal types who rested on their knuckles, underarms bulging as though harboring shoulder holsters. In Europe, these gave way to foxy-nosed characters in homburgs, reputedly Swiss and Austrian bankers, so suave that marzipan wouldn't melt in their mouths. The financial ramifications of any movie are cloaked in mystery; those of *Around the World in Eighty Days* were as impenetrable as the Mato Grosso. To this day, I venture to say, nobody knows where or how Todd promoted the wherewithal to make his chef-d'œuvre, or who got what share of the golden hoard. All I know is that my pittance was extracted only by deep surgery.

European filming began in a village outside Madrid, inaugurated with a Homeric quarrel between Todd and the director, John Farrow, that ended in the latter's dismissal. This stroke of luck raised everyone's spirits—so much so that the bullfight sequences starring Luis Dominguín and Cantinflas were completed ahead of schedule. The company then descended on London, where Todd installed himself in a pad at the Dorchester of such barbaric tastelessness that it must have been shipped piecemeal from Las Vegas to make him feel at home. As with everywhere he roosted, the premises instantly took on the aspect of Donnybrook Fair: phones rang wildly, coveys of actors, agents, and technicians boiled through the rooms, and the air was blue with cigar smoke and maledictions. Concurrently, shooting went on in Knightsbridge and Belgravia, while interiors—the Reform Club, Lloyd's, and Phileas Fogg's residence—were in progress at the studio. One consolation in the uproar was the presence of Candide Yam, Todd's handmaiden from New York. A fetching Celestial strikingly reminiscent of Anna May Wong, Candide inexplicably possessed a fund of colloquial Yiddish, and whenever the turmoil became overwhelming the two of us used to steal away to Isow's, on Brewer Street, and share the inscrutable wisdom of the East over a knish.

Complex as parts of the English production were, they paled beside one exterior, a crowd scene, shot in Paris a fortnight later. The physical action involved was trifling; Phileas Fogg and Passepartout were to arrive in a carriage in the Rue Castiglione and enter the offices of Thomas Cook & Son. Seeking to demonstrate the scope of his AO process, Todd bade his marshals make the scene as lavish as possible. Eight hundred extras were outfitted in the costumes of 1872, and various conveyances of the period—victorias, barouches, berlins, horsedrawn buses—were routed out of warehouses and museums. Since any glimpse of an automobile would have been disastrous, men were employed to clear the area the night before filming; cars were thrust helter-skelter into the streets fringing the Place Vendôme, much to the ire of their owners and the police, who subsequently touched off a lengthy investigation. In any case, by ten the next morning a juggernaut laden with cameras and technicians was positioned against the railing of the Tuileries, seven French assistant directors were rehearsing the crowd with a maximum of hysteria, and our principals had executed so many turns in their vehicle that they were dizzy. Then, just as the whistle blew for the take and the extras started moving, an altogether unforeseen hitch occurred.

Directly above the arcade at the bottom of the Rue Castiglione was a hotel with a number of heavily shuttered windows. Suddenly one of them opened and a fat man in lurid pajamas stepped forth into the sunshine, yawning and scratching himself. His gaze slowly traveled downward into the Rue de Rivoli and, on the instant, he turned to stone. His stupefaction was pardonable; he had retired in 1955 and awakened into a world populated by folk in crinolines and beaver hats. Todd, already overwrought because of the expense and time consumed in the take, suffered a paroxysm. He snatched up a megaphone and screamed at the interloper. "Get back, you dummy!" he shouted. "Can't you see you're on camera, you frog bastard? Close the blind!"

Though Todd's words were inaudible over the din of the extras milling about and the street noises, the man did withdraw, but only momentarily. In an *augenblick,* he popped back with an equally corpulent lady in a peach-colored robe, who reacted as he had. The two of them stood on the balcony gesticulating and chattering nineteen to the dozen while Todd raged up and down, smiting his forehead and inveighing against the French, his subordinates, and destiny. At length, a vassal was dispatched to hale the couple indoors, the multitude was regrouped, and the scene—valueless to the story but quenching Todd's thirst for spectacle—went into the can.

What with another costly crowd scene at the Gare du Nord, involving a number of French screen luminaries, the budget was becoming visibly distended, and Todd decided he had sufficient European footage. In one frantic morning, he organized a second unit to make process shots in India and the Far East, providing its members with tickets to Rangoon, yellow monk's robes, and begging bowls so they could scrounge enough rice to continue onward. Then, distributing a reckless largesse of smiles and handshakes to the technical crew, he raced off to California to do the Western exteriors, and our paths diverged for a spell.

Some six weeks later, I received a midnight telephone plea to join Todd in Hollywood, where he was preparing the Barbary Coast episode and a couple of others in the picture. I complied and, as I expected, was immediately plunged into a courtship unsullied by any hint of money. He urgently needed lines and situations, he confessed, for some exceptional stars he had acquired for cameo roles. I confessed, with equal candor, that I urgently needed bread for my dependents. His eyes took on a glassy, hypnotic stare and he began casting my horoscope. In it he saw yachts the size of the Stella Polaris, racing stables, seraglios full of milk-white lovelies surpassing Jane Russell. Impressed though I was by his clairvoyance, I managed to retain my equilibrium and demanded cash on the barrelhead. He vilified me, rent his garments, and howled aloud, but eventually he consented to a deal on a piecework basis. Nightly in the weeks that followed, therefore, we would meet in a Beverly Hills parking lot, I clutching the pages required for the next day's shooting, he the pro-rata payment. At a concerted signal, we made a lightning exchange, leaped into our respective cars, and drove off.

Five months after the picture had opened and Todd's own picture was appearing on postage stamps, David Niven and I lunched at the Beverly Hills Hotel. As we reviewed the vicissitudes we had undergone in its making, he suddenly interrupted his discourse. "Bless my soul, I almost forgot," he said. "This reunion deserves a special celebration. Waiter—two more Martinis, please!"

"But why?" I asked.

"Because this just came through yesterday." He withdrew his cardcase and exhibited a check. "My final week's salary for *Around the World in Eighty Days.*"

The waiter, engaged in removing our empties, grunted sympathetically. "Well do I know the *boychick* of whom you speak," he said. "The fastest con in the West."

1972

CALVIN TRILLIN

CONFESSIONS OF A STANDUP

SAUSAGE EATER

I SUPPOSE I would have given up the Feast of San Gennaro years ago if I'd had any choice. San Gennaro has always been the largest Italian festival in the city, and for a long time now Mulberry Street during the Feast has been crowded enough to give the impression that, for reasons lost to history, Manhattan folk customs include an annual outdoor enactment of precisely the conditions present in the IRT uptown express during rush hour. In September, the weather in New York can be authentically Neapolitan—particularly on a street that is jammed with people and sealed on both sides with a line of stands where venders are boiling oil for zeppole or barbecuing braciole over charcoal. Occasionally, I have become irritated with the Feast even on evenings when I have no intention of attending it, since I have become one of those Manhattan residents who get testy when some event brings even more traffic than usual into the city from the suburbs. Those of us who migrated to New York from the middle of the country may be even less tolerant of incursions by out-of-towners than the natives are, and I suppose I may as well admit that, in some particularly frustrating gridlock on some particularly steamy fall day, I may have shouted "Go back where you came from, you rubes!" in the direction of a lot of former New Yorkers who now live a mile or two into New Jersey—an outburst that would have been even ruder if the objects of my irritation had not been safely encased in soundproof air-conditioned cars. The traffic congestion caused by San Gennaro is particularly irritating to me because Mulberry Street lies between my house and Chinatown, and the Feast happens to fall at the time of year when I return to the city from a summer in Nova Scotia suffering the anguish of extended Chinese-food deprivation. Practically feverish with visions of crabs sloshing around in black-bean sauce, I detour around the Feast in a journey that seems to get longer every year, as the lights of San Gennaro push farther and farther uptown from the heart of Little Italy toward Houston Street, on the edge of the lower East Side. It would not surprise me, I think, if one of these years commuters from Westchester County pouring out of Grand Central Station some hot September morning walked smack into a line of calzone and sausage stands that had crept up in an unbroken line fifty blocks from Grand Street. The venders, dishing out food as fast as they can, will still have time to complain to the account executives and bank managers they're serving about having been assigned a spot too far from the busiest blocks of the Feast.

I love the elements of San Gennaro that still exist from its origin as a neighborhood festival transplanted practically intact from Naples by Little Italy immigrants—the statue of the saint with dollar bills pinned beneath it, for instance, and the brass band that seems to consist of a half-dozen aging Italians and one young Chinese trumpet player—but the Feast has felt considerably less like a neighborhood celebration in recent years, partly because its size has inevitably brought along some atmosphere of mass production, partly because of the inclusion of such non-Neapolitan specialties as piña colada and eggrolls and computer portraits, and partly because of the self-consciousness represented by "Kiss Me—I'm Italian" buttons. Also, I find that I can usually catch the brass band during the year around the Chinatown part of Mulberry, below Canal Street; it often works Chinese funerals. The gambling at the Feast does not attract me, and the stuffed animals that are awarded for making a basket or knocking down milk bottles hold no appeal for someone whose family policy on stuffed animals is moving slowly, in the face of some resistance, toward what the Metropolitan Museum of Art used to call deaccessioning.

Still, there I am at San Gennaro every year—admitting to myself that I rather enjoy pushing my way down Mulberry at a time when Neapolitan music is coming over the loudspeakers and operators of games of chance are making their pitches and food smells from a dozen different booths are competing in the middle of the street. My presence is easily explained: I can't stay away from the sausage sandwiches. As it happens, I live on the edge of a lower-Manhattan Italian neighborhood where the sort of sausage sandwiches served at Italian feasts—a choice of hot or sweet sausage jammed into a roll with a combination of fried pepper and onions as dressing—can be bought any day of the year in comfortable surroundings, which even include a stool at the counter. I never buy one. Somehow, it has been clear to me since I came to the city that uncontrolled, year-round eating of sausage sandwiches is not an acceptable option for me. It was instinct more than a conscious decision—the sort of instinct that some animals must use to know how many of certain berries to eat in the woods. My wife, who at our house acts as the enforcer for the nutrition mob, has never had to speak on the subject of how much devastation a steady diet of Italian sausage could wreak on the human body. The limits are set. I have a sausage sandwich whenever I go to San Gennaro. I have a sausage sandwich at the Feast of St. Anthony, on Sullivan Street, in the spring. If I'm lucky, I might stumble across one of the smaller Italian feasts in Little Italy to find a sausage stand that has attached itself to some Village block party. Otherwise, I do without. When people from my home town, in the Midwest, ask me how I survive in New York, I tell them that the way I survive is simple: I only eat sausage sandwiches standing up.

I am not the only seasonal eater in New York. There is a time in the fall when a lot of people who have spent August in some rural setting—talking a lot of brave talk about how there is nothing better than a simple piece of broiled fish and some absolutely fresh vegetables—come back to the city and head straight for the sort of food that seems to exist only in close proximity to cement. I noticed one of them during the week of my fall sausage eating while I was waiting in line at Joe's Dairy on Sullivan Street—right across from St. Anthony's, the church that sponsors my spring sausage eating. As it happens, my own mission was seasonal—although one sort of business or another takes me to Joe's all year round. In the early fall, when farmers are still bringing their produce into Manhattan for Saturday-morning markets, it is possible to make a stop at the farmer's market in the West Village, pick up some basil and some tomatoes that actually taste like tomatoes rather than Christmas decorations, stop in at Joe's for mozzarella so fresh that it is still oozing milk, put the tomatoes and mozzarella and basil and some olive oil together to make what is sometimes called a Caprisian salad, and congratulate yourself on having captured the essential feature of Capri without having gone above Fourteenth Street. The man in front of me at Joe's Dairy was looking around the shelves as if he were a Russian defector getting his first look at Bloomingdale's. He asked for Parmesan cheese. He asked for Romano. He bought some mozzarella. "Jesus Christ! I just had a roast-pork sandwich at Frank's!" he suddenly said. "Boy, am I glad to be back in the city!" Everyone in the store nodded in sympathy.

WHEN I walk down Mulberry Street, just below Canal, during the Feast of San Gennaro, I am strongly affected by what I suppose could be called border tensions: I feel the competing pulls of sausage sandwiches and flounder Fukienese style. The street just east of Mulberry is Mott, the main drag of Chinatown. There was a time not many years ago when Mott and a few side streets seemed to constitute a small Chinese outpost in the middle of a large Italian neighborhood; in those days, a Chinese candidate for the New York State Assembly endeared himself to me by telling a reporter from the *Times* that he was running against the Italian incumbent—Louis DeSalvio, the permanent grand marshal of the Feast of San Gennaro—even though he realized that he didn't have "a Chinaman's chance." Over the past ten or fifteen years, though, a surge of Chinese immigration has revitalized Chinatown and pushed out its boundaries—past the Bowery and then East Broadway in one direction, across Mulberry Street in the other. On Mulberry Street below Canal, the calzone stands and beer carts of San Gennaro stand in front of Chinese butcher shops and Chinese importing companies and Chinese produce stores. "They left us three blocks," an official of San Gennaro told me while talking about the Chinese expansion. The blocks between Canal and Broome are still dominated by the robust Italian restaurants that represent the tomato-sauce side against the forces of Northern Italian cream sauce in what has been called the War of the Red and the White. Even on those blocks of Mulberry, though, some of the windows of second-floor offices have sprouted Chinese writing. There are a lot of Italians left in the tenements of Mulberry Street, but a lot of Italians have moved away—returning to shop on Grand Street or sit in one of the coffeehouses or eat sausage sandwiches at the Feast of San Gennaro. The Feast is still run by the grandson of the man who founded the Society of San Gennaro, Napoli e Dintorni, in 1926, but he lives in Staten Island.

Foreign food—non-Italian food, that is—began to creep into San Gennaro and some of the other Italian feasts half a dozen years ago, but not from Chinatown. There were some Korean booths and an occasional taco stand and some stands at which Filipinos sold barbecued meat on a stick and fried rice and lo mein and eggrolls and an unusual fritter that was made of vegetables and fried in oil. At the time, I decided that the purist belief in restricting Italian festivals to Italian food was narrow-minded and artificial—a decision that was based, I admit, on a certain fondness for the vegetable fritters. There was a sprinkling of foreign food at San Gennaro this year—a gyros stand, a couple of stands selling egg creams, a black man selling fried chicken wings, a Pennsylvania-funnel-cake operation, and at least half a dozen stands run by Filipinos. These days, any street event in New York—a merchants' fair on Third Avenue, a block party on the West Side—is certain to have at least one Filipino food stand. At the annual One World Festival sponsored by the Armenian diocese—a festival that has always been so aggressively ecumenical that I wouldn't be surprised to discover someday that a few spots had been assigned to food stands run by Turks—the stands selling Armenian lahmajun and boereg and yalanchi and lule kebab seemed almost outnumbered this year by stands selling what are sometimes advertised as "Filipino and Polynesian specialties." The man in charge of assigning spots for San Gennaro told me that if no attempt were made to maintain a balance—and a Feast that is not overwhelmingly Italian would obviously be unbalanced—Mulberry Street would have had ten Filipino stands on every block. I asked some of the Filipino venders how they accounted for so many of their countrymen being in the street-fair game, but their explanations did not go much beyond the theory that some people made money at some of the street fairs that began being held in brownstone neighborhoods several years ago and other people decided to get in on a good thing. It may remain one of those New York ethnic mysteries that outlanders were not meant to understand. Why are so many fruit-and-vegetable stores that were once run by Italians and so many fruit-and-vegetable stores that previously didn't exist run by Koreans? Why have I never seen a black sanitation man? Why are conversations among venders of hot dogs at the Central Park zoo conducted in Greek?

SELECTING my sausage sandwich requires a certain amount of concentration. At San Gennaro, after all, there are always at least thirty stands selling sausage sandwiches. I don't mean that I do nothing else at the Feast. In the spirit of fostering intergroup harmony, I sometimes have a vegetable fritter. I often have a few zeppole—holeless doughnuts that are available almost exclusively at Italian feasts. I have a couple of beers, muttering about the price, or some wine with fruit. Mainly, though, I inspect sausage stands—walking slowly the length of the Feast and maybe back again before I make my choice. About halfway through my inspection, whoever happens to be with me—usually one of my daughters—tells me that all sausage stands look alike, or maybe even that all sausage sandwiches taste alike. I keep looking.

The stands always look familiar to me. A lot of the food venders at Italian feasts in Manhattan make a business of going from feast to feast around the New York area from spring to fall. In Little Italy, it is assumed that the food-stand operators spend the rest of the year in Florida, living like kings off the sort of profits that must be accumulated by anyone who sells a tiny plate of ziti with tomato sauce for three dollars and has never heard of real-estate taxes. Among New Yorkers, it is practically an article of faith that anyone who runs what seems to be a small seasonal business—the ice-cream man in the park, for instance—can be found on any cold day in February casually blowing hundreds of dollars at some Florida dog track. Although I recognize the stands, I can never seem to keep in my mind which one has served me the best sausage sandwich. The inspection during what had to be my final visit to San Gennaro this year was carried out on a rainy weekday evening in the company of my two daughters—neither of whom has the slightest interest in so much as tasting a sausage sandwich. I was convinced that the stand I had patronized at St. Anthony's in the spring—acquiring a sandwich whose memory I carried with me through the summer—was called by someone's first name. All the sausage stands at San Gennaro seemed to be called by someone's first name. Had it been Dominic's? The Original Jack's? Rocky & Philly's? Tony's? Angelo's? Smokin' Joe's? Staten Island Frank's? Gizzo's? Lucy's? There was nothing to do but inspect each stand—my daughters tagging along behind me, already full of pasta. I looked for a stand that was frying the sausages on a griddle rather than grilling them over charcoal—and displaying peppers and onions that had been sliced and cooked precisely to my requirements. It was amazing how many sausage stands qualified. My daughters began to remind me that it was a school night. Under some pressure, I stopped in front of Staten Island Frank's—or maybe it was the Original Jack's; even now the names run together—and said, "This is it." When I started to eat, I was convinced that I had chosen brilliantly—until we passed a stand that I hadn't noticed before. It was serving sausages, with correctly fried peppers and onions, on marvelous-looking rolls that had sesame seeds on top of them.

"Sesame-seed rolls!" I said. "Nobody told me about sesame-seed rolls!"

"Take it easy," one of my daughters said, giving me a reassuring pat on the arm. "You can have one on a sesame-seed roll next year."

"Not next year," I reminded her as we headed home. "At St. Anthony's in June."

1981

ADAM GOPNIK

A PURIM STORY

I SUPPOSE it is a sign of just how poor a Jew I am that when I got a letter from the Jewish Museum last February asking me to be the Purimspieler at its Purim Ball I thought there must be some kind of mistake. I don't mean that I thought there must be some mistake in asking me. I am enough of a ham that I would not be surprised if a Hindu congregation asked me to come forward and recite choice selec-

tions from the Bhagavad Gita. I mean that I was surprised because I
thought the Jewish Museum was making a mistake about the date of
Purim.

"Isn't that the one in the fall?" I asked my wife, Martha. "With the
hamantaschen? And the little hut in the back yard?"

"No," she said. "No, it isn't. They have hamantaschen all year round.
Even I know that."

"The thing that puzzles me," I went on, holding up the letter and
reading it again, "is how they ever figured out I was Jewish."

She executed what I believe our fathers would have called a spit
take. "That is the most ridiculous question I've ever heard. There's your
name, for one thing, and then the way you use Jewish words in writing."

"What Jewish words have I ever used in writing?"

She thought for a moment. "Well, 'shvitz.' And 'inchoate.' "

" 'Inchoate' is not a Jewish word."

"It is the way you use it. You've got 'Jew' written all over you. It's obvious."

"It's obvious," my six-year-old son, Luke, echoed, looking up from
his plate. "It's obvious." I was startled, though not entirely. We lived in
Paris for the first five years of his life, and ethnic awareness is one of the
first things he's been exposed to on coming home to New York. The
lame and the halt, the meaning of Kwanzaa and the nights of
Hanukkah—all the varieties of oppressed ethnic experience have become the material of his education. He sees the world in groups, or is
beginning to. His best friend, Jacob Kogan, has a sister who was asked
by her grandparents what she wanted for Hanukkah. "A Christmas
tree," she said. Luke reported that with pleasure. He and Jacob have developed a nice line in old, Henny Youngman–style jokes, which apparently circulate permanently in the lower grades of New York schools,
like Mercury space-program debris circulating in outer space, getting
lower and lower in its orbit each year: "Waiter, what's this fly doing in
my soup?!" "The backstroke."

I gave him a look. His birth was the occasion of my realizing just
how poor a Jew I am. When he was born, at Mount Sinai hospital, in
New York, almost every other baby in the nursery had Lubavitcher parents, and in the isolette they had proudly placed a little framed photograph of the Lubavitcher rebbe, Menachem Schneerson, so that the
first thing the baby saw was the thin Russian eyes and the great Rem-
brandt beard of the Rebbe. The Hasidic fathers clustered around the

glass of the nursery, and I felt at once drawn to them and inadequate to their dark-suited, ringleted assurance. They looked wonderful, and I, another member of the tribe, wanted, at least provisionally, to attach myself to them.

"He's crying from the circumcision," I explained to the father on my left, significantly.

He stared at me, and, with the hat and fringe, he looked at first very old and then, as my eye saw past the costume, very young. "He's been circumcised already?" he said. I hadn't known you were supposed to wait.

Still, he grasped the gesture toward commonality. "What's his name?"

"Luke," I said proudly. "Luke Auden."

He backed away from me, really backed away, like a Japanese extra in a Godzilla movie when the monster comes into view, looming up above the power pylons.

I returned to the letter. It was a very nice, warm letter, from the director of the museum, explaining that the "event takes the form of a masked ball in celebration of the Purim holiday, with approximately seven hundred guests gathered for a black-tie dinner-dance at the Waldorf-Astoria." The "highlight" was a "10–15 minute original Purim-spiel—a humorous retelling of the story of Purim, Queen Esther's rescue of the Jews in ancient Persia." In a postscript, the director promised "to send some background information on the Biblical story of Purim."

Looking at the letter again, I began to realize that the Purimspieler barrel must have been thoroughly scraped before the museum people got to me, and also that, getting to me, they knew what they were getting. They had been able to deduce that, though Jewish, I was sufficiently ignorant about Jewishness to need "some background information on the Biblical story of Purim." If they had been asking me to talk on life in France, I doubted that they would have thought to send me a map of Paris.

"Daddy, did I tell you the new version?" Luke said, suddenly.

"Which new version?"

"Man goes into a restaurant, he says, 'Waiter, waiter.'"

"No," I corrected him. "He should just say, 'Waiter!' It's the guy who goes to see a doctor who says it twice: 'Doctor, doctor!' Just 'Waiter!'" What a thing, to be a pedant of one-liners.

"Oh. He says, 'Waiter, what's this fly doing in my soup?' and the waiter, then the waiter says, 'There was no room left in the potato salad.'"

I laughed. "Of course I'm going to do it," I said.

"Is this going to be one of those things where you end up still skeptical but strangely exhilarated by the faith of your fathers?" Martha said. "Because if it is, I don't want you to do it. It's hard enough having you around morose all the time. It would be even worse if you were strangely exhilarated."

THE next morning, a Saturday, I took down the Book of Esther from the shelf—or, more precisely, I took down the old King James Bible, the only one I owned. It has all the words of Jesus picked out in red, as though highlighted by an earnest Galilean undergraduate. I was in charge of the kids, but I felt sure that I would have time to read. Luke was shut in the bedroom, watching Saturday-morning cartoons, struggling desperately to understand; I knew he would interrupt only occasionally, seeking clarification on some cartoon convention. Because of his time in Paris, he missed a lot of cartoon-watching, and now he is frantically trying to catch up. He gets a worried look on his face as he runs into the room and asks about what he has just seen: "Why when people go through walls in a cartoon do they leave holes exactly the same shape as them?" "Why when someone touches electricity in a cartoon do you see his whole skeleton? But only for a second?" The rules of an alternative universe, what there is to laugh at and what is just part of life, remain mysterious.

Meanwhile, the baby, Olivia, was happily occupied at the window, dog-spotting. "Dog! Dog!" came the occasional shout. Breakfast and dinner, she will not stay in her high chair but insists on scanning the skies, or streets, like a scientist in a fifties sci-fi movie, searching for life forms she has identified as alien. She is endlessly excited, and wildly agitated whenever she spots one, which, given the density of dogs on Upper East Side streets, she does, predictably, twice a minute.

"Good girl," I said absently, and went back to my Bible. The story of Purim, I learned, takes place in Persia, and mostly in the court of King Ahasuerus. Ahasuerus, who reigned over a hundred and twenty-seven provinces from India to Ethiopia, has a wife, Vashti, who has a "banquet for the women" and then refuses to come when the King commands. The King overreacts, and his advisers tell him to divorce the queen and hold a beauty contest to choose a new one, which he does. He chooses a Jewish girl named Esther. Esther's cousin, an ambitious fellow named Mordecai, then saves the King's life by exposing a plot against him. But the King gets bored with Esther, and meanwhile his chief councillor, Haman, decides to start a pogrom against the Jews, for all the usual reasons: they are tight and clannish, and obey only themselves. He gets the King's approval, and Mordecai, hearing of the plan, goes out in sackcloth and ashes to protest. He tells Esther that she ought to protest, too, and she says, "Well, what can I do?" "Do something," he tells her. She gets dressed up in her best clothes and goes to the King, and the King, thinking she looks nifty, listens to her. He suddenly learns how Mordecai saved his life, and orders Haman to be hanged on the scaffold he had prepared for Mordecai. Then the Jews, about to be pogromed, massacre Haman's followers, including all ten of Haman's sons, who are hanged or, depending on the translation, impaled on stakes. Then everybody celebrates.

I stopped reading. Send this up? I couldn't even grasp it. I knew that the thing to get was Esther's rescue of the Jews, but that seemed almost incidental to this general story of competitive massacre and counter-massacre and bride-shopping. The trouble, I realized, was not that I did not know how to read in the text but that I did not know, had never been taught, how to read past it. Like Luke with the electrified cat, I did not know what was significant and what was merely conventional—I did not know what were the impaling practices of ancient Near East culture, and what was, so to speak, the specifically Jewish point. Although all our official, school training in reading is in reading in—in reading deeply, penetrating the superficial and the apparent to get to the obscure and hidden—in truth a lot of the skill in reading classics lies in reading past them. The obsession with genetic legitimacy and virginity in Shakespeare; the acceptance of torture in Dante—these are not subjects to be absorbed but things you glide by on your way to the poetry. You have to feel confident saying, "Oh, that's just then"— with the crucial parallel understanding that now will be then, too, that our progeny will have to learn to read past sentences like "After the peace demonstration, they stopped at Joe's for veal scallopini," or, perhaps, "In their joy, they conceived their fifth child," or even, "They immunized the children." Obviously, it was necessary to read past the impaling of Haman's sons, the ethnic pogroms, to some larger purpose—otherwise there would not be Purimspiels and happy Purim balls—but I did not know how to do it. I saw impaled Iranians where I needed to see a fly doing the backstroke in the soup.

I walked over to the baby at the window seat. Out the window, in the near distance, we could see a synagogue. Even now, I thought, in there people were being taught to read past the scaffold. "Dog, dog!" the baby cried, as a dog-walker came up the street, six or seven dogs on leashes held in one hand. She began to cry out in delight. So many dogs! I closed the book, and hoped glumly that a spiel, that whole leashfuls of them, would come before Purim did.

THE next day, I decided to return to the only Jewish tradition with which I was at all confident, and that was having smoked fish at eleven o'clock on Sunday mornings. Every Sunday morning throughout my childhood, my grandfather would arrive with the spread—salty lox and unctuous sable and dry whitefish and sweet pickled salmon. Sometimes he took me with him to shop, and he always had a pained, resigned look as he ordered: "Yeah, I guess . . . give me some of the whitefish." But when he got home he would be pleased. ("He has very nice stuff, Irving," he would say to my father.) For Purimspiel purposes, I thought, I had better get into Jew training, and eat as my fathers had.

Every Sunday morning for the next few weeks, Luke and I went together to Sable's, the extraordinary smoked-fish and appetizer store at Second Avenue and Seventy-eighth Street. Sable's is the only place in my neighborhood where my grandfather would have been entirely comfortable—with the hand-lettered signs and the Dr. Brown's and the mingled smell of pickles and herring—and yet it is owned and staffed by Asians who once worked as nova slicers at Zabar's, on the West Side, and who walked out to claim their freedom. (I imagined them wandering, in their aprons, through Central Park for years before arriving at the promised land.) They sell Jewish food, and with the same bullying, ironic Jewish manner that I recalled from my childhood trips with my grandfather, but they do it as a thing learned.

"They got nice stuff, anyway, Irving," I said to Luke as we walked over.

"Why are you calling me Irving?" he asked.

"My grandfather always called me Irving when he took me shopping for smoked fish. He had me confused with Grandpop, I guess."

"Oh. Is Grandpop's name Irving?"

"No," I said. "His name isn't actually Irving, either. But your great-grandfather could never remember what his name really was, so he called him Irving. I think he thought all small Jewish boys should be called Irving."

Luke wasn't interested. "Oh," he said. I could see he was looking inward. Then, in a rush: "Why in cartoons when someone touches electricity, after you see their whole skeleton for a second, then they go all stiff and straight up in the air and then their whole body turns black and then it turns into dust and then it crumbles while they still look out and smile as if they were feeling sick? Why?"

I said it was just a convention, just the way cartoons are, and was meant to be funny.

"Why is it funny?" he asked.

We walked on in silence.

Later that day, I sat down with a piece of paper. I had one mildly derivative comic idea, which was to adapt the Purim story to contemporary New York. Ahasuerus was Donald Trump: dumb as an ox, rich, lecherous, easily put out, and living in a gaudy apartment. So Vashti must be Ivana—that was easy—and Esther was a Russian Jewish model who had immigrated from Odessa, a beauty, but hardly aware that she was Jewish save for the convenience of immigration. Haman—what if you said that Haman . . . But I couldn't focus. How was it, I wondered, that I could know nothing of all this? For the truth is that Jew *is* written all over me. If on my father's side they were in wholesale food, on my mother's side they were dark-skinned Sephardim who had stayed in Palestine—so busy squabbling that they actually missed the bus for the Diaspora. One of my maternal great-grandfathers, family lore has it, was the rabbi sent from Hebron to Lisbon at the end of the nineteenth century to call the Jews out of hiding and back into the synagogue.

And yet, when I think about my own upbringing, the best I can say is that the most entirely Jewish thing about us was the intensity with which we celebrated Christmas: passionately, excessively, with the tallest tree and the most elaborately wrapped presents. Coming of age in the fifties, my parents, like so many young intellectuals of their generation, distanced themselves from the past as an act of deliberate emancipation. My parents were not so much in rebellion against their own past as they were in love with the idea of using the values unconsciously taken from that culture to conquer another—they went from Jewish high school to Ivy League college and fell in love with English literature. Like so many others, they ended in that queer, thriving country of the Jewish American possessor of the Christian literary heritage: they became Zionists of eighteenth-century literature, kibbutzniks of metaphysical poetry. The only Bible-related book I can recall from my childhood was in my father's office, an academic volume called *The Bible to Be Read as Literature;* the joke was, of course, that in those precincts it was literature that was to be read as the Bible. (We didn't have a Christian Christmas; we had a Dickensian Christmas.) The eradication left an imprint stronger than indoctrination could have. We had "Jew" written all over us in the form of marks from the eraser.

What was left of overt, nameable Jewishness was the most elemental Jewish thing, and that was a style of joking. My grandfather, who ran a small grocery store in a black neighborhood, lives in my memory, apart from Sunday-morning fish, mostly in his jokes, a round of one-liners as predictable as the hands on a clock, and yet, weirdly, getting funnier by the year: "Joe Banana and his bunch? The music with appeal." And "I used to be a boxer. In a shoe store." And "I used to sing tenor—but they traded me in for two fives." And "Feel stiff in the joints? Then stay out of the joints."

The first time I had a sense of Jewishness as a desirable state rather than as background radiation, humming in a Christian cosmos, was when I was thirteen and, turned on to the idea of New York, saw that it was made up of Jewish comedians—of jokes. I discovered the Marx Brothers and then Woody Allen. I bought a book of old comics' routines and learned the telephone spiels of Georgie Jessel. ("Mom, why did you cook that bird? He was a valuable bird; he could speak six languages!" "Oh . . . he shoulda said something.") *The Ed Sullivan Show* fascinated me: Corbett Monica and Norm Crosby and Jackie Vernon, and, hovering above even them, Myron Cohen, the mournful storyteller, and Henny Youngman, genuinely the funniest man, who looked exactly like my grandfather, to boot. The greatest generation. I read interviews with obscure Jewish comedians, old and young—really obscure ones, Ed Bluestone and Ben Blue—and noticed, with a rising thrill, that none of them talked about "jokes" that you "told." Instead, they talked about "bits," which they "did"—and killed "them" doing them. That, for me, explained everything, life and art: life was stuff that happened, art was bits you did. It was the first religion that had ever made sense.

I came to New York to practice that faith, do bits, be a Purim-spieler—only to find that that world was gone. Some time in the decade after my arrival, the Jewish comic culture dried up. The sense, so strong since the beginning of the century, that New York was naturally Jewish and, by an unforced corollary, naturally funny had gone. Of course, there were standup comics, many of them Jewish, but the particular uneasiness, the sense that talking too fast might keep you alive, the sense that you talked as a drowning man might wave his hands, the whining, high-pitched tone and the *r*-less accent—that had gone. Paul Reiser, Jerry Seinfeld, much as I enjoyed and even identified with them, were as settled and as American as Bob and Ray or Will Rogers. This was an event with a specific date, marked in the work of the last great New York Jew comedian. Between 1977 and *Annie Hall,* where being a Jewish comedian is a slightly weary and depressing obligation, to be rebelled against, and *Broadway Danny Rose,* just seven years later, when the black-and-white world of the comics shpritzing at the Carnegie Deli is frankly presented as a Chagall world, a folktale setting, the whole thing vanished. Even Jackie Mason, a rabbi in training and ostensibly a master of the style, was quite different; his subject, when, in the eighties, he returned from obscurity, wasn't the unsuspected power of being a loser but the loss of power in the face of all those new immigrants.

New York Jewish comic manners were still around, only they were no longer practiced by Jews, or were practiced by Jews as something learned rather than as something felt. What had replaced the organic culture of Jewish comedy in New York was a permanent pantomime of Jewish manners. The fly doing the backstroke in the soup was part of a kind of chicken-soup synchronized-swimming event, as ordered and regulated as an Olympic sport: Jewish New York manners were a thing anyone could imitate in order to indicate "comedy."

One sensed this at Sable's, where Jewish traditions of shpritzing were carried on by non-Jews, and in television commercials, where New York taxi drivers were still represented as wise guys, even though they had not been for a generation or more. But it was true in subtler ways, too. On *Seinfeld,* which I had missed while living abroad but now could watch in reruns every night, everything is, at one level, shockingly Jewish, far more than Sid Caesar or Mel Brooks was ever allowed to be, with mohels and brisses and whining fathers who wait all week for their copy of *TV Guide*—but the unstated condition is that there be absolutely no mention of the *J* word, while the most Jewish character, George, is given an Italian last name, Costanza. This is not because Jewishness is forbidden but because it is so obvious. Jewishness is to *Seinfeld* what the violin was to Henny Youngman—the prop that you used between jokes, as much for continuity as for comedy. The Jewish situations are mimed by rote, while the real energy of the jokes lies in the observation of secular middle-class manners. In the old Jewish comedies, it had been just the opposite: the manners of the middle class were mimed by rote—the suits and ties, the altered names, Jack Benny's wife called Mary—while the energy of the jokes lay in the hidden Jewishness. (The comedy of Phil Silvers's great Sgt. Bilko almost scandalously derives from the one thing that no one on the show is allowed to mention, which is that Bilko is a clever New York Jew dominating a kind of all-star collection of dim Gentiles.) New York Jewishness was now the conscious setup rather than the hidden punch line.

ONE Sunday morning, Luke and I walked over to Sable's and bought even more than usual; we were having company. But the cashier was unimpressed. He looked over our order.

"How many people you having?" he asked.

"Eight."

"From out of town?"

"Yes."

He sighed. "Me, I would be ashamed to put this on the table."

"You would?"

He looked at the ritualized bits of cured sable and salmon, and shrugged again—my grandfather to the life!

"This is not worth putting on the table. I would be ashamed."

"What do you think I should do?"

"Get a pound of herring salad. Pound of whitefish salad. Pound of bluefish salad."

I did. "Now I proud to put this on the table," he said. "Now I no longer ashamed for you."

He had learned to do it at Zabar's, I realized as I left—the permanent pantomime of Jewish manners with wings on! Though it cost me nearly a hundred dollars, it was worth it for the lesson. The combination of an Asian sense of face with a Jewish sense of guilt may be the most powerful commercial hybrid in history.

"SO, see, I have an Esther in my family, too. The matriarch of my family. She dominated her sisters, in a grasping way, and then came to die of emphysema in my grandparents' apartment in Florida. We went to see her in, this is in about 1993, I guess. Wheezing and pained, she said, 'People tell me you are doing well, but I lie here in bed at night and worry, oh, I worry about you. How I worry. So now tell me, tell me, so your aunt won't lie here as she is dying and worry . . . tell me . . . how much are you really making?' "

"You can't possibly tell that story," Martha said. "It's anti-Semitic."

"It's true," I said.

"Of course it's true," Martha said. "It's just not appropriate."

I was trying out possible spiels on the more Jewish of our many Jewish friends. We have a certain number of friends who, though coming from backgrounds not unlike my own, have recommitted themselves to Jewishness in a serious way. While Yiddishkeit as a practice had nearly disappeared from New York, one of the things that were replacing it, paradoxically, was Judaism. A number of our friends are what I have come to think of as X-treme Jews, who study Cabala or glory in the details of the lives of Jewish gangsters, and even like to call themselves "Hebes," in the manner of young black men calling each other "niggas."

I envied my friends the seeming clarity of their Jewishness, just as I envied, a little, the clarity of the family of observant Jews who live down the hall from us. On warm Friday evenings, one or two of the adolescent boys in that family will come knocking at our door, galumphing in heavy shoes and with pale faces, and, looking woeful, say, "Could you come and turn on the air-conditioner in our apartment? We can't, 'cause we're Jews." I admired the simplicity of their self-definition: "We can't, 'cause we're Jews." We are unashamed of our essence, even as it makes us sweat.

But, whatever the appeal of that plain faith, I can't say I was inclined to follow them. It seemed to me that my contemporaries, in contrast to the boys down the hall, had chosen Jewish—they were majoring in Jewish, just as my father had majored in English—when the force of the tradition was that it was not elective. I decided to sit down and read what I imagined was the bible on the subject, Alfred Kazin's memoir *New York Jew,* a book that, over the years, I had neither read in nor read past but simply not read, thinking, unforgivably, that I already knew its contents. (The forties, boy! The fifties, joy! The sixties, oy!) In fact, it's an unpredictable, rhapsodic, uncontentious book—but, for all the starkness of its title, its premise is that Jewishness is the board from which one springs, rather than the ground one must dig. To be a New York Jew is, for Kazin, like being a New York tree. It is what you are.

Reading Kazin, I became a little impatient with my own apologetic attitude toward the poverty of my Jewishness. Wasn't it the invigorating inheritance of the self-emancipation of my parents? My father had done the deracinating, to become a devotee of Pope and Swift, Molière and Shakespeare, and to reracinate was to be disloyal to him, to the act of emancipation from tribal reflexes that, with a considerable effort of will and imagination, he had pulled off. What is bracing about Kazin is not his Jewishness but that he makes no effort to pretend that he is something else. His liberation lay in not pretending to be Van Wyck Brooks; the liberation for us surely lies in not pretending to be Alfred Kazin.

In the midst of these bitter-herb thoughts, Luke came in.

"Here's the new version," he said. "Man says to a waiter, 'What's this fly doing in my soup?' 'Sh-h-h,' the waiter says, 'everyone will want one.'" It broke me up. Whether or not there are Jewish essences, there are surely some essentially Jewish jokes. That was one, and I was in the middle of another.

I WAS about to call the Jewish Museum and give it all up, when a friend suggested that I speak to a rabbi. "Go see Rabbi Schorsch," he said. "He's the chancellor of the Jewish Theological Seminary. He's a terrific guy, and I'm sure he'd be glad to help you out with the spiel thing." I vaguely remembered hearing Rabbi Ismar Schorsch on the radio once or twice, so I made an appointment—it felt like making a date with a dentist—and on the day I took the subway up to 125th Street.

The rabbi's secretary showed me into his office, and after a couple of minutes there was Rabbi Schorsch.

"Rabbi," I began, "I was not raised as an observant Jew, but I am nonetheless of a Jewish background, and I am naturally concerned to show some grasp of a tradition that, though familiar in spirit, is still alien to me in many ways." I don't know; that's how I thought you ought to talk to a rabbi. Anyway, I eventually explained that I couldn't make head or tail of the Book of Esther.

"It's a spoof, a burlesque, really," he almost mumbled.

He picked up my Bible, riffled through it as though there were a kind of satisfaction just in touching the pages, and then frowned. "This is a Christian Bible," he said, genuinely puzzled.

He was the kind of hyper-alert elderly man who, instead of putting on weight around the middle, seems to have drawn all his energy upward into his eyes and ears, which gleam, outsized. "Yes. It's a kind of comic chapter, not to be taken entirely seriously," he went on, holding my King James Version in his hand as though it might be loaded. "It's a light book with a serious message. You see, Scripture, the Bible, one of the remarkable things about it is that it contains a chapter about every form of human experience. There's a book of laws and a book of love songs. A book of exile and a book of homecoming. A skeptical and despairing book in Job, and an optimistic and sheltering book in the Psalms. Esther is the comic book, it's a book for court Jews, with a fairy-tale, burlesque spirit."

You could see my whole skeleton underneath my jacket; my hair stood on end; I turned into a pile of black ash, smiling sickly as I slowly crumbled.

"It is?" I said.

"Yes. You see, Mordecai is a classic Jew of the Diaspora, not just exiled but entirely assimilated—a court Jew, really. It's a book for court Jews. Why doesn't he bow down to Haman? Well, it might be because of his Judaism. But I think we have to assume that he's jealous—he expects to be made first minister and then isn't. Have you noticed the most interesting thing about the book?" He looked at me keenly.

"I hadn't even noticed it was funny."

"It's the only book in the Bible where God is never mentioned," he said. "This is the book for the Jews of the city, the world. After all, we wonder—what does Esther eat? It sure isn't kosher. But she does good anyway. The worldliness and the absurdity are tied together—the writer obviously knows that the King is a bit of an idiot—but the point is that good can rise from it in any case. Esther acts righteously and saves her people, and we need not worry, too much, about what kind of Jew she was before, or even after. She stays married to the Gentile King, remember. This is the godless, comic book of Jews in the city, and how they struggle to do the righteous thing."

I was stunned. This was, as they say, the story of my life. A funny book about court Jews . . . I had been assigned to burlesque it, when the text was pre-burlesqued, as jeans might be pre-shrunk.

We talked for a while longer, about the background of Haman as a Jew-hater, and of how the most startlingly contemporary thing in the book was the form of anti-Semitism; even twenty-five hundred years ago in Persia, the complaint against the Jews was the same as it is now. In the end, he gave me a signed copy of the Bible, the Jewish Bible, the Tanach. (Signed by him, I mean.)

We got together a couple of times after that, and eventually I decided to try and go ahead with the Purimspiel. He said, "Why not? What have you got to lose?"

What have you got to lose? It was, I reflected, like the punch line of a Jewish joke.

. . .

IN the ballroom of the Waldorf-Astoria, hundreds of people in dinner jackets and sequined dresses were wearing masks, although this made them look less festive than vaguely embarrassed, as though they were worried about being seen by their friends. I had forgotten the look and feel of a New York benefit: the ballroom made to look like a gym, the chicken, stretched out, mortified, on its plate, with the Indisputably Classy Ingredient—the quince, or sun-dried tomato, or preserved lemon—laid on top of it. The fiftyish women, sexy and intimidating in sports clothes, look wilted in their fancy gowns. The only difference was that at this benefit there was a giant video-projection screen at either end of the hall and one above the podium, and the speakers—who included Rabbi Schorsch, saying the blessing—were projected on them. I gulped. I had thought it would be like a nightclub, where I could play with a microphone in the manner of Rodney Dangerfield, and this was more like a political convention. I was an impostor, even though I had bits to do. I heard my grandfather's voice: *Feel stiff in the joints? Then stay out of the joints!*

At last, just before dessert, I got up and went to the podium. Out of the corner of my eye I could see my own image on the giant screen.

What did I tell them? Well, I did the New York as Persia, Donald, and Ivana bit and then I did a bit I'd made up that afternoon on Haman. That got a modest laugh, and, encouraged, I went on to do the man-goes-to-see-a-rabbi bit. I said that, once I had thought of transposing the story to New York, I had got stuck on Mordecai. Who could Mordecai be in the modern city? I had gone to see a rabbi, and the rabbi had told me that the Book of Esther was in part a spoof, a burlesque: a comedy in which worldly people took risks and did unworldly things, and that Mordecai, if he was anyone, was us—the assimilated court and city Jews. And this was sort of amazing to me, since the idea that the man of the world might be the honest man was an idea that was central to the comic tradition I revered—Molière says it, for instance, just like that—but was not one that I had known had a place in the Jewish tradition. The Jewish tradition, I had always thought, proposed that the honest man was the man out of the world, the prophet crying in the wilderness. But I saw now that there was a connection between a certain kind of comedy, the comedy of assimilation, and a certain kind of courage, the courage to use your proximity to power, bought at the price of losing your "identity," to save your kinsmen. The real moral center of the story, I saw now, lay in the tiny, heartbreaking, and in many ways comic moment when Esther—trayf-eating, dim-witted, overdressed, sexy Esther—appears before the King, who hasn't found her particularly sexy lately. I could see her in her Lacroix pouf dress, I said, gulping for breath and showing up, so to speak, at Donald Trump's office in the middle of a busy day saying that she had to speak to him. But she did, and the Jews were saved, for once.

It went over okay. I didn't kill them, but I didn't die, either. They were expecting something more consistently amusing, I suppose, but no one minds a little moral sententiousness in an after-dinner speaker. "Congratulations, that was unusual," or "You obviously spoke from the heart," or "I knew that when we asked you to do the Purimspiel we would get something different!," or just "Thank you for your interest-ing remarks" was the general tone of the things that people said when I got back to the table. (I still meet people who were there. They give me exactly the look a father might have after seeing his daughter topless in a progressive college production of *A Midsummer Night's Dream;* he re-spects the sincerity of the intention, but it was extremely embarrassing to be there, nonetheless.) I had dessert—fund-raising-benefit dessert, something soft and white interspersed with something red and juicy—and went home. As a thank-you present, I was given a little silver grog-ger, a rattle, meant to be shaken when you heard the name "Haman."

Though I am not strangely exhilarated by my experience as a Purim-spieler, I did find something significant in the Book of Esther, and I am certainly glad I did it. In one way, it was no different from any other ex-posure to an ancient, irrational belief-culture. I suppose I would have felt about the same if I had been a young Athenian who finally goes to Del-phi and hears the oracle: Even if it didn't change the future, it was nice to make the trip. But if there is something particularly Jewish about the experience, it may lie in the odd combination of a narrow gate and a large gathering; the most exclusive and tribal of faiths, Judaism is also the one that sustains the most encompassing of practices, from Moses to Henny Youngman, from Esther to Sammy Davis, Jr., and all us Irvings. Whether it sustains this because, as the rabbi believes, it is in its nature narrow but infinitely various, or because, as I sometimes suspect, any-thing ancient and oppressed must be adaptable, still it is so. At least for a certain kind of court Jew, being Jewish remains not an exercise in read-ing in or reading past but just in reading on, in continuing to turn the pages. The pages have been weird and varied enough in the past to be weird and varied in the future, and there is no telling who will shine in them. The Jewish occasion lay in rising to the occasion. Even if it was too late to be an everyday, starting Jew, one could still be, so to speak, Jewish in the clutch.

We celebrated our own Seder this past spring, and are thinking of joining the synagogue we can see from our window, in part because we want to, in part because there is an excellent nursery school there for our daughter. That is the kind of things Jews do in Persia. I gave the silver grogger to the baby, who holds it at the window and shakes it in warning when she sees a dog. I believe that she now has the first things a Jewish girl in exile needs: a window to see from and a rattle to shake.

2002

DAVID SEDARIS

IN THE WAITING ROOM

SIX months after moving to Paris, I gave up on French school and decided to take the easy way out. All I ever said was "Could you repeat that?" And for what? I rarely understood things the second time around, and when I did it was usually something banal, the speaker wondering how I felt about toast, or telling me that the store would close in twenty minutes. All that work for something that didn't really matter, and so I began saying "*d'accord*," which translates to "I am in agreement," and means, basically, "Okay." The word was a key to a magic door, and every time I said it I felt the thrill of possibility.

"*D'accord*," I told the concierge, and the next thing I knew I was sewing the eye onto a stuffed animal belonging to her granddaughter. "*D'accord*," I said to the dentist, and she sent me to a periodontist, who took some X-rays and called me into his conference room for a little talk. "*D'accord*," I said, and a week later I returned to his office, where he sliced my gums from top to bottom and scraped great deposits of plaque from the roots of my teeth. If I'd had any idea that this was going to happen, I'd never have said *d'accord* to my French publisher, who'd scheduled me the following evening for a television appearance. It was a weekly cultural program, and very popular. I followed the pop star Robbie Williams, and, as the producer settled me into my chair, I ran my tongue over my stitches. It was like having a mouthful of spiders—spooky, but it gave me something to talk about on TV, and for that I was grateful.

I said *d'accord* to a waiter, and received a pig's nose standing erect on a bed of tender greens. I said it to a woman in a department store and walked away drenched in cologne. Every day was an adventure.

When I got a kidney stone, I took the Métro to a hospital, and said *d'accord* to a cheerful red-headed nurse, who led me to a private room and hooked me up to a Demerol drip. That was undoubtedly the best that *d'accord* got me, and it was followed by the worst. After the stone had passed, I spoke to a doctor, who filled out an appointment card and told me to return the following Monday, when we would do whatever it was I'd just agreed to. "*D'accord*," I said, and then I supersized it with "*génial*," which means "great."

On the day of my appointment, I returned to the hospital, where I signed the register and was led by a slightly less cheerful nurse to a large dressing room. "Strip to your underwear," she told me, and I said, "*D'accord*." As the woman turned to leave, she said something else, and, looking back, I really should have asked her to repeat it, to draw a picture, if that's what it took, because once you take your pants off *d'accord* isn't really okay anymore.

There were three doors in the dressing room, and after removing my clothes I put my ear against each one, trying to determine which was the safest for someone in my condition. The first was loud, with lots of ringing telephones, so that was out. The second didn't sound much different, and so I chose the third, and entered a brightly painted waiting room furnished with plastic chairs and a glass-topped table stacked high with magazines. A potted plant stood in the corner, and beside it was a second door, which was open and led into a hallway.

I took a seat and had been there for a minute or so when a couple came in and filled two of the unoccupied chairs. The first thing I noticed was that they were fully dressed, and nicely, too—no sneakers or sweatsuits for them. The woman wore a nubby gray skirt that fell to her knees and matched the fabric of her husband's sports coat. Their black hair, which was obviously dyed, formed another match, but looked better on her than it did on him—less vain, I supposed.

"*Bonjour*," I said, and it occurred to me that possibly the nurse had mentioned something about a robe, perhaps the one that had been hanging in the dressing room. I wanted more than anything to go back and get it, but, if I did, the couple would see my mistake. They'd think I was stupid, so to prove them wrong I decided to remain where I was and pretend that everything was normal. *La la la.*

It's funny the things that run through your mind when you're sitting in your underpants in front of a pair of strangers. Suicide comes up, but, just as you embrace it as a viable option, you remember that you don't have the proper tools: no belt to wrap around your neck, no pen to drive through your nose or ear and up into your brain. I thought briefly of swallowing my watch, but there was no guarantee I'd choke on it. It's embarrassing, but, given the way I normally eat, it would probably go down fairly easily, strap and all. A clock might be a challenge, but a Timex the size of a fifty-cent piece, no problem.

THE man with the dyed black hair pulled a pair of glasses from his jacket pocket, and as he unfolded them I recalled a summer evening in my parents' back yard. This was thirty-five years ago, a dinner for my sister Gretchen's tenth birthday. My father grilled steaks. My mother set the picnic table with insect-repelling candles, and just as we started to eat she caught me chewing a hunk of beef the size of a coin purse. Gorging always set her off, but on this occasion it bothered her more than usual.

"I hope you choke to death," she said.

I was twelve years old, and paused, thinking, Did I hear her correctly?

"That's right, piggy, suffocate."

In that moment, I hoped that I *would* choke to death. The knot of beef would lodge itself in my throat, and for the rest of her life my mother would feel haunted and responsible. Every time she passed a steak house, or browsed the meat counter of a grocery store, she would think of me and reflect upon what she had said—the words "hope" and "death" in the same sentence. But, of course, I hadn't choked. Instead, I had lived and grown to adulthood, so that I could sit in this waiting room dressed in nothing but my underpants. *La la la.*

It was around this time that two more people entered. The woman looked to be in her mid-fifties, and accompanied an elderly man who was, if anything, overdressed: a suit, a sweater, a scarf, and an overcoat, which he removed with great difficulty, every button a challenge. *Give it to me,* I thought. *Over here.* But he was deaf to my telepathy, and handed his coat to the woman, who folded it over the back of her chair.

Our eyes met for a moment—hers widening as they moved from my face to my chest—and then she picked a magazine off the table and handed it to the elderly man, who I now took to be her father. She then selected a magazine of her own, and as she turned the pages I allowed myself to relax a little. She was just a woman reading a copy of *Paris Match*, and I was just the person sitting across from her. True, I had no clothes on, but maybe she wouldn't dwell on that, maybe none of these people would. The old man, the couple with their matching hair: "How was the hospital?" their friends might ask, and they'd answer, "Fine," or "Oh, you know, the same."

"Did you see anything fucked up?"

"No, not that I can think of."

It sometimes helps to remind myself that not everyone is like me. Not everyone writes things down in a notebook, and then transcribes them into a diary. Fewer still will take that diary, clean it up a bit, and read it in front of an audience: "March 14th. Paris. Went with Dad to the hospital, where we sat across from a man in his underpants. They were briefs, not boxers, a little on the gray side, the elastic slack from too many washings. I later said to Father, 'Other people have to use those chairs, too, you know,' and he agreed that it was unsanitary.

"Odd little guy, creepy. Hair on his shoulders. Big idiot smile plastered on his face, just sitting there, mumbling to himself."

How conceited I am to think I might be remembered, especially in a busy hospital where human misery is a matter of course. If any of these people did keep a diary, their day's entry would likely have to do with a diagnosis, some piece of news either inconvenient or life-altering: the liver's not a match, the cancer has spread to the spinal column. Compared with that, a man in his underpants is no more remarkable than a dust-covered plant, or the magazine-subscription card lying on the floor beside the table. Then, too, good news or bad, these people would eventually leave the hospital and return to the streets, where any number of things might wipe me from their memory.

PERHAPS on their way home they'll see a dog with a wooden leg, which I saw myself one afternoon. It was a German shepherd, and his prosthesis looked as though it had been made from a billy club. The network of straps holding the leg in place was a real eyeopener, but stranger still was the noise it made against the floor of the subway car, a dull thud that managed to sound both plaintive and forceful at the same time. Then there was the dog's owner, who looked at his pet and then at me, with an expression reading, "That's okay. I took care of it."

Or maybe they'll run into something comparatively small yet no less astonishing. I was walking to the bus stop one morning and came upon a well-dressed woman lying on the sidewalk in front of an office supply store. A small crowd had formed, and just as I joined it a fire truck pulled up. In America, if someone dropped to the ground, you'd call an ambulance, but in France it's the firemen who do most of the rescuing. There were four of them, and, after checking to see that the woman was okay, one of them returned to the truck and opened the door. I thought he was looking for an aluminum blanket, the type they use for people in shock, but instead he pulled out a goblet. Anywhere else it would have been a cup, made of paper or plastic, but this was glass, and had a stem. I guess they carry it around in the front seat, next to the axes or whatever.

The fireman filled the goblet with bottled water, and then he handed it to the woman, who was sitting up now and running her hand over her hair, the way one might when waking from a nap. It was the lead story in my diary that night, but, no matter how hard I fiddled with it, I felt something was missing. Had I mentioned that it was autumn? Did the leaves on the sidewalk contribute to my sense of utter delight, or was it just the goblet, and the dignity it bespoke: "Yes, you may be on the ground; yes, this drink may be your last—but let's do it right, shall we?"

Everyone has his own standards, but, in my opinion, a sight like that is at least fifty times better than what I was providing. A goblet will keep you going for years, while a man in his underpants is good for maybe two days, a week at the most. Unless, of course, *you* are the man in his underpants, in which case it will probably stay with you for the rest of your life—not on the tip of your mind, not handy like a phone number, but still within easy reach, like a mouthful of steak, or a dog with a wooden leg. How often you'll think of the cold plastic chair, and of the nurse's face as she passes the room and discovers you with your hands between your knees. Such surprise, such amusement as she proposes some new adventure, then stands there, waiting for your *d'accord*.

2006

DAVID SEDARIS

TASTELESS

ONE of the things they promise when you quit smoking is that food will regain its flavor. Taste buds paved beneath decades of tar will spring back to life, and an entire sense will be restored. I thought it would be like putting on a pair of glasses—something dramatic that makes you say "Whoa!"—but it's been six months now, and I have yet to notice any significant change.

Part of the problem might be me. I've always been in touch with my stomach, but my mouth and I don't really speak. Oh, it chews all right. It helps me form words and holds stuff when my hands are full, but it doesn't do any of these things very well. It's third-rate at best—fifth if you take my teeth into consideration.

Even before I started smoking, I was not a remarkably attentive eater. "Great fried fish," I'd say to my mother, only to discover that I was eating a chicken breast or, just as likely, a veal cutlet. She might as well have done away with names and identified our meals by color: "Golden brown." "Red." "Beige with some pink in it."

I am a shoveler, a quantity man, and I like to keep going until I feel sick. It's how a prisoner might eat, one arm maneuvering the fork and the other encircling the plate like a fence: head lowered close to my food, eyes darting this way and that; even if I don't particularly like it, it's *mine*, God damn it.

Some of this has to do with coming from a large family. Always afraid that I wouldn't get enough, I'd start worrying about more long before I finished what was in front of me. We'd be at the dinner table, and, convict-like, out of one side of my mouth, I'd whisper to my sister Amy.

"What'll you take for that chicken leg?"

"You mean my barbecued rib?"

"Call it what you like, just give me your asking price."

"Oh gosh," she'd say. "A quarter?"

"Twenty-five cents! What do you think this is—a restaurant?"

She'd raise the baton of meat to her face and examine it for flaws. "A dime."

"A nickel," I'd say, and before she could argue I'd have snatched it away.

I should have been enormous, the size of a panda, but I think that the fear of going without—the anxiety that this produced—acted like a kind of furnace, and burned off the calories before I could gain weight. Even after learning how to make my own meals, I remained, if not skinny, then at least average. My older sister Lisa and I were in elementary school when our mother bought us our first cookbook. The recipes were fairly simple—lots of Jell-O–based desserts and a wheel-shaped meat loaf cooked in an angel-food-cake pan. This last one was miraculous to me. "A meat loaf—with a hole in it!" I kept saying. I guess I thought that as it baked the cavity would fill itself with rubies or butterscotch pudding. How else to explain my disappointment the first dozen times I made it?

In high school, I started cooking pizzas—"from scratch," I liked to say, "the ol' fashioned way." On Saturday afternoons, I'd make my dough, place it in a cloth-covered bowl, and set it in the linen closet to rise. We'd have our dinner at seven or so, and four hours later, just as *Shock Theater*, our local horror-movie program, came on, I'd put my pizzas in the oven. It might have been all right if this were just *part* of my evening, but it was everything: All I knew about being young had canned Parmesan cheese on it. While my classmates were taking acid and having sex in their cars, I was arranging sausage buttons and sliced peppers into smiley faces.

"The next one should look mad," my younger brother would say. And, as proof of my versatility, I would create a frown.

To make it all that much sadder, things never got any better than this. Never again would I take so many chances or feel such giddy confidence in my abilities. This is not to say that I stopped cooking, just that I stopped trying.

Between the year that I left my parents' house and the year that I met Hugh, I made myself dinner just about every night. I generally alternated between three or four simple meals, but if forced to name my signature dish I'd probably have gone with my Chicken and Linguine with Grease on It. I don't know that I ever had an actual recipe; rather, like my Steak and Linguine with Blood on It, I just sort of played it by ear. The good thing about those meals was that they had only two ingredients. Anything more than that and I'm like Hugh's mother buying Christmas presents. "I look at the list, I go to the store, and then I just freeze," she says.

I suggest that it's nothing to get worked up about, and see in her eyes the look I give when someone says, "It's only a dinner party," or "Can we have something *with* the Chicken and Linguine with Grease on It?"

I cook for myself when I'm alone; otherwise, Hugh takes care of it, and happily, too. People tell me that he's a real chef, and something about the way they say it, a tone of respect and envy, leads me to believe them. I know that the dinners he prepares are correct. If something is supposed to be hot, it is. If it looks rust-colored in pictures, it looks rust-colored on the plate. I'm always happy to eat Hugh's cooking, but when it comes to truly tasting, to discerning the subtleties I hear others talking about, it's as if my tongue were wearing a mitten.

That's why fine restaurants are wasted on me. I suppose I can appreciate the lighting, or the speed with which my water glass is refilled, but, as far as the food is concerned, if I can't distinguish between a peach and an apricot I really can't tell the difference between an excellent truffle and a mediocre one. Then, too, the more you pay the less they generally give you to eat. French friends visiting the United States are floored by the size of the portions. "Plates the size of hubcaps!" they cry. "No wonder the Americans are so fat."

"I know," I say. "Isn't it awful?" Then I think of Claim Jumper, a California-based chain that serves a massive hamburger called the Widow Maker. I ordered a side of creamed spinach there, and it came in what looked like a mixing bowl. It was like being miniaturized, shrunk to the height of a leprechaun or a doll and dropped in the dining room of regular-sized people. Even the salt and pepper shakers seemed enormous. I ate at Claim Jumper only once, and it was the first time in years that I didn't corral my plate. For starters, my arm wasn't long enough, but even if it had been I wouldn't have felt the need. There was plenty to go around, some of it brown, some of it green, and some a color I've come to think of, almost dreamily, as enough.

2007

NOTES ON CONTRIBUTORS

MIKE ALBO (b. 1969) is a novelist, playwright, and performance artist, and VIRGINIA HEFFERNAN (b. 1969) writes the Medium column for *The New York Times Magazine.* They are the authors of the book *The Underminer.*

HENRY ALFORD (b. 1962) has contributed to *The New Yorker* since 1998. He is the author of the books *Municipal Bondage* and *Big Kiss,* which won the 2001 Thurber Prize for American Humor. He is a contributing editor at *Vanity Fair* and also writes for *The New York Times.*

JENNY ALLEN (b. 1955) has written for *The New York Times, Life, New York, Esquire,* and *Vogue.* She is the author of *The Long Chalkboard,* a book of fables for grownups.

WOODY ALLEN (b. 1935) was nominated for an Emmy as a writer for Sid Caesar's television show before becoming famous as a standup comic. He is now best known as the writer and director (and often star) of numerous films, including such classics as *Annie Hall, Manhattan,* and *Hannah and Her Sisters.* He has recently published *Mere Anarchy* and *The Insanity Defense.*

ROGER ANGELL (b. 1920) has been a fiction editor at *The New Yorker* since 1956 and a contributor since 1944. He has been writing about baseball since 1962; his books include *The Summer Game, Season Ticket, A Pitcher's Story,* and *Let Me Finish.*

MICHAEL J. ARLEN (b. 1930) was the magazine's television critic in the 1960s and 1970s. He is the author of a novel and seven books of nonfiction, including *Living-Room War,* an examination of television reportage. In 1976, he won the National Book Award for *Passage to Ararat.*

ANDREW BARLOW (b. 1978) attended Brown University, where he edited the humor magazine. He is the co-author of *A Portrait of Yo Mama as a Young Man.*

NOAH BAUMBACH (b. 1969) wrote and directed the films *Kicking and Screaming, Mr. Jealousy, The Squid and the Whale,* and *Margot at the Wedding.*

ROBERT BENCHLEY (1889–1945) was the editor of *The Harvard Lampoon* and went on to work at *Life* and *Vanity Fair.* One of the wits of the Algonquin Round Table, he developed his famous "Treasurer's Report" monologue for a stage re-view; he performed it throughout his life onstage, and also in one of the first short films with sound, in 1928. He wrote for *The New Yorker* from 1925 to 1940 and was also a popular radio broadcaster, appearing in forty-eight short films, includ-ing the Oscar-winning *How to Sleep* (1935).

BETSY BERNE (b. 1956) is the author of the novel *Bad Timing* and the co-author of *Narciso Rodriguez,* published by Rizzoli. Her writing has appeared in *Vogue* and *The New York Times Magazine.*

ZEV BOROW (b. 1972) has contributed humor and journalism to *New York, GQ, McSweeney's,* and *Spin.* He currently lives in Los Angeles and writes for film and television.

ANDY BOROWITZ (b. 1958) is the founder of The Borowitz Report, a humor website, and the winner of the first-ever National Press Club award for humor. He is the creator and producer of the television series *The Fresh Prince of Bel-Air* and a co-producer of the film *Pleasantville.* His books include *The Republican Play-book, Who Moved My Soap?,* and *The Trillionaire Next Door.*

YONI BRENNER (b. 1980) was raised in Michigan, and writes for film and televi-sion.

MARSHALL BRICKMAN (b. 1941) was a member of the folksinging groups the Journeymen and the Tarriers before becoming a writer for *Candid Camera* and *The Tonight Show*. He collaborated with Woody Allen as a writer on several films, sharing an Oscar for *Annie Hall,* and went on to write and direct a number of feature films, including *Simon* and *The Manhattan Project*. He most recently co-wrote the book for the Broadway musical *Jersey Boys*.

DAVID BROOKS (b. 1961) is an op-ed columnist for *The New York Times*. He is the author of the books *Bobos in Paradise* and *On Paradise Drive*.

CHRISTOPHER BUCKLEY (b. 1952) is the author of thirteen books, including *Boomsday, Thank You for Smoking,* and *Little Green Men*. He is editor-at-large of *ForbesLife* magazine, and has been contributing to *The New Yorker* since 1981.

FRANK CAMMUSO (b. 1965), a political cartoonist, and HART SEELY (b. 1952), a reporter, are writing partners whose comic articles have appeared in *The New York Times* and the *Syracuse Herald-Journal*. *2007-Eleven and Other American Comedies* is a collection of their pieces.

JOHNNY CARSON (1925–2005) was the host of *The Tonight Show* from 1962 to 1992.

CARINA CHOCANO (b. 1968) is a film critic for *The Los Angeles Times*. Previously, she was a television critic for *Entertainment Weekly* and a senior writer for *Salon*.

PETER DE VRIES (1910–1993) was born in Chicago and worked there as an editor of *Poetry* magazine. He was a regular contributor to *The New Yorker* in the 1940s and 1950s. His life in suburban Connecticut provided the setting for many of his popular comic novels, including *Reuben, Reuben* and *The Tunnel of Love*.

LARRY DOYLE (b. 1958) was for several years a writer and producer for *The Simpsons*. He wrote the films *Duplex* and *Looney Toons: Back in Action*. He has also been an editor at *Spy* and *The National Lampoon*. He is the author of the novel *I Love You, Beth Cooper*.

H. F. ELLIS (1907–2000) wrote and edited for *Punch* until S. J. Perelman encouraged him to contribute to *The New Yorker*. He is perhaps best known in England for his book about a hapless British schoolmaster, *The Papers of A. J. Wentworth, BA*.

NANCY FRANKLIN (b. 1956) has been on the staff of *The New Yorker* since 1978. She is now the television critic for the magazine.

IAN FRAZIER (b. 1951) has written humor and reported pieces for *The New Yorker* since 1974. His books include *Dating Your Mom*, *Great Plains*, *On the Rez*, and *Lamentations of the Father*.

BILLY FROLICK (b. 1959) co-wrote the Dreamworks film *Madagascar* and is the author of several book parodies, including *The Philistine Prophecy* and *The Five People You Meet in Hell*.

POLLY FROST (b. 1952) has written on film for *Harper's Bazaar* and *Elle*, and about cooking for *The New York Times*.

FRANK GANNON (b. 1952) has written for *The New Yorker* since 1985. He is the author of *Yo, Poe; Vanna Karenina; All About Man;* and the memoir *Midnight Irish: Discovering My Family and Myself*.

VERONICA GENG (1941–1997) was born in Atlanta and worked as a fiction editor at *The New Yorker* starting in the mid-1970s. Many of her parodies were collected in *Partners* and *Love Trouble Is My Business*. A posthumous collection, *Love Trouble: New and Collected Work*, appeared in 1999.

WOLCOTT GIBBS (1902–1958) was born in New York and worked on newspapers in Long Island before joining *The New Yorker* in 1927. He became known for the varied profiles, parodies, and reminiscences he contributed and for his exacting editing of other writers. In 1940 he became the magazine's drama critic, and in 1950 his play *Season in the Sun* (adapted from his earlier book about Fire Island bohemianism) became a Broadway hit.

ADAM GOPNIK (b. 1956) was born in Philadelphia and began to write for *The New Yorker* in 1986, where he has published under various rubrics, among them The Art World, Paris Journal, and New York Journal. He is the recipient of three National Magazine Awards for his essays and criticism and the George Polk Award for magazine reporting. He is the author of *Paris to the Moon*, *The King in the Window*, and *Through the Children's Gate*.

JACK HANDEY (b. 1949) was born in Texas and lives in New Mexico. He wrote for Steve Martin in the 1970s and 1980s, was a writer for *Saturday Night Live*, and is the author of several books, including *Deep Thoughts, Deeper Thoughts, Deepest*

Thoughts, and *The Lost Deep Thoughts.* His most recent collection is *What I'd Say to the Martians.*

GARRISON KEILLOR (b. 1942) was born in Anoka, Minnesota, and is the host of the long-running public radio program *A Prairie Home Companion.* Keillor was inducted into the Radio Hall of Fame at the Museum of Broadcast Communications, in Chicago, in 1994. He first published in *The New Yorker* in 1970, and his pieces have been collected in such books as *Happy to Be Here, We Are Still Married,* and *The Book of Guys.*

JOHN KENNEY (b. 1962) has been contributing humor pieces to the magazine since 1999. His writing has also appeared in *The New York Times* and the *Los Angeles Times.*

ANTHONY LANE (b. 1962) reviewed books for *The Independent* and films for *The Independent on Sunday,* in London, before coming to *The New Yorker* in 1993. In addition to his biweekly film reviews, he contributes book reviews and other works of criticism, for which he has received a National Magazine Award. His writing for the magazine is collected in his book *Nobody's Perfect.*

JESSE LICHTENSTEIN (b. 1976) teaches writing to high-school students in Oregon. His journalism and poetry have appeared in *Slate, The Economist, The Paris Review,* and *n+1.*

STEVE MARTIN (b. 1945) is a comedian, actor, film director, and writer. He has written and starred in such films as *The Jerk, L.A. Story,* and *Bowfinger.* His writing has appeared in the magazine since 1996, and in 2005 he was awarded the Mark Twain Prize for American Humor. He is the author of *Shopgirl: A Novella* and the memoir *Born Standing Up.*

PATRICIA MARX (b. 1953) is the author of the novel *Him Her Him Again the End of Him* and *Dot in Larryland,* a children's book illustrated by Roz Chast.

BRUCE MCCALL (b. 1935) was born in Canada and came to the United States at the age of twenty-seven. He has been writing and drawing since the age of seven. His writing first appeared in *The New Yorker* in 1980 and his art first appeared three years later. In 1982, he published *Zany Afternoons,* a collection of humor pieces. His memoir, *Thin Ice,* published in 1997, was made into a film. His most recent books are *The Last Dream-o-Rama* and *All Meat Looks Like South America.*

THOMAS MEEHAN (b. 1932) was working in the Talk of the Town department when a friend introduced him to Ina Claire and Uta Hagen ("Ina, Uta"), inspiring his first (and widely imitated) Casual. Later, he wrote the book for the musical *Annie*, which won a Tony Award in 1977. He has won subsequent Tony Awards for *The Producers*, in 2001, and *Hairspray*, in 2002.

LOUIS MENAND (b. 1952) is a professor of English at Harvard University and a staff writer at *The New Yorker*, where he has contributed reviews and essays since 1991. His books include *Discovering Modernism: T. S. Eliot and His Context*, *The Metaphysical Club*, which won the Pulitzer Prize for History, and *American Studies*.

SUSAN ORLEAN (b. 1955) has been writing for *The New Yorker* since 1987 and became a staff writer in 1992. Her work has also appeared in *Outside*, *Rolling Stone*, *Vogue*, and *Esquire*. Her books include *Saturday Night*, *The Orchid Thief*, which was the basis for the film *Adaptation*, *The Bullfighter Checks Her Makeup*, and *My Kind of Place*.

DAVID OWEN (b. 1955) is a staff writer and golf enthusiast. His books include *High School*, *The Walls Around Us*, *My Usual Game*, *The Making of the Masters*, and *Sheetrock & Shellac*.

DOROTHY PARKER (1893–1967), famed as an Algonquin Round Table regular, wrote for *The New Yorker* from its second issue, in 1925, until the end of 1957. She contributed poems, stories, and theater reviews and was also known for her book reviews, written under the pseudonym Constant Reader. Her poetry collection *Enough Rope* was a bestseller in 1926 and was followed by three other volumes. She moved to Hollywood to work with Alan Campbell, her second husband, as a screenwriter. They received an Oscar nomination for *A Star Is Born* (1937).

S. J. PERELMAN (1904–1979) grew up in Providence and attended Brown University, where he edited the humor magazine. When, in 1929, the publisher of his first book, *Dawn Ginsbergh's Revenge*, sent a copy to Groucho Marx for a blurb, Perelman was taken on as a scriptwriter and worked on two Marx Brothers movies, *Monkey Business* and *Horse Feathers*. His first *New Yorker* piece appeared in the 1930s and he went on to contribute nearly three hundred others, which were collected in such books as *Strictly from Hunger* and *The Road to Miltown; or, Under the Spreading Atrophy*. He also collaborated on the stage comedies *All the Good Americans* and *One Touch of Venus*, and shared an Oscar for the script of *Around the World in Eighty Days* (1956).

SIMON RICH (b. 1984), a former president of *The Harvard Lampoon*, writes for *Saturday Night Live*. He is the author of the books *Ant Farm* and *Free-Range Chickens*.

PAUL RUDNICK (b. 1957) was born in New Jersey and graduated from Yale. His plays include *I Hate Hamlet; The Naked Eye; The Most Fabulous Story Ever Told; Mr. Charles, Currently of Palm Beach;* and *Jeffrey*, which was also made into a movie. His screenplays include *Addams Family Values, In & Out*, and *The Stepford Wives*. He is the author of two novels, *Social Disease* and *I'll Take It*, and *If You Ask Me*, a collection of movie reviews written by his alter ego, Libby Gelman-Waxner.

GEORGE SAUNDERS (b. 1958) is a professor of English at Syracuse University and the author of the books *CivilWarLand in Bad Decline, Pastoralia, The Very Persistent Gappers of Frip, The Brief and Frightening Reign of Phil, In Persuasion Nation*, and *The Braindead Megaphone*. He is a four-time winner of the National Magazine Award for his fiction, and in 2006 was named a MacArthur Fellow.

CATHLEEN SCHINE (b. 1953) is a novelist. *The Love Letter*, a national bestseller, was translated into fifteen languages. Her other novels include *Alice in Bed, To the Bird House, Rameau's Niece, The Evolution of Jane, She Is Me*, and *The New Yorkers*.

DAVID SEDARIS (b. 1956) published his first piece for *The New Yorker* in 1995. He is the author of six bestselling collections of stories and essays: *Barrel Fever, Naked, Holidays on Ice, Me Talk Pretty One Day, Dress Your Family in Corduroy and Denim*, and *When You Are Engulfed in Flames*.

PAUL SIMMS (b. 1965) created the television show *NewsRadio* and has written for *Spy, Late Night with David Letterman, The Larry Sanders Show*, and *Flight of the Conchords*.

MARK SINGER (b. 1950) has been a staff writer at *The New Yorker* since 1974. He is the author of the books *Funny Money, Mr. Personality, Citizen K, Somewhere in America*, and *Character Studies*.

WILLIAM STEIG (1907–2003) was a prolific artist and children's book author. He sold his first drawing to *The New Yorker* in 1930, and his first cover illustration in 1932. He then became one of the magazine's longest-running contributors, publishing over 120 covers and 1,600 drawings in his lifetime. His book *Shrek!*, published in 1990, was made into an animated feature film in 2001, which won an Academy Award.

DON STEINBERG (b. 1962) lives outside of Philadelphia. He is the author of *Jokes Every Man Should Know*. His humor writing and reporting has appeared in *GQ*, *ESPN*, *Harper's*, *The Philadelphia Inquirer*, *McSweeney's*, and *Spy*.

JONATHAN STERN (b. 1967) is a screenwriter and producer living in Brooklyn. He produced the films *The Ten* and *Scotland, PA*, and the Web series *Wainy Days*, *Horrible People*, and *Children's Hospital*. He also writes for *Esquire* and *McSweeney's*.

JON STEWART (b. 1962) is the host of the Emmy Award–winning *The Daily Show* and the co-author of *America: The Book*.

RUTH SUCKOW (1892–1960) was born in Iowa and lived there for most of her life. She published her first poetry in 1918 and her first short story in 1921. Her first novel, *Country People*, appeared in 1924. She contributed to *The New Yorker* from 1927 to 1937. She published eleven books in her lifetime, leaving a novel unfinished when she died.

JAMES THURBER (1894–1961) was born in Columbus, Ohio, and joined *The New Yorker* in 1927 as an editor and writer; his idiosyncratic cartoons began to appear there four years later. His books include two children's classics—*The 13 Clocks* and *The Wonderful O*—and a memoir of his time at *The New Yorker*, *The Years with Ross*. He also co-wrote a successful play, *The Male Animal*, and appeared in *A Thurber Carnival*, a miscellany of his works that was adapted for the stage. In 1947 his short story "The Secret Life of Walter Mitty" was made into a film starring Danny Kaye.

CALVIN TRILLIN (b. 1935) has been a staff writer for *The New Yorker* since 1963 and has reported from all over America in his long-running U.S. Journal series. His many books include the bestsellers *Messages from My Father* and *About Alice*, along with comic novels, short stories, a travel book, and three books on food, collected as *The Tummy Trilogy*. He has twice written and performed one-man shows.

GEORGE W. S. TROW (1943–2006) first wrote for *The New Yorker* in 1966 and cofounded *National Lampoon* in 1970. He is the author of a novel, *The City in the Mist*, and a collection of satirical short stories, *Bullies*. He also wrote several plays, including *The Tennis Game*, and co-wrote two Merchant-Ivory films, *Savages* and *The Proprietor*.

JOHN UPDIKE (b. 1932) has written for *The New Yorker* since the mid-1950s, when he was a staff writer for the Talk of the Town. He is the author of twenty-two novels, including the Pulitzer Prize–winning *Rabbit Is Rich* and *Rabbit at Rest*, fifteen books of short stories, seven collections of poetry, five children's books, a memoir, and a play.

WENDY WASSERSTEIN (1950–2006) was the author of two screenplays, four novels, and eleven plays, including *The Heidi Chronicles,* which won both the Tony Award for best play and the Pulitzer Prize for Drama in 1989.

E. B. WHITE (1899–1985) worked as a newspaperman, an advertising copywriter, and a mess boy on an Arctic steamer before coming to *The New Yorker* in 1927. Here, his contributions comprised humor pieces, poems, short stories, newsbreak captions, and even a cover illustration, but he was most associated with the Notes and Comment essays, which he wrote for thirty years. He is famous for three enduring works of children's literature: *Stuart Little, Charlotte's Web,* and *The Trumpet of the Swan.* He received the Presidential Medal of Freedom in 1963 and was awarded a Pulitzer Prize in 1978.

JIM WINDOLF (b. 1964) writes regularly for *Vanity Fair,* where he is a contributing editor. His journalism has appeared in *The New York Observer* and *The New York Times Book Review,* and his short fiction has been published in *The Ontario Review.*